中国政法大学法学实验教学中心法学教育丛书

实践性法学教育论丛 第二卷

Journal of Experiential Learning Legal Education

龙翼飞　潘文军◎主编　　许身健◎本卷执行主编

知识产权出版社
全国百佳图书出版单位

图书在版编目（CIP）数据

实践性法学教育论丛·第二卷 / 龙翼飞，潘文军主编．
—北京：知识产权出版社，2014.4
ISBN 978－7－5130－2652－9

Ⅰ.①实…　Ⅱ.①许…　Ⅲ.①法学教育－研究－中国
Ⅳ.①D920.4

中国版本图书馆 CIP 数据核字（2014）第 053415 号

责任编辑：牛洁颖　　责任校对：韩秀天
特约编辑：王丽莉　　责任出版：刘译文

实践性法学教育论丛·第二卷
Shijianxing Faxue Jiaoyu Luncong
龙翼飞　潘文军　主编
许身健　本卷执行主编

出版发行：知识产权出版社有限责任公司　　网　址：http://www.ipph.cn
社　址：北京市海淀区马甸南村 1 号　　邮　编：100088
责编电话：010－82000860 转 8109　　责编邮箱：niujieying@sina.com
发行电话：010－82000860 转 8101/8102　　发行传真：010－82000893/82005070/82000270
印　刷：北京紫瑞利印刷有限公司　　经　销：各大网上书店、新华书店及相关专业书店
开　本：720mm×960mm　1/16　　印　张：22.75
版　次：2014 年 4 月第一版　　印　次：2014 年 4 月第一次印刷
字　数：390 千字　　定　价：45.00 元
ISBN 978－7－5130－2652－9

认真对待法学教育（代序）

用哪一句话可以形象描述中国的法学教育现状呢？清华大学法学院何美欢教授用英国作家狄更斯的名著《双城记》开篇“这是最好的时代，这是最坏的时代”这句话来描述中国法学教育现状，令人拍案叫绝。

为什么说当下是法学教育最好的时代？因为法学专业还是热门专业之一，法律院校越办越多，至今已将近700所，而在校法科生已达到40余万人的天文数字。法学属于热门专业，这可以确保法律院校有优质生源。得天下英才而育之，这是教育机构梦寐以求的。

中国恢复法学教育不过30余年，回首昨日，发展速度确实突飞猛进，令人瞠目结舌。1978年开始恢复法学教育，那时，法律专业并非文科生首选，现在法学界如雷贯耳的一些大佬，当初他们的梦想是做哲学家或者作家。由于高考技不如人，分不够高，他们先后被强行划入法律系，个别同学估计多少次蒙着被子哭红了眼睛。现在这些法学大佬在心里肯定暗暗感谢上帝当初少给自己分数，否则，想想后果会直出冷汗。由于经济发展以及法治越来越为国家所重视，大佬们很早就实现了出有车食有鱼的舒适生活。假如他们当年如愿进入文史哲专业，那么除非他们出落成口吐莲花的易中天、于丹们，或者满纸小清新的周国平（微博），否则自身生活水准和法律人相比就是非洲和欧洲的差距。当然，年少时的梦想总是美好的，大佬们现在还有埋藏很久的哲学梦或文学梦，他们出版某某哲学或者法律与文学之类的专著就是当年文史哲梦的七彩衣裳。20世纪90年代中叶，在中国政法大学研究生院读书期间，笔者到民办大学讲课贴补家用，放眼班车，讲法律课的都是研究生，而且仅是硕士生，博士生们都在跟着老师奔走法学江湖。高校法学教师早已不屑去民办大学授课，而讲文史哲课的都是正当壮年或盛年的高校老师。目睹此情此景，我心中不禁吟诵："（微博）文史哲在秋风中飘零，法律的春天来了！"现在看，法律专业热度不减，简直是盛夏炎炎。因此，当下是法学教育最好的时代，此言不谬。

为什么说当下也是法学教育最坏的时代？因为法学专业虽然"高烧不退"，但是对之望闻问切，纯属虚热，很快就要打冷战了。媒体不断传出令人揪心的坏消息，法学专业的就业率已经连续很多年垫底。不过，法科生还有一个梦想："只要找到饭辙，高薪还是有保证的。"但事与愿违，今年又传来了更坏的消息，法科生即使千辛万苦、闯关成功后找到了工作，薪酬也不令人满意。据统计，法学专业毕业生已经名列起薪最低的队伍行列。法科生就业难，谋生难，这些都是不争的事实。此外，何美欢教授指出："一方面农村、乡镇闹律师荒，另一方面精英法学院毕业生不能顺理成章地走进占据高端业务的外国律师事务所。外所或者把在中国招徕的业务送到纽约或香港地区处理，或者引进外国律师执业。这就是说，中国法学院还不能培育出大量的高端法律人才，其产品只能囤积在中下档次。"既然法律院校的产品不是高档品而是地摊货，那么这种情况难道不是法学教育最坏的时代？

法学教育存在严重问题，这是不争的事实，它将迫使法律院校及法律教育者走出所谓"法学教育最好的时代"这一错觉，反之，他们应该冷静面对"法学教育最坏的时代"这一严酷现实，认真对待法学教育，并找到应对之策。

目前，法学教育诸多问题的源头是法律院校及法律教育者对于法学教育的培养目标并不明确。虽然法学教育应当定位为法律职业教育，这种观点已经基本达成共识，但是对于职业教育的具体内容仍然存在模糊认识。有人提出，美国法学院的培养目标是职业律师，而中国法科生从事法律职业的比率并不算很高。其实，这种观点是对法律职业的认识过于狭窄。美国司法伦理泰斗 Rhode 教授及 Hazardd 教授认为："法律人的范围除了法律职业者外，也包括下列不从事法律职业的法科毕业生，即从事政治学、新闻、管理、司法行政、法学教育、公务员及非政府组织等的法科毕业生。他们的法学背景对于其视野及社会角色至关重要。在亚洲、欧洲国家，不从事法律职业，而从事上述职业的法科毕业生的比例更高。”换言之，法科生毕业后即使不直接从事狭义的法律职业，但从事上述职业也属于广义的法律人，他们的法律背景使其拥有独特的分析、处理及解决问题的能力，法学教育令其受益终身。简言之，法学教育的培养目标应当是培养具有良好职业技能以及职业价值的法律人。

应当看到，法学教育的短板在于培养法科生的法律职业技能，亦即法律职业教育应该提供何美欢教授所关注的“智能技能（Intellectual Skills）的培育”，具体内容应包括以下知识传授及技能训练：（1）对实体法的足够知识；（2）认定法律问题和就法律问题构建有效和中肯切题的论证的能力；（3）明智地运用一切资料进行研究的能力；（4）明白任何法律的基础政策以及社会环境的能力；（5）分析和阐明抽象概念的能力；（6）识别简单的逻辑上和统计上的错误的能力；（7）书写和讲述清楚简明的汉语的能力；（8）积极学习的能力；（9）认定和核实任何与法律问题相关的事实的能力；（10）分析事实和就被争议的事实构建或批评某论证的能力；（11）对法律实务和程序的足够知识；（12）有效率地适用法律的能力，即解决问题的能力。法律院校及法律教育者应当将上述知识传授及技能训练作为法学教育的具体目标，同时，要寻求行之有效的教学方法，最终还要通过有效的评估方法检验上述目标是否实现。

何美欢教授在目睹法学教育的虚假繁荣之际，中肯地提出了针对法学教育的盛世危言：“中国法学教育需要进行大规模的、深层次的改革。在传统的课程上添加一些律师技巧之类的课程充其量也只能治标，绝不能治本，能骗人于一时，不能骗人一世。国家对高端法律人才的需要是迫切的，如果法学院不能满足这个需求，自然就会出现其他的供应方。为了自救，中国的法学院也应该正视问题，下决心进行改革。”诚哉斯言，看来，法律院校及法律教育者对于目前法学教育的乱象再也不能无动于衷，而应该切实投身教育改革，认真对待法学教育。

本卷出版得到了中国诊所法律教育专业委员会龙翼飞主任以及潘文军秘书长的大力支持。

许身健

2014 年 1 月 26 日于北京

目　录

"卓越计划"背景下的诊所法律教育改革

陈海平　王　倩*

摘　要："卓越法律人才教育培养计划"为法学教育带来了重大发展机遇。缘起于美国的诊所法律教育进入中国以来，成效很卓著，问题也明显，法学教育进入"卓越"时代，诊所法律教育迎来了难得的机遇，也面临诸多挑战。诊所法律教育应当紧抓历史机遇，宜从能力培养、复合培养、拓展案源、扩充经费、加强师资等方面入手，解决旧难题，力免新问题。

关键词：卓越法律人才　诊所法律教育　机遇　挑战

随着中央政法委、教育部联合启动"卓越法律人才教育培养计划"，法学教育迎来了新的发展机遇，法学实践教学必将成为新一轮教学研究与改革的热点和重点，诊所法律教育作为法学实践教学的重要组成部分，必将受到前所未有的重视。在法学教育的"卓越"时代，诊所法律教育制度的改革完善正当其时，刻不容缓。

一、诊所法律教育之实践述评

（一）诊所法律教育的兴起与引入

"诊所法律教育"是 20 世纪 60 年代美国民权运动的产物，起源于美

---

* 陈海平，法学博士，燕山大学文法学院副教授，法学系副主任，研究方向为刑事诉讼法学、法学教育；王倩，河北承德人，燕山大学文法学院诉讼法学硕士研究生。

基金项目：本文系笔者主持的 2012 年度河北省高等学校人文社会科学研究教育规划项目——"卓越法律人才实践教学模式创新研究"（GH121001）的阶段性成果。

国耶鲁大学、哈佛大学等著名学府的法学院。“诊所法律教育”的历史可追溯到19世纪中期，当时，美国律师学习法律的途径有两种：[1] 一种是学徒式的。另一种是经院式的。1830年之后，律师在法学院的集中学习逐步取代了学徒制，在学院接受系统的、统一的、规范性的训练，所采用的教学方法主要是“判例教学法”。20世纪60年代后期至70年代初期，美国的法律现实主义运动学者对法学院的“案例教学法”提出质疑，认为法学教育应当看到法律规则和事实的不确定性，让学生真正接触到社会实践中出现的真实案例。

随后，在美国福特基金会的支持下，许多法律学校开始建立诊所法律教育项目。这是一种实践操作和法律理论相结合的法学教育模式，它模仿了医学院校学生运用诊所实习来培养医生的做法，即由法科学生利用法律为当事人提供专业服务。这种教育模式倡导在实践与经验中学习法律和律师职业技能，强调以学生为主的教学理念，将模拟、参与式、互动的课堂教学以及课后指导相结合，实现法学理论与法律实践的统一。在美国，90%的法学院采用诊所教育方法。[2] 目前，这种教育模式在新西兰、澳大利亚、印度、拉丁美洲等许多国家和地区的法学院校中均已得到了成功地运用。

诊所法律教育是新世纪中国法学教育的一项重大改革，是国外先进教学模式与中国法律教育实际有机结合的成功尝试。兴起于美国的法学教学的新方式“Clinical Legal Education”（诊所法律教育）自传入我国即受追捧，其将医学专业临床实习模式引入法学教育领域，传入初期其中文名称正是“临床法学教育”，强调发挥教师的实务经验，倡导在实践和经验中学习法律和律师职业技能，“帮助学生培养经验式学习的能力以及凭借经验进行反思的能力”，[3] 通过法律实践获得法律职业技能，通过为社会弱势群体提供法律援助，使诊所教学产生广泛的社会效益，培养

---

[1] 李傲：《互动教学法：诊所式法律教育》，法律出版社2004年版，第3页。

[2] 甄贞：《诊所法律教育在中国》，法律出版社2002年版，第19页。

[3] 韩大元、叶秋华：《走向世界的中国法学教育论文集》，中国人民大学出版社2001年版，第765页。

学生的社会责任感和职业道德水准。

在美国诊所法律教育模式的启发和美国福特基金会的鼎力资助下，自2000年以来，已有140多所法学院系开设了诊所法律教育课程，给我国法学教育改革带来了新思路，极大调动了学生参与度和主动性，学生由“要我学”的被动学习变为“我要学”的主动学习。经过10余年的教学实践，诊所法律教育已经在中国高校落地生根，日渐显现出其强大的生命力，并在不同院校中形成了各具特色、有所侧重的专门性法律诊所（如消费者权益保护诊所、社区法律诊所、劳动者权益保护诊所、妇女权益保护诊所等），收获了法律职业技能实践教学和弱势群体法律援助的双重效果。❶

（二）诊所法律教育的优势

与传统的法学教育模式相比，诊所法律教育具有明显的优势。

（1）改变固有的教育模式，培养创造性思维。诊所法律教育与传统法学教育方法不同，强调“从行动中学习”的新型法学教育方法，通过真实的案例，培养学生法律实务思维、法律实务技巧。这种新颖的教学方法的引入，在很大程度上促进了“填鸭式”教育模式的变革，为我国法学教育的不断科学化注入了新的血液和动力。不仅如此，法律教育的宗旨在于发掘学生的创新潜能，培养其创新精神与创新能力，帮助学生形成创新品质。在诊所法律教育中，学生通过实际案例，能够运用自己所学的法律知识，形成分析和批判的思辨能力。诊所法律教育重视培养学生在处理案件过程中的思考能力和懂得放弃的心态，让学生意识到直接经验对于学习的重要性，促使其自觉地发掘自己的创新潜能。

（2）培养法学院校学生的社会责任感，同时提升其实践应用能力。诊所法律教育注重社会责任感的培养，传递正能量，使学生树立公益之心。诊所法律教育的基本特点即通过对贫困以及边缘化群体提供无偿的法律帮助，促进公平正义的实现，培养诊所学生的正义观念和社会责任感。与此同时，在真实的案件材料和真实的当事人基础之上，突出从实

❶ 相关信息请参见中国诊所法律教育网站：http：//www.cliniclaw.cn/.

践中学习，从经验中学习，[1] 也提升了学生的实践应用能力，真正实现学以致用，不致出现学与用的脱节。此外，其也使传统法学教育中无法得到锻炼的法务技能得以培养，如接待当事人、与法官和对方当事人谈判、起草法律文书等。

（3）提升法律职业群体的道德伦理素养，形成独有的职业文化。孟子云："徒法不足以自行。"《圣经》说："我们知道法律体现着正义，但这也要人能正确地运用它。"诊所法律教育致力于将社会良知和职业伦理传递给未来的法律职业群体，从而形成提供法律服务过程中独有的文化。与医学教育相比，法学教育历来忽视职业道德的培养，法律诊所在很大程度上弥补了这个缺失，通过价值培养，使参与者更好地认知自己未来的职业选择。法律职业伦理教育既是法学教育的重要环节，也是培养合格法律人的起点和目标，会推动法律职业群体形成特有的文化。

（三）我国诊所法律教育实践中的问题

注重课堂教学、注重理论传授、忽视实务技能的传统教育模式根深蒂固，诊所法律教育进入中国已10年有余，目前依然面临一系列的困难和问题。

（1）案源不足。在我国，法律诊所通过办理真实案件以实现实践教学和法律援助的初衷。由于主客观多方面的原因，法律诊所尚未获得美国般的社会认同，难以得到政府、公共机构和社会大众的认可和支持，[2] 由于学生阅历和知识方面的不足，说服当事人将其面临的法律难题放心地交给学生"实习"并不容易，这是很多法律诊所共同面临的难题。"从整体上看，法律诊所教育案件来源的特点是民商事案件多，行政和刑事案件少；民事案件多，商事案件少；人身性民事案件多，财产性民事案

---

[1] 甄贞："一种新的教学方式：论诊所式法律教育"，载《中国高等教育》2002年第8期。

[2] 刘小红："我国诊所式法律教育中的困惑与反思"，载《高教论坛》2012年第5期。

件少；一审案件多，二审和再审案件少；本地案件多，异地案件少。"[1]

（2）经费不足。实践性教学方法经费支出大，诊所法律教育的经费在各种实践性教学方法中居首，需要基本的办公条件（一次投入）和日常运作经费（长期稳定投入）。美国的诊所法律教育最初是由美国福特基金会资助的，几乎每一所学校都为他们的学生提供了一个或数个诊所项目的资金支持。[2] 由于诊所法律教育的投入在短期内难有较高回报，在办学经费普遍不宽松的我国，说服所在高校长期额外地"关照"法学专业的实践教学几无可能。诊所法律教育提供的法律帮助以免费为基本特征，自然也不可能通过办理案件获得经济补偿。诊所法律教育能够在我国成功引入并发展，主要得益于福特基金会的大力支持，但从2008年起，福特基金会不再向高校投入资金，仅提供有限资金支持中国诊所法律教育委员会的运作，[3] 由此，经费问题更加严峻。

（3）教师热情不高。诊所法律教育要求教师不仅具备深厚的法学知识素养，还要具备丰富的实践经验，能够对学生实际参与案件的具体情况予以指导。我国目前尚无独立的社科类专业实践教学教师的考核晋升体系，法学教师"两极化"严重，要么只注重理论研究，要么扎在兼职律师业务而无暇顾及教学。但凡谋求职业成长的教师，都有职称评定需求，由此就必须完成相应的科研教学任务，说服专业教师长期保持热情、倾力奉献于法律诊所教学这一"额外"任务亦不容易。

（4）功能缺陷。单一目标设定使诊所法律教育在我国面临重大的功能缺陷，我国法学院仍然以完善法学理论、推动制度建构为主要任务，诊所法律教育推崇的解决实际社会问题对法学的进步和法治的改善并无明显的直接帮助。不仅如此，学生通过法律诊所从事法律实务必然存在风险，学生的"无心之过"可能导致当事人"万劫不复"，教育机构显然

---

[1] 刘加良等："法律诊所教育研究"，载《山东大学法律评论》，山东大学出版社2007年版，第268页。

[2] 张红："学徒制VS学院制——诊所法律教育的产生及其背后"，载《中外法学》2007年第4期。

[3] 李正新："试论法学教育的'临床'培养"，载《教育法制》2012年第2期。

不愿意也无力承担这种风险。基于此，并不是所有法学院系尤其是地方院校法学系都有能力、有动力开展诊所法律教育。

二、法学教育进入“卓越”时代

2005 年，时任总理温家宝在看望著名物理学家钱学森时，产生了著名的“钱学森之问”——“为什么我们的学校总是培养不出杰出人才?”2006 年，时任总理温家宝拿这个问题请教国内最有名的 6 所大学校长和教育专家，但并未得到满意的答案。2009 年钱学森逝世后，安徽高校的 11 位教授联合给教育部部长袁贵仁及全国教育界发出一封公开信：让我们直面“钱学森之问”！“钱学森之问”成为舆论关注的焦点。为回应“钱学森之问”，教育部实施了“基础学科拔尖学生培养试验计划”，即“珠峰计划”，目的在于在基础学科培养拔尖创新人才。2010 年 5 月 4 日，时任总理温家宝访问北京大学，回答如何理解“钱学森之问”的学生提问时说：钱学森之问对我们是个很大的刺痛，大学还是应该由懂教育的人来办，大学还应该改变行政化，按照教育规律办学，大学应该以教学为中心。

为贯彻落实科学发展观，切实提高高等教育质量，教育部 2007 年 1 号文件启动了“高等学校本科教学质量与教学改革工程”，即“质量工程”，这是继“211 工程”“985 工程”之后我国高等教育领域的又一项重要工程，是提高高等学校本科教学质量的重大举措。

2010 年 7 月公布的《国家中长期教育改革和发展规划纲要（2010～2020)》提出：高等教育要全面提高高等教育质量，提高人才培养质量，牢固确立人才培养在高校工作中的中心地位，着力培养信念执著、品德优良、知识丰富、本领过硬的高素质专门人才和拔尖创新人才，全面实施“质量工程”。

2011 年 4 月清华大学百年校庆，时任国家主席胡锦涛发表讲话，从大力提升人才培养水平、大力增强科学研究能力、大力服务经济社会发展、大力推进文化传承创新四个方面重点阐述了“全面提高高等教育质量”的主题，强调高等教育的根本任务是人才培养，把学生的创新精神和实践能力作为高等教育的落脚点，提出注重培养拔尖创新人才。

正是在国家领导高层对高等教育改革的密集变态和顶层设计的推动下，基于培养拔尖、创新人才的需要，高等教育各专业领域的"卓越计划"相继出台，如卓越工程师、卓越医生、卓越农林人才等。2011 年年底，教育部、中央政法委员会共同启动了"卓越法律人才教育培养计划"，首批试点院校审批已结束。

"卓越法律人才教育培养计划"的出台，旨在培养卓越法律人才。所谓卓越法律人才，指的是优秀的法律人才，是既有法学理论知识也有法律实务技能的法律人才，是具有重大可持续发展潜质的法律人才；是指具有完善扎实的跨学科基础知识，具有深厚的法学学科体系知识，能适应我国经济发展、法制建设需要和法律职业特殊要求的新型法律高级专门人才。卓越法律人才教育培养计划要求分类培养法律人才，具体包括应用型法律人才、复合型法律人才、涉外法律人才和西部基层法律人才。

卓越法律人才教育计划给予了诊所法律教育机遇。诊所法律教育作为法学教育中实践教学的重要组成部分，与卓越人才教育培养计划存在契合之处。卓越法律人才教育计划要求加大实践教学比重，提高法律人才的实践能力，加大应用型、复合型法律人才的培养力度。而诊所法律教育的初衷也是改变传统的法学教育模式，践行一种实践操作和法律理论相结合的法学教育模式，将法学理论运用于实践，使理论与实践不脱节。卓越法律人才教育培养计划的提出对于诊所法律教育的发展是一次契机，为诊所法律教育的良性发展提供了机遇。

卓越法律人才教育计划背景下，诊所法律教育面临挑战。卓越法律人才相对于传统法律人才的"卓越性"至少具有三个特点：[1] 第一，具有基本领域更为广阔的知识背景和特定专业领域的知识基础，特别应具有处理环境污染、可持续发展、跨国商务与金融、国际关系、公共服务与政府事务等领域业务的知识和能力；第二，能够参与国际规则的制定、

[1] 杨清望："卓越法律人才的基本类型与培养路径探析"，载《现代大学教育》2012 年 3 期。

表达和维护本国利益和人类共同利益；[1] 第三，能够在处理国内外法律事务中传递中国利益主张，维护社会基本价值，凝结社会共识。若想满足上述特点，现有的法学教育体制是远远不够的，尤其是诊所法律教育在现存的问题还没有得到有效解决的情况下，与卓越法律人才教育培养计划的要求差距甚远。

三、推进诊所教育改革，培养卓越法律人才

基于诊所法律教育现存的问题以及卓越法律人才教育培养计划的目标，应推进诊所法律教育改革，努力培养一批未来的卓越法律人才。

（一）能力培养

要培养卓越法律人才，现代高校必须注重学生能力的培养，但法律职业能力的培养绝非让学生简单接触几个案件、会见几个当事人、写几份法律文书就能完成，[2] 需全方位、多层次展开：

（1）分析能力。法科学生不能满足于被动地“听”老师授课，还要主动地“用”所学知识，通过比较、观察、讨论、阐发、解析法律，洞察各种法律现象的产生、运行、变化和规律。

（2）选择能力。法律领域会呈现多元化竞争，各色各样的法律制度和法学思想适者生存，不适者被淘汰。在学习期间，法典模式与判例模式、个体本位与国家主义、立法冲突与多元纠纷等都摆在了学生面前，需要学生把握博弈的技术，有效地进行甄别。

（3）创新能力。在改革精神的支配下，学生要将主体意识和想象能力结合起来，发挥自己的作用，主动学习，主动思考，主动解惑，而绝非照猫画虎，东施效颦，走抄袭路线。

（4）法律方法。在现代，掌握比较法、实证法、文献法、统计法、调查法、观察法、个案法、经验法等方法，有利于开阔视野，纵横驰骋。就此看来，法学教育的工具性正在于体现“授之以鱼，不如授之以渔”

---

[1] 张文显：“全球化时代的中国法治”，载《法制与社会发展》2005年第9期。

[2] 汤唯等：“国家特色专业建设中的卓越法律人才培养方案及其实施”，载《中国大学教学》2012年第5期。

的基本导向，使各种法律方法作为“工具”，为学生未来的职业有效利用。

（二）复合培养

卓越法律人才与传统法律人才的区别在于“复合”。“复合”是指学科间的交叉、融合、渗透，包括“法律＋英语”“法律＋经济（外贸）”“法律（专利法）＋理科（工科）”的复合等。[1] 因此，卓越、优质法律教育的要求是语言复合、专业复合。卓越法律人才的培养应当更加注重“复合”的专业素养、通识教育、综合素质与能力，例如懂金融工具与金融市场、宏微观经济学、会计、税务等经济学知识。其知识面应当更广，能够成为通识基础上的职业法律人才。

（三）拓展案源

法律诊所要想拓展案源，既要积极向外，与法院、检察院、律师事务所、企事业单位等合作形成合作共建关系，充分利用高校—实务部门合作机制拓展法律诊所案源；还要积极介入司法实务，充分运用“互评计划”，高校教师高度参与司法实务；还可以深入社会矛盾和法律纠纷多发的基层社区，既拓宽案件来源渠道，又及时化解矛盾纠纷。在美国，诊所法律教育正是出于其在为社会弱势群体提供法律援助中的巨大贡献而受到人们的广泛认同。[2]

（四）扩充经费

经费来源可以考虑从以下几个方面扩充：教育主管部门下拨制度性经费，专款专用于法律诊所教育；法学院系积极从所在高校争取稳定的实践经费，用于开办、运营诊所法律教育机构；提升法律诊所在国家法律援助工作中的地位，从司法行政机关那里获得一定的经费资助；通过教改项目申报、申请社会资助等方式，从政府部门、司法实务部门、媒体及社会各界获得经费支持。

---

[1] 王文华：“卓越法律人才培养与法学教学改革”，载《中国大学教学》2011年第7期。

[2] 李正新：“试论法学教育的‘临床’培养”，载《教育法制》2012年第2期。

（五）加强师资

高校应该为从事诊所法律教育的教师提供有针对性的培训和再教育，使这些教师的专业素质达到诊所法律教育要求的程度。对此，可以考虑向司法机关、律师事务所等单位借入师资，聘请优秀的法官、检察官、律师作为兼职教授来指导法律诊所的学生，以实现师资多元化。高校要以一定形式对教师的工作予以承认和肯定，调动教师的积极性，将法律诊所教育绩效考核列入教师评价标准，可以在有关考核和职称晋升中，对诊所法律教育的教师予以侧重。为避免诉讼风险对法律诊所教育的消极影响，应与当事人签订案件代理风险协议，明确责任划分。

作为一种全新的实践教学模式，诊所法律教育有其自身优势，可以弥补中国传统法律教育的缺陷和不足，丰富中国法学教育的内容与形式，积极推动中国法学教育方法和理念的探索与更新。但是，就像新生事物的成长都要经历从不完善到完善的过程一样，诊所法律教育也不例外。诊所法律教育进入中国必然面对困难，对于困难，我们应该迎难而上，抓住机遇，直面挑战，努力实现诊所法律教育的本土化，在卓越法律人才教育培养计划的大背景下，完善我国的诊所法律教育模式。

诊所法律教育与卓越法律人才的培养

李 涛*

摘 要：20世纪60年代在美国法学院兴起的诊所法律教育，以职业技能的训练、职业道德的训练为目标，将理论与实践进行结合，可以弥补目前我国高等法学教育体系在培养法律人才方面的不足，对我国卓越法律人才的培养具有相应的启示。以卓越法律人才的培养定位为基础，如何克服诊所法律教育本身的局限性及我国法学教育现状的局限性，将诊所法律教育的优势与卓越法律人才的培养进行结合，是我国现今法学教育研究的一个课题。

关键词：诊所法律教育　卓越法律人才　实践教学

在当今中国，法律人才的培养体系面临重大的变革。尤其近年来，卓越法律人才的培养成为法学教育中备受关注的课题。起源于美国的诊所法律教育，自2000年在福特基金的支持下，也在我国出现并逐步发展起来。这种教学模式是对传统学院式教学模式的突破，具有全新的教学理念以及较强的社会实践性。此种模式在法学教育与研究中的应用必将为我国卓越法律人才的培养作出一定的贡献，并为我国法律人才培养体系的变革提供一些有益的思路。

一、卓越法律人才的培养定位

由麦可思研究院独家撰写、中国社会科学文献出版社2011年6月出版的就业蓝皮书《2011年中国大学生就业报告》（以下简称报告）显示，

* 李涛，华北科技学院人文社科学院法学系讲师。

2010届本科毕业生半年后就业率最高的专业门类是工学，就业率为93.3%；最低的是法学，为86.7%，低于平均就业率。按照报告的有关数字推断，在法学专业就业率低、有大量剩余的情况下，用人单位应该能够招收到需要的人才，但现实是一些特殊法律人才呈现严重供给不足的状态。显然，法学属于人才培养质量达不到社会需求所导致的就业率较低的专业。[1] 法学毕业生不能满足社会的急迫需求，表现为大部分高校培养的“同质化”法学毕业生过剩，而能够供应市场需要的、具有特殊专业背景的法律人才以及愿意在特殊区域从事法律职业的人才紧缺。

这种情况的出现主要在于各高校在培养目标、培养方案、培养课程的设置中没有注意突出特色、体现多样化，并且缺乏对学生实践能力的培养，因此也造成我国现今法律人才需求与供给的错位。我国高校在法律人才培养方面的不足主要体现在以下几个方面：首先，从宏观上讲，法学教育目标定位不准确。法学教育的目标是整个法学教育发展的核心，直接影响到我国法律人才的培养标准、培养规格、培养方式等方面的定位。目前，我国法学教育对法律人才应该具备的知识结构、能力和职业道德没有明确要求，也未能准确定位法学本科教育是职业教育还是通识教育。这导致我国当前的法学教育带有极大的盲目性、实用性和功利性。其次，从微观上讲，法学教育现状与法律职业要求脱节。法学教育是法律职业的基础，与法律职业有密切关系。我国各高校法学专业在规划及制定具体培养目标时都比较忽视应用能力的培养，重理论讲授而轻能力实训，理论课时较多而实训课时较少，造成学生缺乏相应的实践应用能力。另外，在课程设置方面存在培养目标与课程体系不衔接的问题。一方面，有的高校也认识到了培养学生应用能力的重要性，在培养目标中也提及了此问题，但在具体设置课程时把开设此类课程放在了可有可无的位置；另一方面，即使有些高校设置了此类课程，比如也开设了模拟法庭及各类实习课程，但由于受到经济实力及师资力量的限制，或者由于经验不足，其中的不少课程都流于形式，并没有起到提高学生实践能

[1] 刘丹冰、卞辉：“需求与供给平衡：卓越法律人才培养目标多样化探讨”，载《中国法学会法学教育研究会2011年年会论文集》。

力的作用。而在社会责任感和职业道德素养方面，在日常的课堂讲授过程中，由于授课教师过于注重应试教育（比如司法考试），因而往往忽略了对于学生作为法律职业人应有的责任感和素质的培养。

为了达到法律人才需求与供给的平衡，国家出台了“卓越法律人才培养计划”。卓越法律人才的培养，是在高等法学教育已形成一定规模化、大众化的背景下，将在校法学本科生培养成将来在各个领域起到骨干作用的法律职业人才。所以，其一方面是培养能够提供国际化法律服务、具有行业领军能力并具有国际化视野的高层次法律人才，以适应我国对外开放发展需要；另一方面就是要为各地方培养各类型法律服务的主力军，即为社会提供更多合格乃至优秀的法律实务工作者。因此，应将卓越法律人才的培养定位于复合型、应用型法律职业人才。所谓复合型，强调其具有完善扎实的跨学科基础知识以及深厚的法学学科体系知识，并且能适应法律职业的特殊要求。所谓应用型，强调其实务性，即能很快且很好地适应各类型法律服务工作。这就要求卓越法律人才必须具备扎实的法学基础理论知识和逻辑思辨能力、较强的应用实践能力、相应的创新能力以及较强的社会责任感和环境适应能力。

二、诊所法律教育对卓越法律人才培养的启示

关于诊所法律教育（Clinical Legal Education），早期研究诊所教育的学者将其译作“临床式法学教育”，顾名思义，实际上就是仿效医学院诊所教育而产生的，在医学院就读的学生需要花费相当的时间从事临床实习，从实践中学会诊断和治疗。当法学教育引入这种教学方法时，法学院借用了“诊所”的名称，产生了“法律诊所”这一法学领域特有的名称。学生在“法律诊所”中，在教师的指导下为处于弱势地位的委托人提供咨询，“诊断”他们的法律问题，开出解决问题的“处方”，并为他们提供法律服务。这一做法类似于医学院的临床实习，都是从实践中学习执业技能。[1] 诊所法律教育的主要教学方法有两种，一是课堂模拟

[1] 周凯、王雪皎：“美国诊所式法律教育的起源与课程设置”，载《求实》2011年第11期。

练习，即学生在课堂模拟练习中扮演案件所需要的各种角色，在教师的指导下体验律师、法官、当事人等角色的活动，在这个过程中学会处理具体法律问题的技能；二是真实案件的代理，即由学生在教师的指导下，直接面对社会从事实际的法律服务工作，包括会见当事人、提供咨询意见甚至出庭参与诉讼等。通过这样的实践与锻炼，学生可以将所学的理论知识运用于实践，学会处理和解决实际问题，从而提高法律职业技能水平。

诊所法律教育最早起源于美国，也是对当时法学教育的缺陷进行反思的结果。随着法律的复杂化，一般的案例课程已不足以传授基本法律技能。一些法律界人士批评传统的“判例教学法”太学术化、脱离实际，因此，为改进法学教育的不足采取了各种改革措施，其中诊所法律教育是最为重要的一种措施。与传统法学教育相比，诊所法律教育克服了在培养法律人才方面的不足，凸显出以下几个优势：

(1) 注重素质教育。传统的法学教育侧重于对法律规范内容的理论讲授，而诊所法律教育则立足于增强学生的社会参与意识。参加法律义务咨询，参与法律援助案件代理，有利于培养学生的社会责任感和正义感，增强学生的法律职业道德和职业纪律；并且，参与真实案件的处理有利于学生的批判性及创造性思维方式的形成和分析解决问题能力的提高。

(2) 注重实践教学。诊所法律教育与传统课堂教学方式不同，是一种实践性的教学方式。这种教学方式要求学生掌握比较扎实的法律基础知识，并且能够将所学的法律知识运用于法律实践。因此，其对于学生和教师都提出了较高的要求。对于学生而言，在掌握课堂知识的同时，需要利用课外时间查阅大量资料，寻求问题的解决方案；而对于教师而言，除具备深厚的理论功底外，还必须具有较丰富的实践经验，才能更好地指导学生。

(3) 激发自主学习。诊所法律教育模式能够使学生的学习变被动为主动。在这一过程中，学生是案件的承办人，不得不面对诊所的客户所提出的各种各样的要求，并且需要积极主动地去解决这些实际问题。这些实际问题会激发学生学习的积极性与主动性。问题越多，教学的效果也会越好。学生会主动寻求各种方法去获取各种法律技能，从而找到解决问题的方法，这必然会提高和锻炼学生的综合素质和能力。

（4）培养具体思维。传统的法学教育比较重视理论知识的传授，因而也比较重视对学生的学理性思维的培养，而忽视了相关问题产生的社会原因和各方面的利益衡量，这也使得学生陷入抽象的价值判断，寻找不到解决问题的有效办法。[1] 而诊所法律教育要求学生对每一个细节都应当注意并认真思考，结合具体的事实与证据进行分析，从而得出结论。其要求不仅要考虑相关的法律规定及事实情况，还要考虑法律与事实背后的联系，了解案件所具有的特定的社会背景，进而对案件作出判断。在这样一个判断的过程中，自然就形成了一种实践中的具体思维方式。

由于诊所法律教育具有以上所述优势，结合卓越法律人才培养的定位与目标，其为卓越法律人才的培养提供了有效的途径和思路。其对我国卓越法律人才培养宏观方面的启示主要表现在以下几个方面：

（1）确立以培养法律职业技能为培养目标。首先应明确我国的法学教育为职业教育，而非通识教育。虽然我国现阶段法学教育（尤其是本科法学教育）正在逐渐由学术型教育向应用型教育转变，但是绝大部分高校仍把理论教育作为法学教育的重点。这与国际法学教育的现状是不相适应的，并且不利于学生法律职业技能的提高，无法造就适应社会需求的法律人才，即卓越法律人才。实际上，现代法学教育模式的成功与否应以是否能培养出合格的法律职业人才为标准。

（2）注重培养学生的法律职业道德及创造性思维能力。卓越法律人才需要具备较高的法律职业技能，而较高的法律职业技能就意味着其必须同时具有良好的法律职业道德及创造性思维能力。实践中，诊所法律教育中所代理的真实案件大多都是一些法律援助项目，通过向弱势群体提供法律援助，学生可以切身感受到法律工作是实现社会公正的一个渠道，这使得法学教育远远超出了法律知识和法律工作能力本身，延展到

---

[1] 薄振峰：“诊所式法律教育与中国法学教学改革”，载《黑龙江省政法管理干部学院学报》2007 年第 2 期。

培养学生的社会责任心、公益心和与之相联系的献身精神等思想道德领域，从而培养其法律职业道德素养。另外，诊所法律教育是将学生放置到一个现实的场景中，由于会不断地遇到新问题，需要学生不断地进行解决，在这个不断寻求解决方案的过程中，自然锻炼和提高了学生的创造性思维能力。

（3）转变传统的法学教育理念。传统的法学教育是以理论讲授为主，强调的是课堂讲授。知识是自上而下进行灌输的。在课堂上，占据主动的是教师，学生只是被动地接受，未能进行积极的思考，更谈不上主动地解决问题了。而在诊所法律教学过程中，学生是教学中的主动者，要求具备强烈的参与性和能动性。自我教育和自主学习是教学的通常模式。学生通过办理真实案件学习相关法律知识，教师只是从旁监督与指导。另外，在课堂模拟练习中，教师也是采取启发式的教学方式，引导学生积极进行思考并解决相关问题。引入诊所法律教育理念，必将大大提高学生的法律职业技能水平，并有利于卓越法律人才培养目标的实现。

（4）创立素质教育的法学教学评价体系。传统的教学评价体系对于学生而言，仍以书面试卷考核作为基本考核方式，分数是评价学生的基本标准，而缺乏对学生实践能力的考核。对于教师而言，主要是以教学工作量和科研成果作为评价标准，教师无暇深入从事实践教学。自2008年司法部允许法学本科三年级的学生报考司法考试之后，学生的司法考试通过率也成为相应的教学评价标准之一。而司法考试由于受形式的限制，也只能重在对应试人员案件分析能力和法学理论素养的测试，未能对应试人员的实践能力进行考核。因此，学生与教师都围绕此评价体系调整自己的行为，必然会重视理论知识的加强而忽视实践能力的提高。诊所法律教育学习的评估主体包括指导教师、客户、律师、法官和其他学生等，评估对象主要是学生对实体法和程序法的了解，工作中的行为表现以及这些工作所起的作用等，能够很好地对学生的实践能力进行考核。引入诊所法律教学课程，也必须建立一整套符合实际需要的法学教学评价体系，把对于学生实践能力的考核也作为法学教学的重要评价标准之一，从而激励教师积极投入实践教学、学生认真进行实践，更好地提高学生的法律职业技能水平。

三、诊所法律教育与卓越法律人才培养的融合

经过近一个世纪的实践和发展，诊所法律教育已被美国法学院普遍采用，而且取得了不错的效果。20 世纪以后，拉美、西欧、东欧、澳大利亚、新西兰以及南亚印度等许多国家和地区的法律院校纷纷进行改革，广泛而成功地应用了这种教学方式。2000 年 9 月，美国福特基金会资助中国人民大学、北京大学、复旦大学、清华大学、武汉大学等国内 7 所高校的法律院系开设了诊所课程，受到社会、学校和法学院学生的广泛欢迎。

然而尽管诊所法律教育所倡导的法学教育理念在现代中国高等法学教育中值得认同，但其理论与实践价值并没有它的移植倡导者认定得那么大。在我国，将诊所法律教育融合于卓越法律人才的培养是有一定困难的。究其原因，主要是诊所法律教育本身的局限性及我国现有法学教育现状的局限性所导致的。

（一）诊所法律教育与卓越法律人才培养的融合之困境

首先，诊所法律教育本身有一定的局限性。诊所法律教育的理念与其社会功能存在一定的冲突。[1] 诊所法律教育的目标是把学生培养成社会所期望的各种法律职业角色。学生通过实践法律职业角色锻炼职业判断力，完成高等技能的培养，使学生从经验式教学中学到东西并将这种经验能力应用于将来。也就是说，诊所法律教育的这一理念蕴含一定的社会服务功能。但是，教育理念和服务功能在性质和目标上是冲突的。在这样的教学过程中，若强调教学目的和效果，则当事人的利益有可能受损；若单从当事人角度考虑，则教学的目的可能又会落空。这种教学理念与社会功能之间的冲突是诊所法律教育难以克服的。另外，传统诊所法律教育的教学目标主要还是倾向于提高学生的律师职业技能。但在

---

[1] 周莳文、梁灯："我国诊所式法律教育的价值反思"，载《华南理工大学学报》2006 年第 5 期。

我国，法学教育不仅限于培养律师，还包括法官、检察官、警察、行政执法官和法学理论研究者等在内的各种法律人才。这也体现出诊所法律教育的一定局限性。

其次，在融合诊所法律教育时，我国现有的法学教育现状有一定的局限性。第一，我国的法律文化传统与滋生法律诊所教育的美国有很大不同。我国深受大陆法系的影响，成文法是我国法律的主要渊源，不承认判例法，长期以来法学教育都是以课堂理论学习为主。而美国是英美法系国家，以判例法为主，在法学教育过程中，往往是通过促使学生投入司法实践，让其参与实际办案来运用法学知识、理解法学理论并且树立法律信仰。我国现今的高等法学教育虽然也逐渐重视实践教学，加大了实践课程的比例，但是由于受到法律传统文化的影响，不可能完全照搬美国的模式。失去这种土壤，诊所法律教育在这样一个环境下的发展必然会受到一系列不利因素的影响，可能会难以发挥其应有的一些功能。第二，法学教育的教学条件达不到设立诊所法律教育所需的条件。高等院校开展诊所法律教育首先要设立“法律诊所”，并且需要一定数量的接受过专业训练的教育人员进行专业化的工作。这些都需要相应的物质条件支持。无论是场所、设备及对专门人员的培训，都需要财力保障。而我国高校普遍存在经费不足的问题，难以负担这一大笔支出。另外，诊所教育对师资的要求极其严格，任课教师必须具有较高的法学理论水平和实践能力。但是在中国，各法学院教师的整体水平还较低，普遍缺乏实践经验，很多人不能适应此项工作的要求。除此之外，在实践教学中，案件的来源也有限。在中国，学生只能以公民身份代理案件，因此受各方面条件的限制，诊所教师很难提供充足的案件让学生代理。

（二）诊所法律教育与卓越法律人才培养的融合之具体途径

为了将诊所法律教育更好地融于卓越法律人才的培养，从而发挥其应有的功能，提高我国法律职业人才的职业技能水平，我们除了要注意已在上文中提到的宏观方面的启示以外，在法学教育的微观方面应在以下几个方面进行完善：

（1）多渠道解决资金问题。我国许多著名大学法律诊所的资金都来源于美国福特基金会的支持，但是地方高校是没有这个经费的。地方高校一是可以从这些著名大学获得这方面的财力支持。二是可以整合本校的一些实践课程，将以往用于实践教学的资金投入到法律诊所的建设中去。另外，地方高校应加强与地方社会单位的合作，例如某些公益基金会，也可从它们那里获得一定的资金支持。

（2）加强诊所教师的师资力量。法律诊所的教师可有多种渠道，当然法学院的教师应是主流。学校应鼓励教师参加社会实践，从事法律职业方面的兼职工作，增加其职业技能及经验。学校可以给予对诊所法律教育感兴趣并且有能力从事诊所法律教育的教师专门的培训，确定其为专职的指导教师并保证他们与授课教师有相同的待遇；还可以制定奖励措施，鼓励授课老师担任诊所指导。诊所还可聘请愿意为法学教育做贡献的资深律师或退休在家有丰富职业经验的司法人员担任学生的指导教师。[1] 通过以上方式，可以较好地解决诊所教师的师资力量不足的问题。

（3）建立合作，促使案源多元化。一是取得政府与司法机关的支持。法律诊所可以与政府的法律援助中心建立密切联系，获得法律援助的案源。学生参与代理真实案件的身份，也需要当地司法各界的认可和配合。为此，学校应加强与当地司法各界的联系，或直接建立实践教学基地，或签订合作协议配合教学。二是取得社会的支持。法律诊所可以和当地律师协会、律师事务所和社区组织等建立长久合作关系，以获得较为充足的法律援助案源。

诊所法律教育将法学理论与实践进行了较好的结合，此种法学教育理念可以弥补目前我国高等法学教育体系在培养法律人才方面的不足。如果能将其与卓越法律人才培养进行完美的融合，必将为我国培养出更多符合社会需要的法律人才，使我国整体的法律职业技能及职业素养得到很大的提高。

---

[1] 王菊英："'诊所式法律教育'本土化的思考"，载《河北法学》2005年第3期。

Professional Legal Education in Japan: Achievements and Obstacles

Setsuo Miyazawa*

Introduction

I expect that Professor Shigeo Miyagawa will discuss the development and current issues of clinical legal education in Japan, with a description of the largest clinical program in Japan at Waseda University Law School. Clinical legal education was introduced in Japan as part of the introduction of post-graduate professional legal education (law schools) in 2004 based on the final recommendations of the Justice System Reform Council in 2001. Therefore, I will discuss the background, development, and current issues of law schools in Japan, with an emphasis on clinical legal education.

I will particularly discuss the following:

(1) professional legal education had not existed in Japan before the introduction of law schools;

(2) while progressive and conservative reformers had existed, policy-making process was ultimately controlled by conservatives who wanted to maintain key elements of the old system;

---

* Setsuo Miyazawa, Ph. D. (Yale), S. J. D. (Hokkaido) Professor, Aoyama Gakuin University Law School Visiting Professor, University of California Hastings College of the Law Professor Emeritus, Kobe University Adjunct Lecturer, Waseda University smiyazawa@aoni. waseda. jp

(3) the new law school system has nevertheless produced various positive results including the introduction of clinical legal education;

(4) however, the low and declining bar passage rate has quickly started to undermine the new law school system and retard the development of clinical legal education; and

(5) the recent introduction of an alternative route which does not require graduation from a law school is possible to become a death blow to the law school system.

Considering the brevity of my presentation, I will not cite any references in the text. Instead, I will provide a selected list of background readings at the end of the text in which interested audience can find relevant information.

1. Lack of Professional Legal Education before the Introduction of Law Schools

A total of 74 post-graduate professional law schools were established in Japan in 2004 and 2005. The authorized number of entering students was approximately 5800. This was the first time for Japan to have a system of professional legal education.

It is true that there were approximately 100 undergraduate law faculties and approximately 200000 students were enrolled in the 1990's. However, undergraduate legal education was never intended to train future legal professionals, namely judges, prosecutors, and practicing attorneys. Therefore, there were no courses in legal ethics and professional skills, for instance, while many law faculties taught both law and political science, and other courses in social science, humanities, and foreign languages are also offered at many law faculties.

The National Bar Examination did not require completion of undergraduate legal education. The Bar Exam only required completion of first two years in any undergraduate department. It is true that a vast majority of those who passed the Bar Exam were graduates of undergraduate law faculties, but it does not mean that they were educated to become legal professionals in undergraduate law faculties.

Skill training was provided after passing the Bar Exam at the Judicial Research and Training Institute which was managed by the Supreme Court. The duration of traineeship was initially two years, and it was reduced to one and a half years later. Trainees received a stipend for the entire period. Schooling was provided at the beginning and end of the traineeship, and it heavily emphasized training in doctrines and litigation skills developed by main-stream judges. Trainees were assigned to local courts, prosecutor's offices, and law offices between the two schooling periods. Trainees were treated as apprentices: they observed how judges, prosecutors, and practicing attorneys practiced and occasionally engaged in drafting and other activities. However, there was no systematic curriculum for apprentices, and what they learned varied depending on individual mentors they were assigned to. Faculty members of the Institute were carefully selected from judges, prosecutors, and practicing attorneys. While a vast majority became practicing attorneys, only a quarter of the time was devoted to practicing attorneys: the rest were equally divided to civil judging, criminal judging, and prosecution. Candidates for positions in the judiciary and the procuracy were informally recruited at the Institute. At the end of the traineeship, trainees took the final examination, and the ranking in the final examination was a major determinant for appointment to the judiciary or procuracy.

The Institute was operated with the national budget, the budget determined the capacity of the Institute, and that capacity determined the number of people who could pass the Bar Exam, which was administered by the Justice Ministry. The number of passers only gradually increased: it started with approximately 260 in 1949, reached 500 in 1963, 800 in

1998, and 1000 in 1999.

On the other hand, since the Bar Exam only required completion of the first two years of any undergraduate education, a large number of people took the exam. It reached 29000 in 1976, and the pass rate was only 1.5%.

This extreme competitiveness created an industry of cram schools. Cram schools provided year-round programs at several levels, all of which were focused on the subjects included in the Bar Exam. Therefore, cramming at those schools became the most common educational background of legal professionals in Japan.

Some scholars criticized this old system. A leading example was the late Professor Hideo Tanaka who taught Anglo-American law at the University of Tokyo. He wrote that the training at the Judicial Research and Training Institute was apprenticeship, rather than professional legal education, and argued that Japan still needed a system of professional legal education which provides a broader range of education by faculty members who were guaranteed academic freedom. I took the same position: I argued that theoretically speaking, legal professionals in Japan could not be considered real professionals until they obtain institutions which offer educational programs clearly intended to train future legal professionals.

The Justice System Reform Council reached a similar conclusion from a more practical consideration. A result of the old system was the extremely small number of legal professionals in Japan. In 1988, for instance, Japan had only approximately 13000 practicing attorneys, while the United States had 670000, England 71000, Germany had 49000, and France had 16000. Geographical distribution of practicing attorneys was also highly skewed. In 1998, for instance, Tokyo had one attorney for 1500 residents, while 34 out of 46 other prefectures had one lawyer for more than 16000 residents, including four prefectures that had one attorney for more than 32000 residents. About a half of jurisdictions of district court branches had no or only one attorney, and such jurisdictions were called "zero/one districts". Therefore, one of the major objectives of the Council was to improve public access to legal services by radically increasing legal professionals.

There was also an increasing criticism to legal professionals for their narrowness of educational background and their lack of broader intellectual and social backgrounds which would be required to handle increasingly more complex legal matters. Therefore, the Council also wanted to improve the quality of legal professionals in terms of expanding their intellectual and social backgrounds.

The idea of post-graduate professional law schools was considered the best option to deal with these needs to produce a far larger number of legal professionals who came from broader intellectual and social backgrounds and received broader and more systematic legal education which was clearly designed to train future legal professionals. An alternative was to change undergraduate law faculties to professional law schools. But their number was too large, and their quality varied too much. Furthermore, it would be difficult for undergraduate schools to have a large number of students who already received education in areas other than law or had real life experiences.

Therefore, the Justice System Reform Council considered the introduction of law schools as the most urgent reform which would lay grounds for other reforms, particularly the radical increase of legal professionals and the expansion of their intellectual and social backgrounds. The Council set the target of tripling the number of new legal professionals from 1000 to 3000 by around 2010.

However, there were different models for the new system of post-graduate professional law schools. I will discuss them in the next section.

2. Progressive and Conservative Ideas of Law Schools

When the Justice System Reform Council started its deliberation on law schools, there were two different ideas. I will call them progressive and conservative ideas.

Progressive reformers proposed to establish law schools which would provide education in the entire range of professional legal education, including doctrinal courses, legal ethics, and practice-oriented courses, including live-client legal clinics and other forms of clinical legal education. These reformers wanted to abolish the Judicial Research and Training Institute which had become as a bottleneck to artificially control the number of new legal professionals in Japan and had provided only a very narrow range of litigation-oriented skills. Some of these reformers proposed to replace training at the Institute with training by bar associations like that in Canada. I was one of the most active members of this group. One may be surprised to know that the Korean law school system is very similar to the model proposed by those progressive reformers in Japan.

Conservative reformers wanted to maintain the institutional status of undergraduate law faculties and proposed to create law schools directly on top of undergraduate law faculties, so that those who wanted to enter a law school would start their education from an undergraduate law faculty. They also wanted to maintain the Judicial Research and Training Institute and proposed to provide only a limited range of practice-oriented courses which could be taught in classrooms. Both Tokyo University and Kyoto University, the two most prestigious the pnational universities, took this position. The chairperson of the Justice System Reform Council was a professor at Kyoto University, while another member in the Council was a professor at Tokyo University.

These conservative reformers quickly controlled the policy-making process, and the end result was full of compromises to maintain key elements of the old system. For instance:

(1) A three-year program was proposed as the standard form of law schools, but a two-year program was also permitted to admit those students who had already acquired a high level of legal knowledge. It was clear that students who would enter two-year programs would be mostly graduates of undergraduate law faculties.

(2) Law schools were expected to "bridge theories and practices", but they were not required to provide extensive clinical education. The Judicial Research and Training Institute was maintained as the main place to provide practical training.

(3) The new Bar Exam was to be introduced in 2006 for the first cohort of graduates of two-year programs at law schools, and the old Bar Exam was to disappear after 2010. However, a new system was to be introduced in 2011, in which those who passed the Preliminary Examination would be allowed to take the final Bar Exam without graduating from a law school. The Council proposed to introduce this system, which looked exactly like the old Bar Exam, for those who could not afford to enter a law school or lived too far from a law school. However, when the Bar Exam Act was amended to introduce the Preliminary exam, such conditions were not included. Critical observers like me warned the possibility that this Preliminary Exam would eventually undermine the law school system.

Furthermore, there was no coordination between the Education Ministry and the Justice Ministry. On the one hand, the Education Ministry was working under the general governmental policy of deregulation, and the Ministry approved an application from a university as long as it satisfied a set of standards. That was why 74 law schools were eventually established. On the other hand, the Justice Ministry had no intention to radically increase the number of passers of the new Bar Exam. Law schools opened their doors to the first cohort of students in April 2004, but the Justice Ministry was already reported that it had no intention to triple of the number of new legal professionals by around 2010. A group of law school faculty members including myself lobbied several months to increase the number of new passers, but the pass rate of the first Bar Exam in 2006 did not reach 50%. In other words, the Bar Exam, rather than law schools, immediately established itself as the core of the new system. Given that new graduates will join those who failed in previous exams, it became clear that only a minority of law school graduates would be able to become legal professionals.

3. Positive Results of Law Schools

In spite of the quickly worsening situation, law schools produced various positive results, both inside and outside.

Inside law schools, law professors started pay serious attention to teaching for the first time in the history of legal education in Japan. Even in doctrinal courses, many professors changed the content of their courses and published textbooks that were designed for law school education. Courses on professional ethics were introduced for the first time in Japan, and several textbooks were published, including the one I coedited with two practicing attorneys. Progressive law schools (1) made the three-year program larger than the two-year program, (2) introduced an international program, and (3) established an extensive clinical program, including live-client clinics. As Professor Miyagawa will describe, Waseda Law School was most progressive among largest law schools in Japan and started with all of these characteristics. A few law schools also started with an evening program. As Mr. Yamaguchi will explain, Tsukuba University Law School is an example of small law schools which started with an evening program and a live-client clinic.

Outside law schools, law schools quickly contributed to increase the number of legal professionals, particularly practicing attorneys. The number of practicing attorneys increased from 18000 in 2001, to 22000 in 2006, and 30000 in 2011. Geographical distribution was also improved; while some prefectures had one lawyer for more than 30000 residents in the late 1990's, they now have one lawyer for about 16000 residents. "Zero/one district" virtually disappeared.

However, the low and declining bar passage rate quickly started to take its toll. I will discuss it in the next section.

4. Negative Impact of the Low and Declining Bar Passage Ratc

While the number of applicants to the Bar Exam naturally continued to increase, the number of passers was kept constant since 2008 at arounconitd 2000. The number of passers was only 2074 in 2010 and failed to reach 3000 as expected by the Justice System Reform Council.

The rate was only 23.5% last year and 25.1% this year. This year, the passage rate for graduates of two-year programs was 36.2%, as compared to the rate of only 17.2% for graduates of two-year programs. Even the highest passage rate for a law school was only 57%, and 20 law schools had a passage rate lower than 10%.

This situation quickly damaged attractiveness of legal professionals, and the number of applicants to the Law School Aptitude Test, which is required for all applicants to law schools, continued to decrease from approximately 40000 in 2003 to only about 6000 this year. This decrease means the extremely small and shrinking size of talents from which legal professionals in the future will be recruited.

The proportion new students who have a real life experience also declined from 48.4% in 2004 to less than half of that in recent years. This situation means that a vast majority of new legal professionals in recent years have no intellectual background other than law and no real life experience. This is contrary to what the Justice System Reform Council expected as the new quality of legal professionals.

Facing this reality, many law schools are expanding the proportion of the two-year program. Waseda Law School is a typical example. Many law schools are also expanding the proportion of courses in the subjects covered by the Bar Exam, which makes it difficult for many law schools to expand clinical programs. Those law schools which started with a relatively large clinical program are still maintaining their clinical programs, but it is becoming extremely difficult to introduce a live-client clinic anew.

Five law schools have already decided to close. The Education Ministry is also giving pressure on other law schools with a very low passage rate or very low competitiveness in admissions to reduce the number of students or to close, by reducing financial assistance to such schools. Such a tactics may look too brutal. However, considering the fact that a vast majority of students at such schools have no realistic possibility to become a legal professional, one may realize the existence of an extremely serious consumer problem. A vast majority of students are incurring enormous cost without having any realistic possibility of return. One must at least admit the necessity to find a proper way to protect such students from an enormous waste.

Given the political reality that the Japan Federation of Bar Associations now demands a reduction of the number of passers of the Bar Exam, there is no realistic possibility that the pass rate will go up. The most realistic way to increase the passage rate under the condition of the constant number of passers is to reduce the number of applicants. In order to reduce applicants, we have to reduce the number of law students.

One may hope that the passage rate will rise up again, and those law schools that will manage to survive will regain their idealism and start to strengthen their clinical programs. However, the law school system as a whole may collapse before such law schools start to strengthen their clinical programs. The reason is such a catastrophic scenario is the impact of the Preliminary Exam which I warned ten years ago. I will discuss this problem in the next section.

5. Preliminary Examination as a Potential Death Blow to the Professional Legal Education

The first Preliminary Exam was given last year. Only 116 passed at the pass rate of merely 1. 8%. This year, 85 of them took the final Bar Exam, and 58 passed at the pass rate of 68. 2%, which was higher than the highest passage rate for law schools. This year, 219 passed the Preliminary Exam, and the pass rate increased to 3%. 69 were undergraduate students, and 61 were law school students. It appears that the Justice Ministry intends to gradually increase the number of passers of the Preliminary Exam to the level where their pass rate in the final Bar Exam equals that of the average pass rate of law school graduates. However, a trend has already appeared at top universities that increasingly more undergraduate law students are attracted to the Preliminary Exam, and the attractiveness of law schools is rapidly declining.

It seems possible that no undergraduate law students will apply to law schools in the near future. One possibility for the survival of law schools in such a situation may be to provide opportunities to become legal professional to graduates of non-law undergraduate programs, like JM programs in China. However, it may be more likely that the entire law school system will collapse before making such a fundamental transformation.

We will know the answer in a few years.

Conclusion

Supporters of clinical legal education in Japan are working increasingly more negative environment which is threatening the law school system itself. If the law school system collapsed, it would mean the return of the old Bar Exam and the death of professional legal education. The only hope for clinical legal education may be the possibility of introducing clinical programs into the context of undergraduate legal education. In this sense, it may be important for us to learn situations of clinical legal education in countries where legal education is still provided mostly at an undergraduate level.

Background Readings (in the order of publication)

I would be happy provide a copy of any of my papers upon request. Some of them are, however, available online.

Setsuo Miyazawa with Hiroshi Otsuka, "Legal Education and the Reproduction of the Elite in Japan," Asian-Pacific Law & Policy Journal, Inaugural Issue, 2000, pp. 1～31. (an online journal, http://www.hawaii.edu/aplpj/)

Setsuo Miyazawa, "The Politics of Judicial Reform in Japan: The Rule of Law at Last?" Asian-Pacific Law & Policy Journal, Vol. 1, Issue 2, 2001, pp. 89～121. (an online journal, http://www.hawaii.edu/aplpj/)

Setsuo Miyazawa with Hiroshi Otsuka, "Legal Education and the Reproduction of The Elite in Japan," in Yves Dezalay and Bryant G. Garth (eds.), Global Prescriptions: The Production, Exportation, and Importation of a New Legal Orthodoxy, Ann Arbor: The University of Michigan Press, 2002, pp. 162～208.

Setsuo Miyazawa, "Educating and Training of Lawyers in Japan: A Critical Analysis," South Texas Law Review, Vol. 43, No. 2, 2002, pp. 491～498. (available on LEXIS/NEXIS)

Eiji Tsukahawa, Koji Miyagawa, and Setsuo Miyazawa (eds.), Ethics and Responsibility of Lawyers: A Problem Book, Gendai Jinbunsha, 2004. (2nd ed., 2010) 塚原英治·宮川光治·宮澤節生（編著）『プロブレムブック法曹の倫理と責任』（現代人文社、2004年；第2版、2010年）

Peter A. Joy, Shigeo Miyagawa, Takao Suami, and Charles D. Weisselberg, "Building Clinical Legal Education Programs in a Country without a Tradition of Graduate Professional Legal Education: Japan Educational Reform as a Case Study," Clinical Law Review, Vol. 13, No. 1, 2006, pp. 417～458.

Setsuo Miyazawa, "The Politics of Judicial Reform in Japan: The Rule of Law at Last?" in William P. Alford et al. (eds.), Raising the Bar: The Emerging Legal Profession in East Asia, Cambridge, Harvard University Press, 2007, pp. 107～162.

Setsuo Miyazawa, "Law Reform, Lawyers and the Judiciary," in Gerald P. McAlinn (ed.), Japanese Business Law, Kluwer Law International, 2007, pp. 39～89.

Setsuo Miyazawa, Kay-Wah Chan, and Ilhyung Lee, "The Reform of Legal Education in East Asia," Annual Review of Law and Social Science, No. 4, 2008, pp. 333～360. (Note) I have asked the organizers of this conference to distribute a copy of this paper as the most convenient reference for my presentation.

Shigeo Miyagawa, Takao Suami, Peter A. Joy, and Charles D. Weisselberg, "Japan's New Clinical Programs: A Study of Light and Shadow," in Frank S. Bloch (ed.), The Global Clinical Movement: Educating Lawyers for Social Justice, Oxford University Press, 2011, pp. 105～120.

Setsuo Miyazawa et al., "Outline of the First Mailed Questionnaire Survey of Practicing Attorneys of the 62nd Cohort: Presentation of Descriptive Statistics," Aoyama Law Journal, No. 4, 2011, pp. 57～191. 宮澤節生·他「第62期弁護士第1回郵送調査の概要一記述統計の提

示一」青山法務研究論集第4号（2011年）57～191頁。

Setsuo Miyazawa,“An Archaeology of the Debate over Law Schools: Focusing on the Position of the Judicial Research and Training Institute in Different Models of Law Schools,” Lawyers and Clinical Education, No.5，2012，pp.33～45.宮澤節生「法科大学院論争のひとつの 考古学一異なる法科大学院構想における司法研修所の位置づけを中心に一」法曹養成と臨床教育第5号（2012年）33～45頁。

Status and Prospects of Clinical Legal Education in Korea

Young SHIM *

Abstract: Korea's new legal education system was established in 2007. Korea introduced the US style law school system for improving the problematic legal education and lawyer training system which was a selective system and had created a lot of rising social costs on applicants who repeatedly took the bar exam even if they had very slight chance of passing the exam. The new law school system is intended to educate those who have majored in various areas and have diverse experience to be lawyers. But the new system has limitations on practical trainings compare to the former training system by the Judicial Research Training Institute of the Supreme Court. Now Korean wants to learn lessons from other countries legal practical training system to improve and make up for the weak points its new system.

Ⅰ. Introduction

Before the law school system, resembling that of the United States, was introducing in Korea, Korea had undergraduate law colleges and lawyers were selected by the rigid state bar exams. ❶ The push for a new

---

* Young SHIM, Professor of Law, Yonsei University Law School, Seoul, Korea.

❶ The old system bar exam will be existed until 2017 for the persons who are preparing the former bar exam.

law school system came after long criticism of former legal education because of the intense competition among undergraduate law students and the authoritarianism of legal experts. Introducing new US style law school system had been discussed from 1995. Several judicial reform committees were formed to discuss the legal system reforms. The law school system was pushed ahead with the goals of the quality improvement of legal service and the reform of legal education and the bar exam system. Korean Law School Act was enacted in July 2007.

Ⅱ. Clinical legal education before the law school system

Under the former bar exam system, one can take exam if he/she has taken more than 35 credits of legal subjects regardless of his or her undergraduate major. Therefore there is no condition that an applicant should be a law graduate. Moreover, there is not any graduate qualification for the applicants. Anyone who wants to apply the bar exam needs to take 35 law subject credits. [1] To pass the exam, most applicants seclude themselves from society and focus on learning statutes and court cases by rote. The former bar exam is a kind of "selective exam." From 2001 to 2009, around 1000 applicants have been passed every year. After the law school system was introduced, the number of successful candidates is gradually decreased. [2]

The former bar exam is a three-step exam. At the first-step, an applicant has to take multiple choice tests of three compulsory subjects (constitution law, civil law, and criminal law) and one elective subject

---

[1] During the period of 2003 to 2011, there were five high school graduates who passed the exam.

[2] The number of the applicants who passed the exam was 814 (year 2010), 707 (2011), and 502 (2012). In 2013, 300 applicants will be passed the former bar exam. Afterwards, 200 (year 2014), 150 (2015), 100 (2016), and 50 (2017) will be passed the exam.

(international law, labor law, international transaction law, tax law, intellectual law, economic law, criminal policy, or philosophy of law). The first-step successful applicants are around four times of final pass numbers. At the second-step, applicants have to take essay tests of seven compulsory subjects (constitution law, administrative law, commercial law, civil law, civil procedure law, criminal law, and criminal procedure law). The third-step test is an interview style test, consists of group and individual interviews. Only handful of applicants fails the third-step test. Applicants who fail the third-step test can take third-step test again next year. There has been no applicant who failed the second third-step test until now.

Applicants who passed the former bar exam enter the Judicial Research and Training Institute, which is run by the Supreme Court. The trainees take two-year course curricula. The Institution's education program focuses on training judges and public prosecutors, even if majority of trainees become practicing lawyers. In 2012, the Institute introduced new graduate school style education curricula, focusing on training practicing lawyers.

Under the Institution's program, trainees should take civil litigation practice, criminal litigation practice, criminal law practice, and lawyering together with several basic law and special area law subjects at the first year. At the second year, the trainees have to take practical internship training. The major problem with the Judicial Research and Training Institute's two-year training course is that this program is not designed to meet the diverse demands of society but to meet those of starting judges and prosecutors, including how to write judicial decisions and briefs.

Ⅲ. Bar exam under the law school system

1. Purpose of law school system

The former lawyer selection and train system with the former bar exam and the Judicial Research and Training Institute' training program has drawbacks and limitations on educating desirable lawyers who can adapt to the global environmental change in the legal service areas. The Korean legal education has failed to meet the demands for diverse legal services and wasted human resources to a great extent. [1]Moreover Korean law firms need to upgrade their quality to deal with the openness of legal market in the future.

The new Korean law school system is intended to provide legal education system that those, who have majored in various areas and have diverse experience, take legal education of basic and special area laws together with professional practice. The law school system aims to grant a qualification as lawyers those who fulfill the curricula faithfully.

2. The new bar exam

Only the law school graduates are allowed to take the new bar exam. The new bar exam is an one-step exam. Exam subjects are three compulsory subjects and one elective subject. Three compulsory subjects are public area laws (constitution law and administrative law), civil area laws (civil law, commercial law, and civil procedure law), criminal area laws (criminal law and criminal procedure law). Each compulsory subject consists of three different kinds of tests (multiple choice, essay, and writing a legal documentation). The elective subject test is an essay test. An applicant can choose one subject among international law (including international economic law), labor law, international transaction law (private international law and United Nations Convention on Contracts for the International Sale of Goods), tax law, intellectual law, e-

---

[1] The former bar exam was drawing tens of thousands of young applicants each year, with success being one of the most coveted vehicles of social upward mobility. And so many people repeatedly took the exam, ignoring that they stand little chance of passing, until it was too late to land a decent job elsewhere.

conomic law, or environmental law). It takes four days to take the new bar exam. There is no interview test.

A law school graduate can take five times during five years after graduation if he fails the exam. Currently the Ministry of Justice, which carries out the bar exam, decided that around 75% of law school students quota (2000 every year) passes the new bar exam. The Ministry of Justice announce that the new bar exam tests the legal knowledge and practical ability as a lawyer, and those who pass the new bar exam should have capacity similar to those who complete the first year program of the Judicial Research and Training Institute. In 2012, 1658 applicants took the first new bar exam and 1453 applicants passed. The pass ratio will be decreased every year because the pass rate is decided with the law school entrance quota rather than applicant numbers.

3. Practical training after bar exam

The person who passed the new bar exam has to take a six-month practical training before he/she accepts a case or open an individual law office. The practical training can take at courts, public prosecutor's offices, law firms, state departments, or the Korean Bar Association. The law student who was hired by a law firms or selected as law clerk or as a public prosecutor takes the practical training at the same institution. A law student who was not employed has to take a six-month training course the Korean Bar Association provides.

Ⅳ. Planning of legal education at the law school

When the new three-year law school system was introduced in 2007, the Education Ministry announced that there would be 2000 entrants each year and the issuing licenses to the schools by the competition. [1] Under the plans, there were nine evaluation criteria: educational goals, application process, school curricula, quality of teaching staff, student welfare, school facilities, budget, related academic degree program (such as S. J. D. program), and university's competitiveness and social responsibility.

Under the plan, school curricula took up 34. 5 percent of the evaluation and the quality of teaching staff 19. 5 percent.

The law schools should have at least 20 full-time professors and to appoint more than 20 percent of the statutory required number of professors from professionals who have at least five years of professional experience in the legal field.

The schools had to meet all the requirements before receiving official permission to build the law schools. The Education Ministry granted permission to 25 schools to open law schools. The law schools started to receive the first batch of students in 2009.

All law schools are required to be evaluated in 2012 for the three year result and afterward every five years by the Korean Bar Association. The evaluation criteria are based on the license evaluation criteria. There were eight evaluation criteria: educational goals, application process, school curricula, quality of teaching staff, student welfare, school facilities, budget and supports for teaching and research, and related academic degree program (such as S. J. D. program).

Unlike the Japanese law school system, those university establishing law schools are not allowed to continue have law colleges at the undergraduate departments. Only college graduates with Legal Education Eligibility Test (LEET) scores, similar to US LSAT, can apply for the

[1] The number of law students was limited to 150 per school per year. As a result, only one university had permission to accept 150 students per year.

law school. [1] Law college graduates are also allowed to apply. But a law school can admit law undergraduates up to two-third of its entrance quota.

Ⅴ. Current clinical legal education at the law school

1. Curricula

The Korean Law School Act requires every law school student to take five compulsory practicing subjects. Those are legal ethics, legal research and writings, legal documentation, moot court, and practical training internship.

The legal ethics subject is for providing a good understanding of key concept of professional ethics that lawyers must have. Before taking bar exam applicants need to pass the legal ethics exam. Usually students take the legal ethics exam at the second year.

The legal research and writings course is intended as a basic introduction to research Korean or foreign statutes, court decisions, legal writings, and other information. The legal documentation course gives a good opportunity to understand and practice basic writing method of written arguments. The moot court course is for practicing and enhancing the student's ability to understand how to conduct a real case at the court by becoming familiar with hypothetic cases.

Internship is designed to provide a field study opportunity. Law school should offer various internship programs with out-side institutions, such as law firms, government departments, local governments, public institutions, and company legal departments. The courts and public prosecutor's offices also have their own internship programs.

---

[1] Under the Korean Law School Act, law schools are required that undergraduate GPA, LEET scores, and foreign language ability are included in their evaluation elements.

Students have to complete 160 hours for earn the required credit. Student, who wants to have job at a big law firm, participates more than two internship programs. Big law firms provide general internship programs and intensive programs. Most big law firms recruit new lawyers among students who take their intensive internship programs. At the intensive program laws, firms test the applicant's practicing abilities.

Law schools also provide various kind of practicing subjects. The practicing subjects can be divided into two groups: general theory oriented courses and courses offering opportunities to handle real cases. The law school evaluation criteria require the law schools have to offer comprehensive and up-to-date subjects and there should be a balance of basic subjects and practical subjects. Moreover, law schools should have systematic curricula between theory-based courses and practical-based courses and offer courses combined legal theory and related practical matters.

Courts and public prosecutors' offices also help law school to send judges and prosecutors to teach practicing subjects. Judges teach civil litigation practice and criminal procedure and trial practice courses. Prosecutors teach criminal law practice Ⅰ and Ⅱ courses.

A distinctive feature of Korean law school system is that every law school should have one or more specialty area programs. Among 25 law schools, three schools have three specialty area programs each, two schools have two specialty area programs each, and the others have one program each. There is wide variety of programs. Public governance program, finance law, tax law, gender law, and logistics law are among them. Currently the specialty area programs are not popular to the students because the program enrollment is not compulsory and students are more devoting themselves to the bar exam.

2. Legal Clinic at the law school

Legal clinic is one of three important practical training methods at the law schools. When the law school system was introduced and the licensing criteria were announced, there were no details about legal clinics. But the Law School Evaluation Committee of the Korean Bar Association announced that the legal clinic would be one of the evaluation factors from 2011. In 2012, the Korean government granted a US ＄25000 to ＄46000 to support law schools' legal clinic programs.

Students need to take legal advices program or to participate an actual case litigation. All of law schools have legal advice service for the community or the general public. Some schools send students on field trips for legal advice. The legal advice activities are supervised by the professors who have professional experiences.

Participating actual litigations is very difficult because there are not many cases that the parties permit to handle students their cases. Schools try to find cases to file a suit from the legal advice service, but most of legal advices are simple cases. At least one school has tried to combine its specialty area program and the legal clinic activities, but the school finds out that most parties want to have their own lawyers not students. And it takes long time to finish a case therefore students usually spend their time part of the case process, if there is any.

Therefore many schools provide various kinds of legal clinic classes collaborated with outside lawyers. For example, Yonsei Law School provides more than seven legal clinic classes each semester. A legal clinic class is a small class that an outside lawyer teaches small number of students and work together with the actual case which the lecturer accepted to delegate. Students usually participate to write a petition or briefs to the courts.

3. Role of professors from professionals who have professional experience in the legal field

Under the Korean Attorney Act, an attorney is prohibited to accept a case if he/she works as the public servant. A law professor at the national university is a public servant, therefore he/she cannot accept a case. For the law professors at the private universities, the Education Ministry prohibits them to accept a case as licensing requirement. There is a strong criticism that the prohibition limits to have up-to-dated practical experiences and makes very difficult to teach and supervise students' clinical legal activities.

Ⅵ. Concluding observations

The former Korean lawyer selection and education system is a scheme that focuses on producing judges, public prosecutors, and litigation lawyers. However, the current law school system focuses on educating and training as lawyers who will work at various fields with legal expert knowledge. Therefore, the new bar exam is intended to give a license to individuals who successfully complete their legal education at law schools. [1]

This is the fourth year after the new legal education system was established. The first graduates who passed the first new bar exam have been started working as lawyers in this year. All of them have completed the practical training after the bar exam in October. Now they can open their own legal offices individually or jointly without any conditions. Many of them are working at law firms, big or small ones. Forty graduates were appointed as public prosecutors, and around 100 graduates were appointed as law clerks. We hope that they become competent law-

---

[1] The Korean Judicial Reform Committee, "Recommendation for Judicial Reform," (December, 2004). The Article 2 of the Law School Act provides that : the education goal of the law school is to provide a reasonable legal services to the public by training lawyers who have sound professional ethics and special and effective legal knowledge and capacities to solve complicated disputes.

yers. Until now lawyers who were educated at the law school have been received favorable evaluations. But, there are still some weak points need to be improved, especially in the area of clinical training. Therefore, Korea needs to learn lessons from other countries' experiences.

Purposes of Clinical Legal Education: between Ideal and Reality

MOON, Jaewan*

Ⅰ. Reform of Korean legal education and legal clinic

Korean legal education is undergoing a transition. The previous system of producing lawyers—selecting capable people by examining legal knowledge and teaching them for two years in the Judicial Research and Training Institute—is disappearing and being replaced by the American law school system. This year, the first law school graduates as well as Judicial Research and Training Institute graduates were produced at the same time: Law schools turned out 1361 graduates, while the institute turned out 1030. The number of graduates from the Judicial Research and Training Institute will decrease from now. The judicial examination will be repealed after the last exam in 2017; therefore, after 2020, lawyers will be no longer produced from the institute, but only from law schools.

Legal clinic is a law school course that shows the stark difference between the old and new system in the way of fostering lawyers. Learning from practice did not existed in the old system. The probation course of the Judicial Research and Training Institute is much different from Legal clinic of law school in terms of educational ideal and method. The educational ideal of legal clinic is to deliver social justice by supporting the vulnerable and to learn the meaning of the first article of Attorneys-at-Law

* MOON, Jaewan, Professor at HUFS Law School

Act—— "The mission of an attorney-at-law shall be to defend fundamental human rights and realize the social justice" ——during the process of being a lawyer. On the other hand, the probation course of the Judicial Research and Training Institute is about nothing but teaching lawyering skills to those who have already qualified as a lawyer. In terms of educational method, legal clinic is a student-led education, while the probation course is professor-led.

Law schools in Korea were launched to "cultivate lawyers (…) possessing knowledge and capabilities that enable professional and efficient settlement of complicated legal disputes (…)"[1]. If so, do lawyers from law schools actually have better skills at solving problems than those from the Judicial Research and Training Institute? Korean law society is regarding this issue as serious. For law school system to settle successfully, it is critical that lawyers from law schools receive excellent evaluations. This is possible when the method of legal education by law schools improves to be more effective than the old system.

Ⅱ. Purpose of ideal clinical education

1. Importance of clinical education

Legal clinic performs a key role in the practical education by law schools in Korea. According to Article 13 (2) of Enforcement Decree of the Act on the Establishment and Operation of Law school, every law schools in Korea has to offer courses such as professional responsibility, legal research, legal writing, moot court, and legal clinic. Among these courses, legal clinic is the most effective course that provides comprehensive education about every part of legal practice, gives strong motiva-

---

[1] See Act on the Establishment and Operation of Law School, Article 2 (Ideals of Education).

tion for learning legal theories as well as practical knowledge, and offers an opportunity for experiencing lawyers' mission, the realization of social justice.

Legal clinic are also regarded important in America, the home of law schools. Because the education in law schools completely depends on Socratic case method, there are serious concerns that law schools only focus on thinking like a lawyer, and neglect acting like a lawyer. ❶As a result, there is a problem of students graduating from law schools without learning skills and professional behaviors that they should learn as lawyers. To deal with this problem, it is recommended to reduce the share of courses that uses Socratic dialogue and the case method, and integrate the practical and theoretical education. ❷ Clinical Legal Education Association (hereinafter CLEA) published Best Practices for Legal Education in 2007, which contains the best practical knowledge that law schools should provide. In this book, CLEA pointed out that the problem is that law schools are not teaching best practices while it is clear and natural that they should be. CLEA also expressed concerns that law schools are not doing their best to foster students' practical skills while the license of lawyer does not ensure the ability to defend clients. ❸While CLEA admits that law schools are performing social roles in various sectors, it argues that law schools are failing to perform the most important function of law school: to help new lawyers to develop skills for actual practice. CLEA concerns that poor quality of law school education will lead to producing lawyers with poor skills, and the damage will ultimately fall on clients,

---

❶ Rebecca Sandefur & Jeffrey Selbin, The Clinic Effect, 16 Clinical L. Rev. 57 (2009).

❷ Roy Stuckey and Others, BEST PRACTICES FOR LEGAL EDUCATION (2007).

❸ *Id.* at 11.

i. e., the public.

2. Purpose of legal clinic

The first purpose of legal clinic is education by hands-on experience, in other words, a practical education. Legal education was originally conducted in classroom with textbooks, focusing on examples or cases that come with existing conclusions. However, considering that legal studies pursue practicality and have developed by solving actual cases, practical education is a real legal education. Legal clinic deals with real cases of client and is planned to play a role as real practical education which enables students to experience specific cases and the progresses of them. While encountering actual cases and actual clients, students can research facts, figure out legal issues and find and implement solutions. Mock cases or simulated cases are not as complicated or complex as actual cases. Also, in real cases, clients' purposes are unclear and inclusive, and sometimes change during the process of the case. Legal clinic proceeds this course of consulting and researching an actual client's actual case and solving problems, which is crucial for growing into a lawyer.

In this respect, first, it is needed to view real clients and real cases as very important when participating in legal clinic. Contrary to mock cases or simulated cases, a person's everything—life, body, property—might depend on a real case. Therefore, a real case should not be an object of various experiments. Students have to do their best in every case, try to understand clients' situation, figure out the truth of the case, find solution, and solve the case.

By meeting practicing lawyers in practical courses, students can gain a great opportunity for obtaining basic information that can help them choosing their future path. Legal clinic, along with other practical courses, provides opportunities for contacting with various lawyers. By engaging in legal clinic, students can understand the profession of lawyer and receive help with planning their future for the first time.

The second purpose of legal clinic is to provide motivation for profound learning on substantive law and to actually induce deeper understanding about the law. Understanding of substantive law improves with understanding of procedural law. There is a limit to learning law in a classroom with textbooks. Only when students can understand how substantive law is used in specific practical cases and in solving disputes, they can understand fully about substantive law. Legal clinic gives them opportunities for encountering substantive and procedural law in the field and provides motivation for learning.

For legal clinic to be operated properly, thorough preparation and study are acquired in advance to both professors and students. They should prepare and study for legal clinic class not only personally but also collectively. Students can minimize mistakes and maximize learning effect by group study and activities. Therefore, cooperation is important in operating a legal clinic. Learning effect can be maximized by critically review and discuss different opinions of respective students on a same case. Also, students can improve in expressing themselves and persuading others through opportunities for explaining about the case.

Community service is the third purpose of legal clinic. Especially, helping low-incomers or neglected social groups, who cannot have benefits of legal service, is an important purpose of legal clinic. In fact, to implant an image of lawyer serving society in students who learn law for the first time is more important in clinical education than to teach effectively. Legal clinics at law schools should represent the meaning of law schools' existence as society members by providing legal service for those who are neglected from legal service.

It can be said that the history of legal clinic equals the history of social service. Students at Yale Law School in America have provided legal aid service in New Haven since the 1920s, while students at Berkeley Law School started their practical education by establishing community law office in 1988 to provide legal service to local residents. Empathizing with and serving for community does not conflict with another purpose of legal clinic, education. Students serve for communities by education, with education. Considering that the trend of neo-liberalism and capitalism is being stronger and stronger these days, serving for society is especially important because the number of the neglected is rapidly increasing. Selfishness is surely a nature of human, but overcoming challenges by solidarity and cooperation is also our nature, therefore service becomes an important nature of lawyer as well. The platform for embodying this spirit of service is clinical education.

The fourth purpose of legal clinic is social reform. Social development through reform has been always needed, and is also needed today. Reform of law or system is difficult to be achieved by individual legal practice. Through legal clinic, students represent the poor and vulnerable, and therefore can see society from their point of view. By passing through this process, students do not merely learn about various social systems, but they can view them in a critical perspective. This is because that those who suffer from or are uncomfortable with the existing system are the ones who are first to see the problem of the system, and who can figure out the problem most exactly.

What is important here is critical learning. In fact, as appears by the fact that one of the fundamental ideas of law is legal stability, law does not actively responds to the change or reform of society. Settling for existing points of view makes it impossible to see the problem of law itself; it is possible only by critical learning and critical approach to a case. In this respect, it is very important who a lawyer represents, from whose point of view a lawyer sees the case and the world. Legal clinic trains students to see cases and the world from the view of the neglected social group, therefore enables them to think critically about the existing legal system.

To attempt reform of legal system and, more generally, social reform through legal clinic, it is not enough to see a problem as a fragment, restricting it on to the single case. A problem should be understood more comprehensively by combining it with the entire society. This comprehensive understanding can be obtained with the help from many academic areas other than law, such as sociology, economics, philosophy, or humanities. Creative thinking is often born in the process of combining different experiences of various fields. In addition, higher level of understanding on society in general also helps relating a legal case with overall social problems. Furthermore, discussion with other students or professors can be very helpful in expanding the scope of view by preventing the scope from being fixed on a single case.

Ⅲ. Reality of Legal clinic education: the case of Hankuk University of Foreign Studies (HUFS) Law School

In Korea, legal clinic is only at an early stage, and thus in many ways insufficient for properly embodying ideal purposes that legal clinic pursues. This paper will discuss the challenges of clinical education in pursuing the ideal purposes and how to overcome the challenges based on the case of Hankuk University of Foreign Studies (HUFS) Law School.

HUFS Law School launched Legal Clinic Center as recently as March 2010. However, College of Law, the predecessor of the law school, opened Legal Advice Office on November 1995, and had providing legal service for community and students since then. At that time, students didn't work on lawsuits and only provided free legal consult under the supervision of alumni lawyers. Legal Advice Office started online legal consult service on August 2002, which was once so active that it received 340 cases in 2003, but the number of cases gradually shrank into 20 to 30 a year as of recently. As more and more organizations such as lawyer groups, law firms, internet portal sites are providing online legal consult, college legal advice offices, which seemed relatively less professional, have lost ground.

As law schools were launched on March 2009, some of law school students showed interest in legal clinic. Those who engaged in social service for a long time in college also participated actively in serving for society by providing legal service. This could not be expected under the old system of selecting lawyers by the judicial exam, because students tended to be isolated from the outside world and immerse themselves in studying to pass the exam. On March 2010, when the first law school students became second grade, HUFS reorganized Legal Advice Office into Legal Clinic Center.

When establishing Legal Clinic Center, the university set up three educational purposes. The first is to implement practical legal education course. It was affirmed that internally, legal clinic offers practical experience to law school students; externally, it provides legal service to school staff or local residents. The second is to foster professional lawyers. It was affirmed that legal clinic not only contributes to community by promoting public interest, but also fosters lawyers equipped with practical knowledge and broad perspectives. The third is to realize HUFS Law School's specialization strategy, which is to foster lawyers who have global perspective and knowledge. It means that the clinic aims to contribute to providing legal service to foreigners and foreign companies operating in Korea.

It was hard, however, to find real cases suitable to accomplish these purposes. Students showed great enthusiasm, but there was no actual case to fulfill it. Deciding that it was important to start clinical education as soon as possible, Legal Clinic Center first sought help from the school, not searching for the vulnerable that needs help. The chief of Legal Clinic Center received a case that Center for Interpreting and Translation, an affiliate of the school, provided interpretation service but didn't get paid and directed students to carry out a lawsuit. From 2010 until to day, Legal Clinic Center performed four lawsuits, which claimed respectively for interpretation fee, compensation for damages, revocation of refusal disposition of application for a national merit, and divorce. The clients were school staff in all cases. Legal Clinic Center has been trying since 2011 to specialize the clinic by receiving cases that suit the school's specialization strategy. It has been consulting legal problems of foreign workers, one of which is ongoing as a lawsuit.

The students who have participated in clinical education show high satisfaction. Until now, 18 students have engaged in the education, with five in 2010, another five in 2011, and eight in 2012. Most of them are second grade students at the law school. The students' responses are:

"The process of contemplating on facts, making facts into actual record and filing it to the court was a precious experience that can't be acquired by lectures in class." (A, law school student, the first graduating class)

"I had just learned civil law and civil procedure law when I worked on the case, so it was hard enough to just extract legal issues from the case. Besides, I was flustered by detailed civil suit procedures that are not listed in the textbook. I remember I didn't know even where to file the complaint. I could have never solved the case by myself, but I could solve it with my teammates, not being frustrated." (B, law school student, the first graduating class)

"I would have proceeded faster if the client let me know about some of the facts, more particularly, a bankruptcy of a related agent. But the client may have not believed that the agent was bankrupt, therefore didn't inform me. I totally understand that this can happen. Lawyers should acquire the skill of quickly grasping not only what clients said but also what they didn't say by considering the situation. This is the most important lesson that I was able to learn by this case." (C, law school student, the second graduating class)

"I realized that legal problem is eventually the problem of people. I think that, apart from learning professional legal knowledge, it is most important for solving legal problems to clearly know what my client wants from the consult." (Researcher at Legal Clinic Center)

As seen from the students' responses, it is clear that students are experiencing what clinical education aims for by taking part in the course. It has been successful to teach through practice and induce in-depth learning on substantive law and procedural law. However, social service and social reform, which is another purposes of legal clinic, doesn't seem to have been realized yet. As the cases that students have taken were typical legal cases, students didn't get the opportunity for thinking critically, and the clients could not be seen as the ignored people in Korean society.

However, considering that the history of clinical education is not long, time can be counted on to solve this problem. Students are showing more interest in the cases related to public interest than just simple ones; they didn't work on those cases just because there are no such cases received. In this respect, the fact that HUFS Legal Clinic Center is stepping up to provide legal support for foreign workers in Korea means that it entered the right track of realizing the ideal purpose of clinical education. While the number of foreign workers living in Korea is increasing day by day, there are quite many cases in which foreign workers' human rights are violated; many of them are assaulted or don't get paid. With building close partnership with human rights groups such as Korea Migrant Human Rights Center, it will be not so much hard to find the vulnerable members of society who needs help from law.

Legal Services Activism to Enhance Justice and Remedy Injustice

Thilakanandan. C *

Justice is the most important ideal for which every human being is craving for. The spirit of justice is in fact implanted in man by nature itself. Even though the Law schools are the designated institutions to impart the theory of justice to its pupils all over the world, they miserably fail to assimilate the ideal, philosophy and spirit of justice to their students. It is true that law schools are professional development centers. But at the same time, we should see the objectives of society in establishing these institutions. The most important concern of state and society is to ensure justice to all. How far we were able to achieve this goal so far, how much we will be able to achieve it in the near future, how quickly we can achieve it and what methods we have to adopt for its achievement in the perspective of a law school legal aid clinic are the main concerns of this paper.

In answering these questions, human history proves that earlier when men had only needs the injustice in society were minimal. Peaceful co-existence was the order of the day. Later on when competition became the order of the day, injustice increased. That led to struggles for justice and resultant effects are modern constitutions and laws. These led to a

* Thilakanandan. C, Associate professor in law, Co-ordinator, Clinical Justice Education Organisation (CLIJEO), Governmenr Law College, Calicut, Kerala, India.

revolutionary transformation in enhancing justice. But still it is a mirage to many.

The technological advancement and capitalist globalization in modern times, On the one hand, has made the life of the people easier, faster and more luxurious. On the other hand it has widened the gap between the rich and the poor, created more wastes and polluted environment, provided man with some very serious diseases, and seriously affected the life of many flora and fauna on earth. This loss of flora and fauna again creates more dependency on pesticides and chemicals and it makes life more miserable and expensive. In spite of great attempts to avoid war and bring peace, there are wars in some parts of the world that again leads to human misery.

Now, let us analyse the answer to the second and third question. In the present scenario of highly advanced technology, management and administrative skills, it is actually very easy to provide a reasonable standard of living to every one in the world, if we make a strenuous attempt. In this regard the contribution of the European Union to world peace, harmony and welfare is a great lesson for the whole world particularly Nations in the Asia-Pacific region to emulate. They were able to save millions of money, otherwise should have been wasted for war. Thus in fact they opened a high way towards justice. Thus on a macro analysis, attainment of local, regional and international understanding for reducing tensions and wars is the foremost thing in the achievement of justice for all.

Therefore, instead of aggressive competitive spirit we have to cultivate among ourselves and inculcate among the posterities the spirit of peaceful coexistence. The modern concept of sustainable development is in tune with this idea.

The question of how much we will be able to achieve in the near future that too how quickly is a pertinent one. Dr. Amarthya Sen highlights the idea of remediable injustice. He is addressing the question of enhancing justice and removing injustice, rather than to offer resolutions of questions about the nature of perfect justice. I think for its achievement we need not wait for centuries. Therefore, first of all in the given circumstances, we should come with an international planning and implementation with time bound targeted objectives. Organisations like the United Nations, other international bodies and international community should come forward for this. It is high time for us to think about a General Agreement on Development and Justice (GADJ)

For the last question, In India we have dynamic constitutional provisions, effective legislations, and Court rulings, in support of achieving the goal of justice. In spite of huge budget allocations and government spending why the conditions of many of the marginalized people do not improve according to the expectations of the Government? I would like to attempt to answer this question in the light of the Legal literacy classes, field work and studies conducted by the Clinical Justice Education Organisation (CLIJEO) -the legal Aid Clinic of Government Law College, Calicut. Under its projects 1) one hundred and one Legal literacy classes, 2) field work and fact finding survey conducted in tribal colonies, 3) Eco-friendly village development programme called "Haritha Samrudhi" which means "green prosperity". CLIJEO is working with a twin objective of capacity building of our students as well as empowerment of people. "Legal capacity for empowerment" is our motto.

Our idea is chiefly to enable the people to take appropriate legal steps to utilize all governmental schemes for the deserving ones and also to work together to enhance the quality of living in their area by fostering brotherhood, Humanism and development spirit. We understand that in a democratic country like India unless the people take their own initiatives justice in development will be far away. But creating awareness among the people, particularly among poor and marginalized is a Herculean task. That is why the CLIJEO is conducting legal literacy classes, Field visits, fact finding surveys etc. among people. Through these activities we encourage the local bodies and people to establish legal services clinics and we also extent support to such clinics. We train our students for this purpose on our own and also with the support of the Legal services authorities, practicing advocates in the bar etc.

Under section 4 (k) of the Legal Services Authorities Act 1987 legal services clinics are to be established in all Law Colleges and law Universities in India. The legal Services Authorities have supervisory role over these clinics. The National Legal Services Authority (NALSA) has notified the National Legal Services (Legal Aid Clinics) Regulations, 2011 and has set guidelines for the functioning of such clinics. When good projects are submitted to the Legal Services Authorities by the Legal Services Clinics, they will generously assist in organizing programmes. Earlier the legal aid clinics faced great financial difficulties. Now finance is not a big problem. What we require is willingness, sincerity and honesty.

It is also the responsibility of the local self governing bodies to establish such legal aid clinics in their place. They have to make provisions for office facilities for such clinics. Therefore, these provisions are very much helpful for the legal services clinics functioning in the law colleges and law universities in educating the people to establish such clinics in their place. At this juncture I would like to draw the attention to the words of the Member Secretary National Legal Services Authority Mr. U. Sarathcandran that "the aim of legal literacy classes is not only demystifying the laws but also empowering the disempowered people through the power of law, to know their rights and entitlements and thereby strengthening them to be partners in the economic growth and development". These illuminating words are a great beaming light for me and our legal aid clinic in undertaking and carrying out its various activities.

From our experience we can very well say that in India, the law schools through their legal services clinics have a very important role to play in enhancing justice and also find remedies to injustice. This is chiefly by creating awareness among the people and assisting the local bodies and other authorities in implementing various governmental schemes. By providing legal support to people to get their constitutional and legal rights for certain "actionable entitlements", these clinics can play a vital role in enhancing justice. This is the academic social responsibility of the law schools. I feel that in India we need an activism of legal services to get people their actionable entitlements in the nature of a cultural revolution initiated by legal services clinics supported by the legal services authorities in a constitutional and legal manner through peaceful non-violent means. Mr. Justice V. R. Krishna Iyer in his inaugural address of the Law Liberty and Equality Lecture series organized by CLIJEO said that legal awareness should become part of culture.

In organizing its functions, time is an important factor. We organize our programmes on holidays. In fact I found it very difficult. Another problem is that in these days of competitive spirits and self interest encouraged by market, the students also become more self-centered. The socialist spirit among them is vanishing. Therefore, the only method to encourage students to become activists in legal services is to make it compulsory part of legal curriculum. Attendance, marks and credits should be given to students for their participation in these activities. In my view, all the academic activities other than legal services in a law schools must be finished in the fore noon between 08. 45 A. M and 02. 00 P. M. in the afternoon all students shall engage for legal services activities among the people and internships in law chambers, courts and such other institutions. Apart from this at least one year compulsory legal service among the poor, depressed and marginalized people must be implemented. The students shall be given allowance for this compulsory service. This is the way for Legal Services Activism. Afterwards when these socially sensitized students become lawyers and judges definitely they will be more inclined to the delivery of real and qualitative justice. After all, the modern trend in providing legal services is to spread the idea of Alternative Dispute Resolution methods. The crux of this method is amicable settlement of disputes and enhancement of access to justice for all. Keeping this idea in mind we must be able to thrive for justice education- the idea highlighted in the Global Alliance for Justice Education (GAJE) for the attainment of justice, peace, harmony and happiness for all. Inspired by the GAJE conference we rechristened our Legal Aid Clinic in to Clinical Justice Education organization (CLIJEO). The Beijing forum must come out with an organizational structure to enhance the clinical methods in legal education to wards the attainment of justice for all.

Different Places but Similar Outcomes: the Achievements of Clinical Legal Education in China and Thailand

Panarairat Srichaiyarat*

Abstract

In 2009, an in-depth interview research was conducted at 3 leading law schools in China- Peking, Tsinghua, and Renmin- to find out about the achievements of clinical legal education (CLE) in a civil law country. This research found that CLE in China has been achieved in enhancing students' lawyering skills, knowledge of legal provisions and theories, awareness of legal effect on real people and of the potential and limitation of legal system in real world. The utmost finding of this research is that CLE in China has been accomplished in instilling lawyer values and ethics into their students. Many of student interviewees demonstrated their social responsibility and their responsibility towards clients. Their answers indicated that CLE generates motivation to work for the vulnerable disadvantaged people. In addition, CLE assists students to comprehend the conditions of legal profession and creates students' good attitude towards legal education and the profession.

In 2011, another in-depth interview research was conducted at

* Panarairat Srichaiyarat, Assistant Professor and Head of the Legal Consultation Center at Faculty of Law, Chiang Mai University, Thailand.

Chiang Mai University (CMU), Thailand, to find out if a CLE pilot project at CMU share any similar achievement. The same set of questions were asked 12 CMU law school alumni who graduated between1～3 years ago. Although these graduates did not enrolled in the CMU CLE course and worked for the CMU law clinic as volunteers, they performed community teaching and legal counseling plentifully. Most of them had 2～3 year clinic experience before they graduated.

These alumni had different purposes and motivation to take part in the clinic, however, all of them demonstrated their positive attitude toward their clinic experiences. Most of them stated that the experiences surpassed their expectation. They affirmed that not only their practical skills and knowledge of legal provisions and theories were enhanced, but also their understanding on how the law affects people's lives in the real world. The utmost finding of this research, similar to the former one conducted in China, is that CLE has been accomplished in instilling social justice and human rights values into these alumni. The values and ethics of the legal profession; e. g. , principles of being competent, loyalty to the client, confidentiality, and pro bono are also sustained in their mind. The answers of these alumni also indicated that they gained ethical and moral development, cognitive skills in problem solving and critical thinking, interpersonal skills, and communication skills which is in accordance with the higher education standard of the country.

Introduction

While Clinical Legal Education is well established and has become a core course of law programs in many countries, CLE is barely known in Thailand. To gain more understanding on CLE and to decide whether or not CLE should be introduced to the Thai legal academia, a scholarly investigation is a necessity. Then a research project was initiated in 2009 with the aims to study and comprehend the CLE methodologies, the achievement of CLE in a country having the same legal system and legal education system as Thailand, and to analyze if CLE could reform legal education in the country. This research was conducted by means of documentary research, in-depth interviews with clinic professors, a non-clinic professor, law school executives, and law students, and then data analysis. Three leading Chinese law schools: Peking, Tsinghua, and Renmin University of China, were selected as a field of the study.

Ⅰ. In-house clinics and street-law type clinics

Two types of law clinics- live client legal advice and assistance law clinics or in-house clinics and legal literacy or street-law clinics- were the scope of the study of this research project. Both types of law clinics have two components- academic and service. Their academic components require students to participate in class, seminar, group discussion, and other interactive teaching methods. In addition the students are required to practice lawyering skills utilized in the service components. In case CLE is fully embedded in the law school curriculum, the students will be granted academic credits and grades according to the school regulation. However, some schools implement CLE as a graduation requirement. [1]

The service component of the in-house clinics generally requires the students to provide legal advice and assistance to clients under supervision of the faculty. In some countries clinic students are eligible to represent the clients in courts. [2] The services students provide in the in-house

[1] David Mcquoid-Mason, "The Mission of Clinical Legal Education (CLE) and Its Main Components-Academic and Legal Service-and the Difference between CLE and Legal Aid and NGO Initiatives," (paper presented at Southeast Asia Clinical Legal Education Conference, Phnom Penh, Cambodia, November 26-30, 2005), 33.

[2] Ibid., 34.

clinics may be taken in different forms. A specialized clinic such as an environment law clinic may require the students to do survey research, and a public policy clinic may require the students to draft a bill or to lobby legislators. ❶On the contrary, the service component of the street-law type clinics requires the students to undertake the role of a law teacher in a community. ❷ Their setting may be prisons, detention centers, high schools, or any community of disadvantaged people. The subjects they taught in the community may be varied according to the interests of the community but mainly focus on practical law or law in daily life such as criminal law, criminal procedural law, consumer protection law, and housing law.

Ⅱ. CLE methodologies

At the early stage CLE was basically considered as teaching law students with real cases. ❸At present teaching methodologies utilized in CLE include learning-by-doing and other interactive teaching methods. ❹ In addition CLE methodologies require students to implement legal theories and legal principles in real situations❺, to perform lawyer's roles un-

---

❶ Frank S. Bloch, Mary Anne Noone, "Legal Aid Origins of Clinical Legal Education," in *The Global Clinical Movement Educating Lawyers for Social Justice*, ed. Frank S. Bloch, (New York: Oxford University Press, 2011), 160.

❷ David Mcquoid-Mason, "The Mission of Clinical Legal Education," 35.

❸ Margaret Martin Barry, Jon C. Dubin & Peter A. Joy, "Clinical Education for This Millennium: The Third Wave," *Clinical L. Rev.* 7, no. 1 (2000): 16.

❹ N. R. Madhava Menon, "Clinical Legal Education: Concept and Concerns," in *Clinical Legal Education*, ed. N. R. Madhava Menon et al. (Lucknow: Eastern Book Company, 2008), 10.

❺ Andreas Bücker and William A. Woodruff, "The Bologna Process and German Legal Education: Developing Professional Competence through Clinical Experiences," *German Law Journal*, no. 05 (2008): 589~590.

der faculty supervision[1], and to review and reflect their experiences.[2] The clinic professors are also required to employ many evaluation techniques throughout the course.[3]

Western clinical legal scholars acknowledged the value of CLE that it provides students to learn from experience, to gain necessary basic lawyering skills, and to have self-motivation and development. Furthermore CLE instills ethics and professional responsibility into the students and assists law school to connect with the community.[4] The basic lawyering skills students gain by CLE include client interviewing, client counseling, advocacy, legal research, negotiation, mediation, drafting, oral and written communication, legal analyzing and reasoning, critical thinking, problem solving, communicating with non-lawyers, and identifying and solving ethic dilemma.[5]

Ⅲ. Achievements of CLE in China

China is among many Asian countries that integrate CLE into their law curricular. In 2000 seven leading law schools launched their CLE program to serve the goal of legal education reform.[6] The in-depth interviews with 2 law school executives, 5 clinic professors, 1non-clinic professor, and 13 clinic students at Peking, Renmin, and Tsinghua univer-

---

❶ N. R. Madhava Menon, "Clinical Legal Education: Concept and Concerns," 12.

❷ John Sonsteng et al., "A Legal Education Renaissance: A Practical Approach for the Twenty-First Century," *William Mitchell Law Review* 34 (2007): 405.

❸ Ibid., 407～408.

❹ Richard Lewis, "Clinical Legal Education Revisited," http://www.law.cf.ac.uk/research/pubs/repository/212.pdf, (accessed October 17, 2009): 7～10.

❺ Ibid., 8～9; Lusine Hovhannisian, "Clinical Legal Education: A Practice-Oriented Methodology Developing in New Member States of The European Union," http://www.pili.org/en/dmdocuments/ELFAfinI.doc, (accessed April 11, 2008).

❻ Gong Wendong, vice dean, interview by author, Peking University Law School, May 12, 2009.

sities found that the purpose and motivation of legal educators and students for CLE involvement clearly focused on skill training. Both legal educators and students showed their high satisfaction with achievements. A third-year student at Peking Law School also highlighted the important of skill training. She said: "Law has a life when we practice. We cannot be a good lawyer by learning only theory."❶ Jessica Yang, an LL. M. student at Tsinghua law school shared a similar idea. She said: "Law is for implementing, not just knowing."❷

The in-depth interviews of this research also found that CLE in China has been accomplished in enhancing students' knowledge of legal theories and provisions, awareness of legal effect on real people and of the potential and limitation of legal system in real world. Fu Sini and Gui Lin, Renmin Law School students, demonstrated how CLE enhanced their knowledge. Fu Sini stated: "The clinic course made me realize that some people need help. Legal system and our knowledge can help them. Sometimes I did not have an answer for my clients because we learnt only theory. I had to search for the answer. I had to study more. I had to study what is applicable in real life."❸ Gui Lin stated similar point: "In other classes, it does not matter if we do not understand the lectures. We could hold it as long as it does not affect our exam. If we pass the exam, that's still fine. But when you study the clinic course, you' ve got to help people. You can't say that you don't understand and you will hold on your doubtfulness and not clarify it. If we do not understand, we must try to

❶ Anonymous student, interview by author, Peking University Law School, May 12, 2009.

❷ Jessica Yang, LL. M. student, interview by author, Tsinghua University Labor Law Clinic, May 14, 2009.

❸ Fu Sini, interview by author, Renmin University Law School, May 18, 2009.

understand."[1] An answer from Yu Rong, a retired judge and clinic professor at Peking Law School, reflected another achievement. She said: "Students who took this course learned that our society has many problems. At first they thought everything was so good. Everything was so beautiful. However, after taking this course and having a chance of meeting real people who had problems, they realized that our country has so many problems."[2]

The utmost finding of this research is that CLE in China has been accomplished in instilling lawyer values and ethics into their students. Many of student interviewees demonstrated their social responsibility and their responsibility towards clients. In addition to the answers from Fu Sini and Gui Lin which mentioned above, Hu Jia Yi stated: "When we firstly talked about social responsibility, I felt it was so empty, so ambiguous. However, after I started working with the clinic, I gradually had experience with the poor. People? who came to the clinic? are poor. They are grass root people. University? students have no contact with these people… Before working with the clinic, social responsibility was nothing, so vacant. But after working with the clinic, I know that it's real. It is true. ?"[3]

The Chinese students' answers also indicated that CLE generates motivation to work for the vulnerable disadvantaged people. Gau Yuan, a fourth-year student at Renmin Law School, stated: "I'd never thought about these people because I had never met them. When I met them, especially the one who were in troubles, or got into troubles by the govern-

---

[1] Gui Lin, interview by author, Renmin University Law School, May 18, 2009.

[2] Yu Rong, interview by author, Peking University Law School, May 19, 2009.

[3] Hu Jia Yi, interview by author, Renmin University Law School, May 18, 2009.

ment, or who really had problem but had no one to help, I realized that they exist. I think lawyers are not just a big-money job, but there must be someone who works for these people in our society."❶ Jessica Yang, an LL. M. student at Tsinghua law school, assured that she gained more intention to work for disadvantaged people because of her clinic experience.

In addition, CLE assists students to comprehend the conditions of legal profession and creates students' good attitude towards legal education and the profession. As Gui Lin stated: "Once I felt bad with the career. I thought lawyers met people who quarrel with the other at all times. They were in the dark side of the society. However, after I work in the clinic I realize that lawyers are important for the society. We can help vulnerable disadvantaged people. We may be able to change people life. Changing one life may gradually make the world better."

Ⅳ. Achievements of CLE in Thailand

In 2011, another in-depth interview research project was conducted at Chiang Mai University (CMU), Thailand, to find out if a CLE pilot project at CMU shares any similar achievement with CLE in China. The same set of questions were asked 12 CMU law school alumni who graduated during 2008 to 2010. Although these graduates did not enrolled in the CMU CLE course and they worked for the CMU law clinic as volunteers, they performed community teaching and legal counseling plentifully. Some interviewees stated that they performed community teaching around 70～80 times.❷ Most of them had 2～3 year clinic experience be-

❶ Gau Yuan, interview by author, Renmin University Law School, May 18, 2009.

❷ Maythavee Lertdethanapong and Soracha Santatirat, interview by author, Chiang Mai University Law Clinic, April 25, 2011.

fore they graduated.

These alumni had different purposes and motivation to take part in the clinic; for example, to fulfill the internship requirement of the LL. B. curriculum[1], to gain practical skills[2], and to experiment legal profession. [3]All of them demonstrated their positive attitude toward their clinic experiences. Many of them stated that the experiences surpassed their expectation. Their answers reflected that not only their practical skills and knowledge of legal provisions and theories were enhanced, but also their understanding on how the law affects people's lives in the real world.

When Wathachana Wongsinnak was asked how CLE differed from traditional law courses, he said that in the traditional courses the lecturers hardly talked about the reality of the society, and mainly focused on the legal provisions. On the contrary, the clinic provided him an arena to find out that some legal provisions had loopholes. Some provisions were inapplicable and some are unfair to specific groups of people. He said that he would consider the legal provisions as a god if he only studied in classes. [4]Soracha Santatirat reflected her clinic experience: "I learned that it does not matter for non-lawyers what the law prescribes. What's matter for them is how the law affects them. The law we study in the class is very limited. It cannot make us able to deal with real problems of real people."

Soracha also stated: "The law we study in class is so dry. They have

---

[1] Narudol Wannarat, interview by author, Chiang Mai University Law Clinic, May 21, 2011.

[2] Maythavee Lertdethanapong.

[3] Kathaleeya Jaisrithi, interview by author, Chiang Mai University Law Clinic, May 3, 2011.

[4] Wathachana Wongsinnak, telephone interview with Soracha Santatirat, July 12, 2011.

no life. In the clinic after we put in our heart and our feeling, the law has a life." Her expressions reminded me a part of a clinic journal written by Alfred E. Conard, a Michigan Law School Emeritus Professor when he was a clinic student. He wrote: "Clinical experience puts color in the empty outlines of the legal comic book…. Questions which were dull and meaningless become important and exciting. Answers which seemed black and white become grey, red and green. Dull legal rules become memorable elements of unforgettable events."[1]

The utmost finding of this research, similar to the former one conducted in China, is that CLE has been accomplished in instilling social justice and human rights values into these alumni. The interviewees stated that their attitude toward prisoners and ethnic minority significantly changed by their community teaching clinic experiences. Preeda Saisuparat reflected his experience in a prison that "I had a thought that prisons were overcrowded and dirty. People in there were bad. However, after exposing to them my attitude towards them are changed. Perhaps they were there just because of one mistake in their life. They are not born to be bad"[2]. Similarly, Thidarat Chompuming stated: "I was afraid of them but I changed my attitude after teaching in there. They are not dreadful. They have kids, have families. They talked to us as if they were our aunts, our sisters."[3]

The values and ethics of the legal profession; e.g., principles of being competent, loyalty to the client, confidentiality, and pro bono are

---

[1] A. Conard, "Letter From the Law Clinic," *University of Michigan Law Quadrangle*, 18 (1) (1973): Notes 18, quoted in Richard Lewis, Clinical Legal Education Revisited, 10.

[2] Preeda Saisuparat, interview by author, Chiang Mai University Law Clinic, May 21, 2011.

[3] Thidarat Chompuming, interview by author, Chiang Mai University Law Clinic, May 3, 2011.

also sustained in their mind. Maythavee Lertdethanapong and Soracha Santatirat affirmed that they took their clinic undertaking more seriously than their studies in traditional classes. They reasoned that real practices, real situations, and real persons they had to be responsible for impelled them to do so. They said that in the traditional classes they were responsible just for themselves. If they failed an exam, they could make it up. However, in the clinic their clients and their learners are "a person". Once again the answers from these 2 Thai students are almost identical with the aforementioned answer from Gui Lin, a Renmin Law School Student, when she said "You' ve got to help people".

In Thailand the Ministry of Education issued the National Qualifications Framework for Higher Education in 2009 to be a guideline for the implementation of the National Education Act B. E. 2542 (1999) to serve the goal of education reform. The Ministry proclaimed that the minimum outcomes of learning shall include the following domains: 1) ethical and moral development, 2) knowledge, 3) cognitive skills, 4) interpersonal skills and responsibility, and 5) numerical analysis, communication and information technology skills. [1]Both research projects also found that CLE can be a means for the Thai legal academia to achieve these outcomes.

In addition to the answers from Gui Lin, Fu Sini, Gau Yuan, and others, Mathavee highlighted the achievement of CLE on the first domain, ethical and moral development. She said: "At first, I studied law just because I' d like to get a job and money. After working for the clinic, I learned many things including how to be a human, learned not to take advantage from others. Many people are in trouble. They are in trouble because of the law."

---

[1] Ministry of Education, Announcement on the National Qualifications Framework for Higher Education B. E. 2552, § 4. 2.

The achievements of the second and third domains, knowledge and cognitive skills, are quite promising. By the nature of the clinic undertaking, students are required to provide legal advice or to teach law. They are impelled to acquire knowledge on their own, to be able to comprehend, analyze and differentiate facts, theories, and process. They are required to analyze new situations, apply their knowledge and understanding on the concepts, principles and theories to solve problems.

The fourth domain, interpersonal skills and responsibility, is also well served by CLE. In the clinic, students work in a group with their classmates, professors, and other organization staff. Sarayuth Taechavejaroen, Nathawuth Boonprom, Preeda Saiuparaj, and Thidarat Chompuming, CMU interviewees, all assured the achievement. Many times during the interview, Sarayuth showed his impress on group working experience. He said: "The clinic experience was worth and memorably. It exceeded my expectation. I saw cooperation of people who worked in the clinic. I got more friends."[1]

The achievement of the fifth domain, communication and information technology skills, was assured. To provide legal advice and to teach law require students to communicate with many groups of people, both lawyers and non-lawyers, in different situations. They are required to ask, explain, interview, and contact people by any means of communication. While Nathawuth indicated oral communication skills[2] and Narudol indicated written communication skills, Thidarat confirmed that her both written and oral communication skills were improved by the clinic.

---

[1] Sarayuth Taechavejaroen, telephone interview with Soracha Santatirat, June 11, 2011.

[2] Nathawuth Boonprom, telephone interview with Soracha Santatirat, June 5. 2011.

Conclusion

These two research projects found that CLE is in accordance with the National Qualifications Framework for Higher Education as directed by the National Education Act B. E. 2542 (1999). CLE has potential to make the Thai legal education reaches the goals of the national education reform to enhance students' morality and ethics, as well as their knowledge and necessary professional skills. These research projects, thus, recommend that CLE should be integrated into the Thai law curriculum as a compulsory comprehensive course and CLE teaching methodologies should be utilized in every law course.

American Public Interest Law

Dan Guttman*

Introduction: Public Interest Lawyers and the Public Interest

In America there is now a century old tradition of "public interest law" —— lawyers who use their training and experience to help solve public problems.

The concept of "Public Interest" is universal, but, of course, the meaning of the idea may differ from time to time and place to place; people may disagree a about which people or insitutions can speak for the public interest.

In America, the idea of public interest lawyering arose to describe private (not government) lawyers who help address problems that government and markets cannot fully address by themselves. In America, and probably in most other countries as well, these problems include:

- Assisting the poor, elderly and disadvantaged who cannot afford legal services:
- Helping government make laws work;
- Identifying problems, such as environmental pollution, that government and market have not yet addressed;
- Protecting citizen rights against abuse of power by market and government institutions.

---

* Dan Guttman，北京大学法学院客座教授。

The American law system, of course, is a common law system. Moreover, its traditions differ from other common law systems, as well as civil law systems. To understand the American public interest law tradition, it is essential to understand some of these key differences. Most basically, in the American system the term "public interest lawyer" usually refers to a private (not a government) lawyer. (This is so, even though, of course, government and its lawyers also represent the public interest).

At the same time, in the 21st century public interest law and public interest lawyering is becoming a global phenomenom-there are public interest lawyers in South America, Africa, Europe, Australia and Asia (including China). While the particular nature of public interest law practice differs from place to place, wherever public interest lawyers practice, in common they typically:

• Need to make money——they need to know how to make a career that permits them to practice public interest law.

• Need to know how to go to court, but also how to use other tools used by public interest lawyers-such as social research, lobbying, media, and public education.

• Need to know which tools to use and when——how to craft a strategy for success. It may take years to succeed, and cases may be lost before they are won. Public interest lawyers must know how to put the tools together so that they are most likely to succeed.

• Need to know that the most difficult challenges faced by public interest lawyers are ethical ones. Whenever a lawyer represents people who are unpopular, or opposes powerful interest, he or she may find their own ethics challenged.

In fact, since the early 20th century beginning of modern American public interest law, American public interest lawyers have continually created new career models, and developed and tested new tools and strategies to practice public interest law.

The material that follows;(1) provides some background on the features of the American legal system that must be understood to understand American public interest law; (2) summarizes some of the career models developed by american public interest law-and the related tools and strategies.

I. American Public Interest Law: Some Keys to Understanding the American Tradition

In studying American public interest law it is essential to know (1) that in the American tradition it is common for private citizens to say they represent the public interest; and, as a related point (2) in the American common law tradition, law can be made "from the bottom" as well as from the top.

Americans are comfortable with the idea that nongovernmental groups (or citizens) may advance the public interest. James Madison, the key drafter of the American Constitution, explained (in Federalist Paper Number 10) that the stability of the American government would depend on freedom for competing nongovernmental "factions" (interest groups) to advance their interests.

Thus, in America, there is a long tradition in which nongovernmental interests are expected to compete with ideas and interests. Competing sides to an argument may all say they represent the public interest.

In other countries, the idea that private citizens with their private interests, and not government, can represent the public interest may seem to be a contradiction.

Consistent with the notion that private citizens can represent the public interest, in the (Anglo-American) common law tradition law can be made “from the bottom”, by citizens going to court, as well as from the top (by legislatures and chief executives).

The common law provides basic concepts that lawyers can use to address new problems through court action as times change.

For example, much of modern American environmental law comes from the common law concept of nuisance——the idea that people cannot use their property in ways that injure others was applied to modern industrial pollution. Public interest lawyers use common law theories to seek court relief that pushes the development of environmental legislation.

In the case of environental law, in the 1960's private lawyers began to bring lawsuits against polluters based on the common law concept of “nuisance”. They did not have to wait for the government enactment of a law to do so; they did not have to wait for a statute that said “public interest” lawsuits are permitted. (When, as we will discuss, environental laws were created, they typically did contain “citizen suits” provisions that provide that private lawyers can help government enforce the laws).

In civil law countries, by contrast, it is traditionally said that law is made through codes written by legislatures or executives——and not by courts in response to citizen lawsuits.

Ⅱ. Public Interest Lawyers: Some 20th Century American Career Models, Tools, and Strategies

The American public interest law tradition provides American law students and lawyers with many “models” of how lawyers may make a living while practicing public interest law. American law students can use these models they think about creating a law career for themselves in which they can practice public interest law.

In the early 20th century, these models began with the career of Louis Brandeis, perhaps the most famous American public interest lawyer. Times and circumstances change. Old models have been modified, and new models created. The models evolved throughout the 20th century and they continue to evolve today. Why are there so many different models? As we will see, each one has its advantages and disadvantages.

Some Career Models: The First Part of the 20th Century

1. The Brandeis Model: "The People's Lawyer" Pro Bono Law and the Lawyer as Social Researcher

We will begin our discussion of American public interest career models? with the "Brandeis model". Louis Brandeis (1856～1941) became famous as the "people's lawyer". He pioneered in the practice of "pro bono" law. Brandeis made money representing businesses and individuals who paid him for his work. He volunteered his time to represent the public interest without charge ("pro bono"). In addition to introducing the concept of pro bono practice to modern American law, Brandeis also brought to the practice of law the idea that lawyers should help solve social problems. He believed that social research could help show solutions to social problems. He showed lawyers how they could use social research as a tool in the court, and before legislatures and officials. Brandeis taught that good public information on social problems could itself be a force for reducing corruption and stimulating harmonious change. "Sunshine", he is often quoted as having said, "is the best disinfectant".

(1) *Louis Brandeis: The "People's Lawyer"*.

Brandeis received a law degree from Harvard in 1877. In 1879 he and a Harvard classmate opened a private law firm in Boston. The firm became successful, making money advising companies and individuals.

Brandeis became a successful lawyer in a time (the late 19th century-early 20th century) in American history in which America-like China today-was developing very rapidly. As in China today, there were many new and growing companies, and many new rich people. As in China today, economic development meant things were getting better for many people very fast. However, there were many problems.

As in China today, gaps between rich and poor could be great. The owner of a famous Chicago department store made over \$20000 a week; he paid his clerks \$12 or less for a fifty nine hour week. Workers had to work long hours in conditions that were often not safe. There was little way to make sure that big companies did not charge consumers too much. There was corruption that was hard to control.

In this new world of rapid economic development, Brandeis tried to use the law to help the "people". He showed lawyers how they could use social research, to help officials and legislators know what good policy and law should be, and to help courts decide cases in which new laws were tested.

In Boston, he organized a group of citizens to fight corrupt city government transportation companies. When railroads went to the government to ask to charge more money, he used public hearings to question their claim that they needed more money. At these hearings he questioned companies and their experts. He showed the companies could be more efficient, and could charge lower prices and still make money.

Brandeis most famous social research "invention" was "the Brandeis Brief". In the new age of industrialization, workers often worked long hours for low pay in hard working conditions. Reformers tried enact laws to protect workers. New York State's legislature enacted a law to protect bakery workers. The law limited the hours that the boss could make them work. In the famous 1905 decision in Lochner v. New York, the U. S. Supreme Court decided that the law violated the Constitution. (The Supreme Court majority said it violated the "liberty to contract".)

The state of Oregon then passed a law to limit the hours women could be required to work. Businessmen argued that the law was also unconstitutional. The case went to the U. S. Supreme Court. Brandeis volunteered to represent supporters of the law on a pro bono basis. Brandeis' brief (a brief is a written argument to the court) did not try to tell the judges about the law——about statutes or court decisions. Instead, Brandeis told the court about his research into the conditions of working women. He argued that this research showed that the law was needed to protect women's health.

The Supreme Court found the Oregon law to be Consitutional, pointing to the Brandeis brief. The "Brandeis Brief", as it became known, became famous as the first brief to rely on social research as a tool of legal argument. Today, it is common for lawyers to use social research in arguments to courts. (Indeed, in law schools "law and economics" is a popular subject of legal scholarship and teaching).

Following his success as "the people's lawyer" Brandeis was appointed by President Woodrow Wilson to the U. S, Supreme Court. He authored many memorable opinions and dissents on topics including free speech and the regulation of corporations that provide basic public services. An 1890 Harvard Law Review article he wrote with his law partner introduced the idea of the "right to privacy", which became the basis for important and controversial Supreme Court decisions in the late 20th century.

(2) *Pro Bono Law Today.*

Today, Pro Bono law work is a basic part of American law practice. American Lawyers are not required to do pro bono work. However, many law firms plan each year to allow time and resources for their lawyers to perform bono work. When students apply for jobs, law firms often advertise the opportunities new lawyers have to do pro bono work.

The variety of pro bono projects engaged in by private lawyers is great, and continues to grow. Today, lawyers working in law firms may:

1) Work with nongovernment/nonprofit organizations (NGOs/NPOs) who have need for legal assistance.

2) Work with state or local governments to help advise on policies or the drafting or review of laws.

3) Work globally——helping develop law school programs in coutnries developing rule of law, training judges.

4) Work with law school clinics, helping instruct students and assisting in cases.

2. The NAACP Model: The NGO with long term strategy to address a core social problem

The story of how the courts were used to bring about racial justice is one of the great stories in American history. In the early 20th century a group of people——white and black——created an "NGO" called the National Association for the Advancement of Colored People or "NAACP". [See separate box which explains American NGOs; the box is below] The NAACP's many years of work on behalf of African-Americans led to many court victories, including the U. S. Supreme Court decision in Brown v. Board of Education, perhaps the most important decision reached by the Court in the 20th century.

(3) *The Problem of Racial Discrimination.*

When the US Constitutition was written in 1787 the ownership of slaves was permitted in the Constitution. The enslavement of many African Americans continued until the American civil war, during which Abraham Lincoln issued the "Emancipation Proclamation" which freed all slaves. After the war, Amendments 13～15 were added to the Constitution to assure that state governments would not return to the pre-civil war treatment of African-Americans.

Nonetheless, in the late 19th century many states in the southern US enacted laws to make it difficult or impossible for African Americans to exercise their rights. States passed laws that were designed to deny, or make very difficult to exercise, rights to vote, to go to school with, share public spaces (hotels or restaurants) or marry white people.

In 1896 the Supreme Court, in the case of Plessy v. Ferguson, found that state laws that required "segregation" (separation) of the races in transportation facilities (trains, buses) were permitted under the the U. S. Constitution. The 14th amendment to the U. S. Constitution says that citizens have a right to "equal protection" of the laws. The Court said the Constitutional requirement of "equal protection" was met if the facilities for blacks and whites were "separate but equal". Black people would have seats in the bus, like white people. But black people would sit in the back.

The state laws which restricted African Americans were often enforced against them by threats and violence, including murder (or "lynching.") There was little hope that the Government in Washington——the Congress or the President——would take action to potect african-americans from state laws and local threats and violence. The NAACP sought to use the courts to change the laws not because it was sure courts would help, but because the other branches of government would not.

(4) *The Strategy*.

Beginning in the 1930's, the NAACP and its lawyers developed a strategy for using the courts to end racial discrimination. The strategy was to select lawsuits that would test the law, and ultimately change it. The efforts would begin in areas, such as rights to fair trial, and rights to vote, where the law was clearer. They would move on to the question of segregaton in the schools. There they would begin with cases involving graduate education. Only at the end would the test turn to elementary schools.

In the 1930's and 1940's the NAACP brought cases about laws and practices that prevented African-Americans from voting; it brought cases against laws that prohibited African Americans from buying houses in white neighborhoods; it brought cases against laws that required segregation in transportation; and it began to bring cases against laws that required segregation of schools.

In the case of segregation in the schools, the problems the NAACP lawyers faced were immense. They were dealing with a practice that was both of central importance to southern white society and that was approved by the highest court in the U. S.

The Supreme Court had decided in Plessy v Ferguson that segregation was allowed by the U. S. Constitution in buses and trains. In Gong Lum v Rice the Court confirmed that it was allowed in schools as well. (In Gong Lum, the parents of a chinese-american student wanted her to go to schools for white children; the Courts found that chinese children are "colored", and could only go to colored schools).

So the "precedent" seemed clear that segregation in public schools was lawful. The job the NAACP lawyers faced was——ultimately——how do you get the Supreme Court to directly reverse its own precedent? In the 1920's the NAACP received a donation from a recent Harvard graduate. Part of the money was used to prepare papers on the strategy that might be followed in thee years ahead.

The NAACP lawyers accepted, because they had to, the existing Supreme Court law (that is, they accepted separate but equal as the law). Consistent with the Brandeis model, they then went out to find facts to show the courts that in fact schools for colored people were not equal. They proceeded step by step. First, they brought cases dealing with graduate education, including law schools. Then they began to seek cases dealing with public schools (pre-college) ——showing that separate schools were not equal.. Finally, in Brown v Board of Education, the NAACP argued that schools in which races were separated by law could never be equal. The NAACP directly asked the Supreme Court to reverse it prior decisions.

(5) *NAACP*: *Tools*.

The NAACP is a model of how public interest lawyers can use an NGO to bring about peaceful change in accord with the law. In addition to social research, the NAACP court cases developed other tools that became part of the toolbox of all public interest lawyers. These include:

Test cases: The NAACP looked for cases that would have the most impact. NAACP lawyers spent time seeking "fact patterns" that would best test the law, clients who could show the injustice of the system (and withstand the stress of litigation).

Class actions: African-Americans were discriminated against as a group. The NAACP pioneered in "class actions". It brought cases that would provide relief for a class (group) of injured citizens——and not just a few people.

Court overseen relief: The decision in Brown v. Board of Education declated that segregation by law was illegal. The decision itself did not order schools that were segregated to immediately change to comply with the law. To do so would have produced immediate political and practical problems. The NAACP had to work with courts and defendants to assure that the law would be followed. This effort, which began immediately after Brown v. Board was decided, continues to this day.

(6) *Brown v. Board of Education*: *The decision*.

In Brown v Board of Education, the Supreme Court was finally faced with the need to decide the question of whether segregation was permissible by race in public schools.

When the Court began to think about Brown (actually several cases involving schools in differing states and Washington, DC), political leaders in some southern states threatened to close all schools before they would let African Americans attend schools with white children. The NAACP had to convince the Supreme Court that segregation was unlawful when;1) Supreme Court precedent was clear that it was lawful, and 2) violence and great civil unrest were very possible if the Supreme Court changed its mind about precedent.

Under the leadership of newly appointed Chief Justice Earl Warren, the Supreme Court decided 9 : 0 to reverse its prior precedent. Segregation in the schools was against the law. There could be no "equal protection" of the law if blacks were not permitted to attend schools with whites. The efforts of the NAACP to use the courts and the Constitution to bring about legal change benefited Chinese students, as well as African-Americans. The laws that discriminated against African-Americans also discriminated against Chinese-Americans (and other "colored" people).

In the years since 1954, the NAACP continued to bring court cases to make the decision in Brown v Board of Education work. The NAACP's efforts to assure that African-americans, and now other minorities, have quality education continue to this day.

In the latter half of the 20th century, the numbers of public interest law NGO's multiplied. Today, there are public interest lawyers who work in American NGOs addresssing a great variety of public issues-including environmental health, food safety, migrant worker protections, elderly or the disabled, AIDs patients, and many other groups and public issues.

BOX—American NGOs/NPOs

"NGOs" or "NPOs" play an important role in American public interest law. What is an NGO? What is an NPO? What is the difference?

The terms NGO (nongovernmental organization) and NPO (nonprofit organization) are now used throughout the world. The terms usually refer to organizations whose work is associated with the public interest. However, the meaning of these terms may differ from country to country (or may be misunderstood within a country). The terms must therefore be used with care.

What is an NGO, and what is the difference between NGO and NPO?

In the U. S. an NGO, as the term is usually used, is both a nongovernmental organization (NGO) and a nonprofit organization (NPO).

First, the American NGO is nongovernmental in the sense that it is an organization created and directed by private citizens. NGOs may take money from the government, but the NGO is independent of the government in the sense that the NGO selects its own leaders.

In fact, many of the largest and most successful NGOs in the U. S. work with government, and receive money from it. They provide people with health, educational, and social welfare services, and perform educational and research activities.

Second, the American NGO is also a nonprofit organization (NPO). It is important to understand that nonprofit does not mean that the NGO does not need or seek money. NGOs typically need money to pursue their purposes. However, while a profitmaking organization can take money it gets and distribute it to stockholders to use as they please, NGOs can only use money they get to further the purposes of the NGO. (The purposes of the NGO include providing salaries to NGO managers and staff, so money can be used to pay salaries.)

Do NGOs have to follow any special laws?

In the U. S there is no requirement that an NGO seek special legal status (such as government approval). Anyone can create an NGO, and no special permission is required.

However, many people who create NGOS seek to fulfill two sets of legal requirements.

Just as profitmaking businesses often seek to incorporate, many NGOs incorporate as a nonprofit corporation. This usually means that the person or people who create the NGO fill out the necessary forms and pay the necessary fee (usually small) to obtain nonprofit corporate status in a state-- usually the state in which the NGO is headquartered. The status of nonprofit corporation is useful because, like the status of profitmaking corporation, it limits the liability of the NGO and its officials.

In addition, many NGOs seek approval, for special tax status under U. S tax law. This tax status permits people (including corporations or individuals) to give money to the NGO and receive a tax benefit in exchange. The NGO must provide the Internal Revenue Service (tax agency) with information showing that it will meet the requirements of tax law for exempt status. These requirements are stated in Section 501 of the taxcode. Generally, in order to become a "501" organizaton the NGO must show the government that it is organized for public purpose——for example, education, scientific, research, or charity.

Who is in charge of the NGO?

NGOs are usually governed by a Board of Directors. Depending upon the rules the NGO chooses, the Board may select its own members, or the Board members may be selected by members of the NGO.

NGOs may choose to have members or not to have members. If the NGO is a membership organization, the NGO can have members who vote to elect the Board of Directors, but it also can provide that members do not vote. For example, if they do not have voting rights, NGO members may receive information from the NGO, such as newsletters or magazines, or to participate in NGO activities.

Where do NGOs get their money?

NGOs need money to operate. Depending on the NGO's strategy and needs, it may seek money from Federal, state or local government, from private individuals, from corporations, or from foundations. NGOs may also sell products or services to help raise money. For example, NGOs may sell books or reports they write, tee shirts, calendars. When an NGO engages in a business like activity, this activity may be subject to tax like a profitmaking business.

In the US there are many thousands of NGOs. Larger and more well known NGOs include:

* Schools, hospitals, and research institutions. Many famous universities, such as Harvard and Yale, are nongovernmental and nonprofit organizations. Others, such as the University of California, were created by state government and have directors selected by the state government——they are NPO, but not NGO.

• Organizations that provide vital public welfare services, such as help for poor or sick people or in emergencies.

• Business and professional and worker organizations, such as the Chamber of Commerce (business), American Medical Association (doctors), American Bar Association (lawyers), workers unions.

• Organizations that represent the interests of people with common interests (retired people, consumers, people who use guns, for example).

• Many different kinds of NGOs play a role in public interest law. These include:

• NGOs created to provide legal representation to groups or individuals not adequately served by the existing legal system, and to help make law to protect these groups. These include the National Association for Advancement of Colored People (NNACP), American Civil Liberties Union (ACLU), Mexican American Legal Defense Fund, Asian Legal Defense Fund, Womens' Legal Defense Fund.

• NGOs created to use law to address social problems not yet fully addressed by government or business. For example, these include many environmentalNGOs, such as the Environmental Defense Fund, Natural Resources Defense Council, and World Wildlife Federation——all of which have activities in china These NGOs often include lawyers and non-lawyers, who work together using the law, but also engaging in research and education.

• NGOs that were not created specifically to use law, but that come to see the need to use legal strategies. For example, these include the Center for Science in the Public Interest. This group was formed by scientists to improve food safety and nutrition. It has nearly one million members. It now employs lawyers——both "inhouse" and pro bono volunteers-to further its efforts.

• NGOs that bring together public interest professionals. For example, Taxpayers against fraud is an associatioon of lawyers who bring whistleblower (anti-corruption) lawsuits to help government fight corruption.

• NGOs that are "think tanks" which study and discuss questions on which public interest lawyers may be working.

3. The ACLU and Clarence Darrow Models—Protecting the Rights of Minorities or the Unpopular

The American Civil Liberties Union ("ACLU") and "Clarence Darrow" models will help us think about the way in which private lawyers represent the rights of causes or clients that are unpopular. They may be unpopular because they are minorities or represent minority views. But they may be unpopular because they are bad people——murderers, for example. The lawyer himself may put his or her reputation or career at risk because of the client he or she represents.

The ACLU, like the NAACP, is an NGO created in the early 20th century (One of the first funders of the NAACP legal efforts also funded the ACLU legal efforts).

The ACLU model is similar to the NAACP model in important ways. Both the NAACP and ACLU were created to address problems that would not be easily solved and that would require continuing legal expertise. Both the NAACP and the ACLU came to operate nationally, bringing lawsuits throughout the country, and relying on networks of national and local experts.

Clarence Darrow, like Brandeis, had been a successful private lawyer. He turned his focus to clients and causes he thought important.

A big difference between the Brandeis/NAACP models and the ACLU/Darrow model is that the ACLU and Darrow devoted their efforts to representing the rights of people who are often unpopular. In one of Clarence Darrow's most famous cases he represented two young people who were confessed murderers. The ACLU has often represented the rights of even racists——such as Nazis (followers or Adolf Hitler) or members of the Ku Klux Klan (white racists) ——to exercise rights to speak publicly. The ACLU represents such groups even though ACLU members and lawyers themselves strongly disagree with the views of these people.

The ACLU: Protector of Constitutional Rights

The ACLU was founded in 1920. In its nearly ninety years of existence it has provided continued assistance to those who argue that their rights provided by the American Constitution are in need of protection.

The ACLU's lawyers provide assistance to people who contact the ACLU for help. The ACLU also participates in "test" cases to test and develop legal principles. The ACLU's national office and local "chapters" work with local lawyers and law firms, who provide "pro bono" help to the ACLU.

As a biography of Roger Nash Baldwin, one of the ACLU's founders, explains, the ACLU founders were "overwhelmingly members of America's upper crust, or at the very least, the good middle class". Baldwin himself had studied at Harvard and was a member of the Boston elite (as were Holmes and Brandeis).

The ACLU's initial "statement of purpose" explained that "all thought on matters of public concern should be freely expressed, without interference. Orderly social progress is promoted by unrestricted freedom of opinion."

The ACLU is most famous for its defense of those citizens who seek to exercise their First Amendment rights of speech (including freedom of religion and association).

The Bill of Rights (the first ten amendments, beginning with the first amendment which protects speech) were included in the Constitution when it was written in 1787. However, it was not until the early 20th century that the modern law of the first amendment really began to develop.

Why did it take so long for the Supreme Court to begin to hear the cases that give specific meaning to the words in the First Amendment.

The factors leading to 20th century development of First Amendment law include the turn of the 20th century industrialization of America, and growing differences between rich and poor. The rise of labor unions and worker protests that accompanied industrial growth tested the rights of workers (and their leaders) to speak freely.

In addition, 20th century global developments have continually raised new questions about the right of the American government to limit speech (including the related right of association).

America's entrance into the First World War was not universally popular. ACLU founder Roger Baldwin himself went to prison because——in protest of the war—— he violated the law that required him to register for military service.

Following the 1917 Russian revolution, some prominent Americans expressed support for what they saw as Russia's communist ideals. Support for communist (or socialist) ideals increased when America entered the great depression in the 1930's, and some Americans questioned the capitalist system's ability to provide for America. In the 1940's~1950's, the Cold War lead to official and popular concern that those who spoke in support of Russia or communism were threats to the national security of the U. S. All of these developments raised questions about the ability of the government (state and local as well as Federal) to limit the speech and association of those who spoke on behalf of alternative systems. In many cases the ACLU defended the rights of such people.

In the 21st century, the events following the 911 attacks on the U. S. have raised new questions about the proper relation between rights provided by the Constitution and national security requirements.

Clarence Darrow: Trial Lawyer and "Attorney for the Damned"

Today, American law students may know little about Clarence Darrow (1857 ~ 1938). In the first half of the 20th century, however, Clarence Darrow was the most famous "trial lawyer" in America. (Trial lawyers specialize in going to court, and arguing cases before juries). Even today, American lawyers may say about another lawyer—— "he's a real Clarence Darrow."

In the 1890's Clarence Darrow was a successful lawyer who worked as the top lawyer for a big railroad company. When Eugene v. Debs, a workers leader led a strike against the railroad, Darrow told the railroad management that he could not represent the railroad because he agreed with the workers. He left his railroad job to become the lawyer for Debs and the workers.

In the years that followed, Darrow was involved in many famous cases. These included cases in which he represented workers (or their representatives) who were accused of violent actions.

In the Loeb and Leopold case, Darrow defended two top students who murdered a friend. They did so, it appears, because they wanted to commit the "perfect crime" that could not be solved. They were found out——one of the students left his eye glasses by the body. There was no question that the defendants committed the murder——and that it was premeditated and senseless. The government prosecutors and many of the public wanted the murderers to be put to death. Darrow took the case. He did so not only because he opposed the death penalty, but because of his view that defendants should receive a fair court proceeding-especially where press and public opinion was so strong as to make this almost impossible.. He succeeded in obtaining a sentence of life imprisonment instead of death.

American Public Interest Law Careers, Tools and Strategies: The Second Half of the 20th Century and 21st Century

In the years after the Second World War American society changed greatly. An important part of this change was the use of law to address social problems. Some of these problems, such as racial discrimination and consumer protection, had long been well known, but never been adequately addressed. Others, such as environmental pollution, were just coming to public attention.

Building on the earlier tradition——the Brandeis, NAACP, ACLU, Darrow, and Legal aid models——public interest lawyers worked to develop new career models, tools and strategies to address these problems. They created new areas of law study that were not taught when they went to law school.

Where statutes did not exist to address a problem brought law suits using common law concepts. They tried to push and make law from the bottom. For example, they asked courts to find that a company that used its factory in a way that polluted community water was no different than the kind of "nuisance" that the common law had long provided protection from.

The new generation of public inteerst lawyers was inspired, by the "Warren Court", the U. S. Supreme Court under Earl Warren, who became Chief Justice of the Court in 1953. Beginning with the 1954 decision in Brown v. Board of Education, the Warren Court authored decisions which gave lawyers, especially young lawyers, the confidence that courts could be used to produce needed social change.

(1) Environmental Law: the NGO Model Updated.

The modern American environmental movement emerged in the 1960's. This was a period of great social change. It was the America of the Warren Court, the civil rights movement, and citizen protests against the war in Viet Nam.

At the beginning of the 60's the environmental statutes that are so important today did not exist. NGOs and private law firm lawyers played central roles bringing litigation that led both to Congressional enactment of environmental law and to the interpretation and enforcement of this law.

These NGOs included lawyers. They also included natural scientists and economists who worked along with the lawyers to research and explain the technical issues of environmental protection. The NGOs also worked with private lawyers in private law firms, some of whom also began to develop environmental law as a speciality.

The pioneers among these groups included the Environmental Defense Fund (EDF) and the Natural Resources Defense Council (NRDC). Both of these organizations were created in the 1960's, one by a group that included young law school graduates (who received support from a Founation), and the other by private lawyers and scientists. They also included the Sierra Club, an NGO created in 1892 to protect and preserve America's natural and wilderness resources.

In Sierra Club v. Morton, the U. S. Supreme Court decided that environmental NGOs could represent members in protecting the public interest in environmental protection. However, the NGO had to show that its members had an interest that was damaged by the action complained about in the case. Sierra Club v Morton was the first of important cases in which the U. S. Supreme Court developed the law of "standing" for environmental litigation. The law of standing is now crtical to many efforts by NGOs to bring lawsuits to protect the public interest.

In 1969 the Congress passed the National Environmental Policy Act (NEPA). NEPA provided that when it undertook a "major" action that might have a "significant" effect on the environment, the Federal government has to study the action to mitigate harmful consequences. Lawsuits brought by environmental NGOs established the rights of citizens to go to court to force the government to follow NEPA. The lawsuits also helped define what the law required the government to do.

New Tools: Citizen Suits and Information

The new laws gave environmental public interest lawyers important new tools-citizen suit rights and right to information.

In the 1970's, the Congress enacted environmental laws dealing with specific environmental problems (water, air, solid waste, hazardous waste, pesticides, toxic substances). These laws included "citizen suits" provisions. These provisions give citizens the right to bring law suits to enforce the law. They provide that the citizens' lawyer will receive attorney fees if the suits were succesful. The citizen suits provisions were quickly used by environmental NGOs to assist the government in assuring that environmental law was enforced.

Congress also enacted laws that require companies (including polluters) to provide government and the public with basic information about the hazardous substances they use and the pollution they produce. NGOs use this information to help the government enforce environmental laws.

Today, some of the NGOs that helped create environmental law are often large organizations, employing lawyers, scientists, economists and experts in raising money to keep the NGOs going. They work globally, as well as locally. The Environmental Defense Fund and Natural Resources Defense Council have offices in china, and work with the China government and universities on many environmental law and governance projects.

Box——The Warren Court and the Birth of Modern American Public Interest Law

The "Warren Court" is the name given to the U. S, Supreme Court in the years (1953～1969) when Earl Warren was Chief Justice of the nine member court. The Warren Court is famous for decisions that interpreted the constitution to give new (or newly found) rights to many americans, including african-americans, criminal defendants, those dependent on the government for welfare, voters, students, and teachers.

The Warren court years marked the birth of a new excitement about public interest law, Law students, law professors and lawyers thought the court would help "find" rights in the Consitution to protect the disadvantaged, to assure due process for criminal defendants, to further the rights of minorities, and to protect the environment.

Earl Warren grew up in California and was graduated from the University of California Berkely and its law school (called Boalt Hall) in the early 20th century. He worked as a prosecutor and then entered politics, becoming Governor of California. In 1952, Governor Warren and General Dwight Eisenhower were both thought to be top candidates for President of the U. S. Shortly after Eisenhower was elected President, the Chief Justice died, and Eisenhower nominated Warren to be the new chief justice.

Earl Warren was a lawyer. However, it was said that his best skills were the good skills of a politician. He could help people work together to make common decisions. Warren used these skills as the Court's leader, most famously in the 1954 decision in *Brown v Board of Education*. In that critical case, Chief Justice Warren was able to bring all of the Court's nine judges to agree in a unanimous (9 : 0) decision that reversed the Court's "separate but equal" precedent.

The Warren Court went on to write decisions that established some of the most basic rules of modern American criminal procedure. Its decisions in *Gideon v Wainwright* and *Miranda v Arizona* gave defendants the right to a lawyer and the right to remain silent until they get one.

In addition to the decision in *Brown v Board*, many scholars say the most important decision of the Warren Court was in the voting rights case of Baker v Carr. In that case the *Warren Court* said that voters could challenge the way in which states decided how to "apportion" congressional districts. (States decide how to "apportion" the "districts" from which Congressmen are elected from each state. In some states this was done to make sure that no minority could be elected to Congress.)

The Warren Court also had important decisions on free speech, including many cases in which the government (Washington and states) said the Cold War Russian threat required limitations on citizen rights.

In all of these cases the Warren court had to decide the meaning of key words in the Bill of Rights (the first ten amendments to the Constitution) or in the Fourteenth Amendment, which protects citizens against abuse of their rights by state governments.

The Warren Court's legacy plays a continuing role in modern American poltiical debate. Decisions of the Court were, and still are, controversial. In 1968, when Richard Nixon ran for President successfully, he promised that the judges he would pick would be different from those on the Warren Court. Ever since then, the question of what kind of judges the President will appoint to the Supreme Court (if there is a vacancy because of death or retirement of a judge) has been a hot topic in Presidential elections.

(2) Ralph Nader: Brandeis Model Updated——Pro Bono Lawyer and "Public Citizen".

Ralph Nader "updated" the Brandeis model for the second half of the 20th century. Nader hoped to show that everyone - not only lawyers, but citizens——could help make the law work. Brandeis was "the people's lawyer". For Nader, the idea was that everyone could use the law——everyone should be a "Public citizen".

Nader, like Brandeis, was a Harvard Law graduate. Nader also believed that: 1) lawyers should serve the public interest; 2) lawyers should find the facts about how the world really works. (Nader said, as Brandeis did, that "sunshine is the best dinfectant".)

In contrast to Brandeis, Nader never worked as a "law firm" lawyer. As a young law school graduate Nader became interested in the problem of automobile safety. Every year tens of thousands of Americans died in automobile accidents. The automobile industry said this was because people were bad drivers——they drove too fast and were careless. Nader studied the problem, reading technical reports and talking with experts. He found people were dying not because they drove the cars too fast——but because the cars were not safe to drive. The American automobile industry made new cars to make them look nice and go fast. It did not focus on their safety.

General Motors, then the world's biggest company, hired people to investigate Nader, and to trap him into bad actions. Nader found out that he was being spied on, and sued General Motors, and embarrassed the company greatly. His first book——Unsafe at Any Speed——became famous. Nader testified before the Congresss, and the attention Nader's fame brought to the issue helped Congress to pass new law to regulate automobile safety.

With the money from settling the General Motors lawsuit and the national fame for his work on auto safety, Nader was able expand his activities.

In the late 1960's, Nader brought students to Washington to work during summer vacations to do investigations, and to write books based on their research. The students were divided into teams. The teams studied how government agencies that were supposed to protect consumers worked, they studied the insurance industry, they studied what was being done about air pollution and toxic chemicals, they studied the government's use of private think tanks to do its work, and they studied the Congress itself.

The student reports received attention from the press, the public and Congres. The press called the students Nader's Raiders. The Nader's Raiders showed what young people——including law students could do——to help identify and solve problems that government and business had not addressed or solved.

Along with the teams of Raiders, Nader set up NGOs to provide permanent oversight of the workings of government. These included: (1) Public Citizen——a group that watches what congress does and "lobbies" Congress; (2) Public Citizen Litigation group——young lawyers who became expert in helping other public interest lawyers argue cases before the Supreme Court and other courts; (3) "PIRGS" (Public Interest Research Groups) set up on university campuses so that students could do investigations and research of local problems.

In the 1970's, 80's, 90's, U. S. Presidents and Congressmen came and left Washington, but Nader continued to work. In 2000 he decided to run for President of the U. S. His argument was that there is no real difference between the two major political parties (Republican and Democratic).

Nader's entrance into the world of politics proved controversial. George Bush won the 2000 election because he received a few more votes than Al Gore in the state of Florida. Many people who wanted Gore to win say that Gore would have been President if Nader had not run (people who voted for Nader, they said, would have voted for Gore if Nader had not run).

(3) The Plaintiffs Lawyer Model: Doing Good by Doing Well.

In the late 20th century, "Plaintiffs law" developed as a powerful force in the American legal system and a new model for public interest careers.

Plaintiff's lawyers represent people who are harmed by unsafe cars, cigarette smoking, bad food or bad medicines. They represent stockholders who lose money because of corporate failure, consumers who are cheated by large corporations, and victims of work place discrimination.

Successful plaintiff's lawyers are probably the richest lawyers in America. Plaintiffs lawyers may "do well by doing good," Plaintiffs lawyers can be very effective in taking on problems that the government itself may not be able to address. At the same time, there is continued controversy about whether plaintiffs' lawyers serve the public interest or their own interest (of course they may also serve both).

Contingency Fees: The Heart of Plaintiffs Lawyering

In its literal meaning, a plaintiff's lawyer is any lawyer who represents the plaintiff in a lawsuit-whether the plaintiff is a large institution or a poor individual. In the popular sense in America, "plaintiff's lawyer" is the term applied to lawyers who represent clients on a "contingency fee" basis. The Plaintiffs lawyer does not charge a fee, and will be paid only if he is successful in the case.

Pro bono lawyers also represent clients without charging a fee. In contrast to the "pro bono" lawyer, however, the plaintiff's lawyer hopes to make his living by receiving payment for the case. The payment is "contingent" on the success of the lawsuit. Prior to the lawsuit the lawyer and client enter into a contingency fee agreement. Depending on the kind of case (and the number of lawyers competing to be hired by the client) the contingency fee may be as high as 30%～40% of the total money received by the successful plaintiff.

Because plaintiff's lawyers work on contingency fees, they must be able to take risks. They must have the resources (money and people and time) needed to take the risks. In deciding whether to take a case, plaintiff's lawyers have to consider the likelihood that they will succed. Even if they win, will success provide enough money for lawyer and client to make the case worth doing?(Of course plaintiffs lawyers, like all lawyers, can also decide to do the case "pro bono" ——doing it without expecting to make money.)

Key Tools for Plaintiffs Lawyers

Modern Plantiffs law practice involves continuing efforts by plaintiff's lawyers to find new tools and strategies needed to undertake the risks of contingency practice. Key tools include:

1) class (group) actions (which provides lawyers with the economies of scale for lawsuits in which it would be too expensive to represent

individuals on a contingent basis);

2) creative use of the common law of torts (the law or accidents and injuries) to address the alleged misconduct of corporations, and even entire industries;

3) use of statutory provisions which permit lawyers to work on contingency with hope of getting paid by the defendant if the case is successful (for example, whistelblower statutes, citizens suits and attorneys fees laws);

4) creation of plaintiffs lawyer networks to help locate promising new areas of client represenation, share the costs of developing the expertise needed to pursue the litigation, and share the costs of the litigation;

5) monitoring of legislatures for developments that may affect plaintiff law——as the topic is now one of continued political debate.

The Roots of Modern Plaintiffs Lawyering: Class Action and Personal Injury (Tort) Law

Plaintiffs Law Class Actions

In the 1940's and 1950's the NAACP pioneered in the use of class actions to advance social justice. (Brown v. Board of Education was a class action.) In the cases brought by the NAACP, and later by the ACLU on behalf of prisoners and inmates of mental institutions—— the primary remedies were court orders that brought public insitutions (schools, prisons, hospitals) into compliance with the law. The focus of the lawsuits was on institutional reform, not on monetary damages.

In the 1970's and 1980's Plaintiffs lawyers began to use class actions to seek monetary damages, as well as intitutional reform, for people harmed by corporate misconduct. The plaintiff groups included:

1) consumers who bought products that were faulty, and even caused injury;

2) workers who were discriminated against, and claimed further pay or benefits;

3) stockholders, who claimed the wrongful actions of the company they owned caused the value of their stock to fall;

4) groups of people injured in mass accidents, such as plane crashes or mine disasters ("mass torts".)

Personal Injury Law

At the same time that class action law evolved, there was rapid evolution in the practice of "personal injury" ("PI") law. "Personal injury" lawyers represented victims of accidents. Traditionally, for example, Personal injury lawyers represent victims of automobile accidents, victims of mistakes by doctors or hospitals, and people injured by faulty products.

While many American lawyers do not spend much time in courtrooms, personal injury lawyers often make their reputations as "trial lawyers" ——skilled at going to trial and persuading juries to provide damage awards to the plaintiff.

In the late 20th century, "epidemics" of worker injuries and illnesses provided personal injury lawyers with large numbers of victims whose injuries or illnesses had similar, or the same cause. In parts of Texas and Louisiana where oil and chemical factories abounded, for example, oil and chemical workers provided local plaintiff lawyers with continued supply of clients seeking relief from hazardous chemicals and toxic substances to which they were exposed.

Most famously, the widespread use of asbestos as fire proof material in factories and ships led to the exposure of hundreds of thousands of workers to a substance that can cause lung disease or cancer.

Success in this litigation provided the more successful plaintiffs lawyers with funds which permitted them to take on cases requiring even larger commitments of money and resources. Perhaps like companies engaged in research and developmen, the personal injury lawyers began to search for new patterns of insitutional misconduct, with groups of victims who could provide focus for their growing financial and human resources.

Taking on the Cigarette Companies

In the 1990's Plaintiffs lawyers surprised most Americans by successfully bringing litigation against the source of America's number one health hazard——the tobacco industry.

Since the 1960's the American public had known that cigarette smoking causes cancer, heart disease and other illnesses. However, the tobacco industry is one of America's richest and most powerful industries. It had seemingly endless resources to fight lawsuits. No smoker who was sickened by cigarette smoking had won a lawsuit for damages against the industry. When the Federal government issued regulations that required companies to tell smokers that smoking may cause illness, the cigarette companies claimed that smokers could not claim damages, because they knew the risk and had voluntarily assumed it.

Plaintiff lawyers entered into arrangements with some state attorneys general (the top government lawyer in each state) to represent the states (on a contingency) against the tobacco industry. The basic claim was that the states had to pay tremendous amounts in health care costs for citizens of the states, who were sickened by cigarette smoke,

During the litigation, the plaintiffs lawyers discovered (with important help from whistleblowers) that top industry officials had kept shocking secrets from the government (as well as the public) about their own knowledge of the hazards of smoking. Such discoveries in the tobacco case led to multibillion dollar settlements with the state governments. The plaintiff's lawyers received hundreds of millions of dollars for their work.

Plaintiffs lawyering in the 21st century

In contrast to private law firms that represented corporations, the largest of which now employ over 1000 lawyers——plaintiff's law firms remain small. The most successful have dozens of lawyers, not hundreds or thousands. Thus, law firms often cooperate, with law firms located in differing regions looking for and sharing cases where national patterns of misconduct may be found.

In the interim since the settlement of the tobacco cases, plaintiffs lawyers have used their resources to develop litigation strategies to take on another of america's richest and most powerful industries——the pharmaceutical companies——claiming that the companies have marketed drugs known to be unsafe.

In addition to the potential rewards from class action and tort lawsuits, plaintiff lawyers may use other tools. These include attorneys fees provisions in discrimination laws, the possibility that clients can receive damages multiple times actual losses in antimonopoly laws, and "whistleblower" laws.

As their successes have increased, so has opposition to their work. Defendants (potential or actual), include large corporations, professionals (doctors, accountants, engineers). Representatives of these groups argue that Plaintiffs lawyers seek to help themselves, not their clients. Politicians promise to pass laws that make it more difficult for plaintiff's lawyers to bring class action lawsuits, or to reduce the amounts of money that can be collected. The critics are not limited to defendants (or potential defendants). Ralph Nader and his Public Citizen Litigation group have been among those questioning the fairness of class action settlements.

Ⅲ. Ethics: The Core of Successful Public Interest Law Practice

Perhaps the most important thing for a young public interest lawyer to learn is how success may depend on the ability to understand the special ethical problems and questions that public interest lawyers may face.

Ethical conduct is critical for all lawyers. All lawyers should follow professional codes of ethics. However, especially where they represent unpopular clients or challenge powerful interests, public interest lawyers may often face special kinds of ethical problems or questions that must be dealt with if the lawyer is to succeed. These include:

(1) Why should a lawyer do pro bono or public interest work?

(2) What should a public interest lawyer do when his her idea of what the public interest requires differs from the client's idea—and the lawyer is working for free (pro bono)?

(3) What should a public interest lawyer do when he is working on contingency (or pro bono) and the monetary costs borne by the lawyer become so high that the lawyer's own interests are endangered if he continues the representation?

(4) What should a lawyer do when he represents a group of clients, and differening members of the group have differing views about the way the lawyer should proceed?

(5) What special obligations does a public interest lawyer have where clients may——because they are old, sick, or young—not have sufficient ability to understand the choices before them?

(6) What should a public Public interest lawyers do when the costs to him from representing an unpopular client may become so high as to damage reputation with family, friends, or colleagues?

(7) What should a public interest lawyer do when opposing lawyers (or their clients) threaten that if the lawyer continues the case he may

risk losing his license or be punished?

(8) What should the public interest lawyer do when he seems to win a case, but the client is worse off——for example, the client has lost his job and friends?

(9) What should a public interest lawyer do when he knows that the other side is cheating——should he cheat also in order to win?

The best way to understand how to deal with these kinds of problems is to experience them and, with the help of supervisors or mentors, see how public interest lawyers can deal with them in the real world. However, it is also important to study these problems and understand them. In many cases these problems can be avoided or solved if they are understood in advance. In any case, public interest lawyers, or those who wish to become public interest lawyers, should know about these problems so that they can best serve their clients and the public interest.

Conclusion: Public Interest Law in the 21st Century

In the 21st century public interest law, and public interest lawyering, is hardly a phenomenom unique to the United States. Environmental public interest lawyers, for example, practice in numrous countries throughout the world—including China. At the same time, in the globalizing world, the problems public interest lawyers seek to address-such as climate change and other environmental pollution—are global, perhaps increasingly requiring cooperation among public interest lawyers across borders. The history of public interest law in the 21st century, it is likely, will a history of lawyers in many countries.

论法学教育视野下的公益诉讼

李 轩*

摘 要：随着近年来我国民主法治进程的深入发展和公民意识的不断提高，公益诉讼已经深度介入我们的社会政治生活。在法学教育领域，公益诉讼俨然作为诊所式法律教育和高校法律援助的重要题材登堂入室并发挥着日益重要的作用。作为实现公平正义价值和维护社会公共利益的重要手段，公益诉讼在我国的境遇似乎并不乐观，但我国高校法学教育机构依靠其得天独厚的资源和条件，在公益诉讼的发展过程中具有独特的作用和优势。笔者依据从事多年法学教育的经验以及以兼职律师身份亲身经历和代理的“中国电信”案、“奥运加油”案等公益案件，详细分析了利用法学教育平台发展公益诉讼的独特优势，以及引入公益诉讼元素的法学教育给教学带来的显著成效，归纳总结了公益诉讼在实践过程中可能实施的策略选择，阐明高校法学教育机构若能注重发挥自身优势，借助法律援助平台积极与社会执业律师联合参与和推动公益诉讼，就能收到良好的教学效果和社会效应，并可实现人才培养和服务社会的双重目标。

关键词：法学教育　公益诉讼　法律诊所教育　律师参与策略

一、公益诉讼与法学教育

近10年来，随着我国民主法治进程的深入发展和公民权利意识的不断提高，公益诉讼作为一种新鲜事物在我国悄然落地生根并获得蓬勃发

---

* 李轩，中央财经大学法律援助中心主任，中华全国律师协会宪法与人权委员会秘书长。

展，其倡导者和参与者既有律师界的新锐人物，也有高校法学院系的前卫师生，更有不满于各种违法侵权现象而毅然“以身试法”的普通民众。虽然对公益诉讼的定义还在争论不休，但这并不影响其如火如荼的发展趋势。今天，公益诉讼已然成为我国使用频率极高的一个新词汇：笔者在百度搜索引擎中输入“公益诉讼”一词，跳出的相关网页达641 000篇之多，涉及理论探讨、制度构建和实务操作的方方面面。这间接表明公益诉讼已经深度介入我们的社会政治生活，正在成为民主法治建设的助推器。

严格来说，公益诉讼与法学教育没有必然的联系。但是，随着法学教育职业化倾向日益突出，我国法学教育更加注重实务内容，法学教育机构的社会服务功能日益彰显。尤其是进入21世纪以来，在法学教育全球化的背景下，受西方法治发达国家尤其是美国法学教育理念的日益影响，包括中国、韩国、日本在内的传统东方国家也在逐步尝试以法律硕士教育为主导的法学教育体制和法律教学模式的改革。[1] 公益诉讼由此作为诊所式法律教育和高校法律援助的重要题材登堂入室并发挥着日益重要的作用。

二、通过法学教育平台发展公益诉讼的独特优势

毋庸讳言，近10年来我国公益诉讼的发展已成燎原之势，但是期间或有挫折，作为实现公平正义价值和维护社会公共利益的重要手段，公益诉讼在我国的境遇似乎并不乐观，其发展一直受到观念抵制、制度缺位等因素的制约，公益诉讼实践还存在诸多问题，如主体资格受到限制、法院在公益诉讼受理方面谨小慎微、公益诉讼胜诉的比例较低甚至屡诉屡败、诉讼成本偏高、诉讼成效不大等，凡此种种，不一而足。在某些

[1] 李轩：“论中国法学教育的转向与转型”，载《中国司法》2010年第12期。

时期、某些领域，公益诉讼还呈现出举步维艰的态势。[1]

与此同时，我国公益诉讼还处于自发状态，缺乏有力的组织和协调。虽然律师作为法律服务的中坚力量在公益诉讼中也常常显露身手并取得积极效果，但如果要求律师将公益诉讼作为主业且长期坚守未免过于苛求。要想克服公益诉讼的主客观障碍，带动广大民众共同维护社会公益，需要其他主体的参与。其中，法学教育机构在公益诉讼的发展过程中无疑具有独特的作用和优势。

高校法学院系作为我国主要的法律教育和法学人才培养机构，拥有独特的法律资源优势、良好的氛围与环境，汇聚了众多的法律人才，其中有大量法律专家学者从事相关的教学理论与实务研究，还有广大法学专业本科生、研究生积极从事法律学习和实践。随着职业化教育成为法学教育的共识，以高校法学院系的广大师生作为公益诉讼的推动主体，无疑是水到渠成、顺理成章的事。

事实上，大学法学院参与或主导公益诉讼早在20世纪七八十年代就已经成为西方国家尤其是美国法学教育的一种趋势，法律诊所教育在美国的兴起也天然地与公益诉讼的发展有一种“剪不断，理还乱”的密切关系。笔者曾经访问法律诊所教育成就卓越的美国乔治顿大学，[2] 发现该校不仅设有颇具规模的法律援助机构，拥有堪称世界之最的12学分法律诊所教育课程设置，而且还拥有引领公益诉讼潮流的光辉历史。而笔者访问过的另一所美国著名大学——哥伦比亚大学（Columbia University）还支持创办了具有世界影响力的“公益诉讼研究中心”[3]。随着世纪之交职业化法学教育模式的西风东渐，我国部分知名高校法学院系也在引进法律诊所教育课程的同时逐渐介入法律援助和公益诉讼领域，如北

---

[1] 江伟（中国人民大学法学院）、徐继军（中国社会科学院法学研究所）：“将‘公益诉讼制度’写入民事诉讼法的若干基本问题的探讨”，载中国民商法律网，http：//www.civillaw.com.cn/article/default.asp? id＝44338，最后浏览日期：2010年12月9日。

[2] Georgetown University，或译“乔治城大学”。

[3] Public interest law institute，简称“pili”，该机构目前已脱离哥伦比亚大学独立运作并在中国设有办事处。

京大学、清华大学、中国政法大学、中国人民大学、中央财经大学、武汉大学、西北政法大学、华东政法大学等都先后成立了公益性的法律援助机构，与其他致力于公益诉讼的律师和普通民众不同程度地推动我国公益诉讼的发展。尤其是在民主法治建设不断深化的当下，倡导和坚持公益诉讼甚至应该成为高等法学教育机构的不二使命。

高校法学院系及其法律援助机构参与公益诉讼，具有得天独厚的条件和独特的优势，主要体现在以下几个方面：

其一，包括公益诉讼在内的法律援助活动能够与法学院系的教学工作相互融合与促进。法律援助活动能够与目前法学院开展的“法律诊所”教育相结合，促进法学院实践教学的发展，在为社会提供法律帮助的同时也能满足法学院实践教学的需求。因此，法学院在典型案例的法律实践中会有积极参与的兴趣，借此充实和完善理论及实践教学所需的素材。

其二，高校师生尤其是法学院学生在公益诉讼领域有更多的热情。法学院学生更乐于在法律援助中实践自己的法律知识，有很高的法律热情和较多的课余时间，热衷于提供志愿服务。加上法学院具有兼职律师身份的教师参与指导和辅助，有效地克服学生在知识和实践经验上的不足之后，这些学生完全可以成为法律援助的主力军，发挥重大的作用。他们是法律援助中不可忽视的一批力量，也将是日后法律界的后备人才。

其三，高校法学院系在公益诉讼领域有更大的施展空间，能取得更好的社会效果。相比于其他社会力量而言，其承受的非议和社会压力一般较少，公益诉讼活动的开展能够更加顺利。正如众多媒体所反映的那样，近两年来，中国的法治进程似有停滞的趋势，流弊所及，公益诉讼似亦裹足不前。笔者最近甚至听到一则十分荒谬的流言：有关方面居然禁止媒体使用“公民”一词。流言未必属实，但笔者实实在在听到过不得宣传“公益诉讼”的呵斥，某些人士似乎敏感过度，大有谈“公”色变的意味，很多律师甚至因此而淡出公益诉讼领域。在这种情况下，相对自由和宽松的校园空气更有利于消解和抵御公益诉讼带来的各种压力。同时，高校也具有更多的专业学术资源和社会关注度，高校师生从事公益诉讼活动更容易得到媒体及社会的关注。有了成功的模式和案例后，通过高校的学术交流平台更容易得到推广，取得良好的社会效果。

其四，高校法学院系从事公益诉讼的经济成本较低，便于公益诉讼的可持续发展。由于官方法律援助机构规模有限，援助范围不足，不能充分满足社会需求，而律师事务所由于负担运营成本和经济压力，从事法律援助的时间和精力难以保障，往往不能长期坚持。相比而言，高校在法律援助中的经济成本相对较低，预备一块校内的办公地点和一套办公设备，以法学院教师及学生为主体的援助力量，无需附加多余费用的场地和设施，无需专门支付援助报酬，不仅为高校法援机构的运行降低了成本，也为公益诉讼中被援助当事人降低了成本。再加上高校一些专项经费的支持和当事人适当承担少许诉讼成本的方式，高校的法律援助机构就可以很顺利地运转起来，有了源源不断的学生和教师作为后备力量，法律援助机构的工作就可以持续开展下去。

三、引入公益诉讼元素的法学教育

如前所述，无论是法学院系本身，还是教育主管部门，都已经认识到我国传统法学教育的弊端，开始更多地强调法学教育的职业化。法律诊所教育、模拟法庭、法律谈判、法律文书写作、案例分析等实务类课程得到空前的重视，[1] 教育部和国务院学位办更是明确提出要逐步实现研究生教育从学术型研究生培养到专业学位研究生教育培养的转型。[2] 其中，以法律援助机构为依托的法律诊所教育课程成为新一轮法学教育改革的亮点，公益诉讼也因此得以嵌入高等法学教育。

---

[1] 在全国法律硕士教育指导委员会发布的全日制法律硕士研究生指导性培养方案中，实践必修环节和专业实习占有较大比重，模拟法庭、法律文书、法律谈判等都被规定为必修课程，这已经体现了方案设计者们对职业化人才培养的追求和努力，至于各培养单位实施效果就另当别论了。

[2] 根据教育部2010年10月13日发布的《关于批准有关高等学校开展专业学位研究生教育综合改革试点工作的通知》（教研［2010］2号），共有64所高校的118个专业学位点被批准开始进行为期3年的综合改革试点。其中包括北大、清华、人大、政法、中央财大等5所北京院校在内的全国19所高校的法律硕士点榜上有名。

根据笔者多年从事高等法学教育和参与法律援助、公益诉讼的经验，充分参与公益诉讼有助于开展形式多样的法律实务教学，帮助学生全面培养职业道德意识和实务操作能力，并在客观上起到促进民主法治进程的作用。

众所周知，法学是实用之学，任课教师直接提起或代理公益诉讼并与教学内容相结合无疑是一种非常好的体验式法学教育方式，不少法学院系的教师都做了身体力行的尝试，其收效往往强于一般“纸上谈兵”式的授课方式。例如，笔者曾于1999年作为原告起诉中国电信集团，要求其取消已有移动电话号码“升位加零”的做法，并将该案进程和结果作为民事诉讼法学课程的鲜活素材在课堂上进行深入讨论。该案是笔者有生以来亲自参与的第一起公益诉讼，也自认为是中国早期为数不多的有影响的公益诉讼之一。该案起因于原中国电信集团于1999年7月1日分拆为新的中国电信集团、中国移动通信集团、中国网通集团和中国联通集团，并于分拆之日同时将原10位移动电话号码升至11位，美其名曰为社会提供扩容服务，但其实质显然是为了追求更多的手机用户和更多的经济利益。适逢当时笔者安装的住宅电话也遭到北京电话局的无理改号，一怒之下将北京电话局和中国电信集团分别告上法庭。在审理过程中，法院首先出现了“以调压判”的现象，笔者以此给学生分析法院调解自愿和合法原则以及过分强调调解的不良后果。一审法院调解不成，以被告中国电信集团“一分为四”、移动通信业务已划归当时刚刚成立的中国移动通信集团为由驳回了笔者的起诉，笔者以此帮助学生理解驳回起诉和驳回诉讼请求的区别、裁定和判决的区别等程序性问题；还启发学生运用民法原理分析法院裁定的实体错误：按照《中华人民共和国民法通则》的规定，法人分立的，可以分立后的各个法人为共同被告，共同被告相互之间承担连带责任，这一规定意味着，当中国电信集团“一分为四”之后，笔者仍可以分立后的主体之一为被告，法院不能驳回对笔者的起诉，而最多只能追加中国移动通信集团等另外三个分立后的主体为共同被告。一审结束后，笔者不服，提起上诉，中级法院未经开庭审理即作出维持一审裁定的终审裁定，在一审裁定理由之外还增加了一条理由：中国电信集团“一分为四”有国务院办公厅的文件支持，由此驳回了笔者的上诉。笔者在讲课过程中又借此分析第二审不开庭审理的种种弊端和终审法院对一审裁判所谓“可改可不改的坚决不改”的复杂心理，以及潜在行政力量干预司法的客观现实。因为该案是任课老师的亲身经历，且是课程进行过程中同步发生的新鲜案例，学生们以观察者的身份实时介入其中，投入了极大的热情，对相关知识点有了切身体会，并且学会了法律分析和思考的一些基本方法。甚至现在还有学生记得当年笔者曾经说过的一句话：“虽败犹荣，立此存照。”

值得一提的是，自2000年前后法律诊所教育课程开始陆续引进到国内以来，我国不少高校法学院系都开设了丰富多样的法律诊所课程。据中国法学会诊所法律教育专业委员会的不完全统计，该会现有团体会员130多家，基本都开设了民事（诉讼）诊所、刑事（诉讼）诊所、劳动诊所、社区诊所、立法诊所等不同类型的诊所课程。[1] 但是，笔者认为，典型意义的法律诊所课程应该还是诉讼诊所课程。通过依法参与代理民事或行政公益诉讼，学生不仅可以获得规定学分，更可以获得课堂学习所不能获得的诉讼体会和经验；通过诊所教师的模拟安排、点评、总结和归纳，其他学生不仅可以像教师一样“诊断”当事人的案情，还可以“诊断”参与代理的学生的问题所在，这既有助于培养其实务操作能力，又有助于培养其职业道德意识。公益诉讼通常具有不同于一般诉讼的特殊影响力，更能够吸引参与者的眼球；公益诉讼还具有社会公益属性，所有这些都在一定程度上深化了诊所教育过程对参与学生的影响力。

不过，如何实现法律诊所教育课程与公益诉讼的有机结合，仍然是一个值得探讨和不断实践的问题。在笔者主持的某期法律诊所教育课程的集中课堂上，笔者和其他教师以学生们亲自代理的北京大学某消费者状告圣梦美容院服务欺诈系列诉讼为例，在部分学生实际参与接待当事人、立案和开庭的基础上，先后组织了三次主题不同但又相互衔接的公

[1] 详见CCCLE（中国法学会诊所法律教育专业委员会）主任王晨光教授在“中国诊所法律教育十周年庆典暨诊所教育论坛”上的致辞，载中国诊所法律教育网，http://www.cliniclaw.cn/article_view.asp，最后浏览日期：2010年12月9日。

开课，收到了较好的教学和示范效果，特不揣浅陋赘述如下，或许可为参照：

第一次公开课的主题为学生模拟接待当事人。参与角色模拟的学生都是曾经在笔者指导下同时亲自接待当事人的学生，模拟表演时有人扮演接待律师，有人扮演律师助理，有人扮演当事人，有人则担任观察员。通过这种方式回放实际接待场面，让其他学生现场评价各个角色扮演者的优缺点，还让观察员对比总结，教师最后总结点评。

第二次公开课的主题为学生模拟立案。参与模拟立案表演的学生将他们的真实经历再现出来：学生前往北京某基层法院立案，先后进入三个立案室，充分体会到了老师们平时上课时所批判的法院立案难和法官刁难现象，最后经与庭长交涉才得以立案。作为观众的学生则负责分析评价模拟过程的问题，在了解立案文件要求的同时加深了对当前司法环境的理解。

第三次公开课的主题为学生观摩、点评庭审录像。参与开庭审理环节是法律诊所教育中的重要环节，在两名学生代理消费者开庭之后，笔者将其法庭实况录像拷贝回来在课堂上播放，让其他学生进行评价，并让代理出庭的同学自我总结和参与旁听的同学进行总结，最后由老师进行全面点评。因为观摩的是身边同学的法庭表现场面，学生们普遍认真，并积极投入分析评价。通过老师的归纳、总结，学生们潜移默化地理解了一般诉讼要领和诉讼的策略与技巧。

当然，如前所述，任课教师直接提起公益诉讼或代理公益诉讼，将诉讼实践融入课程内容之中，又或者促成法律诊所教育课程与公益诉讼相结合，将诉讼实践作为主要课程内容，都是公益诉讼嵌入法律实务教学的有效方式，但绝对不是仅有方式。我们还应鼓励学生在教师指导下参与代理公益诉讼，以其亲身经历体悟诉讼过程并相互交流，有条件地邀请公益诉讼代理律师或其他代理人举办讲座，以公益诉讼为题材引导学生组织模拟法庭，让更多的学生参与旁听公益诉讼的开庭审理或者与公益诉讼有关的研讨会、论证会，以便让学生获得更多的启发。如，笔者曾邀请北京市莫少平律师事务所主任莫少平律师、北京市问天律师事务所周泽律师（原中国青年政治学院新闻系副教授）、北京市律师协会消费者权利保护委员会主任邱宝昌律师、北京市汉卓律师事务所秦兵律师等给选修律师制度与律师实务、法律诊所教育等课程的学生举行“公益诉讼的策略和技巧”等讲座，带领学生参与组织和旁听笔者主持的李刚博士状告卫生部及牙防组共同侵权案、财经时报记者状告某地新闻出版局行政处罚不当案、崔英杰刺死城管队长涉嫌故意杀人案研讨会以及笔者亲自代理的一些公益诉讼案件，利用笔者或学生参与代理的公益诉讼案件组织模拟法庭等，都取得了较为满意的效果。

四、公益诉讼融入法学教育的有效例证

如前所述，公益诉讼触动的往往是既得利益者，挑战的往往是强势部门，其发起人或代理人通常会面临方方面面的阻挠和压力，因此，高校法学院系要想在法学教育过程中开展公益诉讼并取得良好的诉讼效果和社会反响，还应当注重诉讼策略的适当应用。笔者所在的中央财经大学法律援助中心曾经成功处理了一起行政公益诉讼案件，在一定程度上可以视为公益诉讼融入法学教育的有效例证。

2008 年北京奥运会开幕前夕，某出版社的官方网站使用了“奥运加油，中国加油”八字以表达爱国情怀和对北京奥运的良好祝愿，不想被某工商局以侵犯奥林匹克标志专有权为由，责令出版社立即停止侵权行为并处罚款 10 000元。笔者以法律援助中心主任的身份接受了该出版社的委托，同时带领一名学生代理出版社向工商局提起行政诉讼，要求被告撤销涉奥不当行政处罚。因为涉奥案件的特殊性，此案一经受理，立刻受到新闻媒体的极大关注。《京华时报》率先对此案进行了报道，此后新华网、央视网、中国新闻网、新浪网、腾讯网、网易网、凤凰网等知名网站纷纷转载，引起社会舆论的广泛关注和讨论。

一审中，笔者曾经认为胜券在握，所以只是按照常规进行了代理，但不想法官滥用职权违法强制变相调解，以工商局少罚款或者不罚款为交换条件劝诱出版社撤诉，并最终作出原告败诉的行政判决。出版社严

重不服，随即提起上诉。在二审过程中，针对本案的核心问题及争议焦点，笔者代表出版社委托中国法学会案例研究专业委员会聘请部分知名诉讼法学专家和行政法学专家召开了一次专家论证会，与会专家一致认为工商局的行政处罚决定认定事实、适用法律法规错误，并且存在滥用行政自由裁量权之嫌。参与论证会的专家们联名提出一份意见书，并将该意见书递交给受理上诉的中级人民法院。《法制日报》《中国青年报》相继对本案及其专家论证意见做了整版报道，全文介绍了这次专家论证会的过程及专家意见的主要内容，社会反响强烈。[1] 为防止二审合议庭不经开庭而草草维持原判，笔者还整理了一份《紧急情况反映》，连同专家论证意见书和相关报道寄给了二审法院审判委员会的主要委员。嗣后，工商局终于意识到自己的错误所在，迫于压力撤销了前述被诉行政处罚决定。二审法院动员上诉人撤回了上诉，上诉人则要求在撤诉裁定中载明鉴于被上诉人已撤销被诉行政处罚决定，该处罚决定及一审判决不再执行。至此，上诉人要求撤销一审判决及行政处罚决定的诉讼请求实际上已经得到实现，本案最终以上诉人事实上的胜诉而告终。

在诉讼进行过程中，不仅先后有两名学生参与本案一审、二审代理，而且有更多的学生到法院旁听，参加专家论证会的材料准备和记录工作，参加专家论证会的现场旁听，还以本案为题材在模拟法庭课堂上组织了模拟行政审判活动。通过这些参与和体验，学生们普遍加深了对行政法和行政诉讼法的理解，也获得了从书本上难以获得的诉讼知识和诉讼

---

[1] 2009年4月19日，受当事人的委托，中国法学会法学教育研究会案例研究专业委员会聘请中国政法大学诉讼法研究院教授兼博士生导师、中国法学会民事诉讼法学研究会名誉会长杨荣新先生，中国社会科学院法学研究所研究员兼博士生导师、中国法学会宪法学研究会副会长莫纪宏先生，中国人民大学法学院教授兼博士生导师、中国法学会行政法研究会副会长杨建顺先生，北京大学法学院教授兼博士生导师、中国法学会行政法研究会副会长湛中乐先生，清华大学法学院法学博士、中国法学会行政法研究会理事何海波先生等人，在北京市义派律师事务所就中国财政经济出版社因诉北京市工商行政管理局海淀分局要求撤销其“京工商海处字(2008)第3942号”不当涉奥行政处罚决定纠纷一案举行了专家论证会。2009年4月24日，《法制日报·周末》整版报道了湛中乐教授、杨建顺教授、何海波博士等知名学者就该案发表的研讨意见。

经验。

五、作为法学教育素材的公益诉讼的策略选择

任何诉讼在实施过程中都需要讲究策略和技巧，公益诉讼也概莫能外。在法学教育过程中开展公益诉讼，更有许多资源优势和有利因素可资借用。总结起来，作为法学教育素材的公益诉讼的策略选择包括但不限于以下方面。

（1）充分利用高校信息资源优势，开发和挖掘公益诉讼。

公益诉讼的特殊意义在于其具有不同于一般诉讼的社会影响力，这种影响力也使得其在法学教育过程中的作用可能成倍增加。但是，如何在众多的法律纠纷中发现并形成公益诉讼，需要我们有目的地选择和甄别，有时还需要对当事人进行引导和说服。作为法学教育的实施者，法学院系教师应当充分利用高校信息资源优势，利用法律援助机构和网上咨询平台，从可能产生普遍意义的纠纷信息中开发和挖掘公益诉讼，并进而作为教学素材有机融入相关教学体系。

（2）积极争取法学专家的智力支持，全面支持公益诉讼。

在“奥运加油”案中，专家论证意见应该起到了决定性的重要作用。众所周知，在司法实践中，法学界专家学者的法律意见是很容易受到关注和重视的，组织法学专家和学者对重大的法律疑难问题和社会热点问题发表专业意见并通过有效的渠道反馈至法院和庭审法官的面前，能够帮助法院和法官了解更多的关于案件的不同观点，引导法官正确地适用法律。在某些时候，专家论证意见甚至能起到防止司法腐败的效果。[1]高校法学院系本身就是法学智力库，具有天然的专家学者资源，因而在开展公益诉讼的过程中必要时要积极争取法学专家的智力支持，以座谈会、研讨会、专家论证会等方式支持公益诉讼。

---

[1] 当然，长期以来，因为专家法律论证意见书可能影响司法公正，理论界和实务界对其正负功能也一直争论不断。参见韩福东：“因刘涌案受质疑 律师田文昌谈专家论证书的是非”，载《新闻周刊》2004 年第 5 期；赵寒春（苏州大学法学院）：“浅议专家法律意见书及解决之道”，载《法制与社会》2007 年第 12 期。

（3）充分利用媒体的力量，积极介入公益诉讼。

媒体的广泛报道和积极参与是案件能得到相对公正的审判的一个重要因素，“奥运加油”案中包括《中国青年报》《南方周末》等知名媒体及大型门户网站对案件案情及研讨论证结果的持续关注和报道，使得行政机关感受到了社会力量的压力，媒体监督充分发挥作用，迫使行政机关作出了让步。媒体监督不仅能够使得这种公益诉讼取得胜利，从根本上还能够限制行政机关滥用权力，实现此类诉讼的最终目的。在公益诉讼中，尤其是面对强权的公权力机关时，适时适当地借助媒体的监督力量，能够为案件争取一个更加公平的结果。[1]

在此颇值一提的是，笔者非常遗憾地发现，国外通常所谓的“律师、法官、检察官和法学家”共同组成的“法律共同体”在中国事实上是不存在的。因为职业身份的异质性，中国的法官、检察官似乎一时还难以和律师、法学家形成“法律共同体”，倒是律师、法学家、法制记者三类群体往往因为都具有民间身份、专业知识背景和共同的公益立场，反而易于结成天然的公益联盟。所以，每当公益诉讼遭遇挫折的时候，律师、法学家、法制记者的结合往往能够形成强大的力量，发挥意想不到的效果。

（4）适时提交情况反映，通过司法监督机制关注公益诉讼。

目前我国诉讼实践中合议庭制度难以发挥民主合议的作用，往往产生审判长或主审法官一人专断的情形。如果遇到独任法官审理，案件的结果更容易受到法官个人意志的左右。及时将案件情况及重要信息向法院审判委员会或主要领导反映，尤其是将案件的特殊情况和重大问题通过适当的方式向法院领导反映，如“奥运加油”案中寄送有关案件的重大新闻报道情况和专家研讨意见等，引起法院领导对案件的重视，启动

---

[1] 必须指出的是，反对新闻舆论随意介入司法过程的研究者亦大有人在，事实上也的确存在媒体过度介入甚至有关方面操纵媒体影响司法公正的现象。参见蔡定剑（中国政法大学）：“媒体审判应该降温——从蒋艳萍案谈起”，载《法制日报》2001年4月17日；王好学（中南财经政法大学）：“论‘媒体审判’与司法独立——以重庆打黑为思维切入点”，载《新疆石油教育学院学报》2010年第4期。

法院内部的监督程序，以保证案件能得到公正审理判决的效果，也是一个行之有效的策略。

（5）以法律援助机构为平台，结合法律诊所教育等实务课程开展公益诉讼。

目前，多数法学院系都开设了若干法律实务课程，旨在服务社会并为学生提供实习实践机会；很多法学院系还设立了对外法律援助机构，比较具有代表性的有原北京大学妇女法律研究与服务中心、北京大学公益法研究中心、武汉大学社会弱者权利保护中心（公益与发展法律研究中心）、中国政法大学环境资源法研究和服务中心、清华大学宪法与公民权利中心、中国社会科学院东方公益法律援助律师事务所、西北政法大学法律援助中心，以及笔者所在的中央财经大学法律援助中心等。高校法律援助机构的日常接待工作是公益诉讼线索的重要来源，法律诊所教育等实务课程的经常性开设是公益诉讼发挥普遍教学功能的必要条件。因此，以法律援助机构为平台，结合法律诊所教育等实务课程广为开展公益诉讼，是保证法学教育中公益诉讼可持续发展的重要方式。

（6）法学院与律师事务所紧密合作，共同推动公益诉讼。

现在，越来越多的人认识到律师等法律实务专家参与法学教育具有非常重要的意义，律师参与高校法律实务教学在西方发达国家更是一种常态。法学院与律师事务所紧密合作，不仅能够为法学院提供师资，为学生提供实习机会，还能够相互结合，共同推动公益诉讼的发展。❶

此外，在法学教育过程中开展公益诉讼还要善于妥协，注重社会影响而非诉讼结果。这一策略在前述手机“升位加零”案、“奥运加油”案中都得到了充分体现。从更高的层次来看，高校法律院系还要全面利用公益诉讼的有效元素，深入挖掘个案的制度价值，必要时将办案过程中发现的重大法律问题整理成文，向有关方面提出制度完善的意见和建议。

---

❶ 例如，笔者所在的中央财经大学法学院及中央财经大学法律援助中心先后与北京市义派律师事务所、北京市国联律师事务所、北京市中闻律师事务所、北京市汇佳律师事务所、北京市资略律师事务所等法律服务机构或其律师合作，致力于推动法律援助与公益诉讼，取得了良好的社会效果。

总之，公益诉讼是当前加强民主法治、推动社会进步的重要力量，但其发展仍有赖于众多主体的参与和相关制度的健全，前景可谓任重而道远。高等法学教育机构在法律实务教学过程中开展公益诉讼具有天然的优势和独特的作用，法学院师生如能注重发挥自身优势，采取适当有效的诉讼策略并借助法律援助平台积极参与和推动公益诉讼，就能收到良好的教学效果和社会效应，从而更好地实现人才培养和服务社会的双重目标。

美国诊所式法律教育的演进

王竹青*

摘　要： 美国诊所式法律教育的产生经历了漫长的发展过程，从学徒式教育、苏格拉底式教育、苏格拉底—案例式教育到诊所式法律教育，历经约200年。在此过程中，无数学者为诊所式法律教育的产生和发展作出了杰出的贡献，如兰德尔、弗兰克、布莱威等，他们在不同的阶段创造了不同的思想，引领了美国法学教育的发展。同时，诊所式法律教育的理念也从单纯培养学生的实践技能到帮助社会的弱势群体、培养学生的职业道德和社会责任感、维护社会的公平和正义等，不断发展与进步。尽管诊所式法律教育存在某些缺陷与不足，但它所蕴含的核心价值是值得我们不懈追求的。

关键词： 美国　诊所式法律教育　演进

一、诊所式法律教育的产生及初期发展

美国的法律教育可以追溯到19世纪，当时正式的法律院校已经存在，但对未来律师的教育和培养是学徒式的。1800年，美国大部分州的法律教育都需要一定的学徒年限（如，马里兰州需要5年的学徒期，有大学学历的可以减少1年）；但是到1860年，随着法律院校的增多（当时有21所法律院校），几乎没有哪个州再要求学徒式教育。❶ 学徒式培养

* 王竹青，北京科技大学文法学院副教授，美国哥伦比亚大学2010～2011年度访问学者，中国人民大学法学博士。

❶ 威廉·奎格利："新诊所法律职业的教学方法初探—来自基层的观察"，载《阿克伦法律评论》1995年第28期，第465～466页。（William P. Quigley，*Introduction to Clinical Teaching for the New Clinical Law Profession*；A View From the First Floor，28 AKRON L. REV，(1995). pp. 465～466.）

方式也有很大的不同，一般包括阅读法律教材和案例，观摩教授或指导老师在代理真实案件时的律师实务等。虽然学徒式教育培养出大量的律师，但对学徒式教育的批评一直存在，包括其不稳定性、不一致性以及潜在的剥削性。

到19世纪末期，大量出现的新的法律院校最终超越了以学徒式教育模式为基本模式的教育理念，这种教育模式的改变也给法学教育提供了新的出路。1870年，哈佛大学法学院院长克里斯托弗·哥伦布·兰德尔（Christopher Columbus Langdell）开始试行案例教学法，学生通过分析上诉法院的判决来学习法律。兰德尔在进行案例教学的同时，对苏格拉底教学法进行了改进。苏格拉底教学法源自19世纪美国三个流行的法学教学方法：源自学徒模式的技能培训；来自欧洲的总体的教学方法；以理性原则进行相互联系的分析及体系化方法。[1] 兰德尔创造的苏格拉底—案例教学法培养学生以分析和批判的方式思考由上诉法院的判决中产生的基本法律原则。这种教学法迅速得到了广泛的认可并且被其他法律院校普遍接受。[2]

19世纪90年代晚期到20世纪早期，当案例教学法被广泛接受时，一些法学院的学生自愿建立了“法律诊所”或法律援助机构，以亲身参与的方式学习和实践法律，同时通过为贫弱群体提供法律服务的方式践

---

[1] 查尔斯·麦克玛尼斯：“美国法律教育的百年历史——一个修正主义者的视角”，载《华盛顿大学法律季刊》1981年第59期，第617～618页。（Charles R. McManis, *The History of First Century American Legal Education*: *A Revisionist Perspective*, 59 Wash. U. L. Q, (1981). pp. 617～618.）

[2] 乔治·格罗斯曼：“诊所法律教育——历史与结论”，载《法律教育》1974年第26期，第162～165页。（George S. Grossman, *Clinical Legal Education*: *History and Diagnosis*, 26 J. LEGAL EDUC, (1974). pp. 162～165.）

行社会的司法使命。[1] 早在1917年，评论家威廉·罗（William Rowe）就发表了一篇法律评论文章，倡导诊所式法律教育是培养学生成为合格律师的最好方式。罗认为诊所式法律教育应该规范化，并且应该置入法学课程之中。他认为法学院落后于医学院、建筑学院、工程学院以及其他提供类似诊所式教育的学院。[2] 在罗撰写这篇文章的时代，大多数法律院校只提供2年的法学教育，他预示了将诊所式法律教育纳入法学教育的可能性，但当时占主导地位的仍然是苏格拉底—案例教学法。

虽然苏格拉底—案例教学法在当时的法学教育中占主导性的地位，但对它的批评自始就存在。第一次质疑兰德尔教学法的运动以法律现实主义为代表，出现于20世纪20年代至30年代。现实主义者认为，学习上诉法院的判决从根本上就是有缺陷的，是不够的，除此之外学生还需要了解法律和法律职业怎样在社会中发挥作用。现实主义者认为，如果法学院的学生能够亲身经历案件发生时及案件判决时的社会生活，他们会受到更好的教育。[3] 现实主义者还认为，法学院有责任培养学生对法

---

[1] 约翰·布莱威："法律援助诊所的特性"，载《加利福尼亚法律评论》1930年第3期，第174页；（John S. Bradway, *The Nature of a Legal Aid Clinic*, 3 S. Cal. L. Rev, (1930). p. 174.）罗伯特·麦克科瑞特："执教一个变化中的职业——从诊所到后续问题"，载《田纳西法律评论》1997年第64期，第1102～1103页；（Robert MacCrate, *Educating a Changing Profession: From Clinic to Continuum*, 64 Tenn. L. Rev, (1997), pp. 1102～1103）；威廉·罗："法律诊所与训练有素的律师——一种必要"，载《伊利诺斯法律评论》1917年第11期，第591页。（William V. Rowe, *Legal Clinics and Better Trained Lawyers-A Necessity*, 11. Ill. L. Rev, (1917). p. 591.）

[2] 威廉·罗："法律诊所与训练有素的律师——一种必要"，载《伊利诺斯法律评论》1917年第11期，第591页。（William V. Rowe, *Legal Clinics and Better Trained Lawyers-A Necessity*, 11 Ill. L. Rev, (1917). p. 591.）

[3] 乔治·格罗斯曼："诊所法律教育——历史与结论"，载《法律教育》1974年第26期，第166～167页。（George S. Grossman, *Clinical Legal Education: History and Diagnosis*, 26 J. LEGAL EDUC, (1974). pp. 166～167.）

律决定所产生的结果的道德和伦理敏感性。❶

二战以后，法律现实主义的意识形态有所改变，以卡尔·卢埃林（Karl Llewellyn）为代表的后现实主义者也声称兰德尔案例教学法与其他教学法一样存在缺陷。后现实主义者对法律教育改革的兴趣既不是诊所教育，也不是传统的法律教育，而是认为法学学生应当以政府部门或决策机构的政策顾问或政策制定者为培养目标。现实主义以及后现实主义的意识形态都没有在法学教育中产生重要的课程改革，❷ 但毫无疑问，现实主义和后现实主义思想对纠正过度注重兰德尔案例教学法产生了积极的影响，而且现实主义的一些影响至今仍在，如对立法的关注在法律课程中的地位仍在增长，但法学院一直在为如何对现实主义的见解注入现实意义而努力。❸

1921 年，卡内基基金会对法学教育进行了一个研究项目，艾尔弗雷德·瑞德（Alfred Z. Reed）撰写了一份报告，被称为“瑞德报告”。瑞德报告把法学教育分为三个部分，即概括性教育（综合教育）、法学理论教育和实践技能教育。案例教学只是这三个部分中的一个，即只为学生提供了理论教育。为满足概括性教育的需要，瑞德报告提出，学生在进入法学院之前至少要有 2 年的大学教育。这种主张一直延续至今，现在美国的法学教育还是研究生教育，进入法学院的学生必须有本科学历，以满足概括性教育的需要。而实践技能教育是缺乏的，这成为诊所式法律教育产生和发展的土壤。

直到 1930 年，诊所式法律教育的概念才出现在学术刊物上。诊所式

---

❶ 洛里·格雷厄姆：“亚里士多德的伦理观与有道德的律师——法律道德与诊所法律教育研究第一部分”，载《法律职业》1995～1996 年第 20 期，第 28 页。（Lorie M. Graham, *Aristotle's Ethics and the Virtuous Lawyer: Part One of A Study on Legal Ethics and Clinical Legal Education*, 20 J. LEGAL PROF.（1995～1996）. p. 28.）

❷ 乔治·格罗斯曼：“诊所法律教育——历史与结论”，载《法律教育》1974 年第 26 期，第 167～168 页。（George S. Grossman, *Clinical Legal Education: History and Diagnosis*, 26 J. LEGAL EDUC,（1974）. pp. 167～168.）

❸ 同上书，第 167 页。

法律教育的拥护者包括杰罗姆·弗兰克（Jerome Frank）和约翰·布莱威（John Bradway），他们撰写学术论文揭示了苏格拉底—案例教学法的缺陷，同时倡导在法学院的课程中开设诊所式法律教育。[1] 弗兰克，一位对兰德尔案例教学法的尖锐批评者，也是法律现实主义的代表人物，[2] 称案例教学法是“无可救药地、绝对地简化”了法学教育，同时他在文章中用诗一般的语言说道：“在兰德尔教学法下学习的学生就像园艺学家学习修剪花草，像建筑学家学习勾画建筑蓝图。他们看起来像未来的狗的饲养员，这些饲养员除了看到吃饱了的狗以外，从来看不到其他的东西。”[3] 他认为学生必须认识到法律是探索结果的手段而不是结果本身。

为了弥补苏格拉底—案例教学法的缺陷和不足，弗兰克建议开设诊所式教育课程以使学生参与现实的法律实践。在弗兰克看来，法学学生应该学习怎样与当事人建立起一种关系，观察证人、法官和陪审团的行为，学习谈判和诉讼技巧。弗兰克并不寻求完全放弃苏格拉底—案例教学法，而是倡导学生参与法律实践以提高对未来律师的培养水平。[4]

约翰·布莱威，另一个诊所教育的拥护者，因创设法律援助诊所的概念并将其置入法学院的课程而广受赞誉。1933 年，布莱威时任杜克大学法学院法律援助诊所主任，在芝加哥大学法律评论上发表文章，概括了法律诊所教育的五大目标：（1）在理论和实践之间建立桥梁；（2）将实体法与程序法相结合；（3）将当事人及其他特性与“法律的学习与实

---

❶ 威廉·奎格利：“新诊所法律职业的教学方法初探——来自基层的观察”，载《阿克伦法律评论》1995 年第 28 期，第 468～469 页。（William P. Quigley, *Introduction to Clinical Teaching for the New Clinical Law Profession*; A View From the First Floor, 28 AKRON L. REV,（1995）. pp. 468～469.）

❷ 罗伯特·麦克科瑞特：“执教一个变化中的职业——从诊所到后续问题”，载《田纳西法律评论》1997 年第 64 期，第 1105 页。（Robert MacCrate, *Educating a Changing Profession: From Clinic to Continuum*, 64 Tenn. L. Rev.（1997）. p. 1105.）

❸ 乔治·格罗斯曼：“诊所法律教育——历史与结论”，载《法律教育》1974 年第 26 期，第 168～169 页。（George S. Grossman, *Clinical Legal Education: History and Diagnosis*, 26 J. LEGAL EDUC,（1974）. pp. 168～169.）

❹ 同上书，第 169 页。

践”相整合；(4) 将学生纳入法律倡导之中；(5) 教育学生从最开始去分析一个法律问题，而不是像苏格拉底—案例教学法那样在最后用上诉法院的判决来教育学生。[1]

弗兰克和布莱威对苏格拉底—案例教学法的批评以及他们所主张的法学院课程的改革，引起了关于法学院的角色应否是培养学生实践法律的大讨论。[2] 学者们关注的是诊所式法律教育本身，而实践者开始要求法学院为学生提供更多的实践技能培训。20 世纪 50 年代早期，阿奇·坎彻尔 (Arch M. Cantrall)，一位有影响的实践家，支持了弗兰克和布莱威的观点，主张学生应该得到理论和实践两方面的培养。[3] 坎彻尔认为，法学院应该指导学生了解当事人的案件发展情况、法律事务所的管理以及法律实践的道德性。[4] 坎彻尔关于法学院应承担实践培训责任的观点是对杜克大学法学院约瑟夫·麦克克林院长的有力回应，[5] 因为麦克克林院长声称法学院不可能对学生进行全面的培训以使学生能够应对只有律师才能处理的问题。[6]

到 1951 年，“法律诊所”的价值问题成为法学教育领域论战的问题

---

[1] 约翰·布莱威：“法律援助诊所课程的一些明显特征”，载《芝加哥大学法律评论》1993 年第 1 期，第 469～472 页。(John S. Bradway, *Some Distinctive Features of a Legal Aid Clinic Course*, 1 U. CHI. L. REV. (1933). pp. 469～472.)

[2] 乔治·格罗斯曼：“诊所法律教育——历史与结论”，载《法律教育》1974 年第 26 期，第 170 页。(George S. Grossman, *Clinical Legal Education: History and Diagnosis*, 26 J. LEGAL EDUC, (1974). p. 170.)

[3] 阿奇·坎彻尔：“法学院与法律人—法律教育发挥作用了吗?”载《美国律师协会会刊》1952 年第 38 期，第 907 页。(Arch M. Cantrell, *Law Schools and the Layman: Is Legal Education Doing Its Job?*, 38 A. B. A. J. (1952). p. 907.)

[4] 乔治·格罗斯曼：“诊所法律教育——历史与结论”，载《法律教育》1974 年第 26 期，第 170～171 页。(George S. Grossman, *Clinical Legal Education: History and Diagnosis*, 26 J. LEGAL EDUC, (1974). pp. 170～171.)

[5] 约瑟夫·麦克莱恩：“法律教育在发挥作用吗? ——一个回答”，载《美国律师协会会刊》1953 年第 39 期，第 120～122 页。(Joseph A. McClain, Jr., *Is Legal Education Doing Its Job? A Reply*, 39 A. B. A. J. (1953). pp. 120～122.)

[6] 乔治·格罗斯曼：“诊所法律教育——历史与结论”，载《法律教育》1974 年第 26 期，第 175 页。(George S. Grossman, *Clinical Legal Education: History and Diagnosis*, 26 J. LEGAL EDUC, (1974). p. 175.)

之一。[1] 罗伯特·斯托里（Robert Storey），时任南卫理公会大学法学院院长，赞美“诊所模式”将学生暴露于现实问题面前，而这些现实问题是他个人及其他人真实遇到的各种麻烦。[2] 然而尽管斯托里院长和其他人努力推进诊所式法律教育，但在 20 世纪 50 年代诊所式法律教育处于迟滞状态。原因在于：首先，法律院校希望自己的教育与学徒式教育模式相区别，而诊所式教育试图创建“法律事务所模式”作为法学教育的组成部分，这种想法并没有深化这种差别。第二，那个时期的法学教育资金非常缺乏。诊所式法律教育需要小班上课，对教师的要求也比较高，而苏格拉底—案例教学法可以大班上课，比较经济。第三，那个时期的法学教师不认可诊所教育的价值及其可行性，很多教师认为教育学生学习律师实务而不是学习法律分析是没有价值的。第四，1920～1940 年，以美国律师协会（ABA）和美国法律院校协会（AALS）开设和提高法律院校的标准为特征，所有标准都不包括鼓励或必须开设诊所式课程。[3] 这四个因素不仅限制了诊所项目的数量，同时由于从事诊所教育的教师不足而阻碍了诊所教育的发展。

二、诊所式法律教育的理念转变及专业化形成

（一）理念转变

诊所式法律教育发展的第二个比较重要的时期是从 20 世纪 60 年代到 90 年代末期。这一时期被称为诊所式法律教育的第二次浪潮，诊所式法律教育在学术界的地位得以稳固。在 20 世纪 60～70 年代，诊所式法律教育的理念从单纯培养学生的律师技能转变为服务于社会的贫弱群体，从伦理和道德的角度培养学生的社会责任感，培养学生从事关涉穷人的

---

[1] 昆廷·约翰斯顿：“法学院的诊所”，载《法律教育》1951 年第 3 期，第 535 页。（Quintin Johnston，*Law School Clinics*，3 J. Legal Educ. (1951). p. 535.）

[2] 罗伯特·斯托里：“法学院法律援助诊所——前言”，载《法律教育》1951 年第 3 期，第 533～534 页。（Robert G. Storey，*Law School Legal Aid Clinics: Foreword*，3 J. Legal Educ. (1951). pp. 533～534.）

[3] 罗伯特·史蒂文斯：《19 世纪 50 年代到 20 世纪 80 年代的美国法学教育》，中国政法大学出版社 2003 年版，第 213 页。

法律实践，在社区中树立法律院校的地位并发挥作用。[1] 这个转变过程中涉及很多因素，比如法学院对社会的关注程度，诊所式教学方法的改进，外界资金的注入，以及有能力、有兴趣从事诊所式教育的教师的增加等。但最重要的因素也许是 20 世纪 60 年代的时代思潮，它要求学生与社会相关联。[2] 当时社会极不稳定，学生运动非常活跃。那是民权激进主义、反战抗议、争取福利权利运动的时代，法律作为促进社会变革的工具的观念开始出现。[3] 有两个因素直接促进了诊所式法律教育的发展，即学生的广泛需求以及私人基金会的大量资金支持。这两个方面均强调通过诊所式教育来实现以社会公正为导向的社会正义。学生中的激进主义者引发了学生对服务于贫弱群体以及通过法律改革来改变社会的强烈愿望。[4] 这些反过来又引发了学生对法学实践教育的需求以及如何成为一个法律活动家的需求。[5]

1965 年，一个诊所教育的拥护者注意到诊所式法律教育与贫弱者对法律需求之间的关系。[6] 这种观点从早期法学院的学生自愿为贫弱者提供法律援助时就开始出现，但在 20 世纪 60～70 年代得到迅速发展。诊

---

[1] 尼娜·塔尔："目前诊所法律教育的问题"，载《夏威夷法律评论》1993 年第 37 期，第 32 页。(Nina W. Tarr, *Current Issues in Clinical Legal Education*, 37 Haw. L. J. (1993). p. 32.)

[2] 查尔斯·阿瑞斯："法律教育与贫穷问题"，载《法律教育》1965 年第 17 期，第 310 页。(Charles E. Ares, *Legal Education and the Problem of the Poor*, 17 J. Legal Educ. (1965). p. 310.)

[3] 明娜·凯特因："妇女暴力行动计划——教育新一代公益律师"，载《法律与政策》1996 年第 4 期，第 446 页。(Minna J. Catkin, *The Violence Against Women Act Project: Teaching A New Generation of Public Interest Lawyers*, 4 J. L. & Pol'y, (1996). p. 446.)

[4] 罗伊·斯塔基："法律实务教育——他们的时代：一种改变"，载《内布拉斯加法律评论》1996 年第 75 期，第 653 页。(Roy T. Stuckey, *Education for the Practice of Law: The Times They Are-A Changing*', 75 Neb. L. Rev. (1996). p. 653.)

[5] 同上书，第 446 页。

[6] 明娜·凯特因："妇女暴力行动计划——教育新一代公益律师"，载《法律与政策》1996 年第 4 期，第 310 页。(Minna J. Catkin, *The Violence Against Women Act Project: Teaching A New Generation of Public Interest Lawyers*, 4 J. L. & Pol'y, (1996). p. 310.)

所项目为贫弱当事人的众多法律问题提供了法律服务。许多诊所项目办理了一些重大案件，这些案件涉及法律改革以及当时社会的一些基本问题。所有这些为探索最基本的理论问题、实质问题以及概念问题提供了极佳的教学方法，它们与真实社会的脉搏一起跳动。[1]

同一时期，批判性法学研究运动从早期的现实主义运动中诞生。诊所教师指导学生将法律当作社会公正和社会进步的工具，而批判性法学研究的拥护者则通过课堂教学将法律去神秘化，教导学生“政治信仰在审判中起着非常重要的作用，而且法律的形成在任何时候都是意识形态、权力以及被错误地称为合理的东西的反映”[2]。马丁·古根海姆（Martin Guggenheim）教授指出，关注社会公平和正义是非常重要的，不仅仅因为它对当事人发挥作用，而且因为它同样对学生发挥作用。诊所式教育不仅仅教育学生学习律师技能，更重要的是教育学生了解法律职业的核心价值，为当事人提供合格的法律服务，促进社会公平、正义和道义，使学生得到持续性的职业提升以及职业化的自我发展。[3] 在学生学习这些职业价值的同时，无数当事人通过诊所项目得到了公平与正义。通过这种方式，诊所项目融合了法律理论与律师技能，学生通过向贫弱当事人提供法律服务学习了律师技能，而这些当事人如果不能得到这种服务，则可能无法获得公正的判决。

20 世纪 90 年代，无偿的公益服务（Pro Bono）活动在律师界和学术界开始出现，对法律职业者（包括法学院的学生）的责任意识的提高起到了很大的作用，他们致力于为缺乏法律途径获得公正审判的群体提供

---

❶ 亚瑟·科诺伊：“法律教育的现实危机”，载《拉特格斯法律评论》1969 年第 24 期，第 7 页。（Arthur Konoye, *The Present Crisis in Legal Education*, 24 Rutgers L. Rev. (1969). p. 7.）

❷ 罗纳德·德沃金：“法律的帝国”，中国大百科全书出版社 1986 年版，第 271～272 页。

❸ 美国律师协会律师教育和管理部：“法律教育和职业发展—持续性教育”，载《法学院与法律职业报告：缩小差距》，1992 年，第 207～221 页。（American Bar Association Section on Legal Education and Admissions to the Bar, *Legal Education and Professional Development-An Educational Continuum*, Report of the Task Force on Law Schools and the Profession: Narrowing the Gap, (1992). pp. 207～221.）

法律服务。[1] 法学院的教师也发动了广泛的学科间的法律改革，将诊所项目与改变贫穷状态的法律教育与研究相结合，并呼吁关注社区的需要。许多公益项目和关注穷人的法律项目得以与诊所项目合作或者得到诊所项目的支持。[2]

基于实现社会公正的基本理念，诊所式法律教育通过三种方法来推进社会公正：首先，诊所项目通过学生代理缺乏法律途径和权利的当事人及社区群体，为他们提供法律服务来追求法律及社会改革；[3] 第二，通过让学生接触公益活动或者公共服务，使法学毕业生热心于公益活动或公共服务事业而实现社会公正的理念。[4] 诊所毕业生充分参与公益活动或公共服务，不仅仅是法学教育培养律师的最终产品，而且通过学生的

---

[1] 史蒂文·鲁伯特，凯瑟琳·斯图尔特：“一种公共财富——公益律师责任理论”，载《宾夕法尼亚大学法律评论》1997年第145期，第1245页。（Steven Lube & Cathryn Stewart，*A "Public Assets" Theory of Lawyers' Pro Bono Obligations*，145 U. Pa. L. Rev. p. 1245（1997）；）米歇尔·雅各布斯：“公益事业与对穷人的正义——真正的改变还是想象的改变？”，载《佛罗里达法律评论》1996年第48期，第509页。（Michelle S. Jacobs，*Pro Bono Work and Access to Justice for the Poor*：Real Change or Imagined Change? 48 Fla. L. Rev. （1996）. p. 509.）

[2] 霍华德·厄兰格、加布里埃尔·莱萨德：“动员法律院校回应贫穷问题——对进步尝试的报告”，载《法律教育》1993年第43期，第199页。（Howard Erlanger & Gabrielle Lessard，*Mobilizing Law Schools in Response to Poverty*：*A Report on Experiments in Progress*，43 J. Legal Educ. p. 199（1993）；）伯纳德·弗里蒙特：“以社会正义为中心的蓝图”，载《西顿豪法律评论》1992年第22期，第1237～1240页。（Bernard K. Freamon，*A Blueprint for a Center for Social Justice*，22 Seton Hall L. Rev. （1992）. pp. 1237～1240.）

[3][4] 罗伯特·迪纳斯坦：“诊所奖学金和正义使命”，载《克利夫兰州法律评论》1992年第40期，第469页。（Robert D. Dinnerstein，*Clinical Scholarship and the Justice Mission*，40 Clev. St. L. Rev. p. 469，（1992）；）弗兰·奎格利：“抓住迷失的时刻——成人学习理论与法学诊所中社会正义的教育”，载《诊所法律评论》1995年第2期，第39～40页。（Fran Quigley，*Seizing the Disorienting Moment*：*Adult Learning Theory and the Teaching of Social Justice in Law School Clinics*，2 Clin. L. Rev. （1995）. pp. 39～40.）

积极参与使学生深刻认识到公共服务工作的重要性。[1] 第三，正如弗兰·奎格利（Fran Quigley）教授所言，诊所教育在社会公正这个问题上不能仅仅局限于倡导参与无偿的公益服务，因为“如果仅仅是鼓励未来的律师参与公益服务，而不是让这些律师在他们的日常工作中为他们社区中的贫弱群体切实提供数小时的无偿服务，那么对学生进行社会公正的教育就是不成功的”[2]；而且，社会公正教育的更大目标应该是学生在广义和狭义的层面上对法律与社会公正之间的关系都有一定的理解。[3] 诊所教育通过让学生亲身经历真实案件、探索公正的意义、发展个人对公正的理解以及发现法律体系对弱势群体的影响、解构法律中的权力和特权等手段来实现社会公正的目标。

（二）专业化形成

诊所式法律教育研究在 20 世纪 70 年代和 80 年代早期得到迅速发展。那个时代的相关研究通过探索律师技能和诊所教育方法而打开了一片新天地，因此对诊所式法律教育的讨论远远超过了早期的学者像布莱威、弗兰克和其他学者主要运用真实案件来教育学生的概括性理念。

直到 20 世纪 70 年代中期，对于诊所式法律教育的方法还没有普遍性的认识，学者们也没有真正努力去构建一个供学术使用的专业词汇库。正如加里·贝洛（Gary Bellow）教授所言，诊所式法律教育的术语来自“任何与法律有关的学生参与的课外活动，以及一些传统的法学教育活动，例如法学研究、模拟法庭甚至对上诉案件的分析”[4]。没有一个普遍

---

[1] 亨利·罗斯：“法学院也应与正义有关”，载《克利夫兰州法律评论》1980 年第 40 期，第 451～452 页。（Henry Rose, *Law Schools Should Be About Justice Too*, 40 Clev. St. L. Rev. (1980). pp. 451～452.）

[2][3] 弗兰·奎格利：“抓住迷失的时刻——成人学习理论与法学诊所中社会正义的教育”，载《诊所法律评论》1995 年第 2 期，第 43 页。（Fran Quigley, *Seizing the Disorienting Moment: Adult Learning Theory and the Teaching of Social Justice in Law School Clinics*, 2 Clin. L. Rev. (1995). p. 43.）

[4] 学术报告会：诊所法律教育——过去 15 年的思考与未来的展望，载《天主教大学法律评论》1987 年第 36 期，第 375～378 页。（Symposium: Clinical Legal Education: *Reflections on the Past Fifteen Years and Aspirations for the Future*, 36 Cath. U. L. Rev. (1987). pp. 375～378.）

认可的教学方法，诊所式法律教育缺乏一个稳固的根基去扩展到所有法学院。20世纪70年代和80年代，贝洛教授和其他人开始致力于构建一个“供教学使用的通用词汇表”。通过把诊所式教育视为一种教学方法，从事诊所式教育的学者开始探索诊所式教育的经验以及未来的发展方向。学者们着重研究怎样使诊所式教学融入法学院的课程，以及确定诊所式教育的目标或目的。❶ 早期的重要范例致力于诊所式教育方法的探索，即学生在法律体系中模拟或从事律师的角色，确定不同种类的律师技能，发展和解释律师职业的理论问题，完善和提高教师的指导方法，以及将教师从事律师职业的经验融入诊所式教育之中。❷

从事诊所式法律教育的学者认为诊所式教育的基本目的是教育学生从实践中学习。❸ 从事诊所式教育的教帅廾始关注怎样“从他们自己的经历中学习成为律师—教师以及律师—学者”❹。他们开始和他们的学生一起探索律师技能和职业价值的理论基础以及实践特征。为帮助学生发

---

❶ 学术报告会：诊所法律教育——过去15年的思考与未来的展望，载《天主教大学法律评论》1987年第36期，第375～378页。（Symposium：Clinical Legal Education：*Reflections on the Past Fifteen Years and Aspirations for the Future*，36 Cath. U. L. Rev.（1987）. pp. 375～378.）

❷ 安东尼·阿姆斯特丹：“诊所法律教育——21世纪的经验”，载《法律教育》1984年第34期，第612页。（Anthony G. Amsterdam，*Clinical Legal Education-A 21st Century Experience*，34 J. Legal Educ. p. 612（1984）.）约翰·巴克：“法律沟通的一个新模式——感性经验与代表性体系”，载《克利夫兰州法律评论》1980年第29期，第575页。（John L. Barkai，*A New Model for Legal Communication：Sensory Experience and Representational Systems*，29 Clev. St. L. Rev. p. 575（1980）.）大卫·巴泽尔：“法律教育的诊所方法——理论与实践”，载《法律教育》1979年第30期，第67页。（David Barnhizer，*The Clinical Method of Legal Instruction：Its Theory and Implementation*，30 J. Legal Educ.（1979）. p. 67.）

❸ 肯尼思·克瑞玲：“诊所教育与律师能力——从适当的安排诊所监督中学习”，载《马里兰法律评论》1981年第40期，第284页。（Kenneth R. Kreiling，*Clinical Education and Lawyer Competency：The Process of Learning to Learn from Experience through Properly Structured Clinical Supervision*，40 Md. L. Rev.（1981）；p. 284.）

❹ 皮特·乔伊：“诊所奖学金——推动法律实践”，载《诊所法律评论》1996年第2期，第393页。（Peter A. Joy，*Clinical Scholarship：Improving the Practice of Law*，2 Clin. L. Rev.（1996）. p. 393.）

展他们的自我反省能力，诊所教师鼓励学生进行自我批评，这个过程被称为“实践的反思”或“行动的反思”。到20世纪80年代末期，在“诊所式教育未来委员会”的报告中对诊所式教育已经达成共识：“诊所式教育是法学教育的首要的、最重要的方法。其原则表现为以下特征：学生面临的问题就是律师在实务中面临的问题；学生参与解决问题的过程；学生必须与他人合作以明确问题并解决问题；也许最重要的是，学生的实践有利于实现批判性思维的目标。”[1]

随着诊所“通用词汇表”以及教学方法的普遍被接受，20世纪80年代后期及90年代，诊所式教育研究得以迅速发展，从而使诊所式教育在法学院得到了永久性地位。1994年，基于广大教师对诊所式教育及其方法的研究兴趣，诊所法律评论在诊所式法律教育协会（CLEA）、美国法律院校协会（AALS）以及纽约大学法学院的资助下诞生。

同一时期，美国律师协会的工作报告以及公众对法律教育的评论对诊所式法律教育的制度化起到了实质性的推动作用，其中最有影响的报告是1992年美国律师协会“法学院和法律职业工作组”的报告：缩小差距。这个工作组以美国律师协会主席罗伯特·麦克科瑞特（Robert MacCrate）为领导，因此该报告又被称为麦克科瑞特报告。[2] 麦克科瑞特工作组发现在培养合格的律师方面存在普遍的缺陷。其强烈建议法学院进行课程改革，同时建议律师协会对于法学毕业新生要加大关注力度，确

---

[1] “室内诊所的未来委员会报告”，载《法律教育》1992年第42期，第508～510页。（*Report of the Committee on the Future of the In-House Clinic*，42 J. Legal Educ.（1992）. pp. 508～510.）

[2] 美国律师协会律师教育和管理部：“法律教育和职业发展——持续性教育”，载《法学院与法律职业报告：缩小差距》，1992年。（Section of Legal Education and Admissions to the Bar，American Bar Association，*Legal and Professional Development—An Educational Continuum*，（Report of the Task Force on Law Schools and the Profession：Narrowing the Gap，1992）.）

保这些律师得到基本的律师技能和价值教育，以胜任法律实务工作的需要。❶

麦克科瑞特报告要求对学生进行职业能力培训，同时要求对学生进行职业价值指导。这些职业价值包括促进“公正、公平和道义”以及“职业提升”。诊所式教育已被证明对培养这些职业价值有非常重要的作用。❷ 事实上，麦克科瑞特报告对实现“公正、公平和道义”的职业价值提供了具体的建议，这些建议包括：（1）在与当事人、证人、团队成员及其他人的交往过程中排除各种形式的歧视，包括性别、种族、宗教、民族、性取向、年龄、残疾等；（2）为职业责任作出贡献，确保为无钱请律师的人提供合格的法律服务；（3）提高法律和法律制度的能力，以实现社会公正。❸

到1999年年底，根据美国法律院校协会下属的诊所式法律教育部（AALS Section on Clinical Legal Education）以及诊所式法律教育协会（CLEA）的统计数据，美国有183所法学院开设了诊所课程，❹ 而美国

---

❶ 约翰·考斯特尼斯：“麦克科瑞特报告：面包、鱼以及美国法律教育的未来”，载《法律教育》1993年第43期，第157页。（John J. Costonis, *The MacCrate Report: Of Loaves, Fishes, and the Future of American Legal Education*, 43 J. Legal Educ. p. 157, (1993).）理查德·马塔萨：“从主任的角度看麦克科瑞特报告”，载《诊所法律评论》1994年第1期，第457页。（Richard A. Matasar, *The MacCrate Report from the Dean's Perspective*, 1 Clin. L. Rev. (1994). p. 457.）

❷ 珍·艾肯：“努力教育正义、公平和道德”，载《诊所法律评论》1997年第4期，第30～46页。（Jane H. Aiken, *Striving to Teach "Justice, Fairness and Morality"*, 4 Clin L. Rev. (1997). pp. 30～46.）

❸ 参见美国律师协会律师教育和管理部：“法律教育和职业发展——持续性教育”，载《法学院与法律职业报告：缩小差距》，1992年，第207～221页。（Section of Legal Education and Admissions to the Bar, American Bar Association, *Legal and Professional Development—An Educational Continuum*, [Report of the Task Force on Law Schools and the Profession: Narrowing the Gap, 1992). pp. 207～221.]

❹ 数据库1993～1995由皮特·乔伊（Peter Joy）编辑，1995～1996由戴维·查夫金（David Chavkin）编辑。

法学院的总数为 184 所。[1] 数据库显示，有 1736 名教师自认为是诊所教师，有 849 名教师称他/她们从事固定的内部诊所教育，有 234 人称他/她们从事外部的诊所教育。总体来看，大约 80%的诊所教育者声称他/她们开设固定的诊所课程。[2] 而大约在此之前 10 年，开设内部诊所课程的法学院只占全部法学院的 33%。[3] 诊所教育发展之迅速由此可见一斑。

三、新世纪对诊所式法律教育的回顾与展望

诊所式法律教育经过了近两个世纪的发展，诊所创建的动机以及诊所项目的多样化随着时间的推移不断融入新的内容。当时空进入新的千年，超越案例教学法的诊所式法律教育进入了更广阔的空间，有了更坚实的基础，诊所式法律教育迎来了第三次浪潮。在此过程中，对诊所式法律教育的评价喜忧参半，不同的法学院面临不同的境况。

自 20 世纪早期第一个法律诊所建立至今，其基于诉讼的总体框架以及目标一直没有改变。[4] 一些法律诊所侧重于为特定的当事人提供代理服务，这些特定的当事人包括贫困者、无家可归者、家庭暴力的受害者、儿童、犯人、老人以及小商人。[5] 一些诊所侧重于某一特定的领域，如

---

[1] 李晶珠、刘李明："哈工大法律系客座教授史蒂芬·巴恩斯（Stephe Barnes）谈美国法学教育与法律职业"，载 http://blog. edwinsky. net/archives/lvshiyingxiao _301. html，2011 年 8 月 18 日。

[2] 数据库 1993～1995 由皮特·乔伊（Peter Joy）编辑，1995～1996 由戴维·查夫金（David Chavkin）编辑。

[3] "室内诊所的未来委员会报告"，载《法律教育》1992 年第 42 期，第 518 页。（*Report of the Committee on the Future of the In-House Clinic*，42 J. Legal Educ.（1992）. p. 518.）。

[4] 道格拉斯·布雷兹："似曾相识——对 15 年诊所教育的反思"，载《田纳西法律评论》1997 年第 64 期，第 854 页。（Douglas A. Blaze，*Deja vu All Over Again：Reflection on Fifty Years of Clinical Education*，64 TENN. L. REV.（1997）. p. 954.）

[5] 迪娜·斯高乐丝伯格："法律诊所与学科之间教育的相互检测"，载《华盛顿大学法律与政策》2003 年第 11 期，第 197～198 页。（Dina Schlossberg，*Examination of Transactional Law Clinics and Interdisciplinary Education*，11 WASH. U. J. L. & POL'Y，（2003）. pp. 197～198.）

移民、税务、破产、知识产权、国际人权、家庭法、环境法、刑法等。[1]美国的许多法学院有着自己独特的诊所教育历史，同时又在为他们的学生创造新的、有意义的诊所课程。总体来看，学生从诊所式教育中获得的经历是非常积极的。[2] 许多因素促使学生热衷于诊所式教育，包括社会意识、为社区服务的愿望、对传统的室内教学方法的厌倦与不满、职业的然而非正式的与诊所教师的关系等。[3]尽管学生需要诊所式教育，但对于法学学生是否应该直接介入律师和当事人的关系一直存在争议。[4]这种争论主要来自法律实践的不可预知性。[5]诊所式教育的其他一些缺点也逐步暴露出来，如学生可能被迫投入时间去处理一个案件而耽误了法学院的其他课程；大多数诊所需要较低的师生比例，导致法学院的成本增加等。[6]而且，评估学时及为学生的表现打分是件很困难的事情。[7]

此外，虽然有些法学院的诊所项目已经成为法学院课程的主流，[8]但案例教学法仍是大多数法学院的主要教学方法。当法学通过案例教学法来建立其学位制度时，案例教学法就取得了不朽的地位。通过分析上诉法院的判决来了解法律的原则，这种方法至今仍主导着大多数法学院的课程，从而限制了诊所式教育的发展。案例教学法的真正价值及其占有统治地位的正当性在于其对法律原则发展概况的有效解释，这种解释为教学和培养学生的法律思维提供了基本方法。然而通过使法律抽象化来学习法律或提炼法律的方法在教与学之间产生了一个鸿沟。这种教学方法先入为主地排除了律师在法律体系中的作用，以及律师在解决法律

---

[1] 迪娜·斯高乐丝伯格："法律诊所与学科之间教育的相互检测"，载《华盛顿大学法律与政策》2003年第11期，第197～198页。(Dina Schlossberg, *Examination of Transactional Law Clinics and Interdisciplinary Education*, 11 WASH. U. J. L. & POL'Y, (2003). pp. 197～198.)

[2][3] 乔治·格罗斯曼："诊所法律教育——历史与结论"，载《法律教育》1974年第26期，第179页。(George S. Grossman, *Clinical Legal Education: History and Diagnosis*, 26 J. LEGAL EDUC, (1974). pp. 179.)

[4][5][6][7] 同上书，第182～183页。

[8] 大卫·赫林："诊所法律教育——能量与转换"，载《托莱多大学法律评论》2000年第31期，第624～625页。(David J. Herring, *Clinical Legal Education: Energy and Transformation*, 31 U. TOL. L. REV. (2000). pp. 624～625.)

问题中所扮演的角色。[1] 正如贾宁·科迫尔（Janeen Kerper）教授所言，将原则性分析及理论性思考与实践相分离是不幸的，因为他们在完善的法学教育中都是不可或缺的。[2] 如果教师在传授知识的过程中不能传递律师在代理案件时所面临的当事人的伤痛，那么法律的原则、理论和技能就不会被学生所领悟。安东尼·阿姆斯特丹指出，从 21 世纪的角度回看，20 世纪的法学教育太过狭窄，因为它缺乏从学生的角度去思考律师的角色——批判性分析、计划、作出决定的方法，这些不是学生自己可以掌握的技能，而是教师培养学生从事法律实务的基本方法，就像案例教学是掌握法律原则的基本方法一样。[3]

尽管诊所式法律教育在法学教育中是一个永恒的目标，但很多时候诊所教育和诊所项目仍处于一些法学院课程设置的边缘地带。[4] 几乎在每一个法学院，这些课程继续被划归为选修课，既不是获得毕业证书的必要条件，也不是获得律师资格的必要条件；而且从事诊所教学的教师

---

❶ 劳伦斯·克里格："什么是我们没有告诉学生和律师的，那些他们必须知道的东西——对从基础恢复法律职业的行动思考"，载《法律与健康》1998～1999 年第 13 期，第 4 页。（Lawrence S. Krieger，*What We're Not Telling Law Students-and Lawyers-That They Really Need to Know*：*Some Thoughts-In-Action Toward Revitalizing the Profession From Its Roots*，13 J. L. & Health，（1998～1999）. p. 4.）

❷ 珍妮·科佩尔："创造解决问题的办法与教科书方法——一个巨大的进步"，载《加利福尼亚西部法律评论》1998 年第 34 期，第 358～359 页。（Janeen Kerper，*Creative Problem Solving vs. The Casebook Method*：*A Marvelous Adventure in Which Winnie-the-Pooh Meets Mrs. Palsgraf*，34 Cal. W. L. Rev.（1998）. pp. 358～359.）

❸ 安东尼·阿姆斯特丹："诊所法律教育——21 世纪的经验"，载《法律教育》1984 年第 34 期，第 612 页。（Anthony G. Amsterdam，*Clinical Legal Education-A 21st Century Experience*，34 J. Legal Educ.（1984）. p. 612.）

❹ 黛博拉·罗德："正义的利益：法律职业的改革"，2000 年，第 198 页。（Deborah L. Rhode，*In the Interests of Justice*：*Reforming the Legal Profession*，p. 198，（2000）.）

在法学院也处于边缘的位置，他们地位较低，权利较少，收入也少。❶而参加了诊所教育的学生经常在申请有声望的书记员职务或赚钱的工作时被排除在外，正如斯科特·韦斯特法尔（Scott Westphal）所哀叹的："律师事务所并不是根据学生的实践技能来评价学生，因为那需要花很多时间来调整他们的录取过程。现代的律师事务所几乎从来不把学生的实际能力当作基本的录取标准，而是继续以法学院的排名以及毕业生的排名为判断标准，同时以鸡尾酒会的方式对学生进行面试，以确定学生是否符合录取要求。"❷ 更为严重的是，一些法官认为，诊所教育是一种负担，对于等待审理的过度积压的案件来说，它减慢了案件审理的速度。❸

虽然从法学院、教师、学生、律师、法官等多个角度来看，诊所式法律教育并未得到其应得的荣誉和尊重，但不能否认的是，诊所式法律教育在培养学生的社会责任及职业技能和职业道德、帮助贫困阶层获得法律帮助、维护社会公平和正义等方面发挥着不可替代的作用。从辨证的角度来看，诊所式法律教育也不可能是完美的，它一定有瑕疵，有不足，但正所谓瑕不掩瑜，诊所式法律教育的核心价值始终是耀眼的，是值得追求的。

---

❶ 安东尼·阿尔菲耶里："反对实践"，载《密西根法律评论》2009年第107期，第1074页。（Anthony V. Alfieri, *Against Practice*, 107 Mich. L. Rev. p. 1074, (2009).）皮特·乔伊，罗伯特·库恩："美国律师协会对诊所教师的评价标准"，载《田纳西法律评论》2008年第75期，第187页。（Peter A. Joy & Robert R. Kuehn, *The Evolution of ABA Standards for Clinical Faculty*, 75 Tenn. L. Rev. (2008). p. 187.）

❷ 斯科特·韦斯特法尔："回应：律师发展合作时代"，载《法律教育》2010年第59期，第645～646页。（Scott Westphal, *Response: Time to Collaborate on Lawyer Development*, 59 J. Legal Educ. (2010). pp. 645～646.）

❸ 梅利莎·布雷杰、吉娜·凯拉布莱斯、特丽萨·休斯："教育职业化：从学生、当事人、顾问和法官角度进行得观察"，载《南卡罗莱纳法律评论》2003年第55期，第343页。（Melissa Breger, Gina Calabrese & Theresa Hughes, *Teaching Professionalism in Context: Insights from Students, Clients, Adversaries, and Judges*, 55 S. C. L. Rev. (2003). p. 343.）

诊所法律教育与社会公益

——兼论法律诊所与法律援助融合的路径

周　凯*

摘　要：诊所式法律教育引入我国后，较为深刻地影响了我国传统法学教育模式，在对诊所法律教育进行了本土化的改造后，诊所教育模式的教学目标越来越清晰化。诊所法律教育实践平台具有天然的公益属性，具体表现在法律援助的过程中。学生们正是在法律援助过程中培养了自身的公益精神，增强了社会责任感。探索和扩展诊所教育和社会法律援助合作途径，才能更好地发挥诊所教育的自身优势，为诊所教育在本国法治环境下的进一步发展打下坚实的基础。

关键词：诊所法律教育　社会公益　法律援助

诊所法律教育从 20 世纪 90 年代末期引进到中国，至今已经 13 年了。法律诊所历经 10 多年的推广和探索，经过了本土化的改造，实践证明这个舶来品完全可以成为法学教育的一种新模式。

对于法学教育来说，作为一种新引进的法学教育模式，它与传统的教育模式的区别是什么？这个问题的答案就是诊所法律教育的目标。

诊所法律教育就是要力图突破现有的法学教育教学模式，现在大学授课内容和教学方式大多数还是单向的知识传播，即教师讲课，学生听课，至于学生听进去多少，能否把知识转化为一种能力，传统方式并不重视，特别是在理论教学与实践教学融合、课内与课外融合、教与学融

* 周凯，中国传媒大学政治与法律学院法律系副教授。

合、内容更新与形式创新融合这几方面还做得不够到位。

诊所法律教育作为法学教育教学中的新模式，诊所课程理应成为法学课程的重要组成部分。经过几年的课程探索，笔者认为，诊所法律教育要实现的教学目标有以下几点。

一是理论知识与实践运用相结合，学习法律实务技能，使得掌握知识的“能力”得到提升。（这种能力有多种表现，有的是应试型的死记硬背，考试时临时突击复习，考完试所学的知识大部分都忘了；有的是把知识融会贯通，善于和社会实践相结合，能够把掌握的知识和技能有效应用于社会，服务于社会。诊所的能力显然指的是后者。）

二是培养法律人的法律思维、职业道德和社会责任感。法律人的思维方式不同于一般社会人的思维习惯，主要区别在于思维方向，法律人的法律思维总是在一个框架体系里，任何要解决的问题对于法律人来说，首先考虑的都是这件事是否合法，受不受法律保护。这里以某人欠他人债务不还为例，分别从道德、经济、政治、法律角度去分析其结果：

道德评价	这人太缺德，跟他要
经济分析	从要债的成本分析，这人能还得上吗？
政治考虑	人际关系、工作关系决定能不能向他要
法律思维	有无证据？能否起诉？时效过没过？

法律人为什么会这么思考？这是法律人所具有的法律思维惯性决定的。那么法律人的思维是怎么培养出来的？答案是主要通过研习法律、案例讨论、法律实践技能训练培养出来的。也就是说，不是学习法律知识就一定能够具备法律人的思维，这需要课堂内的训练和课堂外的锻炼。

法律人的职业道德同样如此，法律人的职业道德是法律职业共同体中所有人都应该遵循的道德规范和行为准则，如维护法治、公平正义等。再进一步扩言之，我们培养的法科学生不管未来是否从事法律职业，都应该成为一个有道德的内心秉持公正的法律人（Building Moral and Just legal Person）。

培养学生的社会责任感是大学的职责，作为法科学生来说更甚。法律人在促进国家和社会的法治进程中发挥着重要的作用，这种作用的表现之一就是他的社会责任感，宣传法治，践行法治，把公平正义的理念传播出去，在日常的工作和生活中去鞭策自己、影响别人，这就是一名法律人社会责任感的体现。而这种社会责任感的培养应该在其学生时代完成，诊所法律教育重视实践的课程特点、扶持弱者的公益之心、弘扬正义的法治理念是培养学生社会责任感的最佳平台。

对法学教育者来说，以上目标具有同等的重要性，而真正实现上述目标确实任重道远。

诊所法律教育在实践中毋庸置疑会体现出公益性。因为它主要是帮助社会上的弱者和边缘化群体，无论是法治宣传、法律咨询、代写法律文书、代理劳动争议仲裁案件、代理民事案件等，都是无偿提供的。在现实环境中，探究法律和公益的关系，特别是法律诊所和公益的结合，就成了下面力图阐述的内容。

一、法律与社会公益

公益，英文 Public，意思就是社会公众的共同利益，[1] 不同的学科领域如伦理学、政治学、法学等对公益有不同的理解和要求。从伦理学角度讲，伦理学运用道德判断去认识公益行为的善恶和道德责任，用公正与偏私、正义与非正义等作为道德评价的标准，对公益的动机与效果、目的与手段给予一种评价和判断。从政治学角度看，是共同利益优先还是私人利益优先，公益和私利的边界何在，实现公益目标的方向和范围如何，体现了政治学不同学派对公益的理解。

从法学的角度看，公益是以社会公平、正义为标准，掺杂有伦理道德要求的权利义务的分配。既然是权利义务的一种分配，在分配过程中就必然带有法律的印记，要体现出法律的价值追求，这就是在公益中实现公平正义。

社会公益的表现形式就是举办和参加各类公益活动，包括环境保护、

[1] 《辞海》（第六版缩印本），上海辞书出版社 2010 年第 1 版，第 598 页。

未成年权益保护、法律援助、传播知识（含法治宣传）、社区服务、紧急救助（如多次参与救助登山驴友野外遇险的著名公益组织——北京蓝天志愿救援队）、慈善活动、专业服务、青年志愿服务等。这里面涉及法律方面的主要就是法律援助。通过向符合标准的社会公众提供无偿法律帮助，就是法律参与社会公益的主要途径。

参加社会公益活动对法律人的影响是明显的，试想如果一个法律人常怀感恩之心，有热情，心地单纯，乐于助人，这里面是不是就有社会公益对法律人的影响呢？

法律和社会公益的结合就是法律公益，法律公益从此具有公益的品格，法律公益自然应该符合公益的整体要求，如扶持弱者、关心他人、扶危济困、爱护环境、保护资源……所有这些公益要求表现在法律领域，就是对经济条件较为困难而又确实需要法律帮助的公众提供法律援助，这是人的基本权利，也是法律所追求的公平正义的价值理念决定的。法律应该平等地对待每一个人，每一个人也有权利得到法律的保障。

在今天，随着民众法律意识的提高，社会关系在各领域发生了深刻变革，法院诉讼量（主要指民事案件）每年都在增长，社会对公益性质的法律服务需求比以往任何时候都迫切。诊所法律教育的实践平台具有公益性，原因在于其接触的当事人一般为经济较为贫困的社会弱势群体，其所代理的案件一般也是其他诉讼代理人不太情愿代理的案件。这种公益属性并不是说诊所代理的案件都是公益诉讼，[1] 即不是说代理的都是影响公众利益的环境污染、消费者权益等案件，而是说通过对各种具体案件的个案解决来体现诊所的社会公益性。公益性特征应该成为现阶段诊所法律教育的典型特征，法律诊所在受理案件的标准、教学实践的方式、教学目标的制定等方面都应该有意识地突出公益性。[2]

---

[1] 公益诉讼的法定界定范围按照2012年8月31日修订的《中华人民共和国民事诉讼法》第55条规定，对污染环境、侵害众多消费者合法权益等损害社会公共利益的行为，法律规定的机关和有关组织可以向人民法院提起诉讼。

[2] 李傲：“诊所法律教育的公益性”，载《法学研究》2006年第6期，第157页。

二、诊所法律教育公益性的体现

诊所法律教育一方面承载着法学教育任务（与一般意义上的法学课程的不同之处在于教学方式），另一方面注重培养、训练学生的实际操作能力（动脑、动嘴、动手、动脚，即想、说、写、走），培育学生的职业伦理，树立学生的社会责任感，通过法律援助这个平台，达到教育者培养人才、服务社会的目的。

（一）诊所法律教育有益于培养公益服务精神

利用自身的优势从事公益活动，帮助需要帮助的社会成员，法律诊所的实践过程就是学生们在教师的指导下接触真实案件，就像律师代理案件一样，并且免除当事人的代理费用。从某种意义上讲，诊所法律教育本身就是法律援助的重要组成部分。[1] 学生代理案件的无偿特性、帮助对象、实现目标、价值理念等都与社会法律援助相差无异。诊所学生代理案件免收当事人费用，援助的对象一般都是社会上经济较困难而请不起律师的弱者，尽力维护当事人的合法权益，实现社会公平正义。无形中，诊所教育成为社会法律援助的组成部分。学生们在为当事人提供法律帮助的过程中，了解到不同层次当事人特别是底层民众的实际状态，加深了对社会的了解，增强了公益服务的意识，诊所法律教育为学生从事法律公益提供了很好的平台。

（二）诊所法律教育公益性有助于解决两个分离

一是法律知识与法律人格的分离，笔者的理解就是学和做的分离，学生们通过课上学习只知道有法律条文，往往不知道其背后所蕴含的法律精神、法律理念。虽然学习和掌握了一些法律知识，但是往往不能把法律内化为自己内心对法律的信仰，不能做到内化于心。法律人格不但

[1] 王立民："法律援助与'诊所法律教育'"，载《政治与法律》2005 年第 1 期，第 27 页。

要求人们了解法律，达到知；而且要实践法律，走向行，[1] 做到知和行的统一。

二是法学理论与法律实践的分离。这是一个老生常谈的问题，此处不多赘述。此现象与上一个问题有联系，学生在课堂上学习的法学理论不会或者不能运用到解决法律实务问题中，分析原因就在于能力上的欠缺。

从事公益性的法律援助成为解决以上问题的途径。因为从事公益活动，一方面能够使人富有爱心，净化心灵，健全人格，培育奉献社会的精神，愿意帮助别人；另一方面为把书本上的法律运用到解决实际法律问题中搭建了实践平台，学生有了实践的机会，有了施展自身智力优势的舞台，从接待当事人、分析案情、事实调查、撰写法律文书到立案、参与庭审，可以说参与了一个真实案件的全过程，在代理案件的各个环节都得到了锻炼，也初步掌握了法律实务技能，逐步积累了办案经验。这对以后的升学、考试（包括司法考试）、就业大有裨益。

三、诊所法律援助应融入社会法律援助体系

为更好地发挥诊所的公益属性，使之能够更好地服务社会，应该挖掘学生的热情，发挥教师和学生的智力优势，让诊所法律教育实践平台与政府部门、社会组织设立的法律援助机构进行合作，这是解决诊所教育目前存在困境的有效方式。笔者从 2006 年从事诊所教育至今，发现除了诊所课程内容和模式难以突破（教师自己的原因）、选用的模拟教学案例陈旧（没有合适的案例补充）外，近年来最大的问题就是诊所实践平台——大学生法律援助中心案源不足，在学生有限的值班时间里很少有当事人来电、来访，代理诉讼案件的数量也很少。尽管诊所教师也想了一些扩大案源的办法（手递手发广告、在一些网站发广告、请一些朋友介绍等），但是收效甚微。没有合适的案源，学生的积极性就会受到影响，诊所的教育效果也不能得到实践检验。

---

[1] 王子龙："论我国公民法律人格的缺失与构建"，载《天水师范学院学报》2003 年第 4 期，第 16 页。

政府部门、社会组织设立的法律援助中心涉及面广，影响较大，当事人一般都知道这些机构，他们也从来不会为案源发愁。社会上需要法律援助的群体还是比较多的，案件数量还是比较大的，法律援助中心只是按照法律规定遴选符合援助条件的案件给予法律帮助，有些案件可能不符合国家的法律援助条件，但是其当事人也可能属于社会相对弱势群体或边缘化群体，而法律诊所对于援助的案件不是那么严格，这些案件可以转由法律诊所的学生代理。

法律诊所一定要积极和政府部门、社会组织的法律援助中心合作，建立一种长效工作机制，或者派学生定期去政府或社会组织的法律援助中心值班，学生通过接待当事人，可以把一些案件带到诊所，或者由政府部门、社会组织的法律援助中心定期选择虽不符合援助条件但适合学生代理的案件，介绍到法律诊所。通过上述方法和途径，可以在一定程度上解决诊所案源不足的问题。至于能否把法律诊所纳入国家法律援助体系，这涉及法律、行政法规的修改，不是短时间内就能解决的问题。从长远看，把法律诊所的实践平台纳入国家法律援助体系，从机制上、经费上给予保障是再好不过的；但是从近期看，解决诊所案源不足问题是当务之急。

中国的诊所法律教育经过10多年的发展成就显著，其中诊所法律教育工作者付出了巨大的努力，正是他们肩负使命，克服各种困难，不断探索诊所课程的教育规律，引导被教育者通过诊所法律教育，深入思考法律是什么、法律职业的价值何在、法律职业群体在整个社会中发挥什么样的作用等重大命题。

笔者曾经看到学生们在接待当事人时，倾听当事人陈述所流下的同情眼泪，帮助撰写法律文书时的冥思苦想，讨论证据效力时的争论不休，听到胜诉结果时的高兴神情。这是因为学生们没有功利思想，有的是热情、激情、奉献，同情弱者，匡扶正义，维护当事人合法权益，正是法律诊所这个平台培养了学生的社会责任感，这就是诊所法律教育要实现的目标。

学生们的无私、激情也许随着他们学业的进步、年龄的增长不会再有，利益的考量也许会消磨他们的热情、激情和追求公正之心，但是作为教育者，还是要感谢他们，他们在青春的某一个时期，通过自己参与的法律实践帮助了社会上需要帮助的弱者，实现了公平正义。

在社会发展的今天，与浮躁充斥、很多“经济人”追求物质目标相反，有这么一群师生，满怀理想，真心实意为需要法律帮助的公众无偿服务，内心秉持公正之心，这是多么弥足珍贵！

随着岁月的流逝，当踏入社会的他们在繁忙的工作之余稍有闲暇时，回想学生时代学习过的印象深刻的课程，应该包括——法律诊所。

诊所法律教育的任务之一就是把学生培养成为一名富有爱心、同情弱者、奉献社会、人格健全的法律人。对此，我们做到了吗？

未完成的规训

——中国高等法学教育实效考察

刘坤轮 *

摘　要：中国法学教育要培养法律伦理和法律技能兼备的法律人，法学教育是否成功地完成了这一使命呢？本文以福柯的规训理论为框架，以中国五大地区具有代表性的五所法律院校的法学教育实践为样本，通过访谈和问卷调查的方式，考察了中国高等法学教育的规训手段的运作，即层级监督、规范性裁决和检查等规训手段的实际效果。同时，本文经验地考察了法科学生对于学校知识传递系统的评价以及对法律的认知。在此基础上，笔者指出，中国的法学教育是一种未完成的规训，因而需要在规训技术上进行改善。

关键词：法学教育　规训　微观权力

一、问题的建构

中国高等法学教育要培养法律人，但培养的效果如何？

在当前法学教育迅速扩张、反思与改革之声充斥视野、改革实践也均被提上日程或在高校零星出现的今天，这看似简单的问题很值得我们进行深刻的思考。[1] 本文则试图通过对这一问题的层层深究，分析当前

* 刘坤轮，中国政法大学讲师，法学博士。

[1] 例如，2008 年，中国政法大学经教育部批准，正式开始 6 年制法学教育实验班，参见 http://news.cupl.edu.cn/news/7860_20080530180419.htm，访问时间：2009 年 5 月 5 日。2009 年，成立不久的上海交通大学凯原法学院也开始进行三三制法学教育改革，参见 http://www.sjtu.edu.cn/newsnet/newsdisplay.php?id=20416，访问时间：2009 年 5 月 5 日。又如中国人民大学法学院开设的法学—工商管理专业，参见 http://news.ruc.edu.cn/102449/102450/102497/66498.html，访问时间：2009 年 12 月 5 日。

中国高等法学教育所存在的问题，并尝试建构一种分析法学教育的新式理论框架，对当前法学教育的不足之处进行分解，并对今后法学教育应当为且能够为的教育实践提出一些警示。

（一）为什么有问题?

之所以以建构来引出问题，是因为本文并不意图去赞同或反对某种法律人才培养的思路。中国高等法学教育职业教育化的呼吁之声与当前法学教育非职业化发展实情的矛盾在当前之紧张关系尤为明显。在我国法学教育研究者的话语范围内，对于“当前法学教育最缺乏的是什么”这一问题没有形成共识，也难以形成共识。因而，本文要立基的前提就是必须宽泛到足以涵括各种主张，反映最不会为人反对的问题。对开篇所提出的“高等法学教育培养法律人的效果如何?”这一问题，当然是最具共识性的回答才可以构成本文问题展开的基础。

对于这一问题，以“合格的法律人”作答应该是最大化的共识，但对于什么是“合格的法律人”又有着不同的理解。这一问题牵涉的范围之广，探讨的领域之宽泛，远非一篇论文所能解决。因而，本文对合格法律人的具体细节要求将不作深究，而是从法律界所能够达成共识的两点要求来限定这个概念。这两点基本要求即“法律技能”和“法律伦理”。对于任何一个法律人来说，合格的基本要求是法律技能与法律伦理的兼备。法学教育界、法律实务界对此基本上是能够达成共识的。

这么说来，问题似乎就无需用建构引出，这两个基本点的问题对于法学教育界而言几乎成为大家所共知的问题，自然也就无需本文来多费周章地再度提起，但常识往往具有欺骗性，并常常掩盖事物发展过程中的真实场景，法律领域的常识也同样如此。[1] 因而，在对这里的“法律技能”和“法律伦理”是否存在问题的疑问前提下，笔者必须以事实来说明其确实存在问题，而对于这里的问题而言，鉴于本文要论证的是一种理想状态的“法律技能”和“法律伦理”的结合，因而问题的挖掘只

---

[1] 关于法律常识的反思，参见［英］搏奥托·迪·苏萨·桑托斯：《迈向新法律常识——法律、全球化和解放》，刘坤轮、叶传星译，中国人民大学出版社 2009年版。

要满足这个接受法律教育的群体并没有达到这种理想状态即可，也就是说，我们完全不必卷入“技能”和“伦理”的具体内涵的争论之中，就能够对具体实践的问题进行描述，这种以实践导出问题甚至论证的做法在学界并不少见，甚至有一个专门的术语称谓，即未完全理论化协议，也就是在对支撑理论不存在合意的情形下对实践问题达成的一致。[1]

这种未完全理论化协议构成了本文从实践中挖掘问题的一个重要前提，也构成了问题可建构性的一个重要前提。

（二）为什么建构？

之所以要以建构来引出问题，乃是因为关于当今法学教育的评判虽多，但实实在在进行调查的极为少见，因而仁者见仁、智者见智的图景在法学教育研究场域随处可见。这也是本文之所以采取一种未完全理论化进路引出问题的一个重要原因，无论主导因子是技能还是伦理，都隐含一个潜在的隐喻，简言之就是德才兼备，转换为法律话语就是“法律伦理”和“法律技能”的一体化。对于法学教育而言，如果要建构起问题的存在，在不深究“法律伦理”和“法律技能”诸多内涵的情形下，必须将这里的问题以一种可以描述、可以测度、可以调查的方式呈现出来。只有这样，它才不致沦为空想的问题，因而在针对空想的意义上而言，这个问题绝不是随便放口就来的，是必须以事实建构起来的。

由上论述，既然高等法学教育所追求的是“法律伦理”和“法律技能”的一体化，那么判断法学教育存在问题就必须指出当前法学教育的产品缺乏法律伦理，或是缺乏法律技能，或是二者兼缺。为了更为方便地说明问题，本文将这里理想状态的法学教育“产品”视为一个兼备法律伦理和法律技能的集合体，而法学教育的目标就在于追求这样一种理想的集合体。既然无需追究法律技能和法律伦理的内涵，就有可能将法学教育体系中所存在的理想目标化约，本文认为这个化约结果可以概括为“去个体化”或“集体化”，即兼备法律伦理和法律技能。为了避免对

[1] 关于未完全理论化协议的一般研究，参见 Cass R. Sunstein，Legal Reasoning and Political Conflict（New York：Oxford University Press，1996）.

笔者这里观点的误读，笔者需要对建构的逻辑再次进行重申。

首先，这里的去个体化或集体化是在未完全理论化协议前提下所做的假定。也就是说，这里的问题并没有否认法学研究界、国内外法律实务界所推崇的个性化法律人。本文的去个体化所去除的是法律“伦理”和“法律”技能的单重或双重缺失。其潜在追求的结果是一种“集体化”了的法律人，这个集体化包含法律技能和法律伦理的最大共识，这个公分母的存在保证了在问题存在的肯定前提下，并不指涉学界具体深究的伦理和技能的内涵问题。

其次，这里的问题设定其实是法学教育所追求的一个目标，这个目标建立在法学教育存在个体化、非集体化的对象前提基础之上，也就是说，高等法学教育的受众尚不具备法律伦理和法律技能。因此，笔者概括出的问题必须是法学教育的受教育者没有实现“去个体化”，这是一个仍然需要证实的问题。但有了化约的问题之后，证实的过程也就具备了一定的可操作性。

接下来，我们需要以事实来塑造这个问题。

（三）问题的最终塑造

在对问题原因和建构前提进行说明后，我们需要进一步塑造这里的问题。也就是说，需要以事实来证明，而不是想当然地设定，当今中国高等法学教育所面对的是一群没有“集体性”的对象。在不深究法律伦理和法律技能内涵的前提下，我们来看一下高等法学教育对象的特征。

由于这里仅是问题的引出过程，因而对于问题分析的材料留待下文介绍。我们看一下经验材料中法学教育对象对于法学学科的基本印象以及态度的问题。这里所要验明的是“集体性”的缺乏，我们可以通过几个问题进行检验。其中，最为直接的就是追问法科学生学习法律的原因，这里的问卷涉及中国法学教育的若干区域，虽然不能说具有完全的信度，但之于总体，这里的代表程度还是相当高的，因而并不缺乏说服力。为了更直观地反映出不同地区法学院中的法学专业本科学生为什么学习法律以及对法律的认识，本文对表1中的数据进行了再次处理，以所占比例来引出“个体化”的问题前提，经过统计与表格化处理之后，得出如下结果，如表1所示。

表1 各地区法学院/系法学专业本科生学习法律原因统计表（%）

选择学习法律的原因		华东政法大学法学院	中南政法大学法学院	西北政法大学国际法学院	海南大学法学院	华北电力大学文法学院	均值
1. 最初原因	个人兴趣	53%	36%	42%	39%	39%	41.8%
	父母要求	16%	29%	13%	8%	5%	14.2%
	亲戚推荐	5%	11%	5%	6%	8%	7%
	他人推荐	4%	3%	8%	6%	7%	5.6%
	其他原因	22%	21%	32%	41%	41%	31.4%
2. 最终原因	个人爱好	31%	21%	28%	23%	36%	27.8%
	可从事法律公职	26%	25%	22%	22%	17%	22.4%
	外人压力	2%	1%	2%	3%	11%	3.8%
	为人解决问题	10%	10%	8%	9%	8%	9%
	可伸张正义	14%	5%	15%	10%	4%	9.6%
	其他	17%	38%	25%	33%	24%	27.4%

笔者必须指出，该调查样本的代表性并不完美，但鉴于此处研究总体特征的单一性，对于引出本文所论证的问题而言，这里要素的描述基本符合条件。这里所欲考察的总体为中国高等法学院校法学本科学生，将这个总体的要素进行处理后，以华东、中南、西北、海南和华北五地区法学院校本科生为样本，以百分比来进行描述，对于塑造这里的问题即法律“集体性”缺乏的问题而言，基本是充分的。[1]

下面我们来对这里的问题略作描述。从表1中所反映的数据来看，选择学习法律的原因多种多样，各地区之间也存在差别。以均值审视，在选择法律的最初原因中，个人兴趣的均值为41.8%；父母要求的均值为14.2%；亲戚推荐的均值为7%；他人推荐的均值为5.6%；其他原因的均值为31.4%。在选择法律的最终原因中，个人爱好的均值为27.8%；可从事法律公职的均值为22.4%；外人压力的均值为3.8%；为人解决问题的均值为9%；可伸张正义的均值为9.6%；其他的均值为27.4%。

[1] 关于抽样代表性以及抽象选择的基本介绍，参见艾尔·巴比：《社会研究方法》，邱泽奇译，华夏出版社2000年版，第243～291页。

对于这些选项的分布，本文无意提出某种原因对于法律伦理和法律技能的培养有多重要，尽管兴趣对于知识的学习确实很有作用。这里，本文只是要指出，高等法学教育所面对的是一个不存在统一性的总体，他们选择法律专业的原因不同，对法学专业缺乏必要的认识，这是进行高等法学教育的必要性之所在。如果使用问题话语来描述此处表1中所反映的信息，由于无意对各种选择的原因进行深究，笔者毋宁将其概括为“集体性”的不足。在笔者看来，这里的集体性就是统一的法律“伦理”和“技能”。

由此，我们就最终完成了问题的塑造。对于高等法学教育而言，这里的问题就是它是否完成了“集体性”的建构，也就是说，高等法学教育是否成功地培育出了法律伦理和技能兼备的法律人。

二、理论框架与假设

（一）福柯规训理论

本文所欲使用的理论分析框架为福柯的规训理论。鉴于分析的必要，该理论可以借用到法学教育分析中的部分，本文将进行有选择性的介绍。

在福柯看来，现代社会中，权力不是一种宏观的占有，而是一种微观的行使。[1] 这种权力的最主要方式就是规训，它的主要功能是“训练”，是为了更好地挑选和征用而训练。规训将各种力量结合起来是为了更好地使用这些力量，并达到增强这些力量的目的。[2] 从一定意义上而言，这是一个逻辑悖论，但规训实际上确实通过一种与传统权力形态完全相悖的形式实现了权力的运作。一定程度上，这种非中心化、非压制性、关系性特征的权力形态通过细微的运作路径达致了14世纪以降民族国家所一直努力实现却一直不尽如意的效果，即国家与个体的面对面。[3]

---

[1] 米歇尔·福柯：《疯癫与文明》，刘北成、杨远婴译，北京三联书店1999年版，第29页。

[2] 同上书，第193页。

[3] 胡水君：“全球化背景下的国家与公民”，载《法学研究》2003年第3期，第3～13页。

但是，它的实现手段不是把所有对象整齐划一，而是进行分类、解析、区分，从而实现必要而充分的独立单位。通过训练，规训权力将大量混杂、无用、盲目流动的肉体和力量变成多样性的个别因素，但赋予这些个体因素独立细胞而使其成为有机的自治体、原生的连续统一体。一言蔽之，规训“造就”了个人。但经过规训的个人，是规训社会所欲的个人，是一种变得更加强壮、更符合规训社会所需要的有机“个体”，是一种深深印刻着集体性的个体。

这个过程的实现借助规训的特殊技术。这种现代权力技术简单却极其精细，具有充分的可测度性、弥散性，能够渗透到社会空间的每一寸微小的角落，因而具备持久的运行力。在福柯看来，规训权力有三种手段，分别为层级监督、规范化裁决以及联结二者的一种机制即检查。在这三种手段中，层级监督是指借助监视实施纪律的一种机制，目的是在规训机构中构建出一个金字塔式的监督人员系统，上一级监督人员监督下一级监督人员的行为。规范化裁决是根据纪律中的规定对规训对象的行为、举止等进行判断，然后根据其是否违反纪律来决定是否受处罚或奖励。规范化裁决是一个双向的规训手段。在规范化裁决中，规训者要制定出一个规范标准，并依据这一标准实现纪律的运行。检查是联结层级监督和规范性裁决的重要程序，也是规训权力得以运行的重要一环。通过检查，可见状态转换为权力的行使，通过检阅仪式将规训对象驯顺化。检查通过个体的文本化实现对个体的改造，即通过个体性书写而将个体物化为既定标准的对比对象，并使个人在充分感知到自身个体性的同时纳入集体性的温和权力网络之中。

（二）为什么可以分析法学教育

对于我们所引出的法学教育问题，即“集体性”的建构是否完成，福柯的理论是一种十分恰当的分析工具。在笔者看来，这主要是基于两个原因。

第一，福柯的规训理论中学校具有重要的地位。在福柯的微观权力观中，学校、军营、医院都是具有代表性的机构，都是知识权力运作的场所。在微观权力的运作并进而重新建构知识体系方面，这几个社会空间都价值不菲，如，医院的微观权力的运作转型导致了近代医学的产生，并产生了与规训场所共生的知识体系和护士类型。而对于学校，规训权力的运作更是促生了现代教育学知识体系的建构，并形成了完备的学科考量体系。因而，对于法学教育效果的考量而言，通过考量与福柯理论中相对照的规训手段效果，就能够对我们所设定的“集体性”建构的任务有所认知。

第二，规训效果测度的可及性。要考量三种规训手段的效果，一个重要的问题就是要描述和测量相应的结果。层级监督、规范性裁判和检查的效果可以通过访谈或问卷形式进行测度，这就使评价具有了一定的可操作性。比如，我们检验层级监督的效果，可以通过对相关规训对象的个体体验的访谈衡量来获得，对检查效果的考察可以通过发放问卷、统计结果来测度。但无论怎样，这些都是可及的，具有可操作性，这也就保证了研究的可能性和可行性。

因而，鉴于福柯理论对学校这一社会空间的可用性，以及调查资料的可及性方面的考虑，福柯的规训理论可以应用到法学教育效果考量的分析中，并应当能够根据具体的结果给出具有建构意义的建议。

（三）假设

在建构起进行分析的理论框架后，笔者对截至当前的交代予以概括，在此作出假设，希望通过下文的调查研究来证成或证伪这里的假设。

本文所欲追寻的问题是“集体性”的建构是否完成，分析的理论框架为福柯的规训理论，考察的路径是对福柯三种规训手段的效果进行描述或测度。因而，将这些糅合在一起，本文可以作出以下假设：

（1）“集体性”建构的规训成功完成。

（2）“集体性”建构的规训没有完成。

这两个假设中，何种将被证成，何种将被证伪，则需要我们通过实践资料来检验。

三、研究对象与研究方法

这里要对本文所涉及的研究对象和研究方法作出一个整体交代。本文主要采取的研究方法是定量研究，并结合一定的访谈。访谈主要针对层级监督这一规训手段，而定量研究则主要针对规范性裁决的感知，以及对检查手段认同度的评价方面。

在定量调查方面，本文采取抽样问卷调查。本文从中国东部、西部、南部、北部和中部五地区挑选出五所统招类法学院校，以问卷调查的方式，从法学本科学生学习法律的原因以及院校中知识传递和校内评价体系的认同度两大方面，对当前中国各区域法学教育的具体运作进行了场域化描述。在进行描述分析之前，为避免不严谨的概率抽样等诸多不必要的口舌之争，笔者首先要对这里的方法和样本进行说明：

首先，此处的考察对象限定为统招类大学法学院的本科生，采用访谈和问卷调查的方式进行，主要采用量化处理方式。这种选“样本”的方式可能在说服力方面还存在欠缺之处。毕竟在现阶段，中国法学教育一定程度上还存在多层次、多渠道、多形式的不规范状态，但这些不规范的情形必将随着中国法学教育体系的逐步完善而消亡。因而，关于样本选择的代表意义，本文在此事先指出，这里的样本选择并不能完全代表中国法学教育的全貌，但代表了中国法学教育主流部分。此外，由于本文所要解决的问题也并不是法学教育的全景，而只是这个法学教育的初级阶段所可能存在的问题，因而，其结论的适用性也仅仅限于法学本科这个总体，甚至可能仅仅适用于这里所选的样本院校。至于一些因地理、人文、民族而相对较为个性化的区域，本样本结论的不适用并不意外。

其次，为节省篇幅，笔者在此对这些数据进行一个总体说明：本文数据来自发放问卷，其中华东政法学院本科生发放问卷 100 份，回收 90 份，回收率 90%，作废 4 份，问卷有效率 86%。海南大学法学院本科生发放问卷 150 份，回收 142 份，回收率 94.6%，问卷有效率 100%。西北政法大学国际法学院本科生发放问卷 300 份，回收 280 份，回收率 93.3%，作废 40 份，问卷有效率 80%。华北电力大学本科生发放问卷 200 份，回收 198 份，回收率 99%，作废 1 份，问卷有效率 98.5%。中南财经政法大学法学院发放问卷 90 份，回收 84 份，回收率 93.3%，问卷有效率100%。统计比例保留到小数点后一位数字。表格统计数据为各选项的比例数据。

四、规训效果考量

我们首先来看一下规训对象对于法学教育规训的认同度。在福柯看来，规训权力的有效运作取决于层级监督、规范性裁决以及检查。要从宏观上考量这些规训手段的效果，最好的方式就是以规训对象的感知为依据进行评价，本文将借助个体考察和宏观问卷的分析来对规训效果分别予以论述。

（一）层级监督

福柯认为，完美的规训机构应能使一切都一目了然。这一切的目的都是为了实现学校纪律的实施，并为之建构起一种借助监视而实行强制的机制，在这种机制中，监视的技术能够诱发出权力的效应，这种机制是一种深嵌（Encastrement）原则的具体运作，它能够使得规训对象时刻感知到权力的印迹，感觉到被监督，但无法发现权力的源头。

在福柯看来，完美的规训机构需要中继站，这些中继站的具备使得规训机构能够完整地形成不间断的网络，增加层次，并使各层次散布在需要监督的整体平面。此外，这种中继站要使规训权力运作的结构合理，不会产生任何对抗规训权力的力量，从而阻碍规训力量对其运作网络的控制。也就是说，中继站应当成为规训权力网络上的有效强化点，因它们的存在而使得规训的权力具体化，从而使得规训对象能够充分“感知”到这种权力，尽管它是温和的、仁慈的。

为了检验这种层级监督是否顺利经过这些中继站而成功地将规训权力传递给了规训对象，本文对所调查对象的其中一所院校的若干学生进行了访谈，访谈内容有关于他们的日常活动和对学校生活的印象，并根据访谈内容整理出代表性的记录，这里权且将这个代表性的学生集合体暂时称为A。以下是笔者所获得的一些信息。

笔者：你们一个班级有多少人？

学生A：56个人。

笔者：平时和学校接触的途径多吗？

学生A：天天在学校，上课、参加各种活动等，挺多的。

笔者：你们有辅导员吗？

学生A：有，是××老师，在教务处工作。

笔者：你们和辅导员联系多吗？

学生A：不多，一般都是开学后、放假前开个会。

笔者：谁负责通知？

学生A：一般由班长通知吧。

笔者：通知到每一个人吗？

学生A：跟同寝室里随便一个人说一下就行了。

笔者：上课严格吗？如果有病或有事情找谁请假？

学生A：一般找同学代一下就可以了，上课老师不点名就没事。平常不在学校基本没人管，只要没人揭发，学校也不会知道。

笔者：课堂点名是怎么做的？老师点名，还是学生点名？

学生A：当然是老师点名，年纪大的教师点名的比较多，年纪轻的老师比较好，很少有点名的。经常点名的老师，我们一般都知道。

我们来分析一下这段对话中蕴含的信息。对于福柯的规训手段而言，最重要的是分层的、持续的、切实的监督。这里访谈的对象是法学专业的本科生，因而话语中所反映的信息对于集体性建构的审视具有一定的说明力。

我们首先来审视一下这里的问题。在层级监督中，学校空间的规训权力若有效运作，就必须有一整套权力的传递系统。与民族国家这种宏大的社会空间相似，高等院校构成了一个微缩版的规训空间。民族国家实现的是国家与社会每一个主体的面对面，而学校空间要实现的是法律知识对于法科学生的面对面规训，这种规训权力的实践路径是柔和却层次分明的主体联结，能够温和地将学校意志和每个学生的生活层层联系起来，并使得这些规训对象时刻感知到学校的存在，尤其是学校所代表的知识权力的存在。但是，从学生 A 所给出的信息中我们可以看到，这种层级监督的层次是有缺陷的，它没有发挥出将每一个点都能够展现在接受关注的平面之上的功能。

具体而言，这里的缺陷首先表现为辅导员的非专职性。对于一个完美的规训机构而言，用于实施权力规训的监督者应当具有一定的专业性。这种监督者的专业存在使得规训的运作变得完美，使得规训对象时刻体味着规训的监督力量。当然，对于法学院校而言，这种规训的监督者即辅导员履行着法学知识建构的监督作用。但无论怎样，文本中所反映的兼职辅导员的做法无疑是破坏了这种层级监督的层次性与连续性，从而使得规训对象无法感知学校规训力量的存在。文本中兼职辅导员与学生见面的频率极低（开学后、放假前各一次），这同样也反映出这种规训力量的失效。

其次，缺陷表现为中继站的缺失。在规训理论中，权力的运作主要是一种温和的关系方式，而不是一种中心外扩的形式，其中发挥重要作用的就在于层级监督中的中继站。辅导员之于学校与学生是中继站，班长之于辅导员和同学是中继站。但这种规训的权力如果到此为止，就无法建构起一整套金字塔式的层级监督体系，也容易使规训权力异化为传统的专制权力，将权力源在某一阶段集中为一个点，从这个点向外扩张。毫无疑问，这种权力运作模式的网络只能是越来越弱，从而无法实现对每一个规训对象的“集体性”规训。访谈中辅导员或班长可能就是这样一个权力中继站，但这些网络联结点的建构没有能够顺利地将学校知识权力和每一个学生面对面地联系起来，从信息通知的随意性上（跟同寝室里随便一个人说一下就行了）我们可以清楚地看到这一重要缺陷。

最后，缺陷表现为层级监督网络的破裂。为了说明层级监督与法律知识规训之间的直接关联，文本中追问了课堂的出勤问题。学生 A 反映的信息表明，在这个社会空间中，联结法学知识和法科学生的法学教师是失职的，“年纪轻的老师很少有点名”这一话语中所反映出的信息正是法律知识规训力量的断裂。作为一个联结法学知识和规训对象也就是联结法律技能、法律伦理以及法科学生的节点，法学教师失却了有效进行层级监督的手段，尽管这一手段未必必须通过点名来反映，但从学生A所反映的“平常不在学校基本没人管，只要没人揭发，学校也不会知道”这一信息里，我们可以清楚地看到，法学知识过渡到法科学生中的有效路径已经断裂了。这种断裂很大程度上在于层级监督网络的破裂，而中继站的缺位是其中最为关键的问题。[1]

（二）规范性裁决和检查

在福柯的规训理论中，规范性裁决是为了保障纪律的运行而制定出的一个规范标准，并依据这一标准来判断规训对象的行为。在福柯看来，规范性裁决能够形成划一的压力，它能够将个人纳入一个整体，将整体既作为一个比较对象，又当作必须遵循的规则。规范性裁决使规训权力的运作同时具备划一和分殊的作用，通过划定严格标准，借助这一手段，规训权力摒弃了传统权力运作过程中所附带的表征地位、特权和依附关系的符号和仪式，取而代之以体系化的规范级别，从而扫清了规训权力运作的路径。

检查则是一种联结监视技术和规范化裁决技术的手段。通过检查，规训对象获得了能见性，并能够以此来区分和判断个人。正因为如此，检查技术在各种规训空间中被高度仪式化，军队的检阅、医院的巡视以及学校的考试就是这种高度仪式化检查的代表。在福柯看来，规训权力借助检查将规训对象客体化，从而实现规训者对被规训者的控制。在学校空间中，这种规训力量就是知识，最典型的检查仪式就是考试，它通过一系列的书写机制将个人变成可描述的对象，成为一个个可比较的文本，并最终使个人成为权力的后果与对象，成为知识的后果与对象。通

[1] 中国人民大学法学博士孟强提出：“密集的、有效的规训有必要吗？会不会扼杀学生的自由?”对此，笔者必须在这里做个声明，这里只是对法学本科生的必要知识规训，对于是否会扼杀学生自由的质疑，本文认为，在未建立牢固的法学基础知识之前，法学思想家的打造基本是不可能的，此外，即便将本文所指责的规训网络全部无缝衔接，学生的自由也是有保障的，因为较之于国外法学教育，在几乎没有课前准备、课下作业的中国高等法学教育中，学生时间是相对宽裕的。

过这种路径，检查成果颠覆了个人化“上升”的传统权力历史，而建构起一个个人化“下降”的规训制度。这是一个悖论，也就是随着权力变得日益隐蔽、日益有效，受其影响的人趋向更为强烈的个人化。❶ 但这种个人化其实是建构在一种“集体性”的对照之下，是规训权力悄然运作的结果。

对于学校空间而言，规训权力核心的运作机制也是联结层级监督和规范性裁决的检查机制。只不过在学校这个社会空间中，规训力量成了知识，所要形成的是一种知识规训的微型社会。考试是一种典型的检查，它是一个永恒的知识交换器，确保知识从教师流向学生，并形成一种供教师使用的知识。那么对于法学规训对象集体性的建构而言，这种规范性裁决以及检查是否确实发挥了它应有的功能呢？学校空间中，规训对象对于这种规训仪式的认同度无疑将能够反映出它的实际运作效果，尽管可能只是在一定程度上。因此，本文对几所院校的法科学生发放了问卷，问卷具体情况和结果如表 2 所示。

表 2　各地区学生对学校评价体系的认同程度（单位%）

学生对学校评价体系的认同度		华东政法大学法学院	中南政法大学法学院	西北政法大学国际法学院	海南大学法学院	华北电力大学文法学院
3. 是否在意在校成绩	不在意	11%	27%	8%	14%	25%
	在意	75%	46%	77%	69%	71%
	不明了，说不清	14%	27%	15%	17%	4%
4. 在意原因	切实反映法律知识掌握水平	29%	22%	29%	47%	29%
	可得奖学金	15%	29%	17%	18%	8%
	有利于找工作	12%	27%	12%	11%	23%
	其他（有利于以后发展等）	44%	22%	42%	24%	40%

❶ 比如，在学校、医院、军队等社会空间中，通过对每个学生、病人、士兵建立文本档案，有形或无形地强迫个体照着一个标准发展，实现的是共性也就是集体性的建构，即实现的是个体性的下降。但同时，对于每一个特定的学生、病人、士兵而言，每个人都有属于自己的文本，这种书写规训所实现的是一人更加个体化的建构，也即个体性的上升。这正是微观权力的精妙所在。

续表

学生对学校评价体系的认同度		华东政法大学法学院	中南政法大学法学院	西北政法大学国际法学院	海南大学法学院	华北电力大学文法学院
5. 不在意原因	反映不了法律知识掌握程度	40%	71%	58%	71%	70%
	和以后无关	50%	24%	15%	24%	17%
	其他	10%	5%	27%	5%	13%

从表2中所反映的信息来看，考试这种规训手段的效果还是很直观的。各个经济地区中，对这一评价机制的在意程度都相当高，即便是最为特例的中南，这个比例也高达46%。其余四个地区的在意度均在70%左右。如从这一数据来分析规训效果，它和学校所在地区的经济差异并没有太大的相关程度，而是与“特定空间限定”的群体文化有着比较紧密的相关关系。此外，课堂教学方式也对学生对成绩的认同度产生相当的影响。比如，中南地区法学院采取自由选课制度，这种制度确实有利于法学教育对人才的尊重和对学生自我发展能力的肯定。不过，对于知识传递的统一性要求而言，现在的效果可能还不是十分理想。无论怎样，作为衡量考试规训力的结果，学校中所给出的成绩在规训对象中的认同程度无疑反映了知识规训的运行能力。因而，如果我们从这里的程度来看，能够得出一个初步的结论，即在学校这一社会空间中，法学知识的检查形式是有着较强的规训力的。

这是一个初步的结论，因为法学知识检查形式的规训力并不代表它的“有效规训”，规训对象内心的接受也不能说明他们在实践中确实有效地认同并接受了这里的规训模式。因而，既然我们所要追究的是集体性规训的完成与否，对于仅仅反映出初步规训力的检查形式——考试，我们必须要深究它之所以被认同以及之所以不被认同的原因。也就是说，它是否圆满完成了联结层级监督和规范性裁决的机制作用。这个衡量标准仍需要从规训对象的反映来检验。

我们首先来看一下认同的原因。在问题4中，问卷隐喻了一个“法律技能”传递与否的问题选项。从各个法学院校学生之所以在意学生成绩的原因中我们发现，选择“认为成绩切实反映了法律知识的掌握程度”选项的学生比例在华东、中南、西北、海南和华北五大法学院校分别为29%、22%、29%、47%和29%。比起其他选项，无论是功利性的还是非功利性的，这一比例都是比较低的，甚至没有任何一所法学院校有超过50%比例的学生认为考试的结果与知识掌握的熟练程度是挂钩的。也就是说，作为一种法律知识规训的技术手段，法学院校的考试制度没有赢得应有的规训认同度，这一制度没有能够实现层级监督和规范性裁决的有机联结功能。

这一判断也可以通过反证来验证。问题5就是对不认同考试机制原因的继续追问。从各个法学院校学生之所以不在意考试成绩的原因中我们发现，选择“认为成绩反映不了法律知识的掌握程度”选项的学生比例在华东、中南、西北、海南和华北五大法学院校分别为40%、71%、58%、71%和70%。从这一结果来看，对于目前的考试机制，法科学生持否定态度的比例是相当高的，虽然经济发展程度对这一结果有一定的影响，但无论是否介入经济因素的考量，如此之高的否定比例也都足以证明了法学知识规训力量的运作不畅。

（三）对法律及法律知识的认识

从以上分析中我们看到的是法律知识规训手段的失效，对于我们所希望证成或证伪的集体性而言，这从一个方面验证了集体性建构的未完成，这个方面就是法律知识的技能方面。当然，这一判断主要是通过对福柯理论中三种规训技术的实际考量获得的，以福柯的权力运作理论来审视，三种技术的实效无疑意味着规训力量的实效，也就是法学知识没有有效地从规训者（学校）这里顺利过渡到规训对象（法学专业学生）那里。这是一个逻辑的推理过程，没有涉及经验的考察，并且，这也只是涉及技能的知识规训，没有涉及集体性的另外一个方面，即伦理的规训。因而，接下来有必要经验地验证一下法学知识传递的实际认同度以及法律伦理的规训效果，从而能够充分地检验集体性建构的完成与否。为此，本文设计了以下两个问题，并仍然以五大地区法学院校的法学本科生为对象，以比例为最终统计结果，具体如表3所示。

表 3　各地区学生对法学知识及法律的认知（单位%）

学生对法学知识及法律的认知		华东政法大学法学院	中南政法大学法学院	西北政法大学国际法学院	海南大学法学院	华北电力大学文法学院
6. 对学校传授知识的评断	用处很大	32%	38%	37%	38%	36%
	有用，但不大	39%	34%	34%	33%	33%
	可能有用	29%	28%	29%	28%	29%
	和工作无关，没用	0%	0%	0%	1%	2%
7. 对法律的认识	学习内容	19%	12%	14%	22%	34%
	生活中必需	56%	66%	53%	55%	36%
	就业垫脚石	8%	13%	15%	12%	11%
	信仰	17%	9%	18%	11%	19%

我们来看一下表 3 中问题 6 所反映出的信息，华东、中南、西北、海南和华北五大法学院校学生认为学校传授的知识“用处很大”的比例分别为 32%、38%、37%、38%和 36%，而认为“有用但不大”的比例分别为 39%、34%、34%、33%和 33%，其他学生则基本不置可否或干脆否定学校传授的知识，当然，完全否定的比例极为少见。但是，这就回应了之前的问题，即从经验上检验，对于学校传授的知识，学生认为用处很大的比例是不够高的。事实上，对于以技能立命的法律职业而言，这一比例所给出的信息反映出目前的法学教育是相当失败的。自有法律职业以来，它就一直与医生和神职并列为专业性很强的职业，三者最重要的特征就在于需要经过特殊的训练。[1] 但从表 3 中所反映出的经验信息来看，目前中国高等法学教育的训练显然没有能够达到满足实践所需的目的，因而我们不能不再次肯定，考试这种规训手段所得出的逻辑推论在经验层面再次获得了支持。法律知识没有能够通过规训技术从规训者那里有效地传递到被规训者那里，即便这里仅仅是技能层面的考量。

那么让我们更奢侈一步，对法律伦理略作简单的考量。实际上，在规训手段的考量中，我们对于法律伦理的建构已经得出了一定的否定结

---

[1] Henry Campbell black，*M. A. Balck' S Law Dictionary*，West Publishing，Com. 2004，p. 1246.

论，即规训对象对规训手段的不认同，尤其是对考试这一检查制度的不认同，这从一个方面反映了规范性裁决的规训技术没有有效地发挥功能，因而，法学知识的伦理也就没有能够有效地形成对规训对象的制约。层级监督的断裂也能够透射出这样的信息，学生不在学校学习没人管的状态就反映了法律伦理建构的细节忽略。事实上，这种细节的忽略能够以一种与规训相同的柔和手段破坏规训权力的运作，从而完全腐蚀掉法律知识的规训。为了经验地验证这一粗糙的判断，本文对五大地区法学院校学生的法律认知设计了一个十分粗浅的问题，这一问题无意严格地探知法律伦理建构的具体程度，只不过想检验一下法律伦理实践的具体情势，因此，对于这一目标而言，问卷选项设计的粗陋并不会有太大影响。从表 3 中问题 7 所反映的信息来看，华东、中南、西北、海南和华北五大法学院校学生认为法律为“生活中必需”的比例相对较高，分别为 56%、66%、53%、55%和 36%；但认为法律仅仅是学习内容的比例也不低，分别 19%、12%、14%、22%和 34%；认为法律不过是“就业垫脚石”的比例分别为 8%、13%、15%、12%和 11%；而与这些相对功利的选择相比，认为法律为信仰的比例则很低，分别为 17%、9%、18%、11%和 19%。笔者不能依此判断法律伦理的建构是完全失败的，即判断依据完全为法科生信仰法律者如此之少，也无意引用早被人说烂的伯尔曼的话支持笔者的判断，但是有一点是可以肯定的，那就是，在可以多选的问卷中，在法学专业的学生对于法律的认知比例中，“信仰”法律者的比例如此之低确实是存在问题的，至少它反映出法律知识规训权力的不足。在一定程度上，这一问题应当引起规训者（法学教育机构）的特别注意。

五、结论：未完成的规训

截至目前，本文经验地考察了高等法学教育的具体运作状况，以福柯的规训理论为出发点，通过对全国五大地区高等法学院校学生的问卷调查以及个别的访谈，分别经验地考量了福柯规训理论的现实版本，从层级监督、规范性裁决和检查三方面，对特殊的社会空间即高等法学院校中所发生的规训效果予以检验，以之主要验证我们假定的集体性中的法律“技能”一面。然后，本文继续以问卷调查的形式对全国五大地区高等法学院校学生对法律及法律知识的认知进行了考察，这里的考察结果主要用以验证集体性建构中的法律“技能”一面。现在，我们重新看一下前文的两个假定。

（1）“集体性”建构的规训成功完成。

（2）“集体性”建构的规训没有完成。

从本文的访谈和问卷调查结果来看，我们可以得出结论，假定1得到了证伪，而假定2得到了证成。也就是说，规训理论的具体运作路径以及对伦理的经验审视都说明，当前我国的高等法学教育没有成功地完成法律技能和法律伦理这一集体性的建构。在高等法学院校的社会空间中，法律知识的传递是一种未完成的规训。当然，这里的考察结果并不具备完美的代表性，对于它所予以说明的总体而言，它的说明力是有限的，但它确实给我们当前的法学教育提出了一个警醒：为什么我们的知识传递是“未完成”的规训？对于建设社会主义法治国家来说，未完成规训的法学教育如何能够承担法学人才供给的重任？在目前的状态下，法学院提供给学生的课程内容乏味，教材陈旧，教师照本宣科，教学脱离实际，考试形式化，改卷评分较为随意并掺杂人情关系。在这样的背景下，通过上课、考试来对学生进行规训，会有好的效果吗？要知道，建构法治国家需要技能和伦理兼备的法律人，需要对法治天下的信仰，如果不信仰法治，如何能够建构法治国家？而如果不能规训出信仰法治的法律人，所有法治梦想都将不过是水中月、镜中花。

因此，我们所应当做的就是终结法学教育“未完成的规训”。而上文所论述的缺陷之处，或许正是我们应当为之的起点。

中美诊所法律教育目标之比较*

齐喜三**

摘　要：源于美国的诊所法律教育，经过近半个世纪的发展，目标渐趋成熟和明确。在这个漫长的发展过程中，从初期的弥补法学教育的不足和传授办案经验技能，发展到创新能力和承担社会责任的培养，以致最后发展到最高层次的目标——律师职业人的培养和推动社会的进步。中国高校在诊所法律教育本土化的过程中，在进行教育目标定位时，既要吸纳美国的经验和做法，又要考虑诊所法律教育的教育本质和教育的阶段性，还要结合各自高校的具体情况来确定本校诊所法律教育的具体目标。同时，各个高校的诊所法律教育目标也要根据不同的诊所类型和发展程度及时予以调整。

关键词：教育目标　诊所法律教育　初始目标　阶段性

教育目标是指学生学习的预期结果或者说预期的学习活动所要达到的标准，它具有指导教学测量与评价、指导教学策略的选择和指导学习活动的进行等基本功能。一切教学活动都是以教育目标为定向。[1] 自2000年中国高校开始逐步推行诊所法律教育，关于中国诊所法律教育的教育目标如何正确定位的问题一直争论不休，困扰着中国高校的许多诊所，特别是一些欲开办诊所教育但又犹豫不决的院校以及白班时间不长

---

* 基金项目：中国诊所法律教育委员会2008年度基金项目“诊所法律教育筹资问题研究”（CCCLE08012）的阶段性成果之一。

** 齐喜三，南阳理工学院文法学院副教授、副院长，研究方向：民法和法学教育。

[1] 教育部人事司组织编写：《高等教育心理学（第2版）》，高等教育出版社1999年版，第374～375页。

的院校。究其原因，主要是我们对诊所法律教育的本质特征、产生背景、核心目标、价值体系、在中国的本土化问题、教育目标的多元化和阶段性问题认识不足，对法学教育改革期望值过高等，其中教育目标的无序与差别尤为突出。

一、美国诊所法律教育的教学目标

（一）初始目标：技能与思维培养

美国的诊所法律教育并非一般的基础素质教育，而是一种非常专业化的职业教育。这种职业教育主要是服从于美国法学教育的需求，为学生毕业之后成为一名合格的律师做准备。这种类似医学院实习医生的培养方案运用到法学教学中，最直接的目的就在于学生的职业能力的养成。

美国法律诊所的教师们从诊所建立的那一刻起，便开始关注诊所式法律教育的目标。J. P. Ogilvy 描述了最初的目标：（1）为提高应变能力而培养预测与分析；（2）提供专业化的技巧训练方法；（3）传授从经验中学习的方法；（4）培养学生的职业责任感；（5）让学生直面所扮演角色的要求与理念；（6）提供学习合作的机会；（7）向学生传授为贫困当事人服务的责任；（8）提供检验法制在真实生活中的影响力的机会，为学生和法学院研究特定的法律领域提供实验室；（9）评价法律工作者和法制体系的能力和局限性。

约翰·布拉德威（John Bradway）提出了诊所教育的 5 项目标：（1）弥补法学院理论教育与实践间的差距；（2）对学生所学的各种实体法和程序法进行融会贯通；（3）在法律学习与实践中引入人的因素；（4）对法律执业中未形成书面材料的辩护实践进行介绍；（5）教会学生对法律问题要从头进行思考，而不是从上诉意见形式出现的结局来进行思考。[1]

---

[1] 约翰·布拉德威（John Bradway 是杜克大学法律援助诊所负责人、早期法律诊所著作最丰富的学者之一）在 1933 年芝加哥大学法律评论中进行归纳。杨欣欣：《法学教育与诊所式教学方法》，法律出版社 2002 年版，第 135 页。

（二）中期目标：责任与意识培养

诊所法律教育在经过漫长的探索和实践之后，仅仅满足弥补教学不足和增加实践技能是远远不够的，培养学生在实践基础之上进行创新和学会承担责任比提高实践技能更为重要。在这样不停的反思过程中，创新能力的培养和学会承担责任成为诊所法律教育目标的核心内容。

1992 年美国《麦考利特报告》[1] 真实地反映了中期目标的全部内容。该报告确立的律师要具备 10 项基本技能：问题的解决、法律分析和推理、法律检索、事实调查、交流、咨询、谈判、起诉和其他纠纷解决程序、法律事务的组织与管理和确认并解决道德困境。通过上述 10 项技能的培训，达到如下价值目标：（1）律师应当提供称职的代理；（2）律师应当努力促进正义、公平与道德；（3）努力完善法律职业，减少职业偏见并扭转这些偏见所造成的影响；（4）律师应当促进法律职业的自我发展，寻求并充分利用各种机遇增长个人知识并提高技能。[2]

华盛顿大学教授 Jane H. Aiken 这样描述诊所法律教育的教学目标："我们希望学生们在结束诊所课程时，已经具备了对'作为一个律师为当事人服务'的更为广泛的认识，已掌握了包括谈判、咨询、会见及实施调查在内的精湛的法律职业技能。我们希望给予他们机会，以发展他们庭前准备与提交证据的技巧，并对有效的法律文书写作有一定的认识。此外，我们想向他们揭露极度的贫富不均与权力滥用。我们致力于让他们产生一种坚定不移的愿望——利用他们的法律技能去纠正这些不公平，运用他们的智慧去了解正在为他们的工作环境进行广泛变革的法律制度的不足……"[3]

---

[1] 英文全称为 The Mac Crate Report，是 1992 年美国律师协会法学教育与律师资格部下设关于法学院与法律职业特别工作组的报告。

[2] 李傲：《互动教学法——诊所式法律教育》，法律出版社 2004 年版，第 75～76 页。

[3] Jane H. Aiken：正义的激发者，7CLINICAL · L. REV. 287（2001），载李傲：《实践型法律人才的培养诊所式法律教育经验》，法律出版社 2005 年版，第 5 页。

（三）终极目标：创新能力与律师职业人的培养

美国诊所法律教育始终要紧紧围绕美国的法律职业人才培养的目标，诊所法律教育在满足学生的技能与思维培养、责任与意识培养之后，必须为社会需求的称职法律人才提供技术支持，必须为律师这一高尚职业服务，这就必然要求诊所法律教育不得不承担培养未来律师的重任，创新能力与律师职业人的培养被赋予到诊所法律教育的历史使命中，同时也是其能够根深蒂固的成长土壤。

Philip. G. Schrag 教授把诊所法律教育的培养目标描述得非常到位。他在《构建一个法学院内的诊所》一文[1]中描述了乔治敦大学法律应用研究中心（简称 CALS）的教学目标有 12 项：（1）责任。这个目标在 CALS 中是首要的，即教导学生对于对真实当事人有重大意义的事件接受和承担责任。（2）原则和制度，即教授学生新领域中的法律，希望学生熟悉该领域中独有的原则、制度、程序、冲突、习惯以及职业道德。（3）免费服务。（4）解决问题。（5）合作。（6）多种文化之间的认知。（7）情绪的重要性。（8）事实处理。（9）思考价值。（10）职业伦理道德。（11）创造力。（12）教授学生学会运用权力。[2]

通过上述描述和对美国诊所法律教育的考察，我们不难发现，美国诊所法律教育的教学目标的确定与其产生的背景和发展过程紧密相连。（1）美国诊所法律教育的教学目标根植于其在美国产生的根本原因。众所周知，美国诊所法律教育产生的重要原因有三个：第一个原因是诊所法律教育本身就属于法学教育中从经验中学习的一部分，[3] 第二个原因

---

[1] 作者 Philip. G. Schrag 系乔治敦大学法律应用研究中心（CALS）法学教授，原文 Clinical Law Review，Fall 1996，载杨欣欣：《法学教育与诊所式教学方法》，法律出版社 2002 年版，第 239 页。

[2] 这里的目标仅仅指的是诊所教师的教学目标，学生的学习目标除了按照上述目标执行外，不可避免地夹杂有其他目标，有时有些目标也是令人费解的。

[3] 诊所法律教育从本质上讲是一种从经验中学习的过程。“法律的生命不是逻辑，而是经验”；“经验是法律举世无双的领袖”；“我听见的事情，我忘记；我看见的事情，我记住；我去做的事情，我理解”。参见杨欣欣：《法学教育与诊所式教学方法》，法律出版社 2002 年版，第 141～143 页。

是为穷人提供法律援助制度的出现大大推动了诊所法律教育，第三个原因是学院式的法律教育对律师职业道德教育的无能为力。[1] 美国诊所教育的最基本的目标——以经验式的学习为基础而进行职业技能的训练是永恒主题。（2）培养学生的社会责任感和职业道德是诊所法律教育弥补学院式教育的不足。法学教育的一个重要方面就是要培养学生对社会进步、公平、自由、程序、理性的道德准则和价值理念。诊所教育的目标恰恰弥补了传统法学教育的缺失，填补了法科学生培养目标的空白。（3）批判性思维能力的培养是诊所法律教育教学目标的灵魂所在。国际私法桥梁中国培训中心主任迈克尔·龚佩斯认为，批判性思维是指一种积极灵活地对信息进行概念化处理，并对信息加以运用、分析、综合、判断以获得解决问题的方案或获得结论的思维过程。[2] （4）为穷人提供法律服务是诊所法律教育教学目标的重要组成部分。在美国，诊所法律教育和法律援助可以说是一对天然的孪生姐妹。

二、中国诊所法律的教育目标

中国诊所法律教育委员会副主任汪世荣教授认为，西北政法大学的诊所法律教育的培养目标是：培养律师，推进法律职业共同体的形成，具体包括：（1）培养“像律师一样思考问题”的思维方式；（2）培养合作精神；（3）训练律师职业技能；（4）推动法律职业道德的发育成熟。[3]

中国诊所法律教育委员会常委牟逍媛教授认为：诊所教育的目标是帮助学生学会如何从实践中学习知识，是进行思考实践的教学，具体为：（1）教授学生“如何行事”，即教授学生如何去做律师所做的事情；

---

[1] 管士寒、刘琴：“诊所似的法律教育的起源与发展”，载《云南大学学报（法学版）》2003 年第 4 期，第 119～120 页。

[2] 迈克尔·龚佩斯：“运用批判性思维进行刑事辩护”，载《2008 年中国诊所法律教育经验研讨会论文集》，2008 年 6 月。

[3] 2004 年 10 月 15～18 日，由中国法学会诊所教育专业委员会主办、西北政法大学承办的“全国法律诊所教学观摩与研讨会”在西北政法大学召开，汪世荣教授在大会上作了发言。汪世荣：《判例与法律发展——中国司法改革研究》，法律出版社 2006 年版，第 169～171 页。

（2）发现学生的律师哲学观，即帮助学生形成作为法律职业者的人生观；（3）提供法律服务；（4）促进社会变革，即充当通过对法律制度的利用实现社会变革的代理人。[1]

中国诊所法律教育委员会副主任李傲教授认为："诊所法律教育不仅要传授给学生法律知识，培养学生的法律操作技能，更要通过特定的法律实践（法律援助）使所有参与者增强公益意识，维护社会弱势群体的合法权益，保障人权，推动社会和谐发展。"[2]

2002年中国人民大学诊所教育的主要教育目标是：（1）从法律技巧和能力方面培养训练诊所学生；（2）从伦理道德和价值取向方面培养训练诊所学生；（3）培养学生以批判和思考的眼光分析其实践经历的能力以及从他们的经历中再学习的能力；（4）培养学生进行批判性思考的能力；（5）实体法知识在诊所教育中的应用。[3]

中南财经政法大学诊所教育的教育目标有两个：（1）教会学生怎样做事。讲授律师从业的技能是诊所教育的原始目标，提高学生的判断与解决问题的能力、法律研究的能力和事实调查的能力。（2）教会学生怎样做人。培养学生公平正义的理念，树立正确的人生观、价值观以及公共服务意识和社会责任感。[4]

厦门大学何丽欣教授认为：诊所法律教育的目标是培养学生成为一名合格的法律人。作为一名合格的法律人，应当具有系统的法律知识，并以特定的法律思维作为职业活动的准则，在价值观上信仰法律的自由、公平、正义、程序、理性之理念。在知识结构上，我国的传统理论教学体系在一定程度上起到了很好的作用，国内法学教育缺失的是法律人的法律思维艺术且价值观念模糊。诊所法律教育的引进应当在这两个方面

---

[1] 甄贞：《诊所法律教育在中国》，法律出版社2002年版，第37～38页。

[2] 李傲："诊所法律教育的公益性"，载《法学研究》2006年第6期，第29页。

[3] 甄贞：《诊所法律教育在中国》，法律出版社2002年版，第323～324页。

[4] 同上书，第372～373页。

体现其真正的价值所在。[1]

尽管中国高校对诊所法律教育的教学目标的描述各不相同，但从这些描述中我们不难发现中国诊所法律教育的教学目标与美国诊所法律教育的培养目标是一脉相承的，既吸收了美国的精华部分，也有自己的特点。中国诊所法律教育在确定教育目标时主要考虑到中国法学教育的培养目标、诊所法律教育的价值本身以及二者之间的互补性，忽视了诊所法律教育的阶段性、层次性和多元化。

三、诊所法律教育目标的多元化

一门课程或者一种教育模式，在确定其培养目标的时候，首先要考虑这种教育方法本身固有的规律性，即自身的本质特点；其次要考虑教育对象问题，即受教育者的接受能力；再次要考虑这种教育的实施环境和有关措施，即实施条件；最后要考虑实施的时间，即持续性，同时也要考虑认可度，即评价性。

（一）诊所法律教育的初始目标

诊所法律教育之所以在20世纪60年代在美国盛行，其根本的原因在于法学教育中理论教学和实践教育的脱节、职业道德的缺失、法律技巧（包括法律思维能力或者说反思性思维能力）的不足以及政府法律援助的无力状况。所以，美国诊所法律教育的教学目标必须考虑其产生的内在动力，必须考虑诊所法律教育的出现要完成的历史使命，否则，这种方法或者这种模式就不会长久，就不会具有生命力。正如四川大学左卫民教授所言："什么是诊所法律教育的目的？在美国，答案一分为三：其一，职业技能训练；其二，职业道德训练；其三，促进社会正义。"[2]诊所法律教育在促进社会正义方面的表现在当时的美国得到了社会的极大认可。中国的诊所法律教育以美国的诊所法律教育为蓝本，理应坚持

---

[1] 何丽新、陈永灿："论诊所教育的价值追求"，载《2008年中国诊所法律教育经验研讨会论文集》2008年6月，第90页。

[2] 左卫民、兰荣杰："诊所法律教育若干基本问题研究"，载《环球法律评论》2005年第3期，第265页。

和发展诊所法律教育的初始目标，这一点应该是毋庸置疑的，即中国诊所法律教育的目标中，最基本的内容应该是职业技能训练和职业道德训练。

（二）反思性（批判性）思维能力是诊所法律教育的本质

一个合格的律师或者“法律匠人”，不仅要具有深厚的法律理论知识，而且要有丰富的实践经验。传统的法学教育完成不了技术风格极强的经验教育，更不能培养出娴熟办案艺术的“法律匠人”。诊所法律教育恰恰能够弥补这方面的不足。反思性（批判性）思维能力正是诊所学生将法律理论知识与实践经验以及案情本身加以分析、综合、判断后获取一种解决纠纷的方案或途径。“诊所法律教育的第一个目标就是教授学生如何去做律师所做的事情”[1]，即我们平常所言的“像法律职业者那样去思考问题”（Thinking Like A Lawyer）。正如 Loyola 大学 William P. Quigley 教授所言：“在法律实践中指导者从他们的经验中得出一个结论，即一个只学习特定技巧但没有学习如何获得这些技巧的律师，注定学习的只是过时的知识。”[2] 美国 Mary Jo. Eyster 教授也认为：“教授学生通过反思性分析以及批判性思考以及从他们自己的体验和观察中学习知识，这是非常重要的……我认为这个目标比起那些普遍表达的目标，例如律师技能、实体法或者审前程序等更加重要。”[3] 一个学习者法律思维能力的建立对其解决法律纠纷起着不可忽视的作用。这个思维能力的建立和学习需要一个漫长的学习和实践过程。

（三）诊所法律教育教学目标的阶段性

诊所法律教育教学目标的阶段性表现在两个方面：一方面是指诊所

---

[1] 甄贞：《诊所法律教育在中国》，法律出版社 2002 年版，第 11 页。

[2] William P. Quigley：“诊所法学教育的最基本介绍——写给新诊所的教师”，载杨欣欣：《法学教育与诊所式教学方法》，法律出版社 2002 年版，第 144 页。

[3] Mary Jo. Eyste：“教学法：大型校外诊所实习法律诊所的设计和教学”，原载 Clinical Law Review Spring，1999；载杨欣欣：《法学教育与诊所式教学方法》，法律出版社 2002 年版，第 316～317 页。

法律教育教学目标与教学活动紧密相连，有一个发展过程。由基本的职业能力学习到批判性思维能力的建立以至职业能力的提高，不是一朝一夕即可实现的，必须一步一步进行。因此，在组织教学的过程中切不可简单从事、一成不变，要强调循序渐进的过程。唯有如此，才可达到固有的教学目标。

另一方面，诊所法律教育教学本身的目标是有层次性的，即从初始目标到中期目标培养最后到终极目标，这个目标必须是递进式的关系，只有解决了初期目标之后，才可以解决终极目标。为什么是一种递进的关系呢？著名心理学家马斯洛认为："一个人的行为或一个有意的愿望，如果只有一个动机，那是不正常的。"[1] 同时，他还认为人的需求是一个金字塔式的递进过程。他把人的需要分成三大级别：金字塔的最底层是最基本的需要，包括生理需要（主要指空气、水、食物、住所、睡眠、性生活等）、安全需求、爱与归宿；金字塔的中部是发展需要，包括尊重需要（自我尊重和他人的尊重）、有意义、自我满足、轻松、丰富以及真、善、美等。金字塔的顶端是自我实现。这些不同层次的需求呈逐渐递减的状态。[2] 马斯洛的"需要理论"给予我们的启示是：诊所法律教育本身是多元化的，诊所法律教育的教学目标也是多元化的，这些目标之间是有一定差别的，只有从最初目标做起才可以达到终极目标，诊所法律教育教学目标的制定是随着目标的逐步达成而实现跨越的。

由此，我们回过头来看一看，关于中美诊所法律教育教学目标的争论也就一目了然了。教学目标的表述一定要结合自身法律诊所的实际情况（主要包括法学教育的整体培养目标、诊所主题、学生对象的层次、开课的时间长短等）来考虑，层次不同的诊所的教学目标是有一定差异的。之所以国内高校对诊所法律教育教学目标有不同的声音，主要是不同类型的法律诊所不能用同一起跑线的标准来确定，当然也存在诸如对

---

[1] 弗兰克·戈布尔：《第三思潮：马斯洛心理学》，上海译文出版社 1987 年版，第 39 页。

[2] 同上书，第 40～57 页。

诊所法律教育的起源、发展背景认识不够以及对诊所法律教育并不十分了解等因素，此外也有人把诊所法律教育的教学目标与法律援助的目标合二为一。

（四）诊所法律教育的教学目标与其价值的误区

教学目标指学生学习的预期结果或者说预期的学习活动所要达到的标准，而法律教育的价值是诊所法律教育主体、客体相互作用的结果，在这个相互作用的过程中，诊所法律教育的主体把自己的教育需求外化为客观存在的东西，诊所教育则把自己的属性和功能内化为诊所法律教育主体享用的东西，从而形成一种特定的需要与满足的关系。[1] 诊所法律教育的核心价值是它的教育价值，除了核心价值之外，诊所法律教育还有社会价值等，诊所法律教育的教学目标要紧紧围绕诊所法律教育的教育价值进行，诊所法律教育在主客体相互作用的过程中还会表现其他价值，这些其他价值的本身并不是诊所法律教育教学目标所应当达到的，如果把其他价值也强加给诊所法律教育的教学目标，诊所法律教育的教学目标就承受不了这一重任，当然也不能实现相应的教学目的。通过上述两个概念的分析可知为什么对诊所法律教育的教学目标表述不清，或者有的学者认为定位不准。究其根本原因，就是把诊所法律教育的教学目标和价值混为一谈。

尽管中美两国的法律制度、文化背景、价值观念和教育理念各不相同，但源于美国的诊所法律教育模式自 2000 年开始在中国高校中相继开展，且呈迅速上升态势。然而一部分高校在诊所法律教育本土化的过程中教学目标定位不准或者目标过高过大，严重影响了诊所法律教育的顺利开展，我们要认真分析美国诊所法律教育的教学目标定位、产生背景和发展过程、价值观念和教育理念，也要结合中国国情和各自高校的具体情况来如何确定各校诊所法律教育的具体目标，同时还要考虑诊所法律教育的目标的多元化，即诊所法律教育的初始目标、教育本质、阶段

---

[1] 章武生等：《司法现代化与民事诉讼的构建》，法律出版社 2000 年版，第 31 页。

性以及中国法学教育的培养目标来分解、细化各自高校的诊所法律教育目标。只有这样，我们的诊所法律教育的教学目标才能符合不同类型高校的实际情况，才能把诊所法律教育的博大精深理念根植于中国的法学教育土壤之中。

法律诊所教育的新发展

——以社会管理创新为视角

谢雄伟　华秋英*

摘　要： 高校法学院作为天然的法律人储备库，应充分利用高校法律诊所让法学院学生参与到社会管理中，使之成为政府购买法律服务的对象。除了完善学校法律诊所与政府法律援助机构的关系，切实保证学校法律诊所真正参与社会法律援助工作外，还要不断扩大法律诊所教育实践的范围，在参与社会管理的同时实现培养法学学生法律实践技能和社会正义感的教学目的，以期在未来高校法学院的教育能与社会法律需求真正链接起来。

关键词： 法律诊所教育　社会管理　社会管理创新

一、我国法律诊所教育的现状与困境

法律诊所教育，是指在法学院建立法律诊所，教师指导学生在法律诊所中为当事人提供法律咨询，诊断案件所涉及的法律问题，提出解决问题的法律对策，进而为当事人提供法律服务，在司法实践中学习和掌握法律实务技能的一种法律教育模式。诊所式法律教育借鉴了医学院学生在医疗诊所临床实习的做法，倡导在实践和经验中学习法律和律师的执业经验及基本技能。

诊所式法律教育起源于美国。目前，诊所式法律教育在美国得到长足发展，美国律师协会认可的法学院均被要求必须开设诊所法律课程。美国在不断发展国内法律诊所教育的同时，也积极向全世界推广诊所式

---

* 谢雄伟，广东商学院法学院副教授，法律诊所教育中心主任。华秋英，广东商学院法学院2011级诉讼法研究生。

法律教育。我国于2000年引进诊所式法律教育模式。我国自恢复法学教育以来，法学教育就是以课堂教学为纲，以闭卷考试为目，学生难以克服被动性、消极性和应付性。[1] 为顺应现实的需要，我国的法律教育既要重视理论讲授，又要重视实践应用。在此种背景下，2000年，清华大学法学院、北京大学法学院、中国人民大学法学院、中南财经政法大学法学院、华东政法学院、西北政法大学和复旦大学法学院在美国福特基金会的大力支持下，首批开设了法律诊所教育课程，拉开了法律诊所教育在中国的发展帷幕。至今，已有114个高校成为诊所法律教育研究会成员。

在我国的法律诊所教育实践中，结合我国的本土情况，各地的法律诊所利用自身的特点用不同的方式来组建法律诊所。清华大学最初的法律诊所是与北京市海淀区消费者权益保护协会共同设立的"调节诊所"；中山大学则充分利用广东外来工集中的优势，开设以劳动法为主的诊所，为以外来工为主的弱势群体提供免费的法律服务。[2] 向弱势群体提供法律援助既是诊所法律教育中通常采用的路径，同时也为社会的纠纷解决提供了一定的帮助。

在理论上，越来越多的学者认识到法律诊所教育的先进性，并致力于研究诊所法律教育的本土化。"可以说诊所法律教育是新世纪中国法学教育的一项重大改革，是国外先进教学模式与中国法律教育实际有机结合的成功尝试，必将对中国高级法律人才的培养产生重要的影响。"[3] 然而在事实上，国内很多本科院校将开设法律诊所式教育定位于检验学生本科阶段理论知识成绩的工具，更多的情况下只是作为理论教学的一种

---

[1] 蔡彦敏："找寻法律诊所教育与中国法学教育契合之路"，载中国法学会法学教育研究会诊所法律教育专业委员会、中国人民大学法学院法律诊所编：《中国诊所法律教育论坛论文集》，中国人民大学出版社2003年版，第50页。

[2] 罗剑雯："诊所式法律教育之功能分析"，载刘星主编：《中山大学法律评论》，法律出版社2005年版，第221页。

[3] 甄贞："中国诊所法律教育的现状与未来"，载《教育部高等学校法学学科教育指导委员会中国法学会法年学教育研究会2007年年会暨中国法学教育论坛论文集》，2007年，第121页。

辅助手段，教育活动开展不充分，且学习时数有限，不能满足全体学生提高实践能力的需求，效果也不明显。[1] 总体来说，现阶段法律诊所教育的最大问题是法律诊所教育的经费问题、法律诊所的案源问题。

（一）法律诊所教育的经费问题

相对于传统的教学方法来说，法律诊所教育是一种比较昂贵的教育模式。以讲授为主的教学模式，一般有上课场所和小型专业图书馆就可以维持教学，但是法律诊所教育需要投入相当大的经费，这些经费主要包括诊所设备费用、办公支出和诊所日常工作管理人员的报酬。[2] 相对于传统课堂讲授形式，法律诊所教育的开展无疑需要更多的人力、物力和财力。首先，在师资力量上，法律诊所教育需要更高的师生比例，也就是需要更多的师资力量。因为每个老师能够指导的学生数量有限，不可能像课堂讲授那样教很多人。其次，法律诊所教育的开展需要专门的办公场所、办公费用和管理费用等。法律诊所提供的法律服务通常是免费的，不仅不能通过援助获得经济补偿，而且实践费用也要诊所自己承担。

法律诊所教育进入我国得益于福特基金会的大力支持，开展得比较好的高校绝大多数也是依赖福特基金会的大力资助。但从2008年起，福特基金会将不再向高校投入用于法律诊所教育的资金，仅提供少量支持中国诊所法律教育委员会运作的有限资金。因此，法律诊所教育经费短缺的问题立即凸现，对我国法律诊所教育的开展产生了一定的影响。[3] 发展法律诊所教育，仅仅依靠外国的资助绝不是长久之计。虽然某些高校的法律诊所教育试点创造的社会价值有利于吸收社会资助，但是这种试点非常有限，体现的价值体有限，难以得到社会资助。法律诊所教育

---

[1] 姜素红："法律诊所教学方法初探"，载《湖南师范大学教育科学学报》2005年第11期。

[2] 韩桂君："诊所法律教育模式研究"，载吴汉东主编：《中南财经政法大学教育思想观念大讨论论文荟萃》，北京大学出版社2006年版，第196页。

[3] 李正新："试论法学教育的'临床'培养——诊所法律教育本土化困境及其应对"，载《教育法制》2012年第2期。

的发展需要经费的投入，没有经费的投入，将导致法律诊所教育在中国夭折或畸形。

（二）法律诊所的案源问题

诊所式法律教育的目的在于让学生通过办理真实案件与解决法律实务来锻炼法律实践技能以及培养社会责任感和正义感。但是在校学生缺乏法律执业经验，大多数当事人对学生存在不信任感，一般不愿意将案件交给学生办理。加之我国现阶段的法制环境不甚理想以及不当干扰、异地办案成本高等多种因素的影响，国内法律诊所的案源范围受指导老师的专业优势和法律院系的优势限制很大，法律诊所教育对案件的需求不可能得到很好的满足，且往往缺口很大。没有真实案件，就无法实现诊所教育的初衷。❶

二、社会管理创新与政府购买社会法律服务

（一）社会管理创新

社会管理创新，是指围绕实现社会管理新目标、新任务，运用现有的各种资源和力量，以先进的、有效的社会管理理念、方法、手段、体制、机制等，对陈旧、落后、不合时宜的管理模式、方式、方法进行改造、改进、改革，构建适应形势发展变化的社会管理框架、机制和制度的行为及过程。其中，所谓的“创新”是指，社会管理工作必须要实现与时俱进、大胆探索，在正确把握国内外形势的各种新变化、新特点的基础上，重点针对社会管理中存在的各种重点难点问题，研究探索加强和改进社会管理的思路和有效举措。❷ 著名法理学家葛洪义认为，社会管理创新的关键是改变国家垄断社会管理的体制，转变为国家与社会分工负责、共同管理的体制；社会管理创新的核心是发挥社会成员的积极

---

❶ 刘加良、刘晓更、米金玲：“法律诊所教育研究”，载《山东大学法律评论》2007年。

❷ 林淼锋：“我国社会管理创新的重点及对策研究”，中国社会科学院研究生院2011硕士学位论文。

作用，提高社会自身的自我管理能力。[1] 我国党和中央政府顺应时代的要求，正在积极推进全社会管理创新。

2011年2月19日，中国省部级主要领导干部社会管理及其创新专题研讨班开班式在中央党校举行，胡锦涛在此次讲话中强调要加强和创新社会管理。胡锦涛在讲话中指出："加强和创新社会管理，是继续抓住和用好我国发展重要战略机遇期、推进党和国家事业的必然要求，是构建社会主义和谐社会的必然要求。"同时，他提出："加强和创新社会管理，就要紧紧围绕全面建设小康社会的总目标，牢牢把握最大限度激发社会活力、最大限度增加和谐因素、最大限度减少不和谐因素的总要求，以解决影响社会和谐稳定突出问题为突破口，提高社会管理科学化水平。"

顺应《中共中央国务院关于加强和创新社会管理的意见》，2011年11月，中央组织部、中央政法委、民政部等18个部门和组织联合发布了《关于加强社会工作专业人才队伍建设的意见》，该意见贯彻和落实了中央加强和创新社会管理的精神。该意见强调，在社会工作专业岗位开发和专业人才使用方面，要积极发展民办社会工作服务机构，通过政府购买等方式引导和鼓励公益慈善类社会组织和民办非企业吸纳社会工作专业人才；各级政府要将应由政府负担的社会工作专业人才队伍建设经费纳入财政预算，加大财政投入；研究制定政府购买社会工作服务政策，引入竞争机制，规范购买程序，完善购买方式，建立综合绩效评价机制。实践中，在加强和创新社会管理的政策下，我国各地方政府不断探索创新社会管理的方式，鼓励社会组织如工会、青年团、妇联、残联等协助人民政府开展各项社会工作。

（二）政府购买社会法律服务

政府购买社会组织服务是指"政府将原来直接提供的公共服务事项，通过直接拨款或公开招标方式，交给有资质的社会服务机构来完成，最后根据择定者或者中标者所提供的公共服务的数量和质量来支付服务费

[1] 葛洪义："社会管理创新与法律方法"，载《法学》2011年第10期。

用”[1]。政府购买社会组织服务，与加强和创新社会管理相契合，与党中央、各部门的政策相契合，更与建设和谐社会相契合。

社会法律服务，包括法律援助、法律宣传等，都是政府的职责。而我国正处于社会急速转型期，社会问题很多，且表现得集中和复杂，导致我国法律服务的社会需求极其强烈，政府提供的服务根本不能满足其需求。[2] 因此，为了创新社会管理，政府就应该购买社会法律服务，既实现社会的自我管理，又解决社会法律服务需求。根据《关于加强社会工作专业人才队伍建设的意见》的规定，政府在创新社会管理的相关措施中可以购买的社会组织服务范围非常广泛，包括社会救助、社区建设、精神卫生、残障康复、教育辅导、就业援助、职工帮扶、犯罪预防、禁毒戒毒、矫治帮教、人口计生、纠纷调解、应急处置等领域。其中，犯罪预防、矫治帮教、纠纷调解等都关系法律服务，在这些相关领域都有政府购买、社会提供的空间。可见，在以上众多领域，法律服务是重要的组成部分。

对社会组织和政府而言，政府购买社会组织服务有助于社区社会组织的发育，社会组织的发展有助于实现社会管理创新，这是一个双赢的格局。政府购买社会法律服务是政府购买社会组织服务中的一类，是创新社会管理的一项具体措施。政府购买社会法律服务将使法律服务的主体多元化，进一步满足社会的法律服务需求，并有效实现政府职能的转变。

三、法律诊所教育在社会管理创新下的新发展

诊所式法律教育模式对于教师和学生来说都是一种新的尝试与挑战，在社会管理创新下，应大胆地将法律诊所教育模式与社会管理创新结合起来。笔者认为，我国学校法律诊所未来的发展应该：首先，完善学校

---

[1] 王浦劬·萨拉蒙：《政府向社会组织购买公共服务研究——中国与全球经验分析》，北京大学出版社2010年版，第3～4页。

[2] 蔡彦敏：“诊所法律教育在中国制度化建设中亟待解决的问题”，载《环球法律评论》2005年第3期。

法律诊所与政府法律援助机构的关系；其次，扩大高校法律诊所参与社会管理的范围，政府在更多领域向高校法律诊所购买法律服务。

（一）完善学校法律诊所与政府法律援助的关系

中国的法学院引入诊所法律教育以后，马上就和法律援助结合在一起，诊所法律教育中所需的案件大量来自法律援助中心。现今的法律诊所大多与政府法律援助中心合作，法律援助中心提供案源给法律诊所。除此之外，也有法律援助中心接收适量的法学院学生，学生在法律援助中心接受实践训练。法律援助让诊所学生置身于现实的社会中把握法律与社会的关系，法学院师生则为法律援助作出贡献。

但是，要保证学生实质性参与真实案例的处理，真正发挥其为社会提供法律援助的功能，就应当完善学校与政府法律援助中心的合作方式。

首先，政府应当为法律诊所提供法律服务创造必要的前提条件。政府社会管理创新的一项重要内容就是发动更多的社会力量参与到社会管理中来，以将部分政府职能分担给社会成员和组织。利用高校的法学院来分担部分法律援助工作，无疑是符合社会管理创新理念的。在政府购买社会法律服务的理念下，政府应有相应的财政预算投放到购买法律诊所的法律援助服务中。

中央组织部、中央政法委、民政部等 18 个部门和组织联合发布的《关于加强社会工作专业人才队伍建设的意见》中就规定：各级政府要将应由政府负担的社会工作专业人才队伍建设经费纳入财政预算，加大财政投入。广东省制定和发布的《关于加强社会工作人才队伍建设的实施意见》进一步贯彻和落实了中央的精神，该实施意见规定“建立公共财政支持体系。加大财政支持力度，合理界定政府购买社会服务范围，建立以政府购买服务为主要形式的财政支持社会工作发展机制。鼓励引导社会资金对社会工作的投入和支持”，“建立合理的薪酬保障机制。以体现专业人才价值为导向，建立健全社会工作人才薪酬保障机制”。

按照政府的相关政策，由政府提供一定的资金给高校法学院用以建设法律诊所，这部分资金可以解决学生的实践经费和法律诊所指导老师的指导报酬；而高校法律诊所分担了政府的法律援助义务。这种“政府购买—法律诊所提供—公民消费”的模式既可以解决高校法律诊所的经费问题和案源问题，促进高校法律诊所的发展，又可以实质性地分担政府法律援助工作，实现政府职能的转移，践行社会管理创新。

（二）法律诊所教育内容的新发展

政府购买社会法律服务的范围是广泛的，不仅仅局限于法律援助工作。根据广东省司法厅 2012 年 7 月 6 日发布的《2012 年省级政府向社会组织购买服务目录》显示，政府向社会组织购买的法律服务有法律援助类、人民调解类、社区矫正类等多种类型的法律相关服务。在政府购买法律诊所服务的同时，法律诊所成为社会建设的主体。我们应充分发挥法律诊所的优势，扩展诊所教育服务的社会范围，在更广泛的领域参与社会管理，这同时也是扩大法律诊所教育的范围。法律援助一般局限于学校这类比较小的范围，而要扩大法律诊所教育的范围，就应该鼓励学生深入社区、街道甚至农村讲授法律知识和运用法律为弱势群体提供法律服务，积极参与社区、街道和农村的普法工作等法律服务工作。广泛参与社会法律服务，能加深学生对法律知识的理解，训练学生利用法律解决实际问题的技能，培养学生作为未来法律工作者应具备的社会责任感和律师职业道德。

北京大学法学院为高校法律诊所深入社区广泛参与社会管理提供了一个很好的范例。北京大学法学院诊所于 2001 年开始与河北迁西县开展合作，成立了北大—迁西社区法律诊所，开始尝试乡村社区法律诊所项目。该诊所参与了基层社会制度的构建和完善、依法治理社区的计划和实施、完善乡村社会的社会治理结构。学生在其中的具体工作包括参与广义的社区立法、行政执法、纠纷的解决、法制教育、法律宣传等。学生在这些工作过程中不仅加深了对法律的理解，培养了解决问题的法律技能和社会正义感，还为该地方的社会管理和建设作出了相当的贡献。

广东省广州市已出台《加快街道家庭综合服务中心建设的实施办法》，该办法要求广州市所有街道都要开展家庭综合服务中心建设，这些家庭综合服务中心以家庭、青少年、长者等重点群体的服务为核心。在此契机下，法律诊所也完全可以参与其中，提供相关的法律服务，成为提供服务的一个主体。

可见，法律作为面向社会的一门科学，法律诊所扩大教育范围、参与社会管理创新的形式可以是多种多样的。根据高校法律诊所的特点，结合相关的政策和实践经验，笔者认为法律诊所可以作为教学范围并成为政府购买对象的范围主要包括政策法规宣传工作、人民调解工作、社区矫正工作、法律咨询工作、安置帮教工作等。以上内容不仅与法学教育结合紧密，是社会实践性很强的法学教育内容，而且在专门老师的指导下在校法学院学生完全可以胜任。

浅析法律诊所的定位与发展若干问题

于连平*

摘　要：法学是社会实践科学，是理论与实践的结合体。法律的生命在于经验而非逻辑。法律经验来源于实践而非理论。法律诊所是高校法科学生在律师或教师指导下参与办理实际案件的平台。法律诊所应当与法学教育现代化、国家法律改革、法律职业伦理、人权问题、法律援助、社会民间机构发展等问题相互促进与影响。

关键词：诊所　法律教育　目标定位　法律改革　法律援助

诊所法律教育（Clinical Legal Education）是一种产生于美国的法学教育模式，在不到半个世纪的时间里风靡世界不同法系、不同发展类型的国家。除欧洲、澳洲等发达国家和地区之外，拉美、非洲和南亚等地的法学院系也积极引进诊所法律教育，并创造了法律援助诊所、刑事辩护诊所、劳动法律诊所、社区法律诊所以及服务于弱势群体的妇女和儿童权利诊所等多种形式，在有些国家，诊所法律教育甚至已经成为国家法治进程中不可缺少的组成部分。受其影响，2000 年 9 月北京大学、清华大学等 7 所院校同时开设了法律诊所课程，标志着诊所法律教育模式正式移植到我国。

中国高校的法律诊所经过 12 年的发展，数量不断增多，而且与法学教育改革、法律援助、弱势群体保护等社会控制与管理问题不断融合。但是不能否认，学界对于法律诊所的定位与发展等问题还没有形成一个明确的权威共识，各高校的法律诊所还游离于学界主流之外，虽然中国

---

* 于连平，东北农业大学法学院副教授。

教育部推出的“卓越法律人才”培养计划包含对法律诊所实践教学形式的肯定，但是对法律诊所运行与发展所必需的环境与条件并没有给予充分的重视与建设。笔者是从事法律诊所教育多年的高校教师，尝试对于法律诊所运行发展的相关问题进行探究，以期学界与社会对高校法律诊所的发展给予更多的关注与支持。

一、法律诊所的目标定位

法学作为一门社会实践科学，是理论与实践的结合体，具有极其鲜明的实践性特点。法学起源于实践，庞德说过：法律的生命在于经验而非逻辑。而经验又从何而来呢？是从纸上谈兵而来吗？书籍当然也是我们获得知识的很重要的途径，但知识不等于经验，知识远没有经验来得更生动与深刻。

美国学者给法律诊所的定义是：在律师或法学教师的指导下，学生在从事实际办案的过程中，学习如何处理人际关系即会晤、辩论、谈判的能力及职业伦理观念的教学模式。借鉴国外的经验，笔者认为高校的法律诊所应当定位于发展学生的实践技能与职业伦理，前者满足学生的现实需求，后者着眼于法律人才市场的需求。

为了实现民主、自由和对人权基本尊重的新社会理念，尝试培养新一代法律人的思想价值规范。这些新的理念与传统的观念立刻形成鲜明对比，既体现在社会价值观念层面，也体现在法学专业教育层面，市场经济改革形成的现实传统观念普遍倾向于个人物质上取得成功的激励，其他观念实际上成为仪式性的蛊惑人心的噪音（多数人的实际想法）。在法律诊所中，这个问题直接关系到学生学习法律的目标与动机。在诊所发展的最初阶段，在诊所经费的赞助商、领导、教师与学生的不断摸索与沟通中逐步确立教学目标与社会目标，教学目标为培养学生的实践能力与职业伦理价值观，社会目标为援助社会弱势群体。

二、法律诊所与法律改革

法律诊所的真正目标隐藏在我国法律改革过程中对于高等法学教育

作用的正确认识之中。传统上，诊所教师也分为“保守派”与“改革派”。前者基本遵守现有法律制度的需要，以“市场经济”为导向，实现大学作为“律师生产基地”的功能，这些大学里制造出来的青年律师能够适应现有的制度、程序、规则以及行为惯例，能够成功融入国家的现有法制体系。后者则倾向于把未来的青年律师培养成社会变革的积极参与者与发起者，即将律师培养为“社会工程师”，实际上，它包括多个层次的转变：实践层次为法律规则适用的转变，制度层次为实体规则与程序规定的转变，系统层次为价值观、愿望与目标的转变。后者往往出于现代法律制度的理解与需要，重新考虑法律与律师在现代社会中发挥的作用。但是关于法律与社会、关于法律改革的争论还没有在专业学术团体中广泛展开，教师与学生对于人文社会科学成果关注不够，人权、自由、民主、正义的概念如何准确界定？对此，律师更多地表现出悲观情绪与玩世不恭的态度，法律改革被认为是纯粹工具性决定，只是一些机构的名称、结构与职权的变化。法律诊所应当成为这样一个地方：学生与教师从实际案件材料中发现法律执行问题、法律制度问题与法律体系问题，讨论法律改革的目标与法律改革的结果，在现行法律改革运动的基础观念中更多体现着实用主义的观念，法律改革运动中没有理想主义的观念是不可能成功的，而青年学生法律改革观念的培养可以从法律诊所的学习中开始。

三、法律诊所与教育现代化

法律诊所提供了新的教育技术手段。现行的法学院必须利用创新的教育技术手段，法律诊所就是在这种情形下出现的，正如在社会经济活动的其他领域创新发展对于传统治理体制的代替，谁来决定教育的变革？国家、专业人士、大学、学生、社会？谁以及如何来配置资源？创新活动的发起者有多大的自由空间？相对独立的法律诊所教育规划与这些问题密切相关。每一个法律诊所都以自己的方式回答了上述问题，例如，法律诊所的学习成果与学院教育的总结果之间的关系，发现法学教育目前的水平高低、专业性、合法性以及教育措施。实际上，在法律诊所中，学生与诊所指导教师可以发现和体会到现行法学教育体制与律师培养制度的重大缺陷，很难说法律诊所可以有效地弥补现行法学教育制度的所有不足，但是法律诊所肯定可以成为社会讨论与关注法学教育改革的催化剂，在法学教育改革的氛围中探讨现行教育制度改革的目标、内容以及方法问题，因此，与其说法律诊所是教育现代化的一个产品，不如说法律诊所是法学教育现代化思想的实验孵化器与未来法律人才的培训基地。

四、法律诊所与职业价值观

由于学生办理案件过程中要面对社会中利益冲突的极端化案例，法律诊所的学生之间以及学生与老师之间经常谈论生命的意义、法律专业的意义这类问题。上述问题的内涵广泛，很难直接准确概括出学生能够认可并效仿的行为规则，实际上可以变换一个角度来间接回答上述问题，例如：律师的作用是什么？律师为谁服务？国家、业务、司法部还是社会？律师的服务宗旨是什么？解决纠纷、胜诉还是追求善良与正义？律师是谁？是善良与正义的实现者，还是追逐个人名利的野心家？

法律诊所的教师应当帮助学生在实践的反思中获得经验，引导学生考虑法律界目前与未来的发展状况与专业要求，使其适应法学未来发展并养成正确的行为规范与价值观念。法律诊所的指导教师应当是具有优秀人格的专业人士，应当是诊所学生行为规范与价值观念模仿的榜样。目前，我们的法学教育的一个严重弊端是学生缺乏行为模式模仿的象征性人物，学生见到的法律体系中的很多法律人士（法官、检察官、律师、商业律师等）都在批评其他同行，似乎批评是使他人接受自己意见的最有效方法。在这种情形下，似乎法律诊所应该形成生产“好律师”的标准模式，但这样做是危险的，可能以丧失学生多样化成长空间为代价。实际上，法律诊所应当是学生通过实际案例反思获得法律经验的场所，诊所教师的人格很重要，他应当避免诱惑，避免学生成为自己的复制品，应当发动和鼓励学生挑战和击败自己，在诊所办理的实际案例中展示这种人格美德，不仅完成法律技能与就业知识的准备，而且注重学生价值观念的引导与塑造。

五、法律诊所与人权问题

法律诊所经常面临各类侵犯人权与保护人权的案例，同时，在法律诊所里学生是准律师与人权捍卫者，外界也称法律诊所是“准人权保护机构”（暗示法律诊所可以通过诉诸法律的范式实现人权保护），也可以按照保护人权的不同种类来划分法律诊所的类别，但是在学术界，对于人权的多样性定义普遍存在于大学的教科书之中，也存在于现实法律活动之中。将人权纳入法学教育的内容、方法与机构中是最近几十年的重大创新，法律诊所可以说是一个探讨人权保护的极好平台。例如，在人权保护的整体规划中，在维权案件的具体工作进程中，在维权案件的工作分析中，均可以讨论人权保护问题。人权是否属于法律教育的核心内容？人权是否属于律师手中的一个工具？是否属于新信仰与绝对价值的综合？或者这些价值不是绝对的，但在不同的文化中有什么不同？什么是歧视人权行为？国际法律中的基本人权（宪法性权利）的具体内容是什么？人权与宪政、法治、民主政治的关系如何？其对于执业律师的工作会产生什么影响？很显然，这些问题的答案取决于对国家法律与律师作用的深入了解，而且，这些问题严肃而意义重大，对人权问题的深入思考有助于学生明确职业目标、认同职业价值观念，因此，法律诊所引导学生对于人权问题进行讨论与思考是值得花费一些时间的。最后，法律诊所在各个大学会形成与本组织文化协调的不同样本，包含人权思想的教学内容与方法，妥善处理伙伴关系、职业关系、相互尊重关系及权利秩序都应当成为法律诊所的一系列特征，但是目前大多数高校仍然是家长式的独裁氛围，人权只不过是有经验教师具有讽刺意味的微笑而已。

六、法律诊所与法律援助

法律诊所的现实社会目的是对公民、组织或地方社区提供法律援助。法律诊所可以与律师、国家法律援助中心以及人权非营利组织进行合作，法律诊所还没有建立相关的社会经济机制，可以帮助学生看到获得司法保护的方方面面的现实情况。法律诊所不能只是帮助有法律援助需要的人员，这些人和这些事每天都会出现，要引导学生看到产生这些问题的根源，激发学生提出对现有法律规则与程序的改革建议。其还可以更进一步引导学生了解，法律诊所的战略目标是以实现社会公正为重点目标，当然这是就法律诊所的整体目标而言，但这与学生的价值观念是相通的。在诉诸法律后应当具有什么样的战略眼光？如何查找法律规范？正义原则的基础是什么？如何设定目标以确保获得法律保护，或者确保解决问题以及取得利益平衡（包括利用解决冲突的替代方法）？与大学生探讨这些问题不是希望可以立即解决所有问题，而是在讨论问题的过程中，要学生在头脑中对这些问题留下深刻印象，不仅仅留下对穷人的悲惨记忆以及同情，或者对法律制度不能处理的无能为力的感慨，而是希望他们能够在未来工作中推动制定或实施确保公正的有效法律制度。

七、法律诊所与民间机构

法律诊所实际上属于社会民间机构的代表或有机组成部分。首先，法律诊所可以提供给学生一个团队工作的环境平台，并积累自我管理的工作经验，在解决社会问题与道德困境中借助学生律师的职业经验与个人经验影响并提高公民的法律素质。在学生之间、学生与诊所教师之间以及学生与诊所客户之间体现与强化社会民间机构成员的基本价值观念：信任、团结与合作。

法律诊所实际上也可以发展成为狭义的专门从事公益活动的民间机构，例如成为专门从事法律援助的非营利组织。有条件的法律诊所也可以改革并从事律师培训工作，这样做不是为了政府机关，也不是为了商业目标，而是为了民间机构力量的发展。很显然，实现这个想法有些困难，需要政府司法行政相关部门的支持，而法律诊所与政府司法行政部门的沟通实际上非常困难，但是诊所教师与学生的沟通是畅通的，可以谨慎地尝试公民权益保护，为今后专门从事公益法律服务积累一些经验。学生会因职业发展的不确定而缺乏动力与热情，因此，法律诊所应当增加学习动机方面的解说。一些法律诊所认为对诊所学生进行法律职业技能培训实际上是现有法律制度框架下的折中选择，律师作为社会民间机构中最活跃的成员，诊所学生是未来律师精英的主要来源，随着社会民间机构的发展，法律诊所会根据法律的框架和社会需求不断修正自己的发展方向，帮助学生为未来的执业需要做好准备。法律诊所教育教给学生的不应只是一些律师的法律适用技能，应有一个更高的目标，即帮助学生成为一个负责任的人，在社会活动中正确行使权利，推动国家法律改革，保护社会公众利益。

法律诊所与法学教育作为一个整体，已经取得许多高校的共识。今天我们对于法律诊所的定位与发展问题应当作出共识性的选择，尽管还有许多困难和外部约束，但笔者相信，在法律诊所定位与发展问题的选择方面，我们是自由的。

诊所法律教育价值论*

齐喜三**

摘　要： 根源于美国的诊所法律教育10年前已漂洋过海，在我国部分高校进行得如火如荼。我国是否可以移植这种模式，首先考虑的是诊所法律教育的价值所在。研究诊所法律教育的价值必须遵循价值的基本原理，要融合法律价值和教育价值的范畴，同时要突出诊所法律教育的特征。基于微观而言，诊所法律教育的价值包括内在价值和外化价值。内在价值最主要的方面是教育价值，这是其核心价值，具体包括学习和继续学习的价值、思维价值、创新价值、职业道德价值。诊所法律教育在具体的实践中，通过办案为社会提供法律服务和促进社会公平正义观念的树立，从而体现法律援助和推动法治进程的外化价值。

关键词： 教育模式　诊所法律教育　教育价值　社会价值

诊所法律教育在中国走过了10年历程，全国已有100余所院校成为中国诊所法律教育委员会的会员单位。尽管如此，对诊所法律教育在中国的开展有相当一部分学者自始至终持有不同的意见，甚至在个别阶段质疑之声呈上升之势。鉴于此，深入研究和再认识诊所法律教育的价值就显得尤为必要和重要。笔者在认真学习诊所法律教育的理念的基础上，借鉴国内外诊所法律教育的研究成果，结合自己在国内从事诊所法律教

---

* 基金项目：中国诊所法律教育委员会2008年度基金项目"诊所法律教育筹资问题研究"（CCCLE08012）的阶段性成果之一。

** 齐喜三，南阳理工学院文法学院副教授、副院长，研究方向：民法和法学教育。

育8年的经验和体会，对诊所法律教育的价值进行了剖析和甄别，以期对研究诊所法律教育之士有所裨益。

一、诊所法律教育价值的基本概念

（一）价值的界定

“价值”这个概念有多种用法。在日常生活中，价值是指一种事物对人的意义或有用性。在经济学上，价值是与使用价值相对而言的，是指凝结在商品中的无差别的人类劳动，即商品的劳动价值。在哲学上，价值是与事实相对应的概念，一般认为是由英国哲学家休谟最早研究的。休谟把人的知识区分为“事实的知识”和“价值的知识”，认为前者回答的是“是什么”的问题，后者回答的是事物“怎么样”的问题，并认为人们对“事实”的研究在于追求“真”，对价值的研究则在于追求“善”和“美”。自19世纪兴起价值哲学以来，西方学者开始对价值问题进行大规模的研究，但并没有对价值形成统一的认识，有的人认为价值是一种客观存在；有的人则认为价值是一种主观追求，是一种应然的东西，不具有什么现实性。❶

马克思主义经典作家并没有对价值下一个完整的定义，但在有关的文献中论述到价值问题。在《评阿·瓦格纳的“政治经济学教科书”》中，马克思指出：“‘价值’这个普遍的概念是从人们对待满足他们需要的外界物的关系中产生的……”❷ 这句话为我们认识把握价值概念指出了方向。马克思在此强调，完备的价值概念既不单纯地来源于外界物，也不单纯地来源于人，而是人和外界物相互影响、相互作用的产物。马克思的这段话揭示了这样的思想：价值的形成必须具备人、外界物和二者的关系这三个基本要素。价值本身包含两层含义：其一，价值是一个表征关系的范畴，它反映的是人（主体）与外界物——自然、社会（客

---

❶ 魏胜强、张玫瑰：《社会主义法治理念解读》，河南人民出版社2008年版，第149页。

❷ 马克思：“评阿·瓦格纳的‘政治经济学教科书’”，参见《马克思恩格斯全集》（第19卷），人民出版社1963年版，第406页。

体）的关系，揭示的是人的实践活动的动机和目的。其二，价值又是一个表征意义的范畴，是用以表示事物所具有的对主体有意义的、可以满足主体需要的功能和属性的概念。在人类的实践中，凡是对人有用、有利、有益，能满足人的某种需要，有助于实现人的目标的东西（实体或精神）就是有价值的，就会得到人们的肯定性评价，反之，则称为否定性评价。总之，从最一般意义上，可以把价值（Value）与善（Good）视为两个大体一致的概念。[1]

通过上述经典著作的考察我们不难发现：价值是一定历史条件下人与外界物关系的范畴，是人们在认识和改造世界的过程中形成的反映客体满足主体需要的一种特殊关系，是主体客体化和客体主体化的统一，它表明了客观对象本身具有的属性对人的需要所发生的效果或作用。可见，价值是客体与主体互动的结果，是由主体向客体提出要求，由客体的属性满足这种要求所产生的主客体关系。

（二）法律价值释义[2]

法律的价值也具有上述一般意义上的价值的两重性质。它一方面体现了作为主体的人与作为客体的法之间需要和满足的对应关系，即法律价值关系；另一方面又体现了法所具有的对主体有意义的、可以满足主体需要的功能和属性。根据价值的一般原理和马克思主义的价值观，我们可以把法律价值界定为：在人（主体）与法（客体）的关系中体现出来的法的积极意义或有用性。

“法律价值”这一术语通常因三种不同的使用方式而有所不同。第一，“目的价值”。“目的价值”是指法律在发挥社会作用的过程中能够保护和增加的价值。这主要是从法律发挥作用的目的出发来考虑法律所追求的理想和目的。第二，“评价标准价值”。“评价标准价值”是指从评价标准角度来研究法律价值。第三，“形式价值”。“形式价值”是指法律自身应当具有的值得追求的品质和属性。在哲学意义上，“评价标准价值”

---

[1] 张文显：《马克思主义法理学——理论、方法和前沿》，高等教育出版社2003年版，第220～221页。

[2] 同上书，第222～225页。

和“形式价值”都是以“目的价值”为基础和原点。因为法律的“目的价值”构成了法律制度所追求的社会目的，反映了法律创制和实施的宗旨，它是关于社会关系的理想状态是什么的权威性蓝图，也是关于权利义务的分配格局应当怎样的权威性宣告。此三种价值有时难以区分，常常交织在一起。相对而言，“目的价值”总是居于主导地位，“评价标准价值”和“形式价值”都是为一定的“目的价值”服务。

（三）教育价值观

教育价值仍然遵循哲学意义上的价值的一般属性，是一个表征关系和表征意义的范畴。

在教育价值概念上，人们普遍认为，教育价值是指作为客体的教育现象的属性与作为社会实践主体的人的需要之间的一种特定的关系，对这种关系的不同认识和评价就构成了人的教育价值观。教育价值在本质上反映的是一种积极的、向上的、肯定的、好的方面的含义，也就是说，研究探讨教育价值，就是在“真”的基础上去追求教育中的“善”与“美”，使人们在教育实践中通过改造教育客体最大限度地满足主体的需要。尽管在教育研究过程中可能要分析某些负面价值或消极价值，但其宗旨在于揭示人们积极的价值意向活动规律，从而使人们对教育价值有一个比较清醒的认识，并在教育实践中自觉地维护教育价值，坚持不懈地追求美好的教育价值。

（四）诊所法律教育的价值

要考量诊所法律教育的价值，必须要把哲学意义上的价值概念应用到诊所法律教育中，同时要注重尊重教育学上的价值观念，要适当考虑法律价值的作用。作为诊所法律教育主体的教师和学生同作为诊所法律教育客体的诊所教育活动之间进行相互作用的过程中，不仅在主体与客体之间形成一定的关系，而且使诊所教育活动更趋向主体、接近主体，为主体的需要及其发展服务，形成一定的价值关系。由此，诊所法律教育的价值可以界定为：诊所法律教育价值是诊所法律教育主体依其内在要求促使诊所法律教育适合、满足和服务于诊所主体的教育目的和需要的一种关系。诊所法律教育主体、客体相互作用的结果是，在这个相互作用的过程中，诊所法律教育主体把自己的教育需求外化为客观存在的东西，诊所教育则把自己的属性和功能内化为诊所法律教育主体享用的东西，从而形成一种特定的需要与满足的关系。[1]

从微观角度考察，诊所法律教育究竟包含什么样的价值呢？诊所法律教育的价值包括内在价值和外化价值。内在价值最主要的方面是教育价值，这是其核心价值，具体包括学习和继续学习的价值、思维价值、承担责任价值、创新价值；外化价值主要指的是社会价值，具体包括提供法律援助和推动法治进程价值。

二、诊所法律教育的核心价值：教育价值

诊所法律教育本质上是一种教育方法或者教育模式。诊所法律教育的对象是人，其最深层次的目的就是提高、发展人的素质。人的自身素质的提高、发展主要是通过教育来实现的，离开了人自身的发展，教育就无从反映和促进社会的发展，教育本身也就不复存在了。因此，诊所法律教育的价值必须以人为本、以知识为本和以社会为本。[2] 所以，诊所法律教育的内在价值主要是教育价值。教育价值主要包括以下几个方面。

（一）学习和继续学习的价值

诊所法律教育涉及如何接待当事人、如何提供法律咨询、如何谈判、如何起草法律文书、如何调查取证、如何进行庭前准备、如何出庭代理、如何解决职业道德困惑等内容，通过这些主题的训练，使学生在经验中学习律师执业技巧和职业道德。学生在训练、讨论、体验活动中，不仅学习了办案的经验和技巧、提高了职业能力，而且可以对已经学习过的法学理论进行加深和强化，对没有学习到的法律理论和知识进行钻研和研究。在这个反复进行的过程中，学生学习能力和继续学习能力有了明

---

[1] 章武生等：《司法现代化与民事诉讼的构建》，法律出版社2000年版，第31页。

[2] 王立民、牟逍媛：《诊所法律教育研究》，上海交通大学出版社2004年版，第71页。

显的增强，对传统法学理论的认识、理解和运用有了更加深刻的体会。同时，对学生本人而言，在今后法律理论的学习过程中会更好地运用诊所的方式进行，学习的效果会大大提高。通过这种互动性、反复性、过程性的学习活动，学生掌握了学习法律的方法和技巧，为今后的继续学习打下了坚实的基础。

（二）思维价值

诊所法律教育使用多种教学手段，培养学生的批判性思维能力。在课堂上，师生对问题解决的方案和途径进行分析、判断，按照不同的角色进行模拟，对解决问题的步骤、细节进行对比和汇总；在课下，学生要像律师一样思考问题并付诸行动，要考虑到当事人的全部利益和利益的最大化，收集对当事人有利的所有法律、法规，分析这些法律、法规之间有无冲突以及冲突的解决办法，面对具体的案例选择一个合理的方案并加以实施。在评价中，评价的方式方法也是一个反思性思维的过程。教师对学生的评价一般分为三种类型：日常评价、阶段性评价和期末评价。[1] 就日常评价而言，在初始阶段也叫制定计划阶段，主要评价计划的目的性、完整性、计划的假设与预测、计划的适用空间与弹性和计划的备选方案；在中期阶段也叫实施行动阶段，主要评价其行为是否达到目的及原因何在、行动的本身是否是最佳选择、行为是否有缺陷、有无补救方案或跟进计划及职业道德问题；在后期阶段也叫讨论与反思阶段，主要评价案件成败的原因及影响案件的因素、准备与预防在实践中的作用发挥得如何以及如何提高行动计划的质量等问题。[2] 美国 Mary Jo. Eyster 教授对思维价值的描述更精彩："教授学生通过反思性分析以及批判性思考从他们自己的体验和观察中学习知识，这是非常重要的……我认

---

[1] 李傲：《动教学法——诊所式法律教育》，法律出版社 2004 年版，第 104～108 页。

[2] 关于诊所法律教育的评价体系问题，可以分为对学生的评价、对诊所教师的评价、对诊所院校的评价，这里仅举例教师对学生的评价，其他内容可参见齐喜三："诊所法律教育评价体系如干问题研究"，载《环球法律评论》2005 年第 3 期，第 304 页。

为这个目标比起那些普遍表达的目标，例如律师技能、实体法或者审前程序等更加重要。”[1] 由此可以说，诊所法律教育的整个活动使诊所教师和学生始终处于一个不停的反思过程中。所以，诊所法律教育中反思性思维能力的培养是诊所法律教育价值的一大灵魂所在。

（三）创新价值

简单地说，创新就是产生某种新的东西，即人们从新的视角、以新的方式、用新的综合为他自己、为社会展现新世界，提示新理想。创新教育是通过教育这种社会有组织、有计划的活动形式，在教育活动过程中构建具有创造性、实践性的学生主体活动形式，通过学生主动参与、主动实践、主动思考、主动探索、主动创造，培养学生的创新意识，并有意识地将潜存于个体身上的无意识或潜意识的创新潜能引发出来，以自己的实践活动实现创新的思想，从而实现社会整体的创新行为，实现社会的知识创新、科技创新和制度创新等。诊所法律教育的创新价值表现在以下几个方面：

（1）教学方法的多样性。诊所法律教育的过程中采用提问式、辩论式、比较式、信息反馈式、大脑风暴式等方式使学生调度自己所掌握的信息，挖掘现有的知识，鼓励学生有勇气跳出一般实践标准；鼓励学生讨论做事的可选择方案，并对各种不同方案进行分析，对各种方案面临的障碍进行挖掘，分类归纳，正确对待，对不确定的事务作出决定等。[2]

（2）教学背景的真实性。诊所法律教育建立在真实的案件背景材料和真实的当事人基础之上。[3] 使用真实背景的意义在于：可以使学生从事物背景提供给他的各种信息中选择有用的东西、有特性的东西，有利于培养学生捕捉事物特点的能力；有背景的学习可以使学生提高发现问

---

[1] Mary Jo. Eyste：“教学法：大型校外诊所实习法律诊所的设计和教学”，原载 Clinical Law Review Spring，1999，转载杨欣欣：《法学教育与诊所式教学方法》，法律出版社 2002 年版，第 316～317 页。

[2] 王立民、牟逍媛：《诊所法律教育研究》，上海交通大学出版社 2004 年版，第 82 页。

[3] 甄贞：《诊所法律教育在中国》，法律出版社 2002 年版，第 7 页。

题、研究问题、分析问题、解决问题的能力；[1] 通过有背景的学习，可以使学生通过比较发现解决问题的最佳方案。

（3）思维方法的批判性。诊所法律教育始终要求诊所学生建立一种批判性的思维方法，从行动的计划到实际行动以及过程后的思考，都是培养一种思维能力和方式，这种思维能力的根本目的是要求学生在事务处理过程中选择更好、更有效的途径。同时，在诊所法律教育的过程中始终让学生有一种思维：通过对比和分析选择一种最佳方案，这个过程同样是一个创新过程。

（4）教学理念的开放性。创新教育的开放性就是在教育过程中始终把学生看作处于不断发展过程中的学习主体，看作一个身心两方面处在不断构建、升华过程中的人；始终把教学过程当作一个动态的、变化的、不断生成新质的过程。开放的教育过程需要创造一个高度自由的思维时间和实践空间，通过学习主体生动活泼、主动的自由活动，使其主体作用得以充分发挥。诊所法律教育的课堂上，所有同学和教师平等地围坐在一起共同完成教学任务，可以听到各种不同的声音；在个案指导中老师不限制学生的思维，不告诉学生现成的答案；在教学进程中可以根据案件的进展和学生的需求进行适当调整。同时，诊所法律教育始终强调学生的独立性、自主性和创造性，充分促进个人能力和素质的发展和张扬。诊所法律教育创设了一个让学生能积极主动参与教育教学过程，并乐于、敢于表现自己所知、所想、所能的民主氛围，以利于共同进行知识的发现、创造和分享的理念。

（四）职业道德价值[2]

公平、公正和正义是法律追求的最高价值，法律职业者应当具备特殊的职业伦理道德。在法律诊所中，有一些课程是课堂教学的固定内容，如“律师与法官的素质要求”“法律职业伦理”“法律与社会公正”等，这些课程内容似乎远远超出了解决法律实务问题的范围，而是注重引导

---

[1] 王立民、牟逍媛：《诊所法律教育研究》，上海交通大学出版社2004年版，第82页。

[2] 同上书，第76页。

学生从社会的角度去思考法律的价值，正确认识和分析社会上存在腐败的问题，从法律的角度追求社会的公正，促使法律教育与职业责任、职业道德相结合。在诊所教育的模拟练习和个案代理中，都会遇到有关伦理的问题，学生由于面对真实的案件、真实的当事人，因而更容易了解职业的责任感，体会进行战略选择的重要。例如，如何处理矛盾冲突和严守保密准则的关系，如何处理律师与当事人之间的关系。这时的职业责任不是假设的、模拟的，学生必须作出正确的决断。这种决断对学生来说，是其对职业道德、职业责任的一种深化理解，是对职业责任的价值判断。由此看来，职业道德的教育价值是对法律职业者（法律人）现行法律教育活动的鲜活补充。

三、诊所法律教育的社会价值：提供法律援助和推动法治进程

诊所法律教育的活动以社会的需求和社会的发展为对象来培养法律人才，因此其所进行的各项教学活动、实践活动离不开社会，离不开具体的案件，离不开具体的法律法规，离不开真实的当事人，所以，诊所法律教育本身就具有社会价值的内容。这些社会价值的内容主要包含在两个方面。

（一）提供法律援助价值

法律援助，又称法律救济、法律扶助，是指国家对某些经济困难和特殊案件的当事人给予减免费用或义务提供法律帮助的一种法律保障制度。高校所开展的法律援助是一种非政府性的法律援助，即民间法律援助。尽管法律援助制度和诊所法律教育在目的、性质、服务范围、机构设置、评价标准等方面存在这样那样的差异，但二者可以互补。诊所法律教育的实践活动可以利用法律援助现成的场所、案源、管理制度等来开展教学活动，学生在免费为当事人提供法律咨询、法律文书代书、个案代理、参与非诉讼事务处理等活动中满足了当事人的需求，解决了法律援助的问题。这些教育活动中，实践部分的价值不仅体现了教育价值的本身，而且具有服务社会的价值。这就是二者双赢的结果，基于这个原因，也有学者称之为法律援助与诊所法律教育共同体。

（二）推动法治进程

诊所学生在具体的教学实践过程中会接触到一些贫富不均、不公平、不合理、社会腐败等问题，这些客观问题的存在，激发学生寻求法律手段去维护社会秩序，解决社会不公平现象，并对这些问题的解决加以分析和研究，提出更加公平和合理的对策和解决途径，从而推动法制向着合理的方向迈进，大大推进我国法治建设的进程，学生在此成为利用法律制度进行社会变革的代理人。[1] 正如华盛顿大学教授 Jane H. Aiken 所言："我们致力于让他们产生一种坚定不移的愿望——利用他们的法律技能去纠正这些不公平，运用他们的智慧去了解正在为他们的工作环境进行广泛变革的法律制度的不足……"[2]

诊所法律教育的价值自产生以来就一直争论不休，争论的实质都不可否认其教育价值和社会价值。在这个价值体系中，关于孰轻孰重的问题要考虑一国的国情、价值追求、产生背景、法律制度和法学教育在国家中的地位等。在现阶段，我国的诊所法律教育的核心价值是教育价值，具体包括学习和继续学习的价值、思维价值、创新价值、职业道德价值。社会价值包括提供法律援助和推动法治进程价值。诊所法律教育的价值所在，为我们开展诊所法律教育提供了一个明晰的思路和选择途径，同时也对我国法学教育改革提供了一个可借鉴的参考模式。

---

[1] 王立民、牟逍媛：《诊所法律教育研究》，上海交通大学出版社 2004 年版，第 38 页。

[2] Jane H. Aiken："正义的激发者"，原载 7CLINICAL L. REV. 287 (2001). 李傲：《动教学法——诊所式法律教育》，法律出版社 2004 年版，第 5 页。

诊所法律教育对中国法科学生的影响

——以诊所教育实例为视角

牟逍媛*

摘　要：诊所学生在参与社区矫正过程中，一方面，培养自身的社会责任感和公益服务意识；另一方面，能观察和思考问题，锻炼能力，为社区矫正事业发展贡献力量。

关键词：诊所法律教育　社区矫正　影响

诊所法律教育是一种实践性的法学教育模式，起源于美国。该模式引入中国后，推动了我国法学教育的改革，弥补了传统法学教育的不足，对我国法学教育产生了积极的影响。现今，诊所法律教育已成为我国法学教育的组成部分，成为广受欢迎和好评的法学教育课程。

一、诊所法律教育对我国法学教育的影响

法学教育是传授法律知识和职业技能等的教育活动，法律职业是提供法律服务的职业。这种职业的基础是建立在对自己所学的法律知识的运用上。要运用法律知识就必须依靠实务操作技能，就必须遵循理论与实践相结合的规律和法律职业技能的共同规律。诊所法律教育将培养法律职业技能、职业素养作为其教育目标之一，将法学教育与法律职业有机地联系起来。

---

* 牟逍媛，华东政法大学教授。

(1) 诊所法律教育推动了我国法学教育与法律职业的互动。法学教育承担着培养法律职业者的重要责任，两者之间的紧密联系决定了法学教育中知识的传授与能力的培养居于同等重要的地位，两者之间有机互动才能完成各自的历史使命。

传统法学教育注重知识的传授，但知识能力的培养只是法律职业者所应具备的职业能力的一部分，同时还须具备职业的思维能力和运用法律能力，这些能力是在知识与实践的相互作用过程中获得的。诊所法律教育把法律职业中知识能力、思维能力和运用能力有机地融合在整个教学和实践过程中，注重在学生掌握法律知识的同时，教会学生获取新知识的方法和能力，使学生能够运用所学的知识和方法，不断充实新知识，解决新问题，最大限度地使知识本身转化为一种认识法律的能力，这种能力赋予了知识无限创造性，能够使知识本身不断升值，以保持法律职业对知识创新连续性的要求，[1] 从而适应社会发展的需要。

(2) 诊所法律教育丰富了我国实践法学教育的方法，同时诊所教育方法也影响到其他法律课程，促进了其他法律课程教学方法的改进。在实践法学教育中，案例教学法是以案例分析讨论形式为主，模拟法庭教学法是以理解程序为主，实习是以师傅带徒弟似的学徒实习为主，但上述方法主要是帮助学生理解和了解法律，缺乏学生亲自参与社会实践，运用所学专业知识解决社会问题的过程。诊所法律教育的开展弥补了这一缺陷，它为法学院学生提供了理论知识和能力知识结合的平台。同时，诊所法律教育中采用的主动思维型、开放型和合作型等多元教育方法，会促使其他法律课程的教师运用诊所教学方法，为我国法学教育方法的创新注入活力。

(3) 诊所法律教育推动了我国法学教育向以学生为本、学生为主体的方向发展。诊所法律教育是一种开放式的教育，其教育模式、内容和方法充分考虑到个人人格的发展。例如，主动思维型、开放性和合作型等教育模式能促使学生充分发挥个人的想象力，探索新事物，其个性在

---

[1] 邹育理："从美国的法律教育谈'判例法教学'"，载《现代法学》2000年第4期。

不断探索中得到发展和完善，创造性也随之产生。

二、诊所法律教育的功能对学生的影响

诊所法律教育具备以学生为本、以知识为本的教育功能和以社会为本的实践功能，这些功能在诊所教育中得到落实体现，并对学生产生了切实的影响。

（一）以学生为本的教育功能促使诊所教育主体性理念的落实

诊所法律教育的活动对象是人，其教育目的之一是提高、发展人的素质，而人的发展是知识发展和社会发展的基础。社会的发展必须依靠人自身的发展，而人自身的发展主要是通过教育来实现的。离开了人自身的发展，教育也就无从反映和促进历史的发展。诊所法律教育有利于促进个人知识与理智的发展及个性的完善。其教育模式、内容和方法充分考虑到个人人格的发展。例如，主动思维型的诊所法律教育模式能够充分发挥诊所法律教育主体的积极性、主动性，使教育主体积极参与诊所教育活动，活跃的思维、创新的精神又为诊所法律教育注入了活力。开放式的诊所法律教育模式使学生不仅学会学习，学会应用，而且学会探索，善于对事物进行观察，关注事物之间的差异性与特殊性，学会创造，为学生施展自己的才能、发挥创新意识提供了广阔的舞台。多元化的、开放型的诊所法律教育满足了学生个性的发展，学生成为学习的主体，主动参与，积极进取，使学生更关注所学法律知识的价值、责任，激发了学生学习的能动性，使其产生强烈的实现社会正义的愿望。

诊所法律教育以培养学生的主体性作为其教育理念。教育主体的含义为：一是尊重学生个体的自主性，让学生主动地、自由地发展；二是尊重教育的自主性，尊重教育的相对独立性，打破以往模式化的教育，用多样化的教育造就富有个性、创造性的人才。教育主体性理念适应市场经济发展的需求，能够发挥个人的主动性与创造性，培养学生的独立意识、责任意识和合作精神。

（1）培养学生的自我意识。自我意识是主体自我对客体自我的认识、体验以及评价。诊所法律教育是一种能够培养和提高学生自我意识的教

育，学生在诊所教育中能够充分认识自我，通过参与实践，体验自己的行为，对自己的行为作出相应的评价，作出符合自身发展需要的选择。

（2）尊重学生的主体地位。对学生主体地位的尊重是培养学生自我意识的基础。尊重才会考虑学生的需求，为学生提供各种发挥主动性的机会，使学生的自主性、能动性得到提高。诊所法律教育尊重受教育者的主体地位，注重受教育者的主动性的发挥。诊所教育能够充分发挥学生的主体作用，体现学生的参与性，激发学生的创造性。

（3）发展学生的主体能力。对受教育者而言，要使自己的主体性得到充分发展，仅仅具有主体意识是不够的，还需要具有与之相适应的能力，即主体能力。诊所学生在诊所教育活动中的自主性，首先表现为具有独立的自我意识，有明确的努力目标和自觉的学习态度，渴望自主、自尊和自强；其次，诊所学生还能够把自己看作教育对象，对学习活动进行自我支配、自我调节和自我管理，充分发挥自身的潜力，主动地认识、学习和接受教育，并能进行自我努力、自我评价，推动自我的不断发展。诊所学生的这种自主性，要求诊所教师在诊所教育中应深入了解和研究受教育主体，掌握他们的认知水平、思维方式和学习态度，并采用恰当的教育方式和手段为受教育主体性的发挥创造条件，使他们真正成为教育的主体、学习的主人。

（二）以知识为本的教育功能推进理论与实践的结合

知识包括理论知识和实践知识。理论知识是法学教育的基础，实践知识是现代社会对法律人才的基本要求。知识的获得与职业技能的培养分别属于诊所法律教育的不同功能价值，但二者具有一致性。首先，二者有相互包含、相互制约性。知识的获得作为诊所教学主体需求的一种价值，其中包含对职业技能的追求。从某种意义上说，职业技能的培养所追求的是以最直接的方式来实现知识的价值。反过来，专业知识对于职业技能具有一定影响，即专业知识的掌握对于职业技能的发挥有重要影响。其次，专业知识与职业技能是相互依存、相互支持的，两者的价值目标形成互补。

诊所法律教育是以培养学生综合素质为目标的教育，它要求学生像法律职业者那样发现问题、思考问题、解决问题，这是对法律理念、法律思想、法律理论不断思索、提炼、升华的过程；是学生感受、理解知识产生和发展的过程；是对职业技能、职业素质的运用、体验的过程。因此，法律知识的学习是诊所法律教育的基础，实践知识、职业技能和职业素质的学习是诊所法律教育的体现；诊所法律教育既注重对法律知识的传授，又注重对法律职业技能的培养。通过诊所法律教育，开发学生认识自我、发展自我的能力，从接受知识、运用知识到发展知识，使职业教育与专业教育互为促进，互为弥补，得到完美结合。学生通过诊所法律教育，能够更深刻地了解社会，理解法律的真谛。诊所法律教育是以知识为本的教育，它不仅包括法律理念、思想、理论和思维的教育，还包括职业技能和职业素质的教育。

（三）以社会为本的实践功能要求学生的积极参与

诊所法律教育的活动以社会为本，为社会培养法律人才，为社会发展服务。诊所教育不仅培养学生在实践中掌握和运用法律方法、法律推理技巧分析解决法律问题以及吸收新知识的灵活反应能力，以应对司法实践中可能出现的各种复杂问题，适应市场经济的快速发展，而且培养学生成为具有良好职业素质的法律人才。诊所法律教育的实践活动中，通过法律援助案件的代理，要帮助学生超越自己的个人利益，发展其公民责任感和社会责任感，使学生不仅成为有才干、有能力的人，而且成为有志于献身社会公共利益的人。诊所法律教育的功能之一在于促进个人的发展，但完整意义上的个人发展应建立在促进社会进步的基础上。诊所法律教育以社会为本的实践功能对促进社会发展、培养学生的综合素质具有重要作用。

诊所教育中紧扣实践的学习，使学生将纯粹对法学理论的关注转向注重理论与实践的结合，更关注“法律与社会发展”“法律与社会变革”“法律与贫困”“法律与社会公正”等社会问题。一方面，其个人能力在参与实践、思考解决社会问题中不断得到提高；另一方面，参与实践需要更广泛的人际交往、掌握人际沟通，促使学生参与社会活动，积累社会经验，并关注社会和个人的命运，将自己学到的知识为社会事业服务，为人类作出自己的贡献，实现个性与共性的平衡发展。

三、诊所法律教育课程对学生的影响

诊所教育课程内容的设置与采取的教学方法，为诊所学生提供了广阔的学习与实践舞台，对诊所学生产生了深远的影响。

（一）互动性激发学生的积极参与

诊所课程重视法律实践教育，这种教育方法显著提高了学生的参与度，从而大大激发了学生自主学习的兴趣。学生由过去的“要我学”变为现在的“我要学”，由被动学习变为主动学习，由严肃学习变为快乐学习；诊所学生和教师体会到这种教学模式带来的教育观念上的转变，即“以学生为主，以学生为本”，“教学互动，教学互补，教学相长”，“平等参与、平等教学”[1]。这种教育方法在理念上的转变，给原本有些枯燥、死板、应试和灌输式的法学教育带来了生机和活力，并直接导致“教”与“学”、“师”与“生”关系的变革。“这种教育方法的理念能适合现代法学教育的需求，培养出社会所需要的法律人。这种理念实际上就冲击了传统法学教育方法的理念，促使其发生变革，推进法学教育方法的革新，推广现代法学教育方法，给法学教育带来新的面貌。”[2]

（二）平等性促使学生主体意识增强

对学生而言，通过诊所法律教育，学生第一次体会到平等对话的好处。传统的法学教育主要采用单向传授的教学方法，教师是课堂上的主角，学生成为配角。这种单向信息传递的结果只能是灌输而不是沟通，学生无法畅所欲言而只是教学的客体，其无法真正满足学生多样化的个别需求。诊所法律教育采取的是平等的沟通，学生可以各抒己见，师生之间可自由地讨论各种问题，教师与学生都是平等的参与者。“诊所法律教育是一种没有讲授者的游戏，师生之间各自就听到的内容发言，双方

---

[1] 甄贞主编：《方兴未艾的中国诊所法律教育——2002年～2004年诊所法律教育文集》，法律出版社2005年版，第5页。

[2] 王立民：“也论诊所法律教育的方法”，载《法学》2007年第11期。

都是接受者，相互影响对方，各自不享有任何特权，各自都不会被对方所吓倒，对话双方处于平等的地位。”[1] 这种教学方式通过平等沟通，体现了对学生的尊重，在教师指导下学生自己办案，从而留给学生独立参与、思考与行动的空间，体现出对学生能力的信任和肯定，这就调动了他们的积极性和潜能。于是，学生从以往只知道接受、认同转变为开始自己独立思考，并学会了质疑和独立行动，其主体意识已逐渐形成。

（三）能力性促使学生法律素质与综合能力的提高

诊所课程给学生提供了一个身临其境的教学环境，学生亲自办理真实案件，参与案件的全部过程和细节，而这样的经历是模拟法庭、案例分析等传统教学模式都无法提供的。这样，学生就可以学习到书本外的知识，掌握灵活处理不同案件的各种技巧，并能加深对法律工作复杂性的认识。[2] 此外，通过学生值班、接待当事人的咨询、定期到社区进行法律宣传等活动，学生可以通过自己所能来帮助那些需要帮助的人，实现自己的社会价值。

诊所学生普遍认为诊所教育锻炼了他们随机应变、处理不同种类法律问题和应对不同类型当事人的能力；不仅锻炼了询问、解答以及归纳总结问题的能力，还让他们学会了制定工作计划、科学地分析问题并提出对策的能力。在整个教学过程中，他们将理论知识和法律实践结合起来，加深了对原有理论知识的认识，此外还学到了书本中没有而司法活动中不可缺少的知识。通过社会实践，他们成为既能说也能干的人，做事认真负责，踏踏实实，并学会为自己的当事人、委托人着想，培养了责任心；在代理案件时，学会了尊重当事人的意见，努力为当事人谋取合法的最大利益。在结束课程后，学生们都认为自己学到了许多为人处世之道，学会了如何倾听与说话等沟通上的技巧，学会了如何调解和出庭诉讼，还学会了如何加强团队合作，增强了办案小组成员间的凝聚力，提高了自己的战斗力和办案质量。

---

[1][2] 陈红梅：“诊所法律教育的特征研究”，载《湘潭师范学院学报（社会科学版）》2004 年第 11 期。

四、诊所教育实践对学生的影响

在诊所法律教育中，诊所学生除接受系统的课程学习外，还参加各类诊所实践活动，参加社区矫正活动就是其中的一种。

自2003年起上海市作为全国6个省（市）之一率先开展社区矫正试点工作，社区矫正作为与监禁矫正相对的行刑方式为越来越多的人所知晓和接受，社区矫正工作的类型和方式也朝着多样化、系统化的方向发展。其中，青少年社区矫正作为社区矫正工作的重要组成部分，具有不同于成年人矫正的特点和需求，更需要人们深入思考和探索具有针对性的矫正方法和教育模式。

基于对青少年的保护和社会稳定的考量，法院对青少年犯罪人多判处缓刑，一方面避免监禁刑的交叉感染，另一方面保持其与家庭、学校、社会的正常联系，消弭犯罪和刑罚对他们成长造成的负面影响。随着青少年犯罪比重的增大，青少年社区矫正已成为矫正工作的重点和难点。上海市某区司法所作为最早开展社区矫正试点工作的单位之一，经过5年的经验积累和总结，于2009年开始组织青少年矫正教育小组活动，旨在探索建立不同于成年人矫正的特别矫正教育模式，帮助青少年矫正对象走上正确的人生之路。作为诊所教育的实践活动，华政诊所学生参加了青少年矫正教育活动小组，他们作为活动小组的成员，与青少年矫正对象近距离接触，对青少年社区矫正有了切身的体悟和思考。

（一）对青少年犯罪成因的思考

个体的成长有赖于自然和人类社会的养分供给和吸纳，性格的养成要受到个体周围人和事物的影响，青少年正处于人格塑造的关键时期，他们在客观的生存环境中不断调节自己的行为活动，从而逐渐形成相对稳定的行为习惯和性格特征。因此，如果生存环境存在许多不良因素，个体的成长没有得到正确的引导，自身又缺乏正面调节的能力和动因，就会形成不正常的人格，甚至作出危害社会和他人的行为。可见，成长环境及个体对自身行为的调节能力对青少年的健康成长起着十分重要的作用。

1. 家庭环境因素

家庭是青少年最主要的成长环境，父母是孩子的第一位老师，家庭教育的好坏直接影响着青少年的性格养成和行为特征。以小组中的6个孩子为例，有5个孩子成长于单亲家庭，还有1个虽然和父母生活在一起，但由于两人都忙于生意而疏于对孩子的教育，孩子虽然生活无忧，却内心空虚，受到社会上游手好闲之徒的引诱而走上犯罪道路。

林某，女，3岁时其母亲因不堪忍受丈夫酗酒后的拳打脚踢而独自一人去了日本，林某从小就对父亲既恨又怕，每天不到睡觉时间就不愿回家，父女之间几无感情可言。15岁的林某因犯盗窃罪被法院依法判处有期徒刑3个月，缓刑1年，在某区某街道接受社区矫正。经过几次见面和交谈，社工发现她的性格算得上开朗活泼，但每当她父亲出现在眼前时，她马上吓得全身僵直，甚至会不自觉地发抖，可见“父亲”这个词对她来说恐怕是与“爱”绝缘了。现在林某在一家宠物店工作，基本可以做到自食其力，她的妈妈捎信来说要接她去日本团聚，希望失落已久的母爱能够为她开启新的人生。

郝某，男，6岁时母亲离家出走，他和身为盗窃惯犯的父亲、伯父和爷爷一起生活，这样的家庭给郝某带来什么样的影响毋庸多言，他的堕落几乎是人人可以预见的结果。在社区矫正过程中，社工多次上门帮助郝某解决生活上的困难，但对他所生活的家庭环境无能为力。

2. 社会环境因素

我国社会目前正处于转轨期，在物质生活极大丰富的同时精神建设没有保持同步的发展，一些错误的观念，如“拜金主义”“金钱至上”等以及不正确的行为方式，对人们特别是青少年产生了误导。他们缺乏判断是非对错的标准和能力，尤其是在家庭教育缺失的情况下，外界的不良诱惑和少数不法分子的蓄意拉拢、乘虚而入，将这些孩子引入歧途。参加活动小组的6个孩子无一例外，都是共同犯罪的一份子，他们或是几个常常厮混在一起的伙伴共同抢劫或盗窃，或是受到成年人的教唆实施犯罪。长期缺位的家庭教育加上社会不良风气的影响，使他们的法制意识淡漠，面对诱惑没有起码的判断力和抵御能力，最终滑入犯罪的深渊。

3. 青少年自身的因素

残缺的家庭和不良的社会影响固然是造成青少年犯罪的重要原因，但不是决定性的，真正酿成犯罪恶果的还是青少年自身的性格和行为缺陷。通过观察不难发现，小组中的6个孩子普遍有好逸恶劳、贪玩厌学、不服管教的缺点，好攀比、图享受、怕吃苦是他们的共同写照。求学时，他们艳羡好工作和高收入，对老师和同学皆不屑一顾，甚至恃强凌弱；辍学后，残酷的就业现实和复杂的社会环境时刻考验着他们本就脆弱的心理防线，在种种诱惑面前，这些缺乏自控力又贪图虚荣的孩子选择了犯罪来摆脱生活的窘境。

（二）对青少年社区矫正的思考

1. 对青少年矫正监护人的思考

相对于收监执行而言，社区矫正是在社会上服刑，矫正机关和社区矫正机构依照社区矫正管理办法，定期对矫正对象进行集中教育和个别教育，并通过走访、慰问等形式及时了解其生活和思想状况等。在矫正过程中，具体实施这些工作的是社工，他们扮演的是监督者和教育者的角色，尽管每一位社工都全心全意、事无巨细地为矫正对象解决诸如户口、住房、就业等实际困难，但有限的精力和庞大的工作量决定了社工不可能“无微不至”地照顾到每个矫正对象的方方面面。对于成年矫正对象而言，他们大都有自己的工作和生活，能够定期参加矫正教育和公益劳动，除此之外并不需要社工给予额外关照。但青少年矫正对象特别是未成年人，由于年龄、家庭等因素，仅有社工的监督和教育是远远不够的，他们还需要一个负责任的监护人，[1] 他（她）应当与矫正办公室

[1] 这里的监护人应当具有与《民法通则》中未成年人的监护人不同的含义，前者对应的被监护人不仅包括未成年人，还应当包括19～25岁的青少年；监护职责的履行期间比后者为短，仅限于矫正期内；监护的职责也比后者更为艰巨，因而需要更严格的资格限制和选任机制。如果不考虑社区矫正的特殊性而一概沿用《民法通则》关于监护人的规定，仍以不负责任的父母为青少年矫正对象的监护人，这种监护很难起到实际作用。

签订社区矫正监护协议书（承诺书），负责对青少年遵规守纪和接受矫正情况进行监督，督促其遵守社区矫正规定，及时发现和掌握青少年的情况，同时还必须定期向社工反馈相关信息。由此可见，监护人在青少年社区矫正过程中发挥着非常重要的作用。

实践中，青少年在社区矫正中的监护人角色多由其父母担任，但复杂的家庭情况和不负责任的态度使得相当一部分监护人没有实际起到监督、保护的作用。如，在父母离异的情况下，青少年的监护人是父母中的一方，但孩子的居住地变换不定，时而随父亲住，时而跟母亲住，时而随亲戚住，时而又在朋友处寄宿。这种情况下，监护人难以与孩子保持正常的沟通交流，更谈不上了解其遵守矫正规定的情况了。又如，有的孩子与父母关系紧张，平时根本不愿待在家里，行踪飘忽不定，而父母由于工作忙等原因疏于对孩子的管教，只从物质生活上关心而从不过问其心理状况。更有甚者，把保护变成溺爱，拒绝配合社工的工作，对集中教育、个别教育的通知置若罔闻，帮助孩子找各种借口逃避社区矫正教育。

这样的监护人显然形同虚设，甚至会产生负面影响，因此有必要设置监护人的考察和筛选机制，社区矫正机构应当本着负责任的态度了解青少年的家庭状况，选择与青少年长期居住、有能力担负起监护责任的家庭成员为其监护人，并适当考虑青少年的意愿；在现有监护人不适当履行监护职责时，给予批评教育，督促其及时改正，对情节严重者，应当更换监护人。当然，这需要法律赋予社区矫正的执行机构选任和变更青少年矫正对象监护人的权利，并制定具体的实施办法，将社区矫正期间监护人的责任落到实处。

2. 对青少年矫正场所的思考

相对于监狱矫正的封闭性而言，社区矫正是一个开放的环境，目的是使矫正对象保持与社会的联系，特别是有利于青少年继续求学和工作，给予其正常的成长空间。但不容忽视的是，比起监狱这种较为单纯的环境，社会的复杂性呈现给青少年更多的诱惑，这些诱惑曾经是促使他们犯罪的“黑手”，在矫正期间也仍然构成他们重新犯罪的潜在危险。

青少年由于年纪小、阅历浅，又正处于叛逆期，对于师长包括社工的教育存在习惯性的抵触心理，要求他们和成年人一起接受社区矫正的集中教育、公益劳动等并不能有效地实现矫正目的。不仅如此，大部分青少年的家庭都是不完整的，家庭成员间关系或疏离或紧张，父母不能给他们树立正确的榜样，在这样的内因和外因的双重作用下，为青少年建立专门的“矫正基地”无疑更有利于对他们进行有针对性的矫正教育。基地的主要作用是为青少年提供阅读、集中学习和劳动的场所：应当有专门的阅读室，为孩子们准备符合其年龄和知识水平的书籍、杂志，目的是在矫正期内帮助青少年养成良好的读书习惯，补上家庭教育缺失的一课。

集中学习的内容主要包括心理健康知识、法制教育等，并能根据青少年在矫正过程中表现的问题和需求安排有针对性的课程内容，而授课老师则可由社工和志愿者共同担任。志愿者可能是退休教师、学生、企业家、白领、公务员等各种扮演不同社会角色的人，他们的人生经验和阅历本身就是极为丰富的教材，可以根据他们的专业知识和职业经历为青少年安排不同主题的讲座。其中，学生志愿者由于时间较为宽裕，可以承担更多的工作，如，为青少年提供升学、考试、求职方面的知识和经验；与青少年一起阅读，分享读书心得；参与基地的建设和管理，从事一些辅助性工作等。

社区矫正虽然重在教育，但仍然是一种刑罚执行的方式，必须体现惩罚性。对一般矫正对象安排的公益劳动是社区服刑的内容之一，每个矫正对象都必须完成一定量的工作时间。目前实践中缺乏专门针对青少年矫正对象的劳动场所和项目，也没有特别的工作时间规定，[1] 因此法律法规应当弥补这方面的空白，可以要求青少年社区矫正基地设置具有

---

[1] 澳大利亚新南威尔士州《儿童社区服务令法》对于18岁以下儿童的社区矫正工作时数作出了具体的规定：“对于不满16岁的人实施的犯罪，不得超过100小时。对于16岁以上的儿童实施的犯罪：如果对相关犯罪行为法律规定的最高监禁刑期不超过6个月的，为100个小时；如果对相关犯罪行为法律规定的最高监禁刑期为6个月以上1年以下的，为200个小时；如果对相关犯罪行为法律规定的最高监禁刑期为1年以上的，为250个小时。”

一定劳动强度又不乏趣味性和益智性的劳动项目，并定期组织青少年到图书馆、孤儿院、敬老院等公共事业单位提供服务和帮助，在劳动中获得启迪和教育。

3. 对青少年矫正中学生志愿者作用的思考

目前实践中青少年和成年矫正对象由相同的社工帮教，平均一个社工要对 20～40 名矫正对象负责，很难在日常工作中给予青少年更多的特别照顾。为解决这一问题，上海市某区组织成立了青少年活动小组，小组成员除了社工和 6 名青少年之外还吸纳了一部分学生志愿者，诊所学生参与了该活动。小组针对青少年的特点专门设计了阶段性的活动内容，既有室内的圆桌座谈和讨论，也有户外的参观和主题活动。在每一次活动中，诊所学生作为学生志愿者全程参与每一个细节，不仅仅是旁观者，也不仅仅是策划者或组织者，而是作为小组的一份子，用自己的亲身体验衡量活动的意义和对青少年的影响力。

学生志愿者的身份定位不同于社工，他们在年纪上与这些孩子相差不多，彼此之间有着相近的兴趣爱好，也比较容易揣测他们的喜恶，此外，社工囿于其监督者、教育者的双重身份不宜与青少年过于亲近，而他们权威的形象也不容易获得青少年的接纳和认可，而学生志愿者则可以试着与青少年做由浅入深的交流，尽可能多地了解他们的想法，并及时反馈给社工，协助社工制定有针对性的矫正方案。因此，虽然学生志愿者在社区矫正中只是从事辅助性的工作，但这一群体可以凭借自身年龄、知识和比社工更为超脱的定位对青少年矫正工作发挥更大的作用。

学生志愿者不是专业意义上的社会工作者，利用课余时间投身于这项事业凭借的不仅是身为社会一员所应有的责任心、公益心，还有对专业知识的探求和继续研究的热情，这也是学生志愿者不同于一般志愿者的地方。在参与社区矫正特别是青少年社区矫正的工作中，作为法科学生更注重从法律乃至法制层面考虑这一工作的现实意义，不仅关注社区矫正这一刑罚执行方式在实践中的操作是否符合法律的程序和实体规定，更以发现相关法律法规的不周详、不完善之处为己任，并致力于思考法律的相关规定是否能够满足目前社区矫正工作的现实需要，并探索可能的解决方法。以青少年矫正为例，目前我国相关法律法规阙如，没有对青少年矫正对象给予不同于成年人的特别关注。理论界虽然对这一问题有所重视，但还没有形成具有系统性的看法和具有权威性的立法建议。这也为学生志愿者提供了更大的研究空间。

综上所述，诊所学生在参与社区矫正的过程中，一方面，培养自身的社会责任感和公益服务意识，学会倾听和交流，在帮助他人的同时不断校正自己的人生航向；另一方面，以专业的视角观察和思考工作中遇到的问题，锻炼研究能力，也为推动社区矫正事业的法治化贡献自己的力量。

法律诊所参与社区矫正的制度构想

李俊刚*

摘　要：《中华人民共和国刑法修正案（八）》和《社区矫正实施办法》的出台，结束了实施8年的试点工作，标志着我国社区矫正法律制度的确立，为改革完善我国刑罚执行制度奠定了重要基础。而社区如何开展服刑人员的矫正工作成为一项在实践中不断完善的课题，法律诊所（尤其是社区法律诊所）在参与社区矫正工作时可以发挥自身的资源优势，促进社区矫正工作的顺利进行。首先要做好社区矫正的平台建设、培训工作、心理矫正工作，建立健全社区法律诊所的值班制度、登记制度、走访制度、汇报制度以及电子档案的管理工作。

关键词：法律诊所　社区矫正　心理矫正　可行性

一、社区矫正制度在我国的建立

社区矫正（Community Correction）是一种不使罪犯与社会隔离并利用社区资源教育改造罪犯的方法，是所有在社区环境中管理教育罪犯方式的总称，简单地说，就是让符合法定条件的罪犯在社区中执行刑罚。社区矫正是一个外来语，是西方国家首先推行的一种刑事执法模式，其理念正式始于19世纪末近代学派的行刑社会化思想。近代学派的大师们认识到监狱刑罚的缺陷和不足，提出了非监禁刑罚措施和对罪犯人格的改造，社区矫正便由此发端。20世纪50年代兴起了罪犯再社会化思潮，以安塞尔为代表的新社会防卫学派提出对罪犯实行人道和再社会化，这使社区矫正思想由孕育走向成熟，并逐渐由学说渗透到立法，再转化为各国的行刑实践。注重对犯罪人的改造、完善而不是报复，刑罚的目的

---

* 李俊刚，哈尔滨理工大学法律诊所责任人。

是将社会人格不完善、不能正常进行社会生活的犯罪人再社会化，这已成为现代社会的共识。社区矫正比监狱矫正具有更大的优越性，目前已成为西方国家占主导地位的行刑方式，也已成为世界各国刑罚体制改革发展的趋势。

国外较常见的包括缓刑、假释、社区服务、暂时释放、中途之家、工作释放、学习释放等。中国的“社区矫正”，是指将符合社区矫正条件的罪犯置于社区内，由专门的国家机关，在相关社会团体和民间组织以及社会志愿者的协助下，在判决、裁定或决定确定的期限内，矫正其犯罪心理和行为恶习，并促进其顺利回归社会的非监禁刑罚执行活动。从国外视角来看，社区矫正是一种比较成熟的制度，但在我国，由于制度建立时间还比较短，各个负责的机构间还缺少实务上的经验，加之司法所与社区工作的繁重压力，这些都给社区矫正工作提出了巨大的挑战。

现行的法律规定主要见之于 2011 年 2 月 25 日通过的《中华人民共和国刑法修正案（八）》和最高人民法院、最高人民检察院、公安部、司法部于 2012 年 1 月 10 日颁布的《社区矫正实施办法》，这些比较详细的规定结束了实施 8 年的试点工作，为我国进行社区矫正工作提供了根本上的法律依据，标志着我国社区矫正法律制度的确立，为改革完善我国刑罚执行制度奠定了重要基础。社区矫正工作注重整合力量对社区矫正对象实施人文关怀，坚持做到“三不三多”，即不嫌弃、不歧视、不纠缠旧账，思想上多交流、生活上多关心、就业上多帮扶；基层司法所针对部分矫正对象家庭困难的情况，联合社区积极开展对点帮扶活动，在共同矫正其犯罪心理和行为恶习的同时，努力帮助矫正对象解决实际问题和困难，使矫正对象感受到社会的温暖。

全国的社区矫正工作从试点开始逐步走向全面试行，初步取得了成效。我国于 2003 年开始了社区矫正试点工作，2009 年在全国全面试行，社区矫正工作发展迅速，覆盖面稳步扩大，社区矫正人员数量不断增长。截至 2010 年 12 月底，全国 31 个省（区、市）和新疆生产建设兵团已开展社区矫正工作，覆盖全国 91%的地（市、州）、72%的县（市、区）和 65%的乡镇（街道）。北京等 13 个省（区、市）已经在全辖区开展社区矫正工作。各地累计接收社区矫正人员 59.8 万人，现有社区矫正人员 27.8 万人。

但我们也应该看到社区矫正工作面临的难题。比如，司法行政机关进行矫正工作无相应的法律依据和强制措施的保障；社区群众的认同度不高；矫正对象本人的心理障碍；矫正经费的短缺和无着落；解决实际问题的有限性；社区矫正工作志愿者短缺；等等。这些问题的解决需要全社会的人给予更大的关心与关注，因为对于社区矫正的对象来说，没有社会的关心与爱护，他们是不可能顺利融入社会大家庭之中的。法律诊所的出现，可以为社区矫正工作提供大量的志愿者并提供理论与实践的深入探索。

二、法律诊所参与社区矫正工作的可行性

首先，法律诊所拥有丰富的人力资源，可以弥补社区矫正工作因志愿者缺乏而产生的不足。从现在社区矫正工作的试点情况来看，担任矫正工作的主要是司法行政人员。但司法行政人员在从事矫正工作时也需要培训，而且还面临人员短缺、工作强度大的问题，这在一定程度上也使我们的社区矫正工作在利用社会资源的问题上不够充分，使得社区矫正的心理矫正难以完成。从本质上说，社区矫正工作就是积极利用各种社会资源，整合社会各方面力量，对罪行较轻、主观恶性较小、社会危害性不大的罪犯或者经过监管改造、确有悔改表现、不致再危害社会的罪犯在社区中进行有针对性的管理、教育和改造的工作。法律诊所参与社区矫正工作具有很大的发展空间。法律诊所的学生主要来自大三，他们具备了初步的法律素养、健全的法律人格、基本全面的综合能力、比较充裕的工作时间，最为关键的是投身社区矫正工作的工作热情。

其次，社区法律诊所为社区矫正工作提供了良好的平台。社区法律诊所是法律诊所中的一种新兴形式，它具备调解与服务的双重功能，随着社区法律诊所的普及，在很多社区中都建立了这样的组织。该组织扎根于社区之中，掌握学校、社区民警、律所等多种资源，为社区矫正工作打造了一个良好的平台。

再次，法律诊所为社区矫正工作提供了强大的智力资源。社区矫正在中国还只是处于雏形阶段，管制、缓刑、假释等虽然具备一定的社区矫正因素，但与之相去甚远。因此，我国的社区矫正工作任重而道远。20世纪七八十年代以来，各国都在不断进行刑罚制度的创新，尝试用最有益的方式处理犯罪和犯罪人，社区矫正就是这样一种刑罚方式的探索和实践。从试点走向实现，社区矫正还需要在实践中进一步完善，如果说社区矫正工作在很多方面还只是空白，也并不为过。法律诊所依靠强大的大学，可以作为研究社区矫正行为的平台，作为一个研究社区矫正效果的场所。一方面是理论的升华，另一方面是实践的探索，两者完美结合将大大促进社区矫正工作的顺利完成。

三、法律诊所参与社区矫正的制度构想

法律诊所参与社区矫正工作并不是一个新课题，在全国各地已经有很多试点。武汉大学、中南民族大学、北京师范大学等学校法律诊所参与了社区矫正工作。很多学校还建立了专门的社区矫正法律诊所。社区矫正是刑事诉讼中执行阶段的重要组成部分，需要高素质的志愿者队伍，法学院本科生非常适宜参与这一工作。以武汉大学为例，它把社区矫正作为刑事诊所的教学方向，一方面与省法律援助中心、区法院合作，积极寻求指导学生参与刑辩工作的模式，另一方面与区司法局共建社区矫正教学实习基地，积极参与开展社区矫正工作。在黑龙江省，法律诊所参与社区矫正工作仍然处于初创阶段，但一些学生参与社区的实践活动已经涉及一些社区矫正活动。社区矫正是一项庞大的体系，很多制度的建立还需要在大量的实践活动中去发现和总结。这里仅就哈尔滨理工大学的法律诊所参与哈尔滨市社区矫正工作的实际情况，结合社区矫正所面临的困难，略谈一点制度的构想。

首先，做好法律诊所参与社区矫正的平台建设。

2009年哈尔滨理工大学与哈尔滨市南岗区政府签订了“互设法学研究实践基地促进地校合作”的协议。2010年5月21日，哈尔滨理工大学法学院与南岗区政法委、南岗区综治办、南岗区法学会联合创办了“社

区法律诊所”，并举行了揭牌仪式。该社区法律诊所属于外挂型的法律诊所模式，依托社区获得案源、资金等资源。如今，南岗区的所有社区几乎都设立了法律诊所，学生有固定的值班时间安排。两年来，在南岗区政府、相关街道办事处及 12 个社区的支持下，社区法律诊所通过开展普法宣传、法律咨询、诉讼代理等形式为居民提供法律服务，尤其在处理拆迁纠纷等群体性事件中起到了良好的沟通、协调作用，取得了较好的社会效果。在这种模式之下，政府搭台、社区主持、社区法律诊所唱戏的基本格局初显雏形，而两年来社区法律诊所参与社会管理的活动也初具规模。这以充分的事实证明了地校合作模式的正确性，同时也说明该模式具有巨大潜力。在社会管理方式上，社区法律诊所是一次有益的尝试。社区中的法律诊所由此成为处理社区矫正工作的良好平台。

其次，法律诊所参与社区矫正的学员选择与培训制度。

目前，法律诊所学员的选择主要来自大三，实际上每个学校的法律诊所学员的选择都各不相同。如，有的学校实行一学期一期，学员的选择主要来自大三。若法律诊所的学期是一学年，则法律诊所的学员从大二下学期开始比较合适。参与社区矫正的学生也有特殊要求，如，男学生的比例要适当提高，以降低接触犯罪人员过程中的风险；应当主要安排大三的学生，这样的学生具备更多的实践经验和交际能力。

参与社区矫正的学生需要提前做好必要的培训。其培训内容，主要是由社区矫正工作人员针对日常管理的任务和工作程序、社区服刑罪犯的行为约束、审前调查评估、社区矫正罪犯的交付和接收、社区教育矫正和解除矫正、矫正工作的法律责任等方面展开的。尤其是在如何对犯罪人员进行心理干扰方面，需要进行有针对性的培训。

再次，成立专门的心理矫正中心。

心理矫正是面向全体社区服刑人员，通过开展心理教育、心理辅导等活动，使他们对心理矫正和心理健康有一个正确的认识，激发和强化自我矫正的积极性，改善和提高自身的心理素质，加速再社会化进程。如制定心理矫正方案、进行心理评估与诊断、制定心理矫正计划、签订心理矫正协议、制定心理矫正方案等。

成功的心理矫正应当注意做好两项工作：在心理矫正前先要做好服刑人员的人身危险性评估，包括入矫前的人身危险性评估、人矫后的人身危险性评估、解矫前的人身危险性评估。这样不仅可以加强对服刑人员的信息的了解，还可以降低学生参与社区矫正的危险性。然后要做好心理矫正的工作方案。社区矫正具有极高的价值，可以对有心理问题和心理障碍的社区服刑人员及时实施辅导、教育、咨询和治疗，帮助他们消除心理障碍，缓解心理矛盾，摆脱心理困扰，改变问题行为，促进心理健康。

四、法律诊所参与社区矫正的具体工作

社区矫正的工作人员包括三类：矫正工作的专职人员（司法行政干警）、社区矫正工作中的社会工作者和社区矫正中的社会志愿者。其中，法律诊所的学生属于第三类人员。其参加的主要工作是在专职人员和社会工作者的指导下，进行初级的社区矫正基础工作。

（1）参加统计分析、信息报告、档案管理和情况通报工作。这些活动是社区矫正的基础工作，该项工作任务繁重，工作量大，需要大量的志愿者参与，尤其是没有直接面对服刑人员的危险性，法律诊所的学生比较适合分担此项工作。

（2）参与定期报告工作。定期报告是为了保证矫正机构全面了解服刑人员的情况。服刑人员必须定期向矫正机构报告，汇报自己的思想、工作、学习、生活情况，汇报自己认罪伏法、遵守社区矫正纪律以及参加学习、培训、公益劳动等情况以及下一步努力的方向。定期报告与定期走访工作的性质是相同的，学生在参与定期报告工作时主要是及时记录、反馈，必要时要进行及时的心理干预。

（3）心理辅导工作。经过一定培训的学生可以参与服刑人员的心理辅导工作。“人是可以改造的”，这是我国刑罚执行制度的基本理念。教育矫正是社区矫正工作的重要任务。当服刑人员遇到自己无法解决的难题和困惑时，要根据社区矫正罪犯的心理状态、行为特点等具体情况，采取有针对性的措施进行个别教育和心理辅导，矫正其违法犯罪心理，

提高其适应社会能力。在坚持依法、严格、科学、文明管理的基础上，对不同犯罪类型、不同情况的社区矫正罪犯，因人施矫，实施个性化教育矫正，是将社区矫正人员改造成为守法公民的重要方法。

（4）监督服刑人员的公益劳动工作。社区矫正罪犯应当自觉参加教育学习，有劳动能力的还应当参加社区服务，增强法制观念，培养责任意识和自信意识。社区矫正罪犯参加社区服务，不是惩罚，是培养社区矫正罪犯的劳动习惯、集体意识和纪律观念，强化其社会责任感，纠正其不良习性，促使其认罪悔罪，走向新生。

（5）做好社区矫正的预警及紧急事态处理方案。

社区矫正是一个新兴事物，其制度还需要在实践中不断完善。学生参与社区矫正工作可能会面临无法预料的突发事件，还可能会发现新的无法预料的危险。这就需要法律诊所学生做好工作记录，做好服刑人员的风险评估，从而安排预警和紧急事态的处理方案。

从未来的发展趋势来看，刑罚制度已经从以监禁刑为主的阶段进入以非监禁刑为主的阶段。在许多国家，适用社区矫正的人数大大超过监禁人数。国外社区矫正的方式主要包括缓刑、假释、社区服务、暂时释放、工作释放、学习释放、电子监控等。社区矫正是以惩罚为基础、以恢复性矫正行为为主的刑罚制度，以实现社会和谐作为其基本价值目标。和谐意味着合理地界定利益关系，合理地分配利益主体的权利与义务，切实保障各个利益主体合理的利益，平衡各个利益主体之间的利益关系。法律诊所在承担社区矫正工作时，应侧重于对社区矫正对象的教育矫正，通过多种形式矫正其不良心理和行为，促使其弃恶从善；帮助社区矫正对象解决就业、生活、心理及维权等方面的问题和困难。这对于提高罪犯的教育改造质量、维护社会稳定等都具有全方位的意义。可以说，法律诊所参与社区矫正工作既有很长的路要走，又可以大有作为。

困境与出路：诊所法律教育的本土化命题

——基于广东法学专业的考察

江保国*

摘　要： 诊所法律教育的引进有助于克服法学教育小成本、低门槛运作的弊端，提高法科学生的实践能力。广东各校法学专业的实践表明，这些新建的法律诊所有着不少共性和特色，也在发展中面临教学理念、教学资源和实际操作等方面的短板，无法对概念法学教学模式带来根本性变革。完全普及美式诊所法律教育不切实际，也无此必要，走出本土化困境的出路在于积极进行相关具体制度的培育。

关键词： 诊所法律教育　本土化　广东

十余年来，我国的法学本科教育规模经历了跨越式的发展。据统计，截至2008年11月，全国共设有法学院系634所，30年来增长了105.67倍；法学本科在校生规模达到30万人左右，法学专科在校生超22万人，30年来增长了200多倍。[1] 而这一数字尚未包含成人教育和高职高专院校等其他层次的法学教育。由此，我国历史上出现了民国以来的第二个法学教育高峰期，体现了教育界对市场经济和法治国家目标的有力响应。规模的急剧扩大在另一方面也导致法学本科教育教学质量的显著下滑、与就业市场供求关系的脱节等一系列问题。因而，近年来改革法学本科

* 江保国，安徽全椒人，法学博士，华南农业大学人文与法学学院副教授，主要研究方向为国际法学。

[1] 中国社科院法学研究所：《中国法治发展报告No.7（2009）》，社会科学文献出版社2009年版，第331页。

教育模式和教学手段方法的呼声此起彼伏，激进者甚至提出了取消法学本科教育的主张。[1][2]

在此背景下，从国外引进的以诊所法律教育为代表的一些新型法学教育方法在我国得到热捧，并迅速在法学教育中得以推广。2000年9月北京大学、清华大学等7所院校同时开设了法律诊所课程，标志着诊所法律教育模式正式被移植到我国，后来又有中山大学等3所院校加入。[3] 10年间，在广泛开枝散叶的同时，诊所法律教育在我国的发展也时常遭遇诸多水土不服的症状和诸多困境。本文意在对我国诊所法律教育的现状及其困境进行检讨，同时为了便于分析，特将范围主要限定于具有一定代表性的广东法学专业，但其研究过程及结论也大体上适用于全国其他地方的法学专业。

一、广东诊所法律教育的背景和现状

广东开设法学专业的历史始于作为今天中山大学法学院前身的广东法政学堂，它成立于清末律法改革期间的1905年，仅比我国第一个官办的法律学堂——京师法律学堂晚一年。这批早期的西式法学教育学堂开创了我国法学教育近代化的先声，[4] 为国家培养了一批社会精英，同时也决定了起步阶段我国法学教育对国外经院式法学教育的全盘因袭，难

---

[1] 例如，2006年7月中旬在上海举行的第三届中外大学校长论坛上，厦门大学校长朱崇实先生提出法学专业不应该在本科设置，因为本科层次培养的法学毕业生很难从事相应的工作，专业的法律人才需要更高层次的知识结构。法律应该作为大学生的基础课来学习，而不是专门设置一个专业，如果学生希望从事相应的职业，可以有了一定的知识背景后到硕士阶段再学习法律。在美国的高等教育中，很多专业是没有本科生的。

[2] 代小琳、韩娜："大学专业目录正在调整 法律、管理类本科专业酝酿取消"，载《北京晨报》2006年7月18日。

[3] 左卫民、高跃先、兰杰荣等：《诊所法律教育在中国：本土化与多元化探索》，四川大学出版社2008年版，第6～7页。

[4] 侯虹斌："广东法政学堂：广东现代法制的起步"，载《南方都市报》2005年11月7日。

以从我国历史上长期存在的师徒式律学教育中汲取营养。[1] 其后的连年争战和政治运动导致广东法学教育的发展也是波折不断，甚至长期处于停滞状态。直到改革开放后广东的法学教育才逐步进入正轨，中山大学、暨南大学、华南师范大学、汕头大学和深圳大学等一些综合性院校先后恢复或开设了法学专业。2000 年时全省设置了法学本科专业的高校共计 8 所。然而世纪之交的高校扩招打破了广东法学专业发展的进程，仅到 2006 年全省招收法学专业的高校就激增到 35 所之多，其中 23 所新增的法学招生院校集中在 2002～2005 年。[2]与庞大的招生规模形成反差的却是全省法学专业总体办学层次不高以及法学专业毕业生连年低迷的就业率。虽然近年来包括广东商学院、广东外语外贸大学等数所高校取得了法学硕士一级学科点，中山大学和华南理工大学甚至取得了法学博士学位授权一级学科单位资格，[3] 法学教育的重心开始从单一的法学本科向硕士、博士层次转移，但是对比全国其他地区，广东仍然是法学教育和研究的“低洼地带”，与它在全国的经济发展地位、丰富的立法和司法实践资源非常不相称。这种洼地效应也导致了长期以来内地法学界人士和法学专业毕业生“孔雀东南飞”的现象。目前广东法学教学和研究机构、法律实务界的精英大多非本地法学院系培养，这一事实使广东法学界在学缘结构上具有较高的生态多样性，有利于造就充分竞争的环境，但也从另一角度说明了本地法学教育的乏力。而法学专业毕业生就业的情况也同样不容乐观。以 2008 年为例，据麦可思研究院的统计，广东该年度本科各专业大类中，法学专业毕业半年后就业率仅为 79%，远低于广东（90%）和全国的本科毕业生毕业半年后平均就业率（88%），在各专业

---

[1] 以广东法政学堂为例，它聘请了日本教习授课，同时用的也是日本的课本。

[2] 符启林、宋敏：“广东高校法学教育存在的问题与对策”，载《法治论坛》2007 年第 2 期，第 12～22 页。

[3] 根据国务院学位委员会 2011 年 3 月 3 日发布的《关于下达 2010 年审核增列的博士和硕士学位授权一级学科名单的通知》，我国法学博士学位授权一级学科单位由原来的 11 所猛增至 38 所，其中华南地区从无到有一举斩获 3 个名额，除中山大学和华南理工大学之外，海南大学也挤入了这个日显拥挤的法学高端教育俱乐部。

中垫底。[1][2]

对办学层次、办学特色的追求和传导自就业市场的压力从正反两个方面促使广东各法学院系尝试新的人才培养模式。诊所法律教育以实务操作为主要内容，将培养目标直指法学教育的终端产品——合格的、富有动手能力的法律人，并将能否达成这一目标作为衡量法学教育成功与否的重要标准。而学生的动手能力往往又与其被就业市场和社会接受的程度甚至与其经济收入直接正相关，因此就不难解释诊所法律教育传入我国后广东各法学院系对于这一教学模式的关注热度了。至 2012 年 7 月，全国共有 146 所高校的法学院系成为中国法学会诊所法律教育专业委员会的单位会员，而广东就有中山大学法学院、广东商学院法学院、广东外语外贸大学法学院、华南农业大学人文与法学学院、广东嘉应学院政法系、华南理工大学法学院、华南师范大学法学院、深圳大学法学院、汕头大学法学院、五邑大学政法系和私立华联学院法律系等 11 个单位会员，占总数的 7.5%，高于各省、直辖市或自治区的平均水平。[3] 其中，中山大学更是我国首批 10 个引进诊所法律教育并获得福利基金会资助的高校之一。

根据课题组的调研，这些先行设置的法律诊所各有特色，同时也具有不少共性：

(1) 法律诊所的名称和设置。由于“法律诊所”这一名称属于舶来品，在中国社会中的认知度不高，广东各法学院系在命名时不少考虑到对外交往的需要，对命名作了变通性处理。如，华南师范大学法律诊所的名称为“华南师范大学法律援助中心（法律诊所）”；汕头大学法律诊所的名称为“汕头大学法律援助研究中心”；广东外语外贸大学法律诊所

---

❶ 全国范围内 2008 届本科各专业大类毕业生的就业率排名中，法学（79%）也仅略高于哲学（76%），排名倒数第二。

❷ 麦可思中国大学生就业课题研究组：《2009 年中国大学生就业报告》，社会科学文献出版社 2009 年版，第 67 页。

❸ 中国法学会诊所法律教育专业委员会：“诊所法学教育专业委员会会员单位目录”，载 www.cliniclaw.cn，发布时间：2012 年 6 月 29 日，最后访问日期：2012 年 9 月 3 日。

则干脆采用了两个名称——对内称为“法律诊所”，对外则称为“法律援助中心”。由名称也可以看出，广东内的各法律诊所都将法律援助服务作为自身发展的重要切入点。广东商学院法学院甚至直接与广州市法律援助处（我国首家政府法律援助机构）签订了合作协议，由后者根据实际情况接收并安排该校法律诊所派出的法律志愿者参与接待咨询工作，或作为法律援助承办律师的志愿者助理参与办理诉讼、仲裁案件和非诉讼法律事务。前者则聘请广州市法律援助处的部分律师担任法律诊所的兼职指导老师，对法律诊所学员通过讲座等方式进行业务培训和指导。此外，双方还通过合作立项、共同研究、举办研讨会等途径在法律诊所教育和法律援助工作的理论研究方面进行多样化的合作。

（2）案件来源及性质。适当而稳定的案件来源是诊所法律教育成功的关键因素之一，而各法律诊所在运作过程中特别是在初创时期面临的主要困难之一也是如何获取适当而稳定的案源。就广东业已设立的各法律诊所来看，除了与法律援助机构合作以获得支持外，还在实践中发展出了多种拓展案件来源的渠道：其一是通过法律诊所本身直接接收案件。多数法律诊所设有专门的工作场所，配备了专门的值班人员，经过一段时间的信誉积累和业务扩展，往往能够形成自主接案的能力。其二是通过法律诊所指导老师个人或其他相关人员介绍案源。法律诊所指导老师（包括来自实务界的兼职导师）通常具备一定的法律从业经验，甚至拥有较为丰富的案件来源，将其中一些案情较为简单、难度不大的案件交由诊所学生处理不失为一个多赢的举措。其三是通过其他途径接收案件。例如，华南师范大学法学院法律诊所将提供法律服务的对象首先指向本校师生，为发生交通事故的本校学生提供诉讼代理服务；广东商学院法学院法律诊所选拔综合素质较好的学生进入广州市总工会劳工法律服务队，为职工群众提供法律宣传、法律咨询、法律调查以及其他法律援助服务。

（3）教学对象和规模。诊所法律教育面对的是来自现实社会生活中“原汁原味”的不规整的案件，办理这类案件要求较全面的法律素养和应变能力，因此进入诊所学习的学生一般是高年级的本科生或研究生。由于诊所法律教育具有一定的师徒制性质，每名教师所能指导的学生的数量必然十分有限，总体上限制了法律诊所的规模，使其只能面对小部分符合条件并且有志于法律实践的学生。就广东各法学院系法律诊所的规模而言，通常在30人左右。例如，广东嘉应学院政法学院法律诊所的学生均从三年级本科生中选拔，配备了6名指导教师，每个诊所教师负责指导4～6名学生。广东外语外贸大学法律诊所则在诊所内分设了劳动法小组、民法一组（主要负责民事侵权类案件）、民法二组（主要负责民事违约类案件）和行政法组等方向，参与学生俱为具有一定法学理论基础的本科生及研究生，以法律援助者的身份对外开展工作，从事诉讼与非诉讼法律服务活动。

（4）教学内容的设置。与传统教学方式相比，诊所法律教育将学生置于教学的中心位置，包括集体讨论、小组讨论、单独询问等部分，可以使用案例分析、角色扮演、模拟法庭、阅读、游戏和心理测验等多种多样、不拘一格的方法，甚至鼓励学生走出课堂投身法律实务，与社会各阶层进行即时互动。[1] 但在严格意义上说，诊所法律教育的特有教学方式是对真实案件的处置。广东各高校现有的法律诊所均综合运用了多种教学方法，不少诊所将教学内容分为课堂内教学和课堂外教学两个模块。如，中山大学法学院法律诊所将课堂内教学分为若干专题，由富有理论和实务经验的法学院诊所教师、资深法官和律师等主持，以小组讨论、模拟或真实案件演练等诊所式教学方法为学生传授法律职业技能、责任和道德观念，课堂外教学则包括免费为当事人提供非诉和诉讼代理服务等。此外，广东各高校法律诊所还承担了不少传统意义上的实践教学活动，如法制宣传、法律咨询和社会调研等。

二、诊所法律教育本土化中的短板

诊所法律教育模式的引入给素来以课堂讲授为主的我国特别是广东的法学教育吹入了一股新鲜的空气，促使人们反思既有法学教育模式的

[1] 李傲：《互动教学法——诊所法律教育》，法律出版社2004年版，第79页。

目标设置与方法体系。许多法学院系表现出对于这一来自异域的法学教育新路径的浓厚兴趣，其中不少更是勇敢地对之进行了摸索和尝试，但与此同时也发现自己或多或少地面临不少困境。

（一）教育理念上的困境

（1）法学本科教育的性质。有关法学本科教育的性质，历来有通才教育与专才教育两论之争。“从大的方面来说，法律教育的目标不外乎两个，一是为法律行业培养新人，一是为更广泛的社会成员提供法律知识与意识上的训练。”❶ 前者为专才教育模式，重在职业训练，为社会培养具备操作能力的专门型人才；后者为通才教育模式，意在提高国民素质，培养宽口径的复合型人才。近年来，法学专业在招生中取消了过细的专业划分，统一为法学专业，不少学校强调在低年级阶段进行大平台的“打通”教育，似乎在朝着通识教育方向发展，但与此同时对法学专业实践性的强调和实施也呈不断强化之势。诊所法律教育的引入无疑顺应了法学专才教育的要求，在某种程度上也加深了法学教育定位上这种两难抉择的困顿。

（2）法学教育的本土化要求。“法学和民族志，一如航海术、园艺、政治和诗歌，都是具有地方性意义的技艺，因为它们的运作凭靠的乃是地方性知识。”❷ 作为法学知识传承重要方式的法学教育，同样无法回避“地方性”实践的问题。诊所法律教育产生于美国的普通法土壤，锻铸于学徒式传带与经院式教学的历史合流，是现代法学院向曾经培养出“最好的律师”的学徒式法学教育模式致敬的产物。❸ 它以解决问题和实务操作为指向，带有深沉的美式实用主义哲学印记。而我国的法学教育却历来重视对理论体系的系统讲授，从概念规则到原则制度再到其间的逻辑推演等，无不体现了经院式的风格。我国的成文法传统也为这种概念

❶ 贺卫方：《中国法律教育之路》，中国政法大学出版社1997年版，第114页。

❷ 吉尔兹：“地方性知识：事实与法律的比较透视”，转引自梁治平：《法律的文化解释》，北京三联书店1998年版，第73页。

❸ 张红：“学徒制Vs. 学院制：诊所法律教育的产生及其背后”，载《中外法学》2007年第4期，第498～512页。

法学教育提供了坚实的合理性语境。虽然这一模式单向度的知识传授路径饱受诟病，但成功地为我国在短期内批量培养了急需的法律人才，其低廉的运作成本也支撑起我国法学教育的突飞猛进。与此相应的是，在概念法学教育模式中，我国也已形成社会实践、专业见习和毕业实习等实践教学环节，用以培养学生的实际操作能力。诊所法律教育的引进及其铺陈如何与现有的实践教学环节接合也是其无法回避的一个问题。

（二）教学资源上的短缺

（1）合格的师资。美国法学院系的法律诊所教师队伍主要从实务界延聘，且大部分为专职，无须承担诊所之外的其他课程的教学任务，在职称晋升上也有一套不同于其他教师的评价体系。[1] 而广东各法学院系现有的法律诊所教师普遍是从原有的专业教师中选拔，通常要求具有一定的司法实务经验，他们除了诊所法律课程外，还要承担起其他课程的教学任务。同时，为了应对职称晋升和科研考评等需求，诊所教师还要完成大量的课题研究及论文撰写任务。诊所法律教育的特点在于其成本的人力投入，教师需要在课堂外花费大量时间用以指导学生进行作业，这些投入常常无法计入现行的工作量统计体系。其结果必然是由于缺乏足够的驱动力，诊所教师甚至无法专心于诊所教学本身，更勿论致力于提高诊所的教学质量。

（2）适用的案源。在传统的法学课堂教学中，教师所使用的案件往往经过了刻意的裁减、简化或假定，以使其具有内容上的适用性。与此不同，诊所法律教育要求将学生置身于真实的案件情境中，在教师的指导下完成会见当事人、书状写作甚至出庭等活动，通过这一过程去体验现实法律案件的复杂性和生动性。此外，法律诊所的首要目的毕竟在于教学，由于学时和性质等因素的限制，法律诊所只宜接收部分案情相对简单、难度不是太大的案件。虽然广东不少法学院系努力通过各种途径拓展案源，包括与法律援助机构合作，但从效果来看并不十分理想，不

---

[1] 蔡彦敏："诊所法律教育在中国制度化建设中亟待解决的问题"，载《环球法律评论》2005 年第 3 期，第 270～274 页。

少诊所的教学方式仍以课堂讲授或案件模拟为主。

(3) 充足的经费。诊所法律教育的运行成本较高——固定的办公场所和设施、值班人员、差旅、打印复印乃至更高的师生比都使其较概念法学模式消耗更多的经费。对于不少法学院系而言，启动诊所项目首当其冲的便是经费问题。尽管中山大学法学院法律诊所等曾获得福特基金会的一定资助，但从长远来看，维持法律诊所正常运转的经费必须源自教育体制内部资源的切分，源自教育决策层对法学实践教学的真切重视。

(三) 实际操作上的障碍

(1) 诊所的规模及对象。出于对单一课堂教学的“审美疲劳”和对投身法律实践的热望，不少法律诊所都出现了学生踊跃报名甚至人满为患的情景。而教学资源上的限制又使得各法学院系不得不对法律诊所的规模进行一定的限制，以使其不至于流于形式而变成大课堂法学教育的翻版，由此就提出了诊所的规模控制及遴选参与者的标准问题。就实践来看，各法学院系几乎无一例外地将诊所法律教育的对象限定于高年级学生和研究生，这显然具有相当的合理性，因为只有基本完成了法学核心课程的学习、掌握了一定的法律理论基础之后，才谈得上较全面的法律实践。然而入选诊所的标准很难精确量化，因此不少法学院系采取了个人申请加面试筛选的办法，如，中山大学首期诊所即通过这一方法选择了40名“有兴趣、素质高的学生”参加，[1] 其他法学院系的规模也大致如此。这使诊所法律教育只能作为相对较为昂贵的小众教育而存在。

(2) 诊所的实体化与课程化。法律诊所不仅是一种教学模式，还要作为一个实体而存在，除了必要的场所和设施之外，还需要配备一定的管理和值班人员。在编制普遍较为紧张的各高校，为法律诊所配备专职的管理和辅助人员存在一定的困难，因此多数法律诊所的工作人员由专业教师和诊所学生兼任，如，广东外语外贸大学法律诊所设置了诊所主任、导师和顾问、主管、业务部门和助理团等岗位。此外，将诊所法律教育引入我国现行法学教育体系还面临如何将其课程化的问题。不少学

[1] 甄贞：《诊所法律教育在中国》，法律出版社2002年版，第391页。

校名义上设有法律诊所，但实际上只是将其作为实践教学的点缀，没有进行常规化、制度化的设置。只有将诊所法律教育课程化，才能够为其稳步发展提供保障。由于规模和资源上的限制，将诊所法律教育作为必修课程存在困难，因此已完成法律诊所课程化的学校将其定位于专业选修课程。如，广东商学院将法律诊所课程列入法学专业教学计划并为其分配了 3 个学分，中山大学则为法律诊所课程分配了 4 个学分。

（3）伴生的法律问题。法律诊所的目的在于为学生提供实务技能的培训，其接手的案件主要是免费的法律援助案件，但是我国尚未制定专门的法律援助法，对参与法律援助的社会团体和个人的法律地位缺乏规定，现有的《法律援助条例》存在位阶低、较为原则等不足。[1] 在法律诊所实践中，为当事人提供代理服务的学生往往面临身份上的尴尬。他们由于不具备律师身份和相应的执业经验，一方面在获取当事人的信任方面存在一定的难度，另一方面在与司法机关接触时也存在一些法律上的困难，例如，刑事案件中不少诊所学生在会见犯罪嫌疑人和调查取证方面不易取得相关主体的配合。而对于法律诊所与当事人之间的潜在纠纷及法律诊所可能的损害赔偿责任等，更是无所依据。

三、诊所法律教育的制度培育

中美两国的法学教育有着不同的生存土壤。美国的普通法传统、实用主义哲学乃至主体性教育理念等都为美式诊所法律教育提供了营养充足的土壤，从经院式法学教育向诊所法学教育的衔接过渡非常自然顺畅，况且诊所法律教育在美国也经历了近半个世纪的发展历程。而在我国，历史上的律学传授尽管有学徒式的风格，但从来未达到一定规模，也未能形成特有的教学模式。法学教育则基本是近代以来舶自西方的概念法学传统，迄今其学制和教学安排与其他人文社会科学并无二致。这一状况在短期内仍然不会有大的变化。广东法学院系进行诊所法律教育的实践也说明，到目前为止诊所法律教育在我国的功能还仅仅在于对现有概

[1] 赵宏伟："法律援助法：我国法律援助制度的完善路向"，载《中国司法》2010 年第 3 期，第 92～94 页。

念法学的具体教学方式进行改革和补充，它与模拟法庭、毕业实习一样均是作为实践教学的一个环节或手段，难以对法学教育的基本模式产生冲击。完全普及美式诊所式教育只能是不切实际、一厢情愿的想法，诊所法律教育也并非一劳永逸地解决法学教育所有问题的灵丹妙药，但它对实践技能和社会服务意识的高扬倒完全可以作为对僵化、低成本的概念法学教育的一剂解毒剂。

综合广东各法学院系诊所法律教育的实践，在对其进行本土化吸收借鉴的过程中，需要因地制宜地对其进行适当改造，特别是要培育以下制度：

（1）经费支持制度。一是建立常规经费支持制度，将诊所法律教育的成本列支专业教学或实践经费，也可以通过教改项目形式提供专项启动资金支持。二是拓宽外部经费支持制度，与基金会、律师事务所等民间机构合作，获取资金支持，如，华南理工大学法学院通过与律师事务所合作，现在每年能够获得较稳定的经费支持。三是从法律援助经费中抽取一定数额支持和鼓励高校等社会团体承担法律援助职能。《法律援助条例》第7条规定："国家鼓励社会对法律援助活动提供捐助。"该条例第24条第2款规定："法律援助机构收到结案材料后，应当向受指派办理法律援助案件的律师或者接受安排办理法律援助案件的社会组织人员支付法律援助办案津贴。"据此，法律诊所对于其承担的法律援助案件可以要求一定的办案津贴，以贴补诊所的经费开支。

（2）师资培训与拓展制度。合格的师资力量不足严重制约着诊所法律教育的教学质量和覆盖范围。培养诊所教师的途径不外乎内部培育与外部引进两种：内部培育包括定期选派部分教师到国内较为成熟的法律诊所甚至国外进行集中培训，鼓励法学教师接触法律实务，有条件的甚至可以直接去实务部门挂职；外部引进则包括从实务部门引进具有学术能力和教学意愿的从业人员，而合理聘用具有诊所教学经验的外籍教师可以使诊所迅速进入正轨。例如，中山大学法律诊所的建设过程中，雅礼协会派驻的具有美国律师资格的外教就作出了“令人难忘的贡献”[1]。

（3）特色办学制度。为解决适合案源不足的问题，各法律诊所采用了多种办法拓展接收案件的渠道，其中，积极承担法律援助职能是最有效同时也是最具有社会服务意义的。虽然自《法律援助条例》颁布以来，我国成功获得法律援助案件的数量有了巨幅增长，[2][3] 但是总体上仍处于供小于求的局面。特别是广东在2010年年底颁布了《广东省法律援助经济困难标准规定》，将法律援助覆盖的人口扩大到4000万，[4] 这对专职法律援助机构将是不小的压力。有效利用高校法学院系的法律诊所知识和人力资源将是惠及多方的共赢之举。此外，为避免法律诊所发展的过分同质化，有条件的高校可以建立一些立法诊所、劳动争议诊所、农民工权益保障诊所等特色诊所。

（4）参与者的选拔制度。在诊所教学资源总体供小于求的情况下，可以引入合理的准入竞争机制，在综合考虑学生的个人职业定位和综合素质的基础上，有重点地培训一些有志于进入法律职业的学生。

（5）多样化的教学制度。在适合案源不足的情况下，可以将法律诊所与模拟法庭、课堂教学等相结合，改进教学案例的仿真性，特别是要充分考虑实践中存在的诸多不确定性，提高学生的应变能力。

（6）合理的课程化制度。合理配置诊所教育的学时和学分数量，使诊所式教育形成对课堂教学的有益补充，同时也能够调动教师和学生参与的积极性。

（7）日常管理和成绩评估制度。科学的管理制度能使相关资源和设

---

[1] 甄贞：《诊所法律教育在中国》，法律出版社2002年版，第390页。

[2] 2009年全国办理的法律援助案件总量达到641065件，几乎是2003年的4倍。

[3] 中国法律援助网：“全国历年法律援助数据图”，载 http://www.chinalegalaid.gov.cn/China_legalaid/content/2010－08/27/content_2263187.htm?node＝24953，发布时间：2010年8月27日，最后访问日期：2012年9月3日。

[4] 刘冠南等：“粤1/5居民将可免费打官司”，载《南方日报》2010年12月29日。

备发挥最大效能，包括值班接待和登记制度、案件管理制度、指导监督制度与文件归档制度等。而科学的成绩评估制度则要能够体现各环节、多方面的表现和努力程度，特别是重视来自委托人和同伴对参与者的评价。

法律诊所公益诉讼现状分析

——以中国矿业大学法律诊所为例

汤道路[*]

摘　要：在过去的几年中，中国矿业大学法律诊所成功发起了多起公益诉讼，引起了公众广泛关注，产生了良好的社会效果，提高了参训学生的法律应用能力，也培养了学生的公益精神。实践证明，公益诉讼是法律诊所培养法科学生的专业知识与公益精神的最佳途径之一。然而案源问题是制约法律诊所公益诉讼的最重要因素之一。在民事诉讼法最新修订并实施以后，法律诊所的公益诉讼将有可能得到更好的法律支持与发展。

关键词：法律诊所　公益诉讼　法律实践

中国矿业大学大学生法律援助中心成立于1996年，是淮北地区第一家大学生法律援助中心。1999年，经徐州市司法局批准，其成为徐州市第一个由学生组成的具备法人资格的事业团体。2005年，以援助中心为基础，成立了中国矿业大学法律诊所，并于当年6月成为中国法学会诊所法律教育专业委员会第105位单位委员。其后，法律诊所教育被正式列入学校法学本科教学计划中，法律诊所教育得到了更大的支持与更快速的发展。

自成立以来，中国矿业大学法律诊所共办理各类诉讼案件百余起，提高了学生的法律应用能力，较好地服务了社会，尤其是系列公益诉讼案件，不仅在客观上达到了公益诉讼的社会效果，培养了学生的公益精

---

* 汤道路，硕士生导师，中国矿业大学副教授，法学系主任，中国矿业大学法律诊所负责人。

神，也更好地展现了诊所法律教育在中国的当代使命。

一、中国矿业大学法律诊所公益诉讼案情况

中国矿业大学法律诊所自成立以来，特别关注社会弱势群体利益以及公共利益的维护，已经成功代理多起公益诉讼案件。

（一）陈某诉“新一佳”超市强制存包人格权纠纷案

1. 案情简介

2004年12月，原告陈某在去“新一佳”超市购物时，遭到该超市保安人员的阻拦，要求其存放包裹。陈某正急着要赶火车，所以与保安商量可否不必存包，但超市保安人员态度强硬恶劣，强制其必须存包。陈某认为自己的时间受到耽搁，而且超市保安的言行举止让他感到自己被当成了小偷，被强制存包就是怕他偷东西，因此他的人格受到严重的侮辱。事后，陈某以超市强制其存包，使其人格受到损害为理由，委托中国矿业大学法律诊所代理，将徐州市“新一佳”超市诉至徐州市泉山区人民法院，要求认定被告侵犯了原告的人格尊严权，赔偿精神损失费10元，并承担本案的诉讼费用。

2. 审理过程及结果

在庭审过程中，原被告双方就被告“新一佳”超市要求原告存包的行为是否构成强制、是否侵犯了原告的人格权展开了针锋相对的举证、质证及法庭辩论。原告所委托的法律诊所的两位学生代理人，运用平时所学的专业知识，凭借精心的准备以及临场镇定、敏锐的反应，表现相当突出，与对方律师据理力争，赢得了包括法官、旁听人员的好评。

经审理，一审判决认定“新一佳”超市工作人员的行为虽然构成了强制，但没有侵犯原告的人身权。原告陈某不服一审判决，上诉至徐州市中级人民法院，后二审法院维持原判。

3. 社会影响

案件受理后，《扬子晚报》《徐州日报》《彭城晚报》、徐州市经济生活频道等各大媒体都相继对此事做了报道，在社会上引起了很大的反响，很多人表示在购物时也遇到过类似的情况，但没想到通过法律途径来解

决。该案在泉山区人民法院公开开庭审理那天，法庭座无虚席。这场被称为“第一起学生状告超市的案子”，自始至终都受到了社会各界的关注、认可与好评，虽然最终没能取得预期的诉讼结果，但社会效果明显，从该案被广为宣传以后，全国超市开始逐步取消强制存包制度，这标志着中国矿业大学法律诊所走出了公益诉讼的第一步。

（二）许某诉中国电信徐州分公司114查询台侵犯隐私权案

1. 案情简介

原告许某在中国电信徐州分公司购买了一部小灵通，但是使用了一段时间以后，她的小灵通经常收到一些骚扰短信和不良广告，还经常会接到一些陌生男人的骚扰电话。许某咨询至中国矿业大学法律诊所，经分析，诊所人员认为与电信的114查询台有关，因为任何人向114查询台提供一个姓名，都可以查询到该姓名注册的电信小灵通和固定电信号码。经诊所讨论后，由诊所代理许某以中国电信徐州分公司侵害了用户的个人隐私权为由诉至徐州市云龙区法院，要求被告停止侵权行为，并赔偿精神损失1元钱。

2. 审理过程及结果

庭审中原、被告双方在被告向公众提供姓名及电话号码服务是否构成侵权以及原告是否遭受损失等焦点问题上展开了激烈辩论。法律诊所的出庭代理人员指出，向公众提供查询服务也必须以保护用户隐私权为前提，除非用户明确要求公开，否则就应当对该用户资料予以保密，这一观点得到了法院的支持。但在原告的精神伤害方面，因证据不足难以认定。最后，在法官的主持下，双方达成调解协议，被告同意为原告提供保密服务，原告放弃了1元钱的精神损害赔偿请求。

3. 社会影响

案件最终以调解结案，重要原因之一就是原告对证明自身精神伤害的证据信心不足，也说明法律诊所的代理人员对案件的准备不够充分细致，但调解的结果双方都能接受。最为重要的是，该案件被社会各媒体广为报道宣传，东方卫视的《律师视点》还以此为题专门制作了一期节目。在此影响下，电信部门最终改变了原来的强硬立场，更加重视用户的合理要求，客观上也提高了为社会服务的质量。

（三）刘某诉中国移动江苏有限公司徐州分公司话费有效期合同纠纷案

1. 案情简介

2010年原告刘某发现其办理的中国移动号码在卡内剩余金额为11.7元的情况下被停机，后经查询被告知因为话费已经超过了有效期而被停机。而刘某认为当时办理入网手续时自己并未被告知这一约定，故委托法律诊所作为代理人，对中国移动通信集团江苏有限公司徐州分公司提起诉讼，请求法院判令其继续履行合同并取消有效期限制。

2. 审理过程及结果

案件审理过程中，双方围绕本案件是否属于民事诉讼受案范围，以及被告是否对原告进行了告知展开了辩论。随着案件审理的进展，被告的傲慢态度逐渐转变，并开始对其行为的违法性进行反思。2011年6月一审法院判决被告于判决生效之日起10日内取消对原告刘某手机号码为159052×××××的话费有效期的限制，恢复该号码的移动通信服务。

一审宣判后，被告向徐州市中级人民法院提出上诉，后又提出撤回上诉，徐州市中级人民法院于同日裁定，准许中国移动通信集团江苏有限公司徐州分公司撤回上诉。随着中国移动的撤诉，这起针对“霸王条款”的诉讼正式画上了句号。经过此次诉讼，刘某的合法权益得到了保障，更重要的是达到了公益诉讼的目的，使人们更深刻地认识到消费者权益保障的重要性。

3. 社会影响

本案受到了社会的极大关注，各种报纸、电视及网易、中新网等著名网络媒体都进行了大量跟踪报道，也在社会及网络上引发了激烈的讨论。法律诊所负责出庭代理本案的王同学等代理人也一时成为网络红人。考虑到本案的社会影响，该案先后被《徐州审判》和《江苏审判》推荐为典型案例。在本案审结以后，电信、移动、联通三大通讯集团都已经或表示将要取消话费有效期制度。这说明公益诉讼真正起到了消除“霸王条款”等不公平社会现象的目的。

(四) 杨某诉中国移动江苏公司徐州分公司“话费余额转现”合同纠纷案

1. 案情简介

2011年12月，原告杨某在被告处办理了一张手机卡。2012年2月，原告停止使用该卡并向被告要求退还卡内的剩余话费，被被告拒绝。经多次协商无果后，在中国矿业大学法律诊所的支持下，原告将被告诉至法院。

2. 审理过程及结果

本案于2012年5月15日在一审法院进行了诉前调解。在调解过程中，原告要求被告承诺今后对所有用户都实现“话费余额返现”方案，但被告只承诺对原告实现此方案，诉前调解无果，进入一审开庭审理程序。

3. 社会影响

法律诊所是中国矿业大学法律实践教学的重要环节，提高学生的法律应用能力、维护社会公共利益是进行公益诉讼的最终目的，所以案件胜负并不是唯一考核标准。本案最终拒绝调解结案，并选择以诉讼的方式解决纠纷，正是希望通过这一个案件引起社会公众的关注，并达到公益诉讼的最终目的。

二、取得的成绩与存在的问题

经过多年的持续努力，中国矿业大学法律诊所在公益诉讼方面展现出一些特色，也取得了一定的成绩。

(一) 公益诉讼案件收到了良好的社会效果

这几起公益诉讼，无论纠纷在法院处理的结果是否胜诉，都经过媒体宣传而被社会公众广泛关注，引发了公众对一些社会不公平现象的群体反思，在法律诊所的带动下，公众开始尝试用法律武器去对抗一些社会强权组织及其损害公众及广大消费者的不公正做法。诉电信114查询台案迫使电信部门改变了其保护客户隐私权的做法，诉移动公司话费有效期案更是在很大程度上迅速推动了三大移动公司宣布取消话费有效期制度。社会公众的认可以及侵犯公益的不公平现象的点滴改善，都是对法律诊所全体师生的最高褒奖，也是法律诊所全体师生的最大精神收获。

（二）学生的法律实践能力有所提升

法律诊所的各项活动都以提高学生的法律应用能力为直接目标。但与其他诉讼相比，公益诉讼往往面临的困难更多，阻力也更大，对代理人的能力要求也更高。在中国矿业大学法律诊所代理的以上几个公益诉讼中，在审理过程中都既涉及法学实践前沿问题争议，也涉及法学理论前沿问题争议，要求代理人不仅要有深厚扎实的法学理论功底，也要有较为丰富的司法实践经验。因此，这几起公益诉讼的代理人都是从有过多起诉讼代理经验的学生中选出的。而且，经过这几次诉讼以后，代理学生都反映像是经历了一场法律大考，其语言与文字表达能力、法庭应变能力以及法律应用能力都有了很大提升。

（三）有利于法科学生的公益精神培养

公益精神是社会现代化的重要标志之一，其发达程度也昭示了一个社会的文明程度。我国传统儒家思想中本不乏公益精神的描述与要求，马克思主义、社会主义以及我们共产党人的共产主义理想更是对公益精神有着更高的要求。然而改革开放以来，在拜金主义、个人主义等西方思潮的冲击下，加之国内在公益精神培养方面的忽视，当前社会中的公益精神严重缺失，并伴生出诸多违法与失德现象。在推进精神文明建设的语境下，加强青少年公益精神的培养已经刻不容缓。

法科学生是一个特殊的青少年群体，作为准法律人群体，他们承担着建设与发扬社会主义法治事业的光荣使命，因而其是否具有强烈的社会责任感，是否具备深厚的公益精神素养，甚至事关我国法治发展的前景与未来。我们的法学教育不仅要授以法科学生法学知识与技能，更要培养与提升法科学生的公益精神与社会责任感。与常见的学生公益活动相比，公益诉讼形式是培养学生社会责任感与培养学生法律能力的完美结合，具有极强的专业性与公益性，因而应当是法科学生公益精神培养的第一选择。在经历过几次公益诉讼以后，中国矿业大学法律诊所的受训学生对公益事业有了更直接的认识与体会，而且先后有 3 名学生在毕业后选择了去一些社会公益非政府组织就业。在我们的毕业生回访中，他们都表示工作在推进社会公益事业的最前线很快乐，而在校期间的法律诊所公益诉讼经历对他们的选择有着很直接的影响。

（四）促进了法学理论的学习

诊所法律教育本质上是一种实践教学方式，但反过来也能促进学生的理论学习热情。在法律诊所的具体案件讨论中，总是无法回避一些法学理论的前沿争议；而且，通过公益诉讼，学生们对法学之外的社会学、经济学、管理学等学科也有了更多的了解。公益诉讼在学生的社会实践与理论学习之间搭起了较理想的桥梁。

中国矿业大学法律诊所在取得这些公益诉讼的成绩的同时，也发现了许多困难与问题，主要有：

1. 新民事诉讼法中公益诉讼制度与法律诊所公益诉讼的定位问题

长期以来，公益诉讼在我国并无法定概念。学理上通常认为，对违反法律、侵犯公共利益的行为通过民事诉讼程序或行政诉讼程序向法院起诉以追究其法律责任的活动均可归入公益诉讼之列。对于原先虽然与案件有直接利害关系，但其诉讼目的明显在于为谋求公共利益的，亦可归为公益诉讼。例如，中国矿业大学法律诊所发起的诉电信 114 查询台侵犯隐私权案的诉讼要求仅精神损害赔偿 1 元钱，诉移动话费有效期案诉讼标的也仅仅数十元，但这些案件背后类似的受害公众规模则是十分庞大的。因而从理论上说，中国矿业大学法律诊所的这些所谓公益诉讼，在形式上仍归属于传统的原先与案件有直接利益关系的民事诉讼，只不过在实质上代表了更广泛的公共利益。

2012 年 8 月，我国最新修订的《中华人民共和国民事诉讼法》（以下简称《民事诉讼法》）第 55 条规定："对污染环境、侵害众多消费者合法权益等损害社会公共利益的行为，法律规定的机关和有关组织可以向人民法院提起诉讼。"这一规定很容易被解读为公益诉讼的法定形式，由此法律诊所的类似诉讼活动则很难再被称为法定的公益诉讼。再者，根据该条规定，公益诉讼的主体应当是"法律规定的机关和有关组织"。而我国法学教育实践中，绝大多数法律诊所并没有在国家社团管理部门登记注册，其是否可以被认定为“有关组织”并获得诉讼主体资格仍有待明确。

2. 公益诉讼的案源问题

法律诊所的前述各项诉讼均发生在此次《民事诉讼法》修订以前，当时考虑到《民事诉讼法》关于原告资格的规定，都是选择法学系师生作为原告来提起诉讼的。这样的操作方法固然简便，但也存在不少问题。首先，它限制了案源。例如，中国矿业大学法律诊所曾经计划对调整公路的不合理收费方式提起诉讼，但最终未能付诸实践，适格原告的选择则是取消计划的现实问题之一。其次，公益诉讼往往跨时较长，少则一两年，多则三四年，如果学生作为原告，可能在结案之前已经毕业，从而给案件审理带来不便。例如，前述诉电信 114 查询台案，案件最终以调解结案，现实原因之一是诉讼过程中作为原告的学生已经毕业并在一个很遥远的城市就业，这就给案件审理带来了一些不便。再次，有些诉讼中，由于被告在社会上处于强权地位，可能会给原告个人施加一些不该有的社会压力与影响，甚至会干预新闻媒体的正常工作，这些都是法律诊所工作实践中不得不考虑与重视的问题。

3. 法院的配合问题

既然是诉讼，则法院的态度与行为对于公益诉讼将会产生十分关键的影响。在中国矿业大学法律诊所发起的以上几起诉讼中，不同的法院，不同的法官，态度亦不同。大多数情况下法官对这些公益诉讼是支持的，但也有个别法官表示难以理解，甚至予以排斥，指责这种诉讼是无事生非，是浪费司法资源，是给法院和法官找麻烦。针对这种情况，诊所要求每一起公益诉讼都要先经过指导老师研究决定，并且提前与法院做好沟通工作，从而避免法院的不配合情况。

三、展望

总体来看，中国矿业大学法律诊所在公益诉讼的探索之路上，克服了种种困难，取得了一定成绩，产生了良好的社会影响，也培养出一批专业扎实、富有公益精神的法律人才。实践证明，公益诉讼是法律诊所培养法科学生的专业知识与公益精神的最佳途径之一。随着新《民事诉讼法》的修订与实施，我们相信，困扰法律诊所发展的案源与诉讼主体问题将会得到更好的解决，我们的法律诊所公益诉讼必将迎来更好的发展与未来。

地方性大学法学院法律诊所教育改革的探索与实践

——“社区法律诊所”的成效与困惑

蔺　妍[*]　梁丽芳[**]

摘　要： 地方性大学法学院为了培养适应社会需要的应用型基层法律人才，需要加强实践教学，推进法律诊所教育。本文结合大连大学法学院尝试开展“社区法律诊所”所取得的成效及遇到的困惑，探讨在地方性大学法学院开展法律诊所教育的可行性及对策。

关键词： 法学教育　实践教学改革　社区法律诊所

如何培养适应社会需要的高素质的应用型法律人才是法学教育面临的重要课题。我国传统的法学教育是以理论教育为主，以“灌输式”的课堂讲授为主要教学方式，其结果是忽视了法学教育本身的实践性，缺乏从法学学科本身的实践性出发培养学生的实践能力，制约了学生的主动性和想象力。20 世纪 70 年代兴起于美国、2000 年起在我国北京大学等 7 所院校开始尝试的诊所式法学教育则是一种通过学生参与解决实际案件锻炼学生的实践能力、提高学生的综合素质、陶冶学生的职业道德的教学方法，为全国各类院校法学专业尤其是旨在培养服务地方的应用型法律人才的地方性大学法学院提供了创新法学实践教育的新思路。大连大学法学院 2008 年年底在大连市经济技术开发区马桥子街道创设了 14 个“社区法律诊所”，开始了具有地方大学特色的诊所法律教育的尝试，

---

* 蔺妍，大连大学法学院讲师，法律诊所教学负责人，法学博士在读，兼职律师。

** 梁丽芳，大连大学法学院讲师，法务实训教研室主任，法学硕士，兼职律师。

在不断地探索与实践中取得了一定的成效，但如何进行诊所法律教育改革，以更好地实现地方性大学法学院人才培养目标，仍旧是我们亟待解决的重要难题。

一、地方性大学法学院法律诊所教育改革的必要性

（一）地方性大学法学院人才培养目标定位

法学教育是现代高等教育的重要组成部分，承担着培养法律人才、发扬一国法律传统和法律理想、传播法律知识和职业技巧、弘扬法治精神的重要任务。而教育的理念问题是关于人的培养目标和价值取向的问题。[1] 从20世纪70年代，中国就开始构建当代法学教育体系，已经培养了大批法律人才。我国现行法学教育对人才培养的目标的基本定位是：法学专业本科是一种法律专业人才教育。[2] 这种人才培养目标定位已经渐渐不能满足社会变化对法律复合型人才的需求。2011年12月23日教育部和中央政法委员会发布的《关于实施卓越法律人才教育培养计划的若干意见》中指出：卓越法律人才培养计划的总体目标是“经过10年左右的努力，形成科学先进、具有中国特色的法学教育理念，形成开放多样、符合中国国情的法律人才培养体制，培养造就一批信念执著、品德优良、知识丰富、本领过硬的高素质法律人才”；同时又提出：“培养应用型、复合型法律职业人才，是实施卓越法律人才培养计划的重点”。这就要求各类高等院校法学专业在人才培养方面需要找准自己的定位，形成自己的特色法学教育体系。

大连大学是大连市唯一的一所综合性、地方性大学，大连大学法学院在不断的成长与探索中，始终贯彻“服务地方”的法学教育理念，将法律人才培养目标定位在努力培养具有丰富法律知识、优良法律职业道德、较强法学实践能力的复合型、应用型基层法律人才，并在此基础上，

---

[1] 曾宪义、张文显：《中国法学专业教育教学改革与发展战略研究》，高等教育出版社2002年版。

[2] 周世中、倪业群等著：《法学教育与法科学生实践能力的培养》，中国法制出版社2004年版。

努力探索法学人才培养模式的改革，以“社区法律诊所”为平台，加强法学实践教学，构建合理的法学实践教学体系，逐步形成了地方性大学法学院的法学教育特色。

（二）地方性大学法学院法律诊所教育改革的必要性

法律诊所教育（Legal Clinic Education）是建立在法律诊所基础上的一种实践性法学教育模式。广义上讲，其是指有关法律职业的任何经验的、实践的或者积极的训练，它将教学的焦点放在如何教授法律技巧之上，属于实践教学范畴。[1] 法律诊所教育模式自 2000 年在美国福特基金会的资助下开始在我国北京大学等 7 所高校践行以来，已经在中国实践性法学教育中发挥了重要的作用。10 多年来，中国各类开设法学专业的院校分别成为中国法学会法学教育研究会诊所法律教育专业委员会（CCCLE）的会员，其中许多是地方性大学法学院。这些院校在对诊所法律教育的不断探索与实践中遇到了一些亟待解决的问题，面临一定程度的改革与创新。

1. 服务地方的需要

以大连大学法学院为例，作为大连唯一的一所综合性、地方性大学，需要有服务地方的意识，在法律诊所教育平台的构建上，需要有针对性地考虑让学生在法学实践中尽可能地运用自己的法律知识为地方建设做贡献。

2. 培养基层法律工作者的需要

作为地方性大学法学院，人才培养的目标定位在培养复合型、应用型基层法律工作者，需要在法律诊所教育中尽可能让学生深入基层，尤其是作为社会最底层构成元素的社区，培养学生做人做事等多方面能力。

3. 克服现有诊所教育弊端的需要

作为地方性大学，大连大学法学院在探索诊所教育过程中遇到许多难题，尤其是需要“诊断”的案源问题，设立“社区法律诊所”可以由

---

[1] 理查德·J. 威尔逊，美国华盛顿大学法学院国际人权法律诊所教授、导师。摘自《诊所式法律教育教学参考资料》，美国福特基金会 2000 年。

学生直接接触各类案件，能够在一定程度上有效地克服这方面的困难。

综上，考虑到地方性大学法学院人才培养目标定位的特殊性，法律诊所教育改革具有一定的实际意义。作为地方性大学法学院，我们也在积极地不断探索与尝试。

二、大连大学法学院“社区法律诊所”的尝试

（一）“社区法律诊所”的建立

2008 年，大连大学法学院在学生培养方案中开设了“法律诊所”课程作为专业选修课，2008 年年底与辽宁锦连律师事务所合作，在大连经济技术开发区马桥子街道 14 个社区建立了“社区法律诊所”。法学专业的学生从第三个学年的第一学期开始，分成 14 个组到“社区法律诊所”进行为期一个学年的“挂职锻炼”。具体做法是：法学专业学生进入“大三”后，第一学期（暑期）学生提前一周返校到所分配到的社区“挂职锻炼”，开学后实行每周一次（星期四）到社区；第二学期学生正常返校，开学后实行每周一次到社区“挂职锻炼”。学生在社会实践过程中根据各个“社区法律诊所”的不同特点，运用所学法学专业基础知识为社区居民提供法律服务。

（二）“社区法律诊所”的运行方式

五年来，大连大学法学院学生一直坚持在 14 个“社区法律诊所”与社区干部一道走访居民，送法到户，“社区法律诊所”为大学生参与社会实践活动提供了理论与实践相结合的有效平台，现已初步形成以法学专业大学生为有生力量、常年在社区开展法制宣传活动的实践教学环节基本运作形式。

（1）根据各个社区的不同特点，学生运用法学专业知识开展形式多样的法律服务活动。开学以后，学生按照已划定好的小组到各社区参加社区的活动，每周四，大学生充分利用“社区法律诊所”这一平台，同社区工作人员一起开展法制宣传工作。如开展模拟法庭、知识竞赛、知识讲座、普法宣传等活动，尤其是在老师以及律师的指导下为社区居民代理法律案件，解决法律纠纷。

(2) 定期开展普法宣传活动，实现法学教育与普法常态化相结合。每月的最后一周的周四上午，学生分成三个大组，在街道划定的三个区域集中开展大型普法宣传活动。届时，法学院诊所课程教师、律师事务所律师、社区书记都亲临现场参加活动，指导学生接待法律咨询、受理各类案件。

(3) 坚持每周一次的案例收集与设计。诊所教师与律师事务所指派的专门律师分片负责“社区法律诊所”，要求学生在本社区内收集鲜活案例或根据社区的特点设计案例，在限定时间内递交案例分析报告。在此基础上，诊所教师或律师要对交上来的每一份案例分析报告进行评价，及时将意见反馈给学生。对需要调解或进入诉讼程序的案例，则由诊所教师或律师直接带领“社区法律诊所”的学生参与整个案件的处理过程。

(三)“三位一体”的共同管理机制

(1) 将“社区法律诊所”实践教学环节纳入学校的实践教学管理体系之中。2008 年 5 月，法学院向校教务部门递交了关于法学院设置法律诊所实践教学环节课程的申请，同年 6 月，学校教务部门批准了法学院制定的大学生“社区法律诊所”社会实践活动的教学改革方案，并将其作为一门实践教学课程纳入学校的实践教学体系。法学专业大三学生从第 5 学期到第 6 学期，被派到马桥子街道 14 个“社区法律诊所”开展社会实践活动。设定每学期 32 课时，2 学分。

(2) 建立“每周例会制度”“巡查制度”。为避免大学生在“社区法律诊所”的实践教学环节流于形式，法学院针对这门课程的特殊性，先后建立了“每周例会制度”和“巡查制度”。所谓“每周例会制度”，即每周由院里的专门指导教师召集各“社区法律诊所”的小组长召开例会，及时掌握学生的思想动态，鼓励学生树立正确的人生观和世界观；分析和解决前一周学生遇到的各类问题；如果遇到需要解决的案件，进行分组讨论；需要代理的，组织学生接受委托。所谓“巡查制度”，即每学期要有至少 3 次的不定期巡查，由诊所教师带队，抽调 3 个小组的小组长组成巡查小组，对学生在“社区法律诊所”的实践活动状况进行检查。巡查的内容主要包括学生出勤情况、学生在社区活动中的表现、社区交给学生的任务完成情况等。

(3) 实行“三位一体”共同管理机制。即由学校、律师事务所和街道三方共同对学生的“社区法律诊所”活动进行管理。

第一，大连大学法学院成立了由主管副院长和诊所教师组成的“社区法律诊所”指导小组，对学生的社区实践环节全面负责。第二，参与指导“社区法律诊所”学生实践活动的14个社区的书记和辽宁锦连律师事务所的律师，被学校聘为校外“大学生实践活动指导教师”。学生到了社区以后，他们要承担指导学生参与社区社会实践活动的工作任务。第三，每年举办一次由大连大学、马桥子街道和辽宁锦连律师事务所三方参加，以大学生“社区法律诊所”社会实践活动为主题的理论研讨会，把对法学专业大学生实践能力培养、大学生在法制宣传中的作用以及如何在社会实践过程中提升大学生的人生观、社会价值观和就业观等问题作为主要内容，探讨如何培养适应社会发展需要的复合型、应用型法律人才。

(四) 三方合作的评价体系

第一学期，法学院为每名学生发放《“社区法律诊所”社会实践管理手册》，学生对每次到社区的情况在管理手册上做详细记录，期末，由社区、律师事务所和指导教师三方根据学生在社区的表现、办理案件的具体情况等，在管理手册上对学生进行鉴定，由法学院组成的考核小组综合三方意见，评定本学期学生的最终成绩。第二学期，从增强学生专业知识水平和提高分析解决问题能力的需要上考量，以划分到各社区的小组为单位，每个组设定本组在社区所要研究的课题（创新立项的方式），指导教师承担对各个组研究课题的指导任务。期末，由社区、律师事务所对各小组的课题完成情况进行评定，由法学院组成的考核小组综合社区、律师事务所的评定结果和指导教师的意见，评定本学期学生的最终成绩。

三、地方性大学法学院法律诊所教育改革的探索

（一）尝试法律诊所教育改革的效果

几年来，大连大学法学院在推进法律诊所教育创新、尝试“社区法律诊所”的过程中取得了一定的效果。

1.“法律诊所”的课程体系设置趋于合理

大连大学法学院现已开设校内“法律诊所”课程，大三学年每学期16学时，1学分（主要侧重于案件模拟、技能培养）；校外“社区法律诊所”实践课程，大三学年每学期32学时，2学分（主要侧重于学生在社区的法学实践）。教师也有相应的工作量。整个法律诊所课程体系趋于合理。

2.学生“扎根基层，服务地方”的意识逐渐增强

学生在社区接触的人和事都源于基层，通过琐碎的事情（不仅仅是案件）培养学生树立正确的人生观和世界观，平和浮躁情绪，提高“服务地方”意识，符合地方性大学培养基层法律人才的目标。

3.学生法学理论与实践相结合的能力显著提高

作为法学实践教学的重要一环，“社区法律诊所”为学生践行法律知识提供了广阔的平台，通过各种活动，通过处理真实案件，把所学的法律知识与实际相结合，分析问题能力、处理问题能力、语言表达能力、社会交往能力等都得到显著提高，学生在研究生考试、司法考试、公务员考试中都取得了好成绩。2005级学生考研率达28%；2006级学生一次司法考试通过率达29%，其中4人以400分以上高分通过；2007级学生一次司法考试通过率达58%，大连大学法学院一次司法考试通过率连年位居大连高校法学专业前列。

4.社会对院校的认可度日益突出

“社区法律诊所”由大连市司法局、大连市开发区政府相关部门领导亲自参与挂牌仪式，由学生组成参加的大型普法宣传活动在大连市“五五普法”“六五普法”、消费者权益保护日、宪法日等活动中表现突出，受到大连市相关部门的极大重视，也被相关媒体报道过多次，使得社会

对地方性大学的重视程度、认可程度日益突出，充分发挥了地方性大学“服务地方”的优势。

（二）法律诊所教育改革探索中遇到的困难

作为地方性大学法学院，在对法律诊所教育改革的尝试中取得了一些成效，但在诊所教育的规范化、科学化发展进程中还是遇到了诸多困难，面临严峻的挑战。

1. 课程设置上的困难

在目前的尝试中，虽然已经开设校内外“法律诊所”课程，但与真正意义上的“法律诊所”课程设置尚存较大偏颇。由于案源不具有稳定性，校内“法律诊所”模拟的案件有时不完全是接受委托的案件；而且，虽然学生在社区实践的课时已经设置，但学生接受委托处理案件的课时尚未设置，教师指导学生办案的工作量亦未设置。此外，学生选课人数较多，是否需要开设不同类型“法律诊所”，在今后的培养方案制定中也需要斟酌。

2. 平台搭建上的困难

“社区法律诊所”已经为学生搭建了“社区”、律师事务所这样的平台，但完整意义上的“法律诊所”课程为学生搭建的实践平台范围应更为广阔，正在构想成立法律咨询中心、市法律援助中心、校内法律援助站，同时也在积极与消费者权益保护协会、知识产权协会等社会团体进行沟通，希望能共同为学生的法学实践搭建更广阔的平台。

3. 经费来源上的困难

虽然目前“社区法律诊所”处理委托的案件不是很多，但学生每周去社区、接待咨询、办理案件、复印资料、组织活动等都需要一定的费用，现在这部分费用基本都由律师事务所、各社区以及学院承担，甚至有些是由诊所课程指导教师个人承担。因此，在整个课程体系构建中，财务制度建设日显迫切。

4. 师资建设上的困难

诊所教师是诊所法律教育制度化建设中最为关键的主体性要素，塑造一支严格训练的师资队伍成为成功开展诊所法律教育的关键。无论诊所教育如何改革，都需要有具有事业心、公益心、包容心、懂得奉献与付出的教师队伍。[1] 作为地方性大学法学院，“社区法律诊所”师资力量比较薄弱，在聘任社区书记、律师事务所律师为指导教师的同时，仍需要培养更多的诊所教师，加强培训，甚至还需要吸纳更多的社会热心人士来担任兼职指导教师，以推动诊所教育的发展。

结 语

“社区法律诊所”是大连大学法学院立足于地方性大学法律人才培养目标定位而对法律诊所教育模式改革的一次大胆尝试，也是对地方性大学提倡改善大学教育环境、加强人才培养模式改革的一次创新型的实践探索。经过几年的尝试，“社区法律诊所”丰富了法学专业实践教学的内容和形式，增强了学生对专业知识的学习热情，锻炼了学生的意志品格，基本达到了预期设计的效果，但是也需要看到改革尝试过程中遇到的诸多困难。对此，相信地方性大学法学院仍会秉承“服务地方”的理念，努力解决困难，迎接挑战，推动改革，最终实现人才培养的目标，为社会培养更多的具有法律职业精神和素养的复合型、应用型基层法律人才。

---

[1] 邓建民：“在法律实践中学习法律——论诊所法律教育对法学教育改革的意义”，载《西南民族大学学报（人文社科版）》2003年第10期。

少年司法视角下的本土广义街道法律诊所的运作探析

——来自江苏警官学院诊所式法律教育的报告

杜洪海*

摘　要：产生于美国的街道法律诊所运用多种实践教育方式，与法制宣传、教育紧密结合，在为弱势群体提供法律帮助方面独具特色。江苏警官学院（以下简称苏警院）法律诊所在本土化的过程中探寻了广义街道法律诊所的运行模式：包括课堂训练、以培训为主要形式的对未成年人的法制宣传及法律帮助、未成年人刑事案件辩护及代理、非法律援助的参与诉讼模式，在广义少年司法领域作出了探索。本土广义街道法律诊所的运作在诊所学生参与诉讼的身份定位、少年司法实践平台建设等问题上值得探讨。

关键词：法律诊所　法律帮助　法律援助　少年司法　运作

产生于20世纪20年代末的美国南加利福尼亚大学法学院诊所法律教育，借鉴医学教育的模式即医学院学生临床实习的做法，倡导在实践、经验中提升法科学生的法律素质及律师职业技能。诊所学生利用法律诊所——这个法律职业道德教育最好的平台，在鲜活的法律现实、实践中以准法律人的思维思考问题，以准法律人的行为方式来处理法律问题，并为弱势群体[1]提供看得见、真实的法律援助。而属于法律诊所类型之一的街道法律诊所的运作与少年司法制度建设息息相关。

未成年人是国家的未来，各国均重视对其的保护。未成年人犯罪问

---

* 杜洪海，江苏警官学院法律系讲师。

[1] 包括未成年人，又称少年。

题一直以来都是社会热点问题，切实完善各具特色的少年司法制度更是各国的当务之急。所谓少年司法制度，是指专门少年司法机构或者其他司法机构应用法律处理少年犯罪和不良行为案件，以达到保护和教育少年健康成长、防治少年犯罪和少年不良行为这两个目标的专门司法制度。[1] 立法方面，我国还未有独立的少年法，目前相关的法律规定只散见于《中华人民共和国刑事诉讼法》[2] 及《中华人民共和国未成年人保护法》《中华人民共和国预防未成年人犯罪法》中。虽然在立法层面新刑诉法确立了未成年人特殊刑事诉讼程序，因少年法的缺失及司法运行、未成年人社会保护等存在很多不足，少年司法制度在我国的完善是一个比较艰巨的过程。笔者赞成少年司法制度应向社会（社区）延伸的观点。[3] 街道法律诊所中，诊所学生应针对普通意义上的未成年人及违法、犯罪等失范未成年人进行法律咨询、法制宣传和持续性的同伴教育；以辩护人、代理人及社会调查员、合适成年人、社区矫正社工等身份介入未成年人刑事诉讼程序，促进少年司法制度的完善。

一、街道法律诊所的内涵

在美国，广义上的诊所式法律教育模式分为四类：虚拟的法律诊所、

---

[1] 姚建龙《长大成人：少年司法制度的构建》，中国人民公安大学出版社 2003 年版，第 20 页。

[2] 2012 新《刑事诉讼法》规定了未成年人特殊刑事程序，明确规定了对犯罪的未成年人实行“教育、感化、挽救”的方针，办案人员专业化，对未成年犯罪嫌疑人、被告人实行强制辩护，确立社会调查制度，严格适用逮捕措施和分案处理，实行讯问和审判未成年人时的合适成年人在场制度，设立附条件不起诉制度，规定了犯罪记录封存制度。“未成年人特殊刑事程序的设置，体现了我国对未成年当事人的特殊保护，使办理未成年人案件的程序更有针对性，更有利于通过诉讼活动为犯罪的未成年人改过自新和回归社会创造有利条件。”宋英辉：“专家解读新刑诉法：特别程序彰显对未成年人特殊保护”，载 http：//news.jcrb.com/jxsw/201204/t20120402_836636.html.

[3] 冯锐：“少年司法保护及其向社区延伸的理论与实践”，载云南省昆明盘龙区人民政府、救助儿童会编：《为了明天——未成年人保护与违法犯罪综合预防研讨会文集》，中国检察出版社 2007 年版，第 68 页。

真实当事人法律诊所、校外实习诊所以及街道法律诊所。[1] 自2000年初北大、清华、人大等高校率先在美国福特基金会的资助下开展诊所法律教育试验以来，诊所式法律教育的价值越来越被国内法律教育界认可和重视。相较于美国的四类模式，国内亦发展了模拟法庭实践教学模式、“诊所式”实践教学模式、法学专业教育实习模式与法律咨询、社会调查模式。其中，法律咨询、社会调查模式与街道法律诊所相似，但在中国的实践较少。[2]“街道法”是美国法学院开设的一门法律实用课程，被安排在诊所法律教育中。[3] 广义街道法诊所运用真实案件辩护及代理、模拟角色、模拟法庭、演讲、头脑风暴式游戏等多种教育、实践方式，通过学生承担社会责任，宣传法制并力所能及地为弱势群体提供法律帮助。[4] 街道法律诊所培养诊所学生在一个完整课程体系下参与主动学习和实践，具备或加深与被服务人群的沟通、理解能力，在训练团队合作精神的过程中学会共享、倾听，分析信息、观点，以及整合资源、资料的方法和技巧。

公益精神、社会责任感的具备和强化是街道法律诊所学生为未成年人等弱势群体提供包括法律援助在内的法律帮助质量的有效保证，应有专业教师的指导。[5] 学生在社区、街道、律所、其他司法机构开展街道法实践，明了法律职业道德与法律所代表的社会公平及正义的密切关系，向弱势群体传授法律知识、提供法律咨询，不仅提高了授课对象的法律水平，维护了弱势群体的合法权益，且能够在诉讼程序层面，用在诊所学到的专业知识帮助相关涉罪少年自我成长，使其更好地回归社会，也

---

[1] 韩爱芹、付云岭：“美国诊所法律教育的类型与中国法学实践教学模式”，载《科教文汇：下旬刊》2009年第6期，第284页。

[2] 韩晋、刘英：“‘街道法律诊所教育’的本土化模式”，载《经济研究导刊》2010年第22期，第221页。

[3] 王胤颖：“美国的街道法与青少年法制教育”，载《青少年犯罪研究》2001年第6期，第56页。

[4] 显然，此取广义街道大律诊所之义，这里的“法律帮助”亦是包括法律援助在内的广义的形式。

[5] 翁跃强、雷小政主编：《未成年人刑事司法程序研究》，中国检察出版社2010年版，第295页。

在一定程度上缓解了公安司法等工作人员的压力。

二、街道法律诊所模式

（一）平等、互动式的教学模式

建立于2009年的苏警院法律诊所（少年刑事法律诊所）带有显著的街道法律诊所性质，迄今为止共开设了8期诊所培训，共培训学员近300名左右。

在街道法律诊所，学生成为课堂的主人。讨论、分析和评判式的教学改变了传统灌输式教学方式的不足。教学过程中，有效利用小组合作的方式，设立观察员、评论员，就法律实务操作中出现的问题、疑点，教师引导学生进行思考，并控制学生讨论的进度、节奏。学生在平等的氛围里积极主动地发表意见，并能将小组讨论的合作成果展示给课上其他学生，教师需并联每一个小组代表性的意见，最后进行总结性评判。可以说，解决问题的方案是在学生主动探寻的条件下产生的。

在苏警院法律诊所的课堂上，教师引导以组为单位的学生设计会见未成年被告人（犯罪嫌疑人）场景，制作会见笔录，研讨辩护词、教育词的制作。基于头脑风暴课堂游戏的设计使学生在讨论抑或在欢愉中引发诸多思考，寓教于乐。如，绑腿奔跑游戏、拼图游戏考查了诊所学生作为律师的复述能力、理解能力及动手能力。比如，在语言表达方面如何做到准确，让委托人理解自己的真正意思；在观察能力方面如何做到细致入微，不放过任何一个细节等。头脑风暴游戏引发的学生对补强、传闻、直接言词等证据规则以及调查取证、会见、阅卷等律师权利的深思是活泼而深邃的。

（二）少年司法视角下的法律服务

诊所式法律服务具有专业化、持续性、便民性和公益性等特点，弥补了依靠政府行政力量的相关部门所组织的街头、社区、乡下不定期的法律咨询、宣传活动的临时性、流动性、形式化、功利化的不足。街道法律诊所更具有个案问诊的务实性及针对性的特色。具有街道法律诊所独特属性的苏警院法律诊所培养的诊所学生，在学习过程中通过第一步

“深化对法律理论、案例的认识”、第二步“系统、全面地对未成年人进行规范化的法制教育”的两步走方式，在实践过程中反身将系统的知识传授延续在广义少年司法、社会保护活动中，由法律教育客体转变为培训授课主体，同时也为少年司法制度的完善贡献了力量。

街道法律诊所的运行与青少年法制教育紧密相连。在美国，“街道法”课程被安排在街道法律诊所中，学生选修了“街道法”课程就意味着要承担对青少年的教育义务。[1] 促进少年在成长过程中建立公正观、秩序观、善良观并能在日常学习生活中不断实践、不断提高、不断升华，是培养有法治精神的社会主义接班人的必由之路。让未成年人具备基本的法律知识，懂得自己拿起法律武器以维护自己的合法权益，是街道法律诊所学生要做的基本工作。街道法律诊所的学生以己所学，以法律老师的身份来到未成年人身边，对其进行法制培训；进入社区为未成年人的家长提供未成年人法律保护方面的咨询，传授法的内涵、属性及守法、普法的重要性，对有失范倾向的未成年人的行为起到较好的“医治”和预防作用。[2] 未成年人懂法后对自己的行为有了主动的法律约束意识，这不仅有利于思想道德建设，而且更会促进广义少年司法制度建设。

苏警院法律诊所的学生通过进驻中小学、社区表演法制情景剧、演讲、课堂授课的方式，传授未成年人保护法、预防未成年人犯罪法、刑法、刑事诉讼法及民法等系统法律知识。教师在前期主要引导诊所学生从多种渠道深度了解被服务对象的法律需求，根据不同对象的需求，督促、辅导学生制定培训服务对象教学大纲和课程内容，设计贴近对象实际的实践策划书。[3] 比如，对普通中小学生及工读学校的学生，采取多媒体授课、讲解法律知识并穿插互动、游戏、知识竞赛、情景剧，其中

---

[1] 王胤颖：“美国的街道法与青少年法制教育”，载《青少年犯罪研究》2001年第6期，第56页。

[2] 诊所学生在为未成年人被告人辩护的过程中，曾从实证的角度总结过案件发生的原因，发现绝大多数的当事人都存在法律意识薄弱、法律知识存在盲区的状况。

[3] 苏警院法律诊所的街道法律帮助对象有普通的中小学生，还有特殊（培智、聋哑）、工读学校的少年。

针对高年级的中小学生可以采取展现或合办模拟法庭的方式，在授课过程中充分发挥案例的作用，采取多种“教学方法”将法律问题、法律知识讲清、讲透。根据农民工子弟学校、培智学校的特殊属性，大多采取形象、生动的游戏、情景剧的方式。这些孩子的家长法律素质的重要性引起了法律诊所的重视，因此街道法律诊所培训对象中也包含家长。长期以来，苏警院法律诊所的学生在培训相关家长法律素质学校的建立和健全过程中洒下了辛勤的汗水，得到了所服务的中小学及社会的较高评价。

在发挥诊所学生主动性的同时，特别是涉及情景剧角色扮演、模拟法庭等，教师对诊所学生的引导、辅导也很重要，如良好人际关系、沟通的能力及概括归纳问题中心和重点的能力、较快时间适应教师角色的能力。特别是适应教师角色的能力，直接影响街道法律诊所法律服务的形象、生动及同伴效应等优势是否能够彻底发挥出来。街道法律诊所的法律帮助模式培养学生面临培训授课对象对讲授内容质疑时的能动处理能力、在培训授课各项工作中的自我管理能力、在培训授课过程中展示优良品格和专业素养的能力，帮助发展诊所学生在培训授课过程中的自我认知和批判性思维能力并在活动中找到自身的价值。[1]

街道法律诊所教师的教学设计应包括帮助、指导学生在经验与教训中学习、成长。而学生对突发问题的处理能力强弱，对整个授课、活动的控场及自我管理能力强弱，均是诊所课堂后期进行实践综合反馈、评价的项目。每次从普法实践中总结出来的经验包括与此相关的未成年人社会、司法保护等实证调查，[2] 不仅使公平、正义、尊重人权等司法理念深植于诊所学生的内心，而且法治精神在这样的双向熏陶中得到发扬，健康、向上的法律职业性格在法律经验的积累中得到锤炼。街道法律诊

---

[1] 韩晋、刘英：“‘街道法律诊所教育’的本土化模式”，载《经济研究导刊》2010 年第 22 期，第 222 页。

[2] 值得一提的是，苏警院法律诊所每次法律实践活动都做到了发放问卷调查，内容涉及服务主体对法律的认识、社区矫正项目及效果评价、融入社会状况及未成年人保护等问题，有的问卷还涉及对家长的法律咨询知识调查以及征询家长对街道法律诊所学生在“社会、家长、孩子共成长”活动中的评价。

所的学生在达到街道法律诊所的“公共服务”教学目标的过程中，从法律诊所课程的学生变成了未成年人群体的“教师”，实现了理论与实践的双向互动发展，真正诠释了准法律人“以我所学，服务社会”的精神。他们身上所洋溢的为实现法律理想而作为准法律人的满足感和成就感、职业责任感不仅感染了诊所教师、服务对象，也征服了他们自己。

2009年以来，苏警院法律诊所学员走入了南京外国语学校、树人国际学校、南大附中、宁工小学、鼓楼特殊学校、育英第二外国语学校、芳草园小学、白云园小学、六一小学、浦口实验小学、顶山中心小学等十多所中小学为未成年人进行法制宣传，江苏卫视少儿频道、江苏卫视早安江苏频道、南京电视台18频道、浦口电视台、江苏法制报及法治鼓楼等电视、报纸、网站均有报道，收到了很好的社会效果，不论是广义少年司法的犯罪预防还是未成年人法制宣传教育，带有街道法律诊所特点的苏警院法律诊所成了新兴法律诊所中一道亮丽的风景线。

（三）未成年人案件刑事法律援助

刑事法律援助是国家以法律化、制度化的形式，为经济困难或者特殊刑事案件的当事人提供免费或者减费的法律帮助，以保障其社会基本权利得以实现的一项法律制度。作为国家应尽的义务和公民实现其社会基本权利的重要途径，刑事法律援助作为一种重要的司法救济制度被世界各国普遍采用。[1] 虽然在国家制度中担负着不同的使命，诊所式法律教育以在真实的案件中为弱势群体提供法律帮助（援助）为目标，拓展了法律援助的人力资源渠道，一定程度上缓解了供需矛盾，与刑事援助制度的宗旨、任务有契合之处，两者在理论和实践上互相促进，相辅相成。法学院诊所在法律援助工作方面所起的作用也许并不是很大，但是诊所本身所负有的教育任务得到了律师业和法律援助团体的普遍认可。[2] 苏警院法律诊所的未成年人刑事案件法律援助模式不仅成为少年司法之

---

❶ 沈凌、叶晓辉：“‘法律援助——诊所式法律教育’模式的研究”，载《辽宁行政学院学报》2009年第12期，第37页。

❷ 杨欣欣主编：《法学教育与诊所式教学方法》，法律出版社2002年版，第75页。

刑事法律援助制度中不可忽视的部分，也为街道法律诊所的运行找到了崭新的途径。[1]

围绕真实未成年人刑事案件的辩护与代理，教师根据周密的课程设计，训练学生法学专业思维能力，引导学生在占有资料、资源的基础上，主动找到解决怎样圆满履行辩护、代理职责等问题的途径，培养其通过检索法律条文、整理和研究资料、阅卷、会见以及制作阅卷笔录、会见提纲、调查笔录等，掌握对法律资源、资料进行占有、阅读、分析及概括的能力，收集事实材料和相关证据的能力，分析案件事实、构成要件和刑事责任的能力，发现案件事实与相关法律条文之间联系的能力，主动、积极地发现案件中“法律真实”的能力，使学生成为学习的主人。[2]

例如阅卷，教师指导学生仔细研究从司法机关复制得来的证据材料，[3] 主要包括拘留证、逮捕证、传唤证，起诉意见书、起诉书等诉讼文书，犯罪嫌疑人供述和辩解、证人证言、被害人陈述等言词证据，以及书证、物证、鉴定意见、现场勘验笔录等，通过寻找这些证据是否达到确实充分的标准、证据链是否存在问题，从而为了为被告人做无罪或者罪轻辩护打好事实基础。值得一提的是，在一起盗窃案件的证据审查中，诊所学员仅是在教师引入性的指导下，就对该案所涉及的诉讼行为时间上的衔接和公安机关的起诉意见、检察机关起诉时罪名的变化等问题进行了热烈讨论和研究。一名法律诊所学生曾这样对教师说：“每一份放进案卷的笔录都是为了证明该案件的某一个或几个点，能不能互相印证就是关键了。口供在公检法办案人员心目中一直是证据之王，所以，我们一定要认真、细心，一字一句，不要放过任何一个细节，认真阅读分析。”在阅卷的时候，法律诊所的学生注意到应将证人、被害人对有关事实的陈述与犯罪嫌疑人、被告人的供述、辩解进行综合比较，找出自

---

[1] 如前文所述，笔者认为，街道法律诊所模式应该包括法律援助，与不包括法律援助模式的通说有差别。

[2] 杨文丽、高凛：“诊所式法律教育与法律人的培养”，载《江南大学学报（教育科学版）》2007 年 6 月第 2 期，第 34 页。

[3] 目前，法律诊所学生作为指定辩护人对未成年人刑事公诉案件的阅卷，仍仅限制在案件移交到法院以后。

相矛盾的地方，并以小组讨论的方式分析矛盾产生的原因。除了紧密围绕案件事实的讨论之外，小组成员还对涉及案件诉讼卷、证据卷中时间、地点、人物、告知、签名问题，制作笔录的时间是处在案件的什么阶段，制作了几次，每次的时间间隔，被告人的供述发生了什么变化，为什么会有这种变化，笔录的制作时间、制作主体、制作程序是否规范合法等问题进行细致的分析、研究。如，在一起涉及被告人年龄问题的案件中，法律诊所的学生在笔录中发现被告人的出生日期存在农历和公历不对应的情况，在庭审中得到了法官的肯定。

又如写辩护词。从法律、事实层面找到被告人无罪、罪轻或者减轻、免除其刑事责任的意见是一名辩护律师最基本的技能。建立在以上实务训练的基础上，教师引导学生思考如何将动态的分析案件事实、刑事责任的过程演变成静态的辩护词，同时还要严格遵守法律文书的格式，注意在辩护词中使用法言法语，辩护条理清晰，有理有据，做到以法说理、以情动人。

再如出庭。教师持续训练学生具备使命感和责任感，法律职业道德和职业素质的效果在出庭这一环节得到非常深刻的体现。每一位诊所学生均能认真负责对待，全力以赴，自发做到每一个行为都受这样的使命感的支配和统领，敢辩慎辩。同时，少年案件特殊的庭审方式如法定代理人出庭、法庭教育环节包括合适成年人参与诉讼等问题，都是法律诊所学生特别注意的。可以说，每经过一次辩护、代理，街道法律诊所的学生就是与少年司法制度近距离接触了一次。

苏警院法律诊所学生在真实案件中体会法律知识、法律技能的运用，同时在为涉案未成年人提供法律援助的过程中也直观感受到法的力量及法律人的职业道德和社会责任感的真谛。自该法律诊所成立 3 年来，诊所学生在故意毁坏财物、诈骗、盗窃、抢劫、破坏电力设备等真实案例中，零距离接触、援助了近 20 名涉罪未成年人，达到了较好的“同伴教育”效果。其中，有几起是比较复杂的共同犯罪及数罪并罚的案件，在诊所教师的悉心指导下，承担案件辩护、代理任务的诊所学生开庭前认真分析案件事实证据、阅卷、会见及精心撰写辩护词、教育词，圆满履行了辩护职责。庭审结束后，主审法官、主控检察官、当事人的法定代理人对法律诊所学生认真、敬业的态度及庭审中的表现等都给予了高度评价。

法律诊所的学生在真实的案件中融入少年司法制度，这种与司法制度近距离接触的方式对诊所学生的影响是巨大的。通过以下笔者摘录的法律诊所一学生的辩护心得可窥见一斑："在接到法律诊所援助的案子后，心情格外激动，这是我学习法律以来第一次真真正正地接触法律事务，对一切都充满了好奇和期待。我终于可以身临其境地去感受法律的威严，去体会威严背后的公平与正义，去触碰未成年被告人内心的悔恨。作为未来的法律人，信仰法律是我的追求，法律精神在于惩恶扬善，在于定纷止争，在于促进和谐。现阶段的我在掌握了一定的法律理论基础后，对一切法律事务充满了好奇和期待。这次有机会接到这个援助的案子，我感到很荣幸，感受到自己内心汹涌澎湃的动力，感受到作为法律人的那份荣耀。在我将要为这个案子效力时，我真切地知晓这个案子的分量，它既是锻炼我的一次绝佳机会，同时也教会我作为法律人如何更好地履职。从中我也可以感受到身上那份沉甸甸的责任，它关乎未成年被告人的未来，关乎我的职业信仰，我必定会发挥我的所长，切实履行好辩护人职责，为被告人争取到最公平的法律判决。"

（四）非法援性质的介入诉讼

1. 社区矫正

"未成年人社区矫正，即是把符合条件的不满 18 周岁的违法犯罪人置于社区内，由专门国家机关在相关的社会团体和民间组织以及社会志愿者的协助下，矫正其犯罪心理和行为恶习，使其在正常的生活环境中接受帮助和教育，从而改变原有的不良思想和行为，接受正确的道德规范和行为准则，同时从生活、学习、心理等各方面给予帮助，并促进其顺利回归社会的非监禁刑罚执行活动。"[1] 很显然，未成年犯社区矫正不

---

[1] 桑爱英："未成年人社区矫正制度比较研究"，载《云南大学学报法学版》2011 年 1 月第 1 期，第 89 页。

仅是监管、考查，教育、改造亦是其应有之义。该项工作是非常严肃、专业性很强的工作，直接影响受矫正的未成年人的成长，也在一定程度上影响社区的正常生活秩序。❶

社区矫正工作者的选取采取专业工作者与志愿者相结合的模式是很多地区的做法。司法社工的介入是少年司法制度的创新，社工的身份能让未成年矫正对象更轻松地进行自我认识、自我剖析、自我开放以及自我成长，❷ 同时在一定程度上缓解公安司法等工作人员的压力。笔者认为，司法社工亦包含很大一部分志愿者，街道法律诊所的学生理所当然可以成为这样的志愿者，在参加由相关司法所定期的关于法律知识、谈话技巧、心理疏导、矫正技能、组织协调、危机应对、突发事件预防等方面的培训后，❸ 用在诊所学到的专业知识协助这些涉罪少年进行自我成长，更好地回归社会。特别是大学生与涉罪未成年人年龄相仿，有共同语言，相较于其他身份的志愿者具有不可比拟的同伴教育优势。3 年来，苏警院法律诊所在两个社区参与的对涉罪未成年人的社区矫正所做的访谈、问卷、心理疏导等工作得到了司法所、街道干部及社区民警的高度赞扬。同时，法律诊所的学生在社区矫正工作中，还能够就现实状况提出完善我国未成年人社区矫正制度的看法和建议，对少年司法制度的完善与时俱进地做较深程度的思考。

上文所提的社区矫正制度的适用范围限于刑罚执行领域。笔者赞同学者及相关实务人士的观点，将相对不起诉的涉罪未成年人也列入其中，并尽早设立专门机构，构筑立体的社区矫正网络。❹ 随着刑法修正案八的施行及 2012 新刑诉法的通过，未成年人社区矫正及刑事诉讼全面调查

❶ 北京规则：以社区观护办法替代少年司法诉讼程序的可行办法，通过短时期监督和指导以避免将来触犯法律事件的方案。

❷ 席小华：《少年司法社会工作理论与实务研究初探》，中国人民公安大学出版社 2011 年 2 月第 1 版，第 259 页。

❸ 当然，此类培训业可以充分利用法律诊所与司法实务部门的合作优势，将相关的专业、实务人员请到法律诊所来，对学生进行针对性的矫正技能培训。

❹ 马柳颖：《未成年人犯罪刑事处遇制度研究》，知识产权出版社 2009 年版，第 250 页。

原则在少年司法制度中占有的地位越来越重要，而具有街道法属性的苏警院法律诊所的学员在未成年人社区矫正运行及诉讼中承担了审查起诉环节的涉罪未成年人品格证据社会调查员以及刑罚执行环节的矫正志愿者社工的职责，笔者认为，这是在司法人员指导、带领下贯彻新刑事诉讼立法精神的一种呼应。

未成年人刑事案件社会调查是少年司法制度的一个重要组成部分，[1]世界上许多国家和地区都对少年刑事案件实施社会调查做了明确规定。从长远来看，未成年人案件的社会调查工作对于全面掌握未成年人的犯罪情况和各种动态、探索研究预防未成年人犯罪提供了素材。可以说，从少年司法制度的角度，街道法律诊所的运行对侦查、[2]审查起诉、审前的未成年人社会调查制度以及附条件不起诉的后续观护制度的完善起到了有益的促进作用。司法人员在审查起诉、审前环节选取社会调查员时，苏警院法律诊所的学生因纪律严明、责任感及保密意识强更受人民检察院、人民法院的青睐。

2. 合适成年人参与刑事诉讼

合适成年人制度是指在刑事诉讼中，司法机关在讯问未成年犯罪嫌疑人时，必须要有合适的成人在场的制度。作为维护未成年人权益的一项重要的司法制度，它在西方刑事诉讼中具有重要意义。英国、美国、澳大利亚、新西兰、我国香港地区等国家和地区都有关于此项制度的立法。[3]根据2012新刑诉法的规定，对于未成年人刑事案件，在讯问和审判的时候，如法定代理人不能到场的，可以通知未成年犯罪嫌疑人、被

---

[1] 《联合国少年司法最低限度标准规则》即《北京规则》第16条规定："所有案件除涉及轻微违法行为的案件，在主管当局作出判决前的最后处理之前，应对少年生活的背景和环境或犯罪的条件进行适当的调查，以便主管当局对案件作出明智的判决。"

[2] 根据目前的司法实际，侦查阶段的社会调查、合适成年人制度的运行有较大的难度，但笔者相信，随着相关法制的逐步健全，其会逐步引起重视并有较大改变。

[3] 姚建龙："英国适当成年人介入制度及其在中国的引入"，载《中国刑事法杂志》2004年第4期，第5～6页。

告人的其他成年亲属，所在学校、单位、居住地基层组织或者未成年人保护组织的代表等合适的成人到场，并将有关情况记录在案。合适成年人制度作为一种新的制度，在我国的司法实践中被证实具有非常大的应用和发展空间。2011 年，苏警院法律诊所的学生曾作为南京中院指定的合适成年人参与到该制度试点工作中。在一起检察院指控罪名为故意杀人，被告人是外来性质未成年人的刑事案件中，远在东北的被告人法定代理人无法到场，诊所学生作为合适成年人以诉讼参与人的身份介入刑事审判程序，在审前的法官讯问未成年被告人时在场，并参与了全部庭审过程，一定意义上减少了外来涉罪未成年人由于家人不能到场、亲情上的缺失而产生的心理恐惧。合适成年人的介入虽然不能替代家人的关怀，但是能够在心理上给予涉罪未成年人极大的安慰，同时也能更好地帮助其认识到自己行为的危害性，使其能够平等地得到国家的关怀。

三、少年司法视角下本土街道法律诊所的运作与完善

本土街道法律诊所的运作无一例外都存在案源瓶颈、学生辩护和代理人身份定位、经费及实践平台建设等方面的问题。一方面，2012 新刑诉法强化了未成年刑事案件法律援助的规定，严谨了指定辩护人参与诉讼的程序，民诉法也对代理人参与诉讼提出了较高的要求，而学生是以志愿者的身份参与到法律援助工作中，必然面临身份不合规定的矛盾。为充分发挥街道法律诊所在少年司法中的作用，笔者建议《法律援助条例》及刑诉法司法解释应对高校法律援助机构的法律地位、职能作出明确的规定。对于未成年刑事案件指定辩护，可以考虑由公安、司法机关在侦查、起诉、审判等环节，通知法律援助机构指派律师或由律师与适格人员共同为其提供辩护。[1] 此外，还要有相关的具体条例对法律诊所学生参与刑事诉讼作出具体规制，并对相关的调查取证权、阅卷权、会见权、参与诉讼权等作出明确的规定。同时，法律诊所委员会或各院校法律诊所也应对诊所学生参与诉讼的范围、形式、责任作出严格、细致

---

[1] 这里的适格人员即指高校法律诊所学生。

的规范。

法律诊所教育教学活动通过真实的实务操作，能够夯实和提升学生的理论知识，积累执业经验，培养法律职业能力和责任感。为此，法律诊所教育活动的开展需要首先搭建好实践平台。法律诊所的实践平台是实现法学教育培养目标、培养学生的创新精神和实践能力的关键环节，对于法律诊所教育活动的顺利开展具有举足轻重的作用。苏警院法律诊所积极努力健全与律师事务所、公安机关、检察院、法院、司法局（所）、社区、街道的合作机制，为诊所学生提供了很好的实践渠道，所合作的实务部门在少年司法领域也因法律诊所学生的加入而完善了相关制度。当然，在合作的层次、范围及评估机制上，还有许多需要探讨的地方。

四、结语

总之，广义本土街道法律诊所的建立健全，充分实现其独特的有别于传统法学教育的教学价值，不仅仅能够为探索出一条符合我国国情的法律诊所的运作模式作出贡献，苏警院法律诊所致力于少年司法制度中的犯罪预防与控制的努力也较大程度上彰显了法律诊所的社会价值。少年司法制度的进步无疑也会促进以维护未成年人权利为己任的街道法律诊所更趋强大。

北京科技大学诊所式法律教育探索

王竹青*

摘　要： 诊所式法律教育于2000年开始传入我国，目前已有100多所大学成为诊所法律教育专业委员会的成员。北京科技大学法律系于2009年3月在校级教改项目的支持下开始探索诊所式法律教育，并于2010年4月成为专委会第130个会员单位。经过3年的探索实践，课题组从硬件设施的利用与资源整合、实践型法律课程的定位与衔接、诊所主题的确定与升华三个方面总结了自己在诊所式法律教育领域的经验与体会，希望对我国诊所法律教育的发展起到积极的推动作用。

关键词： 北京科技大学　诊所式法律教育　探索

诊所式法律教育起源于美国，20世纪60年代在美国得到迅速发展，成为法学教育中不可或缺的一门实践课程。我国于2000年在美国福特基金会的资助下开始开设诊所课程，最初有清华大学、北京大学、武汉大学等7所大学开设，后逐渐扩展到几十所大学，而尚未开设诊所课程的会员单位更是多达100多所大学。北京科技大学法律系于2010年4月加入中国法学教育研究会诊所教育专业委员会，成为第130个会员单位。

2009年3月，"诊所式法律教育"在北京科技大学校级教学改革项目中立项，开始对诊所式法律教育进行尝试性探索，到2012年3月，项目顺利完成。项目执行期间，笔者有一些经验和感受值得总结，以期与其他大学的法律诊所课程进行交流，共同推动我国诊所法律教育的发展。

---

* 王竹青，北京科技大学文法学院副教授，美国哥伦比亚大学2010～2011年度访问学者，中国人民大学法学博士。

一、硬件设施的利用与资源整合

诊所式法律教育是为真实当事人提供法律援助的实践教育，因此需要有接待室、案例研讨室以及电话、电脑、打印机、传真机等基本的办公用品。诊所式法律教育通常有校内诊所和校外诊所之分，校外诊所大多设在社区，依赖社区资源服务于社会的弱势群体；校内诊所则需要配备房间及上述硬件设备，因此需要大学给予先期投入。北京科技大学的诊所为校内诊所，在项目立项时学校尚未给予这些支持，只是作为普通教改项目给了很少的经费，这远远不能满足教学的需要。为了解决这一基础问题，课题组与“北京科技大学公共政策与法律研究中心”相结合，解决了房屋和基本办公设备的问题。

北京科技大学公共政策与法律研究中心（以下简称研究中心）是挂靠在北京科技大学的一个研究机构，自筹经费，自主管理，从事妇女和老年人权益保护工作，属于 NGO 性质。2008 年 1 月文法学院为中心安排了办公室，配备了办公桌椅等基本用品，其他电话、电脑、打印机等电子设备则在不同的项目中逐渐配置，到 2009 年研究中心已经具备了基本的办公条件。诊所式法律教育作为教改项目立项后，因课题组负责人是研究中心的主任，课题组其他成员也是研究中心的工作人员，因此利用研究中心的资源来开展诊所教育成为当然的选择。

这种最初的救急之举，在后来的诊所教育中体现出未曾预料的优势。研究中心的主要工作是从事妇女和老年人权益保护，因此诊所教育的主题可以在这两个领域中选择。考虑到妇女权益问题已经广受关注，而且已有其他大学的诊所以其为主题开展诊所教育，而老年人权益问题尚未引起社会各界的广泛关注，在当时的诊所主题中也没有涉及这一领域，因此课题组决定以老年人权益为诊所主题，由此创建了我国第一个老年人诊所。

将诊所的主题与研究中心的工作领域相结合，可以起到事半功倍的效果。首先，在案件来源上，因研究中心在执行项目过程中已经与相关机构建立了合作关系，如，就老年人权益问题，研究中心与全国老龄委、北京市东城区法院建立了合作关系，合作单位将需要法律援助的老年人案件介绍到研究中心，研究中心将案件分配给诊所学生，由指导老师对学生给予指导，为当事人提供专业的法律服务，这种模式使诊所教育的案件来源得到保障。其次，在法律服务水平上，与研究中心的结合使诊所学生的法律服务水平达到较高的程度。研究中心因专职从事老年人权益保护工作，对相关领域的法律法规和政策较为熟悉，在适用法律上基本可以做到全面、有效。另外，研究中心的老师大多从事律师工作，对案件代理有着较为丰富的经验，在指导学生代理案件上可以做到游刃有余。因指导老师长期关注并从事老年人权益保护工作，其专业知识水平和实际操作水平都相对较高，在其指导下的学生为当事人提供较高水平的法律服务就成为一种必然结果。

北京科技大学的这种模式并非只能在研究中心工作人员与课题组成员重合的情况下才能实现，在研究中心的人员与课题组成员不重合的情况下依然有实现的可能。目前各大学都设有不同主题的研究中心，特别是关注社会弱势群体、关注社会公平正义、关注人类可持续发展主题的研究中心更是不胜枚举。尚未开展诊所法律教育的大学在开设这一课程时可以考虑对现有研究中心资源的利用与整合；已开设诊所课程的大学可以考虑将诊所的主题与研究中心的主题相契合，或者在诊所教育的基础上创办一个研究中心。这样可以有效地解决诊所经费不足、教师投入多而回报少的问题，因为研究中心作为一个平台可以申请到一些项目，特别是关注社会弱势群体、关注社会公正的研究中心容易得到国外资金和国内资金的资助。目前诊所教师面临很多困境，各高校对教师的年度考核和职称评定都以科研为标准，课题的经费和性质、论文发表的级别和数量成为衡量教师资质的标准，法律实务技能的有无和多寡在所不问。这一体制的直接影响是：强化了教师在学术上的研究而弱化了其从事法律实务的愿望，使教师获得实务技能的可能性更为降低。[1] 而诊所与研究中心的结合，使教师在做项目的同时，对相关领域的研究更为深入，可以写出有价值的研究报告，同时指

---

[1] 陈思琴："中国法学院不能承受之重"，载《福建论坛》2009年第2期，第180页。

导了学生，还让当事人接受了免费的专业法律服务，可谓事半功倍。如果不能达到这种完美状态，诊所教育也要尽可能借助研究中心的资源，努力达到各种资源的最佳配置与利用。

二、实践型法律课程的定位与衔接

目前我国高校开设的实践型课程主要包括模拟法庭、律师实务、法律诊所、专业实习等。其中，模拟法庭、律师实务和校内法律诊所在校内开设，功能和作用各有侧重，但有些内容相互重叠，若不能做好协调工作，将达不到应有的教学目的。

北京科技大学法律系目前开设的课程包括模拟法庭和律师实务，校内法律诊所尚未正式列入教学计划，处于试行阶段。在教改项目执行期间，课题组对上述3门课程的功能和作用进行了讨论，确定了各自不同的教学内容和教学重点，以期达到各门课程的最佳效果，并实现3门课程之间的有效衔接。

律师实务主要以律师业务为教授内容，包括律师职业道德与职业规范、与当事人的沟通、调查取证、法律文书写作（主要是起诉书、答辩状、代理词）、案例分析、法庭辩论、参与调解、以当事人利益最大化为导向等。律师实务课程的功能是让学生了解律师的职业理念、操守、工作技能等方面的知识，用律师的思维方式去解决问题。

模拟法庭源于外国法学院的 Moot Court/ Mock Court/ Mock Trial 课程，是为法学院学生举办的讨论模拟或者假设案例的虚拟审判，是教授审判程序、证据规则、法律辩论、庭审技能、具体审判制度以及法律文书写作等职业技能的一种教学方法和课程，是法学本科专业重要的实践性教学环节。[1] 模拟法庭的功能主要是指导学生了解法庭审理程序，同时在模拟法庭上学习法官驾驭庭审的能力、检察官作为国家的代表提起公诉的方式以及律师出庭的技巧和方法。

从中可以看出，律师实务和模拟法庭在内容上有重叠之处，因此在

---

[1] 孙德强、李文沛："本科法学专业的实践教学方法的完善"，载《中国劳动关系学院学报》2011年第6期，第93页。

课程讲授上模拟法庭侧重于对法官角色的理解和把握，包括法官的职业道德和职业操守、法官主导庭审走向的能力、归纳总结庭审焦点的能力以及组织双方当事人举证、质证、辩论、调解的能力等。另外，检察官的法庭地位和作用也是模拟法庭要讲授的内容，以使学生了解检察官的角色、与律师的关系以及在司法中的地位和作用等。律师的职业道德和职业操守、职业技能等内容则主要由律师实务课程讲授。模拟法庭和律师实务是2门独立的课程，因此在律师实务课程中以讲授专业知识和方法、案例分析为主导，模拟开庭的教学任务主要由模拟法庭课程来完成。在课程设置上，模拟法庭和律师实务可以同时安排在第5学期或第6学期，2门课程在同一学期开设，学生对模拟法庭和律师实务的学习进度基本可以保持一致，在模拟法庭的训练中加入律师技能的运用；或者可以将律师实务安排在第5学期，模拟法庭安排在第6学期，这种安排可以让学生先掌握律师的职业技能，之后在模拟法庭课程中得到运用。对于只开设模拟法庭课程或只开设律师实务课程的大学来说，则可以将2门课程的内容整合起来，在专业知识讲授的基础上进行模拟开庭，达到模拟实践的目的。

诊所课程与模拟法庭和律师实务的区别在于，诊所课程不再是模拟实践，而是真实的实践，其内容侧重于将模拟法庭和律师实务课程中学到的知识运用于实践，在实践中体会、深化书本上学到的知识。诊所教育是最完整的实践课程，从与当事人第一次接触了解案情开始，直到作为代理人出庭参加诉讼，前两门课程中学到的知识都将在这门课程中得到运用，从而帮助学生检视课本中学到的知识与实际运用之间的差距。诊所课程最好安排在第7学期进行，此时所有的专业课程已经完成，学生不仅学习了各实体法、程序法，也学习了模拟的法律实践，对于代理真实的案件已经做好了充分的准备。虽然大四的学生有找工作的压力，但诊所课程为学生提供的实践机会将成为学生找工作的有利支持。因诊所课程以案件办理为主要内容，不再有定时上课的安排，因而也解决了大四学生出勤率低、上课效果差的教学问题。将3门课程整合后的教学效果非常突出，学生对3门课的定位极为清楚，也对模拟法庭和律师实务中的知识有了切身的体会，法律不再是书本上陌生的东西，而成为学生现实生活的一部分。

北京科技大学将诊所教育与模拟法庭、律师实务有机结合，构成了较为完善的法律实践教学体系。在其他大学开设的诊所课程中，模拟法庭通常被涵盖在诊所教育之中，因其占用的课时较短（往往是为要开庭的个案进行模拟开庭），因此缺乏系统性和理论性，对法官的职业道德、职业素养、庭审的目的和功能等内容往往不予涉及。而律师实务与诊所教育是独立的2门课程，诊所教师往往不承担律师实务的教学工作，因此很难将这些相关的课程整合起来。本课题组的成员同时担任模拟法庭和律师实务的教学工作，对3门课程重新定位，使得诊所课程的功能更为突出，学生对当事人、法官、检察官和律师等角色的理解更为深刻，对自己未来职业生涯的定位更为明确。

三、诊所主题的选择与升华

诊所法律教育的目的是服务于社会的弱势群体，同时培养学生的社会责任感和正义感。早在19世纪90年代晚期到20世纪早期，美国的一些法学院的学生就自愿建立了“法律诊所”或法律援助机构，以亲身参与的方式学习和实践法律，同时通过为贫弱群体提供法律服务的方式践行社会的司法使命。[1] 在20世纪60～70年代，美国诊所式法律教育的理念从单纯培养学生的律师技能转变为服务于社会的贫弱群体，从伦理和道德的角度培养学生的社会责任感，培养学生从事关涉穷人的法律实践，

---

[1] 约翰·布莱威：“法律援助诊所的特性”，载《加利福尼亚法律评论》1930年第3期，第174页。（John S. Bradway, *The Nature of a Legal Aid Clinic*, 3 S. Cal. L. Rev, (1930). p. 174.）罗伯特·麦克科瑞特：“执教一个变化中的职业——从诊所到后续问题”，载《田纳西法律评论》1997年第64期，第1102～1103页。（Robert MacCrate, *Educating a Changing Profession: From Clinic to Continuum*, 64 Tenn. L. Rev, (1997), pp. 1102～1103.）威廉·罗：“法律诊所与训练有素的律师——一种必要”，载《伊利诺斯法律评论》1917年第11期，第591页。（William V. Rowe, *Legal Clinics and Better Trained Lawyers-A Necessity*, 11. Ill. L. Rev, (1917). p. 591.）

在社区中树立法律院校的地位并发挥作用，❶ 强调通过诊所式教育来实现以社会公正为导向的社会正义。当时的诊所项目为贫弱当事人的众多法律问题提供了法律服务。许多诊所项目办理了一些重大案件，这些案件涉及法律改革以及当时社会的一些基本问题。所有这些为探索最基本的理论问题、实质问题以及概念问题提供了极佳的教学方法，与真实社会的脉搏一起跳动。❷

在上述理念的指导下，我国诊所教育开展十余年来，几十所大学确定了不同的主题作为诊所教育的特点和依托，如，武汉大学开设了社会弱者法律诊所，清华大学开设了劳动者权益保护法律诊所、弱者权益保护法律诊所以及公民权利救助法律诊所，北京大学开设了民事法律诊所，人民大学也以社会弱者为诊所主题，中国政法大学开设了刑事法律诊所，西北政法大学开设了农村社区诊所，西南政法大学以“所有人的正义”为主题，还有的大学以环境保护、社会可持续发展为主题，内容丰富，主题多元，形成了具有一定规模的中国诊所式法律教育。

北京科技大学地处北京，京内一些知名大学的诊所教育开展得较为成熟，因此选择诊所主题成为课题组面临的首要问题。诊所主题的选择不是以追求新奇为目的，更不是为了媒体效应，但从诊所的发展及服务于社会的功能来看，选择合适的主题是扩大诊所影响、有效服务社会的必要条件。诊所主题的选定原则应以社会弱势群体为服务对象，以实现社会正义为诊所目标。在此前提下，应考虑各地的实际情况，如，环境污染严重的地区可以考虑以环境保护为诊所主题，农民工集中的地区可以考虑以农民工劳动权益为诊所主题等。在对我国诊所式法律教育的现状进行分析的情况下，结合本校研究中心的现有资源，课题组决定以老年人权益为诊所的主题。

---

❶ 尼娜·塔尔：“目前诊所法律教育的问题”，载《夏威夷法律评论》1993年第37期，第32页。（Nina W. Tarr, *Current Issues in Clinical Legal Education*, 37 Haw. L. J. (1993). p. 32.）

❷ 亚瑟·科诺伊：“法律教育的现实危机”，载《拉特格斯法律评论》1969年第24期，第7页。（Arthur Konoye, *The Present Crisis in Legal Education*, 24 Rutgers L. Rev. (1969). p. 7.）

中国已经进入老龄社会，但老龄社会所面临的问题尚未引起社会各界的充分关注。怎样让这个群体引起社会各界的关注以及怎样保护这个群体的合法权益，是当前亟须研究的问题。北京作为经济发达城市，医疗条件较为优越，人均寿命高于全国大多数城市，老龄化程度相对高，老龄问题较为突出，因此以老年人权益为诊所主题有地缘优势，可以通过法律援助案件的代理，了解老年人的生存状况及面临的困难，对我国未来出台老年人社会保障政策和法律提供第一手资料。课题组以敏锐的视角注意到这一问题，并引导学生通过个案代理和访谈等形式对老年人群体的权益状况进行调查，学生代理的案件涉及老年人赡养、房屋侵权、人身损害、婚姻自由等诸多问题，具有典型性和代表性，一定程度上反映了我国老年人目前的生存状况和面临的困难，具有积极的现实意义。

在诊所主题的选定上，除要考虑服务于社会弱势群体外，还需考虑对社会公平与正义的追求，要引导学生学会发现现象背后存在的社会问题。以老年人权益为例，在诊所学生接触到的当事人中，同样都是70～80岁的老人，有的老人是从机关干部岗位退休的，有的老人是从企业管理岗位退休的，但退休金的差异很大，机关干部的退休金大约为每月5000元左右，而企业管理人员的退休金大约为每月2000～3000元。同样是退休人员，同样参加工作30多年，退休金的差距为何如此巨大？这是否反映了我国分配不均的社会现状？此外，城市的老人大多有退休金，生活基本都有保障；而农村的老人基本没有经济来源，主要依靠子女养老。没有经济来源的老人生活较为困苦，在子女经济条件差或不孝顺的情况下更是如此。这种城乡差异的存在是否合理？让农村人口承担社会发展的主要成本是否公平？为什么牺牲的是他/她们？这些问题会引起学生对社会现实的反思，使学生学会批判性思维，明白法律的真谛，并且懂得追求社会正义是法学学生的天然使命。

四、结语

尽管诊所式法律教育在美国法学教育中是一个永恒的目标，但很多时候诊所教育和诊所项目仍处于一些法学院课程设置的边缘地带。[1]几乎在每一个法学院，这些课程继续被划归为选修课，既不是获得毕业证书的必要条件，也不是获得律师资格的必要条件。从事诊所教学的教师在法学院也处于边缘的位置，他们地位较低，权利较少，收入也少。[2] 这些负面作用在中国的诊所法律教育中同样存在，到目前为止，几乎所有诊所课程都是选修课，而诊所教师比其他专业课教师投入了更多的时间和精力，但在评价体系上却无不同，诊所教师得不到相应的收入和教学认可。一些大学因缺乏愿意从事诊所教育的教师而不得不外聘退休法官或退休律师担任授课任务，这又使得教师的专业性受到影响。

北京科技大学的法律诊所模式在某种程度上解决了上述问题，与研究中心的结合保证了教师的经济收入和科研需要，同时也解决了诊所教师不受重视的问题；在课程的设置上，虽然诊所课程是选修课，但因其较强的实践性以及弹性的工作时间而受到学生的认可与欢迎。

在 3 年的项目执行过程中，课题组从陌生到熟悉，指导学生一步步走进诊所教育的崭新领域。参与的学生从大三到大四，反馈着参加诊所课程的心得与体会，诊所课程与模拟法庭、律师实务课程的定位也逐渐清晰，指导老师对诊所教育的理解和把握更为成熟。源自美国的法律诊所课程在经过本土化的改良后，其弊端将会越来越少，而其体现的核心价值将受到越来越多的认可与关注。学生普遍认为，诊所课程是大学四年不可不学的一门课程。一位清华大学法学院的学生在诊所教育的报告

---

[1] 黛博拉·罗德：《正义的利益：法律职业的改革》，2000 年，第 198 页。(Deborah L. Rhode, *In the Interests of Justice*: *Reforming the Legal Profession*, p. 198, (2000).)

[2] 安东尼·阿尔菲耶里："反对实践"，载《密西根法律评论》2009 年第 107 期，第 1074 页。(Anthony V. Alfieri, *Against Practice*, 107 Mich. L. Rev. p. 1074, (2009).) 皮特·乔伊、罗伯特·库恩："美国律师协会对诊所教师的评价标准"，载《田纳西法律评论》2008 年第 75 期，第 187 页。 (Peter A. Joy & Robert R. Kuehn, *The Evolution of ABA Standards for Clinical Faculty*, 75 Tenn. L. Rev. (2008). p. 187.)

中提道："清华法学院的学生几乎形成了一种心理惯性：读了四年法律，没选过任何课都没关系，但若没选过法律诊所，你的这四年就是不完整的。"这对法律诊所课程而言是无与伦比的赞誉。[1]

---

[1] SRT 小组："清华大学法学院诊所式法律教育开展状况调查及初步研究成果报告"（正文节选），载 http：//oa. law. tsinghua. edu. cn/LegalClinicalEdu/ReadNews. asp? NewsID=28724，2012 年 4 月 1 日。

我国法律诊所模式的本土化与多元化趋势

李　傲　马立群*

摘　要： 诊所式法律教育已逐步被国内诸多高校接受，成为法学教育改革和发展的趋势。法律诊所教育的内容、方法与法律诊所的模式密切相关。当前，法学院校在诊所的类型、教师配置、课程设计与管理、资金支持以及与法律实务部门的合作方式等方面，正在做着有益的探索。法律诊所未来的发展，应在保障其独有的教学目标的前提下，提倡诊所类型的专业化趋势，发挥诉讼法律诊所与非诉法律诊所的特点，鼓励诊所类型的多元化发展。同时，规范法律诊所课程的评价机制，在制度上保障法律诊所教学的可持续发展。

关键词： 法律诊所教育　诉讼法律诊所　非诉法律诊所

法律诊所教育肇始于美国，是20世纪60年代民权运动的兴起与法律现实主义的推动等因素共同作用下的产物。事实上，早在1901年，俄国教授亚历山大·琉布林斯基（Alexander Lyublinsky）已提出法律诊所教育的设想，他认为可以参照医院诊所模型在法学院设立法律诊所。[1]时至今日，法律诊所教育被以美国为主的许多国家所借鉴，呈现出全球化发展的趋势。我国法律诊所教育10余年来发展迅速，截至目前，已有140余所高校法学院系开设了诊所法律教育课程。我国高校设立的法律

---

* 李傲，法学博士，武汉大学法学院教授，博士生导师。马立群，法学博士，西南政法大学行政法学院讲师。本文为初稿，部分论证和资料还需补充修正，请勿转发转引，谢谢。

[1] Richard J. Wilson: *Training for Justice: The Global Reach of Clinical Legal Education*, Penn St. Int'l L. Rev. 421, 2004.

诊所模式偏疏各异，运作方式也各有不同。探讨适应国际发展、符合国内法律教育的法律诊所模式对我国法律诊所教育的完善和发展具有重要意义。

一、国外法律诊所的设置方式

法律诊所教育最突出的3个目标在于专业技术训练、专业经验学习、社会正义和价值观的灌输。[1]法律诊所的设计形式与其所欲达到的目的密切相关，是法律诊所教育首先要解决的基础问题。国外法律诊所的设置有不同的形式，基本可以做如下归类。

（一）校内诊所与校外实习地诊所

校内诊所（In-House Clinic），也可称为内置式诊所，是指依托学校法学院，将其诊所活动中心置于学校中的法律诊所。校内诊所是法律诊所最初的形态，最常见的是依托学校法学院所成立的法律诊所。在校内法律诊所中，诊所教师负责指导学生参与实践活动，包括会见当事人、提供法律咨询、代写诉讼文书、调查和分析案件事实、提供政策依据、出庭代理诉讼等。学校为了支持法律诊所教学活动，会在校内或学校附近设置接待处，以保障诊所学生参与实践所需要的案源。

校外实习地诊所（Externship Clinic），也可称为外置式诊所，这类诊所是法律诊所教育向社会逐渐扩展的过程中产生的。校外实习地诊所的主要场所通常在学校之外，通过法律诊所与其他社会机构的合作完成教学任务。如法律诊所与政府机构、社会组织、公司、社区、法院、律师事务所、医院、劳教部门、监狱等单位进行合作。校外实习地诊所通常将上述单位作为实践场所，学生在合作单位派出的指导教师与法学院诊所教师的共同指导之下从事法律实践工作。这类法律诊所使学生走出校园，最大限度地融入法律实践工作，直面社会问题。其形式类似于国内法学院的实习，但强调在此阶段中法学院法律诊所教师的教学指导作

[1] Frank S. Bloch, *Access to Justice and the Global Clinical Movement*, 28 WASH. U. J. L. & POL'Y 111, 121, 2008.

用，要求校内外教师分工和配合，诊所教师的教学活动贯穿于校外实习地诊所学习的始终。

（二）诉讼法律诊所与非诉法律诊所

诉讼法律诊所（Litigation Clinic）也是法律诊所产生较早的形态，这类诊所主要是通过指导学生亲自代理法律援助案件，完成法律诊所的教学任务。诉讼法律诊所的目的在于让学生“像律师那样行动和思考”，通过接触当事人，参与真实案件的代理，让学生有机会从教室走进法庭，在实践中检验自身对法律知识的掌握，训练法律职业者应当具备的技能。诉讼法律诊所中的一个核心目的在于培养学生的法律思维，训练学生的法庭代理技能，同时也培养了学生的法律援助意识与社会责任感。

非诉法律诊所（Non-litigation Clinic）不以学生参与诉讼代理为途径，而是将注意力集中在培养学生解决实际问题的能力，对法律法规的熟练掌握成为非诉解决纠纷的知识背景。同时，注重训练学生的逻辑思维能力与沟通表达能力。非诉法律诊所关注社会、文化、传统、道德伦理以及习俗的作用，提倡在自愿、平等、公平的前提下创造性地解决纠纷。

（三）综合性诊所与专业性诊所

综合性诊所（Comprehensive Clinic）的特点是不对受援助对象做特殊限制，通常是以“社会贫弱者”为服务对象，以受援助人的要求为标准，以法律允许为前提，在不同的专业领域提供法律服务。其主要服务方式包括提供法律咨询、代理诉讼等内容。

专业性诊所（Specialized Clinic）是依托学校的优势学科或根据社会需求成立的专门领域的诊所。有些学校由最初的综合性法律诊所逐渐发展为多个专业性诊所。与律师事务所的专业性发展趋势类似，专业性诊所同样是随着社会结构的发展以及法律分工的细化而产生的，这类法律诊所更注重法律知识的专业性和特殊性，注重特定领域法律实务技能的积累。专业性诊所如反性别歧视法律诊所、农村法律诊所、刑事社区矫治法律诊所、街道法诊所、低收入纳税人诊所、老年人（未成年人、精神病人、外来务工者、残疾人、消费者、医院患者、行政诉讼案件原告等）权利保护法律诊所、环境法诊所等。

（四）国内法律诊所与国际法律诊所

国内法律诊所（Internal Clinic）是指围绕国内法和国内法律事务为核心而成立的法律诊所。目前我国的法律诊所以国内法律诊所为主。

国际法律诊所（International Clinic）是随着全球化运动而被提出，以服务涉外法律事务为目标的法律诊所。国际法律诊所教育可以为法学院的学生特别是国际法专业的学生提供国际法律实践的机会，学生在这些诊所运用国际法知识，与国际法律机构、国内外律师一起工作，或为涉外求助者提供法律服务。在美国的国际人权法领域、移民出入境法领域，法律诊所学生的实践活动非常活跃，例如哈佛大学法学院的国际人权法律诊所（International Human Rights Clinic）。

上述法律诊所的设置模式，从形式上对法律诊所进行了区分，目的在于明辨差异，但不同类型的法律诊所之间亦有交叉之处。如，诉讼法律诊所既可以是校外诊所，也可以是校内诊所；专业性法律诊所有可能是诉讼法律诊所，也有可能是非诉法律诊所，或者是两者兼备。

二、我国法律诊所的特色

2000年我国首批高校开展了诊所式法律教育。法律诊所教育作为借鉴移植的产物，需要不断改进以适应中国的法治教育土壤。目前，我国法律诊所的设置模式各异，总体而言具有如下特色。

（一）高校法律援助中心与法律诊所的良性互动

依托高校的民间法律援助实践早于诊所法律教育。国内较早依托高校的法律援助机构——“武汉大学社会弱者权利保护中心”成立于1992年，其宗旨是“为求社会公正，以最优秀的法律人才为最需要法律帮助的人提供最佳的法律服务”。该中心各部门负责人为法学院的教师，提供法律援助的主体是一届届的法学院学生。由于缺乏系统的法律实务课程的讲授和规范的训练，援助中心的学生志愿者采取“学徒式”的方式，在中心各部门指导教师或有经验的志愿者的“传帮带”中获得技能，在代理案件中积累经验。在弱者权利保护中心，教师的指导工作是义务的，学生的法律服务是无偿的，师生凭借法律人的社会责任感，以无比的热忱数十年如一日，投入于法律援助与公益事业中。

法律诊所的出现得到了高校法律援助中心的极大支持。法律诊所将法律援助中心作为实习基地，作为接受案件的窗口，解决了案源问题；法律援助中心将法律诊所作为培训基地，选拔完成了诊所学习且表现优秀的学生作为志愿者进入中心工作，保证了中心援助案件的服务质量。而教师指导学生提供法律服务的工作发展为规范的课程，工作量得到认可；学生在诊所的学习和在中心的法律实践活动也相应地获得了学分。这无疑是一个“多赢”的结果，也是法律诊所规范化、持续化发展的保证。

上述模式已在国内得到普及。由于法律诊所教学日益受到高校法学院的重视，因诊所教学需要也催生了一批高校法律援助中心的成立。

（二）校内法律诊所与校外实习地诊所并存

校外实习地诊所通常需要与校外的机构取得合作，在法律诊所教育发展初期，单一的校外实习地诊所相对较少。部分高校尝试校内诊所与校外诊所并列设计的模式，比较有代表性的是北京大学的法律诊所。北京大学引入法律诊所教育之初，共建有两个正式法律诊所。一个是建立在北大校园旁的以民事案件为主的民事法律诊所；另一个是建立在河北省迁西县的以社区法律服务为主的社区法律诊所。其中，民事法律诊所主要依托高校，兼具教学机构与法律援助服务组织的双重性质；社区法律诊所则是与迁西县地方政府合作，旨在推动基层社会法治发展。社区法律诊所有助于实践学生开展调查研究，获得基层社区样本，探索法治在乡土社会推进的道路，以此方式完成诊所学习任务。

（三）凸显学科优势，设置专业性诊所

基于社会需求、师资力量和专业学科优势，部分高校成立了专业性法律诊所。清华大学、中南财经政法大学法律诊所利用诊所教师的学科优势，成立了专业的消费者权益保护诊所和劳动者权益保护诊所。西北政法大学曾经尝试立法诊所，武汉大学的行政诉讼法律诊所、四川大学的刑事诊所等同样利用学科优势确立了专门的诊所模式。

三、我国法律诊所近年来的发展趋势

法律诊所教育在中国经过10余年的发展，效果显著，也积累了大量的经验。法律诊所教育在法学教育以及法律援助领域的作用已得到法学教育界以及司法实务界的普遍认同。近几年来，各地高校法学院系在积极探索更具本土化的法律诊所模式，并不断实现突破和创新。

（一）校外实习地诊所逐渐增多

法律诊所教育最显著的优势在于通过实践平台培养学生的法律经验，加深他们对法律和社会的认知，对此，校外实习地诊所无疑是理想的实践平台。近年来，中国政府机构、事业单位以及民间NGO组织设立了大量的法律服务平台，为民众提供法律服务工作。这些服务机构通常需要法律专业人才，为法律诊所提供了参与的机会。如政府成立的法律援助中心、社区服务站、妇联、残联、未成年人保护中心、社会救助站、民间调解中心等。很多高校法律诊所已经走出校园，与校外机构合作，成为校外实习地诊所。

（二）专业性诊所形式多样

法律诊所教育的发展与国家的法治状况、法学研究关注的领域有着密切的关系。随着近年来我国立法内容的不断细化、民众法治意识的不断提高以及受援助群体的社会需求，我国的专业性诊所设置各具特色。中国政法大学于2010年成立了控烟法律诊所，这是全国第一家在高等院校设立的以控制与减少烟草危害为主要目标的公益性法律诊所；武汉大学的司法调解诊所与民事调解诊所不同，学生的身份由当事人一方的代理人转化为法院中的调解法官，在真实法官的指导下帮助争议双方当事人达成调解协议，之后由法院出具正式的司法调解书。

（三）非诉法律诊所发展迅速

国内最初的一批法律诊所是以无偿提供法律援助、代理诉讼为主要运作形式的，学生通过法律诊所的实践活动，为当事人提供法律咨询，代写诉讼文书，参与谈判和调解，出庭参与诉讼，从而接触法律实践。

随着中国法律诊所教育的发展，法律诊所服务的范围和形式在逐渐拓展，已不限于指导学生参与诉讼案件。如民事调解诊所，学生在老师的指导下居间充当调解员，经过系统的有关调解技能训练，帮助夫妻、邻里、用人单位与劳动者等具有特定关系的纠纷双方消除矛盾，寻求双赢、互益的纠纷解决方式，减少诉累，达成协议，构建和谐的关系。

四、我国法律诊所设置存在的问题与建议

（一）存在的问题

法律诊所的设置不仅应与其功能和目的相匹配，同时也应结合中国法学教育自身的特点不断改进完善，使其能够成为拓展我国法学教育的重要途径。我国的法律诊所教育起步较晚，在设置与运行方面还存在一些问题，需要进一步完善。

1. 法律诊所亟需更明确的定位

目前，一些法律诊所的设置缺乏相关的法律和制度规定，导致法律诊所的性质和地位定位不明确。各高校法学院系通常根据自己的学科优势设置法律诊所，其形式差异较大。依托高校法律援助中心的法律诊所为常见的诊所设置方式，尽管法律诊所教育与法律援助制度具有类似的教育和服务目标，但两者毕竟是不同的组织体系。高校中的法律援助组织通常具有明确的法律地位，如属于学校的组织机构或注册的民间机构；而法律诊所教育则强调其独特的互动式、参与式、实践性的教学方法，它是一门课程，还可能由此成立一个专门的教研室。法律诊所与高校法律援助机构在性质、主体、范围与方法诸方面有很大的差异。[1] 因此，不能将法律诊所与法律援助混为一谈，法律诊所应在高校法律教育中有更明确的定位。

2. 法律诊所模式仍需创新

法律诊所的生命力在于为社会和高校法学院校之间搭建了桥梁，因此得到受援群体、广大师生以及用人单位的欢迎。也就是说，社会需要

---

[1] 牟逍媛："法律援助制度与诊所法律教育"，载《法学》2002年第8期。

是法律诊所存在的基础。凡是符合诊所的教学目标、有社会需求并符合法律规定的法律实践形式，均可能成为新兴的法律诊所。目前，我国的法律诊所主要是与法律援助相结合的形式，法律诊所的设置以诉讼诊所居多，诊所实际办理的案件也以诉讼案件为主，非诉案件类的业务则较少。案件的类型主要以民事案件为主，刑事、行政案件相对较少。法律诊所设置形式的局限限制了法律诊所教育的范围。

3. 法律诊所教师缺乏身份认定

法律诊所的设置，除了需要有明确的组织机构和法律地位外，还需要有固定的包括专职、兼职从事法律诊所教育的教师。如果说组织机构是设置法律诊所的外在形式，那么从事法律诊所教育的教师则是法律诊所的核心。法律诊所的教师应该是专业教师还是兼职教师？符合哪些条件的教师才能成为从事法律诊所教学的教师？耶鲁大学法学院法律诊所教授的评估体系不同于其他专业的教授，对教学效果的重视程度远远高于对科研成果的要求。[1] 在耶鲁大学，法律诊所教育的教师人数已经达到法学院教师的25%以上。[2] 我国也有学者主张，诊所教师的评价和职称评聘机制与专业课教师区分开，法律诊所教师不应适用现行的评价和评聘机制，可以另行制定单独的评价和评聘制度，对诊所教师和专业教师的科研任务不做“一刀切”式的要求。[3]

4. 外置式诊所法律责任界定不清

高校依托校外的政府机构、社会团体、民间组织设置的外置式诊所，可以让学生更加深入地参与社会实践。但是，外置式诊所通常涉及高校与其他机关或组织的合作，对外代表的主体需要进行法律上的确认。同时，对于学生在提供法律服务时所产生的法律责任，需要有明确的规定。

---

[1] 徐显明、郑永流主编：《六年制法学教育模式改革》，中国法制出版社2009年版，第44页。

[2] 陈建民：“实现司法公正的重要保障——美国法律诊所提供的法律援助模式对完善中国法律援助制度的启示”，载甄贞主编：《方兴未艾的中国诊所法律教育》，法律出版社2005年版，第415页。

[3] 张峰振：“当前诊所法律教育的中国问题和出路”，载《江苏行政学院学报》2011年第6期。

笔者认为，外置式诊所与其他机关或组织的合作可以通过协议或合同的方式，对学校、院系、诊所教师、诊所学生的责任予以明确确认。

5. 法律诊所的设置与运作存在资金障碍

法律诊所的设置与运作存在三方面的资金障碍。首先是组织机构的日常运作机构需要配置相关的场所、办公设施、图书资料等。其次，学生必要的办案经费不足。法律诊所学生代理案件不得向当事人收取报酬。办案中产生的必要费用需要法律诊所负担。再次，教师的指导经费不足。对于法律诊所实践教育，指导教师在课堂外付出了大量的时间和精力，法律诊所教师基本上都是在日常的教学工作外无偿地承担诊所教育。付出与收入存在很大的差异，这也影响了法律诊所教育的可持续性发展。

（二）若干建议

法律教育的移植需要考虑移植体与受体之间的共性与差异，尤其是基于不同法律教育背景的本土文化基因。[1] 除了法律教育的发展程度以及文化差异外，我国法律诊所的设置还有待进一步完善。

1. 法律诊所的身份独立

目前，我国高校设置的法律诊所存在身份独立与身份定位的挑战。国内最普遍的设置方法是法律援助与法律诊所合二为一，法律诊所与法律援助不仅在工作场所、机构设置上相同，而且在运作过程和管理制度上完全一致，可以称其为援助与诊所的“共同体”。许多高校法律诊所即采用这一形式，不管称呼上是“诊所”还是“援助中心”，或对外称为“法律援助中心”，对内是法律诊所课程，都同时具备两方面的职能。[2] 法律诊所的身份如何确认是高校开展法律诊所教育必须回答的问题。

2. 法律诊所种类多元化配置

目前，法律诊所的种类主要以诉讼法律诊所为主，学生参与诊所实践教育也主要以诉讼案件为主。可以讲，法律诊所的单一性必然会限制

---

[1] 李傲：“论诊所式法律教育与儒家治学思想”，载《法学杂志》2011 年第 8 期。

[2] 李傲、许炎：“法律援助与法律诊所之甄别与整合”，载《法学杂志》2003 年第 24 卷。

法律诊所教育的授课方式与范围，也势必限制学生接触法律实践的空间。截至目前，非诉法律诊所尚属少数，外置式诊所需要摈弃原有实习制度的不足而走向规范化，专业性诊所也未能全面发挥作用，国际法律诊所目前尚在酝酿阶段。法律诊所教育的发展需要多元化。丰富法律诊所的类型才有可能拓展学生法律实践的范围。

3. 重点培育非诉法律诊所

在美国，诉讼法律诊所的出现与呼应民权运动等特殊的历史背景有关，但是诉讼法律诊所作为法学教学实验基地，有其存在的局限性。由于诉讼法律诊所教育存在案源单一、法律风险较大、介入滞后等问题，近 30 年来，非诉法律诊所在美国蓬勃发展。非诉法律诊所设置领域广泛，案件风险可控，参与方式灵活，在中国转型时期社会矛盾增多的情况下，非诉法律诊所应当获得更广阔的发展空间。高校法学院系应重点培育非诉法律诊所，使其成为法学实践教育与疏解、研究社会问题的有效平台。

4. 专业性诊所的设置进一步细化

随着法治社会的不断发展，法律诊所向专业性发展是必然的趋势。目前，我国的专业性诊所的设置种类逐渐增多，但是依然不够细化。依托学科成立的法律诊所，在诊所设计上可以进一步细化。例如，我国有学者认为，从行政法领域来看，可以开展诊所法律教育的领域就包括行政立法、听证、行政诉讼、行政复议、行政赔偿、信息公开等诸多领域，但这些领域的诊所并不多见。[1]

5. 法律诊所教师配置制度化

法律诊所教师的配置是法律诊所教育能否实现目标的核心。目前，我国法律诊所教师的聘任，随意性比较大且教师流动性较快，不利于法律诊所的持续性发展。笔者认为，法律诊所的教师应包括专职教师与兼职教师两类构成，专职教师在学校教师中选择，兼职教师可以在行政机关、社会团体、法官、律师等有经验的法律从业人员中聘用。此外，法律诊所教师的资格确认与聘任以及评价体制同样应该走向规范化。

---

[1] 王青斌："论我国诊所法律教育存在的问题以及改进——以行政法领域为视角"，载《行政法学研究》2010 年第 3 期。

试论诊所法律教育中影像资料运用的价值

刘建明[*]

摘　要：“法律不是逻辑，而是经验”，“像律师那样思考”，甚至“像律师那样工作”，这些曾经在西方社会流行的法学教育理念已经被中国的法学院校普遍接受，特别是已经成为中国诊所教师的基本共识。对于中国的诊所法律教育而言，树立“像律师那样思考”的教学理念固然重要，但更为重要的是要研究在诊所教学过程中贯彻和落实这些理念的基本途径和具体方法，即如何精心设计教学方案，选择教学方法，从而培养学生能够像律师那样思考，像律师那样工作。影像资料回放教学法具有信息量大、形象直观、便于操作的特点，较多地运用会见当事人、法律咨询和法庭抗辩等教学环节。本文通过分析影像资料回放教学法在诊所教学中的功能与作用，努力摸索与探讨影像资料回放教学法在诊所法律中的基本方法与步骤，以期在诊所教学中更好地激发学生学习的积极性，获得最佳的教学效果。

关键词：诊所法律教育　影像资料　教学法

众所周知，法学教育主要是为了培养法律专业的应用型人才，为法制建设服务。但是，我国现行的法学教学体系，无论是教材的编写和课程的设置，还是具体的教学内容的设置和教学形式的选择，都依然是一种重视理论而轻视实践能力的法学教育模式。近几年来，法学实践教学尤其是诊所法律教育被提到了重要的议事日程上，“像律师一样思考”的

---

* 刘建明，浙江工商大学法学院讲师。

教学理念对于从事法学教育的同仁来说早已耳熟能详，不再陌生；“提升学生实务能力”“提高学生的法律运用能力”等口号和提法充满整个法学教育界。但遗憾的是，往往是“雷声大，雨点小”或者“只听雷声，不见下雨”，缺乏落实这些教学理念的具体管道和具体方法，所谓的“加强和提高学生的能力培养”往往止步于理念的传播和媒体的宣传，缺乏具体的实施步骤，缺乏法学实务教学的研究与探索。

诊所法律教育的主要特点是根据教学内容的需要，打破传统课堂授课的单一形式，将教学方法由课堂讲授转向实践体验与课堂讲授的结合，教学内容由依赖教材变为尊重学生的自我体验与感受，使整个学习过程从以“教师为中心”转向以“学生为中心”，学生从传统的以教师为主体的“教学中学习”转向以学生为主体的“实践中学习”。正如华盛顿博物馆墙上所写：“I hear，I forget，I see，I remember，I do，I understand.”实践对于学生的成长具有重要意义。实践的过程也就是学生体验司法实践的过程，诊所法律教育总是与学生的实践与体验并行，主要的教学活动在学生的实践与体验中展开，学生的体验与经历成为诊所法律教学的起点，学生的经验与感受成为实践教学的背景。然而时至今日，我们仍然对实践教学的教学方法与教学手段缺乏足够的重视和必要的研究。

诊所法律教学的核心是法律职业技能的培养，诸如法律思维、法律职业操守、法律职业工作能力等，具体而言，诊所法律教学的目标就是培养法科学生两种基本能力，即用脑的能力和用嘴的能力。用脑的能力，即法律思维能力，即严谨的法律推理和论证能力、观察认知能力、证据分析和判断能力、归纳概括能力等；所谓用嘴的能力即法律表达和论辩能力，运用专业理论知识、职业语言和思维进行论证、辩驳以说服对方的能力。诊所法律教学从教学内容的设置到教学手段的选择都应该围绕这些目标展开。目前，我国诊所法律教学比较普遍的教学方法大体有传统的讲授式教学法、头脑风暴教学法、讨论式教学法、案例教学法（案例研讨教学法）等，但从便利程度、教学效果等考虑，笔者首推影像资料回放式教学法。

影像资料回放法是教师对相关录像（包括国内外影片资料、庭审实况录像、学生代理案件的录像等）进行编辑，选取某些录像资料的片断，学生通过观看录像片断，借鉴、模仿他人的成功经验，或者反思他们的行为，从而帮助学生掌握法律技能的一种教学方法。

影像资料回放法的资料来源可以是现有的影视资料，采集适宜的影视资料，经编辑整理后呈现给学生，可用于会见当事人和法庭抗辩的内容，目的是让学生分析、模仿和学习；也可以是法庭审理现场录像；还可以是学生在课堂模拟练习的录像等。指导教师对录像资料进行剪辑，对亲历现场的学生来说，观看录像是为了更好地发现不足，总结提高；对非亲历现场的学生来说，这是一种在真实再现的环境中获得感性的真切体验。

一、影像资料回放法在诊所法律教学中的作用与功能

目前，影像资料作为教学辅助工具在高校各学科中开始得到广泛运用，但使用较多的也只是文学类和医学类的专业，[1] 而在诊所法律教学中使用影像资料作为教学辅助材料，或者说直接以影像资料作为诊所法律教学的对象尚且不多，如果能更多地将影像资料加以运用，有利于完善传统的实践教学方式，更好地培养学生的法学专业素养。

（一）信息量大，形象直观，有利于将抽象法学概念具象化、形象化，将法律学习融入生活

在以往的法学专业课堂中，学生通常是听与记。所谓听，即将教师的解释说明听懂；所谓记，就是将一些重点和难点记录下来。影像资料回放，以声像结合的形式来传输知识，有利于克服传统书本教学的弊端。尤其是当需要解释一些难以理解的抽象概念时，通过影像资料的回放，融入影像资料，将抽象概念中的定义制成具象的动态形式重复给学生播放，能够带来视觉和听觉上的冲击，使学生对法律概念的内涵有一个更

[1] 赵宏波、何新民、王凯："浅谈数字化影像资料在多媒体幻灯片教学中的应用"，载《教学研究》2005 年第 14 卷，第 1 期。

加直观和深刻的理解，使原本抽象的概念变得具体而生动，将知识变得“立体化”[1]。只有当抽象的概念得到了理解与掌握时，学生学习法律的兴趣才会增强，学生才更有身临其境之感，容易引起共鸣，加深对法学理论和法律条文的了解，把法学知识渗透到平日的学习和生活中。

（二）激发学生的学习动机，诱发其学习兴趣，提高其学习效率

对学生的指令和要求要明确、具体、清晰；要注意评价的教育性，保证评价的公正度和信度；要保护学生的自尊心、自信心，尊重学生的隐私，关注学生的处境和需要，注重发展变化的过程，以鼓励为主；与教学协调统一。要有利于促进教学，有利于学生反思不足，促进其思维水平的提高，从而调整学习策略，明确方向；同时，要关注学生的发展性和差异性。

由于目前我国的诊所法律教育受到案源、经费等因素的困扰，相当多的诊所还无法保证充足的案源，部分学生仍然无法真正参与真实案件的代理，因此，可以通过对案件过程进行录像，让当时未能参加和观摩的学生在事后可以通过视频影像观看全过程，体会到真实审判中那种你来我往、唇枪舌剑的感觉，弥补以往未能参加或者“旁听”的遗憾，也让参加的学生能够在法庭庭审结束后不断地回放和定格观看，好好揣摩，找出自身不足，找出同学优点，从而取长补短。

（三）有利于教师全面、客观地观察、掌握学生的实践表现

诚然，诊所法律教育强调学生学习的主体作用，但是，教师在实践教学中的作用同样也不能忽视，学生法律思维能力和法律语言表达能力的提高需要反复练习，其间要经历无数演练、反馈、指导、完善的过程，指导教师在法学实践教学中的主要作用应该是督导。“督”具有监督、督促、检查和评估的意蕴，主要是督导对学生学习情况进行及时的检查，包括是否清楚案件事件，是否明确当事人的具体诉求，对证据的分析和解读是否全面、准确，案件的策略是有效可行，代理意见的法律依据是

---

[1] 黄瑞耀：“探索大学法治教育新模式——开创影视法学课”，载《现代远距离教育》2005年第4期。

否充分，法庭论辩演练是否到位等；“导”则具有指导、帮助的职能，具体是指对在检查过程中发现的问题以及办案过程中可能遇到的问题进行启发和引导，寻求解决问题的方法与途径。教师的启发和引导的准确与否的关键在于能否及时发现学生存在的问题，录像回放教学法由于具有可重复性，方便存储、复制和传播，使得指导教师有充足的时间反复多次观看学生实践技能演练的情况，掌握学生领会、掌握实践技能的客观素材。

（四）真实、客观，有利于提升教师评价的公信度

诊所法律教育离不开指导教师对学生学习情况的评价，评价的目的在于通过评价学习，将评价融入学习之中，确保评价在学生学习中发挥作用。教师对于学生法律实务演练情况要及时组织评价，积极地反馈给学生，使学生改进实际操作能力。指导教师的评价基本要求就是客观真实，言之有据，言之有物。特别是对于学生语言表达能力和庭审庭辩能力的训练，指导教师可能通过录像回放的方式，直观、形象地观察学生语言表态的准确和论辩能力的掌握，指导教师的评价工作有根有据，让学生对自己存在的问题心悦诚服，对指导老师的建议和指导有客观清晰的印象。

二、影像资料回放教学法的方法与步骤

影像资料回放教学法可以根据录像的内容分为影像教学法与录像反思反馈法。

影像教学法主要是指通过多媒体手段为学生展示、播放法律专业类的电教片或影视。相对于枯燥的课堂授课，影像教学方法深受学生的欢迎。该方法可分为两类：一类为电教片教学。目前适合教学的电教片已为数不少，较早的有中央电视台推出的《中国法庭》《今日说法》等系列光盘，中华全国律协组织录制的《律师视点》系列光盘等都是反映较好的电教片。教师可以在授课过程中有针对地选择适合的案件进行播放。另外，现在也有不少电视台和网站开办了“法庭直播”类节目，组织学生收看或下载后整理播放也不失为一种好方式。另一类为影视教学。教

师可以收集中外有关的法律电影或电视连续剧，进行必要的剪辑，为学生放映或安排自己观看，如，想了解域外法治状况，可以观看《杀死一只知更鸟》《失控的陪审团》《肖申克的救赎》等经典大片；想了解我国近代的司法状况，可以观看《审死官》《九品芝麻官》《杨乃武与小白菜》等影视；想了解我国的司法现状，可以观看《被告山杠爷》《秋菊打官司》《马背上的法庭》等电影。这些影视资料在法学实践教学中的作用主要是对传统教学方法的丰富和延伸，能够带来视觉和听觉上的冲击，将知识变得“立体化”。学生通过多重感官的配合，更容易理解和记忆所接受的知识，从而提高实践教学的有效性。

录像反思反馈法是将学生会见当事人的场景、出庭辩论的情景以及学生出庭前的演练准备等利用录像设备录制下来，经过适当的剪辑，作为学生自我反思和课堂反馈的依据。

录像反思反馈又可以按照主体的不同分为自我反思和课堂反馈两种，自我反思是指学生回顾自己的演练录像，仔细观看自己的表现，这有助于准确发现自身存在的不足与错误。传统意义上的反思只不过是学生对自己在实践中的言行举止在自己的脑海中进行回放，受到学生固有思维模式的影响，传统的自我反思往往有较大的局限性。而录像自我反思是将学生的活动瞬间定格，它像一面镜子，可以自我对照、自我检查、自我完善，可以发现很多以往难以发现的问题。不少学生反映，第一次看到自己上法庭的表现，很多问题都是过去不曾注意到的，甚至是从未想到的，而录像反思则给了自己一个直观的反映。从实际的运用效果来看，录像自我反思法对学生庭辩能力的提高有很好的促进作用，在实践中，许多老师发现学生掌握庭辩技能的障碍和困难并不在于庭辩的核心知识和技巧，而是克服内心的焦虑和恐惧。学生由于缺乏实战经验和体会，每当与当事人会谈、参与庭审工作时难免出现肢体颤抖、手心出汗、声音发抖、口干舌燥、心跳加速、脸红等内心焦虑的现象，甚至在法庭上忘记自己要讲什么、语言表达不流利、表情动作不自然等。由于在录像中可以清晰地看到自己的不足之处和优势所在，学生往往在第二次模拟训练时就会有意改正错误，发挥长处。

课堂反馈法主要是指教师对学生的各个实践活动忠实地进行记录，并且进行适当的剪辑，在课堂进行回放，由学生进行互相间的评价。通过录像媒体的直观影像和声音，可表达出一些用语言无法描述的知识内涵，使法律操作过程中的各个环节及存在的问题更加细致，生动直观地展现在每个学生面前，通过观看录像进行互相评价，取长补短，相互促进。录像设备可以踏实地将各种表现及时、准确和完整地记录下来，不放过任何微小的差错，并能通过存储设备保存，信息不会“丢失”，这为学生进行客观评价创造了条件。在评价过程中，学生的实践活动能够逼真地再现，为学生进行客观评价提供素材和依据，培养学生言之有据、言之有物。

当录像资料积累到一定程度，可以建立一个相对比较完整的学生录像资料库。录像资料库建立后，录像反思教学法还可以有进一步的发展，即形成纵向录像反思和横向录像反思。纵向反思是指学生将自己在不同时期、不同阶段的录像都剪辑出来，一起播放，进行研究与反思，其目的是总结原来发现的问题现在是否已经得到了解决，反思自己的法律实践能力是否提高。让学生经常进行纵向录像反思，有助于学生发现自己的进步，确立自信心。横向录像反思是指对不同年级、不同班级的学生在同一主题中的录像（如会见当事人、法庭辩论等）进行剪辑，一起播放，通过录像比较进行反思，目的是发现别人的优点，借鉴、学习他人的长处，弥补自身的不足。

三、影像资料回放教学法需要注意的问题

根据教育部《高等教育面向21世纪教学内容和课程体系改革计划》，现代教育技术被纳入高等教育教学改革的重要内容，而作为重要组成部分的法学教育，在教学改革中也面临如何从传统实践教学向现代化教学转变的重大问题。近年来，随着高校法学教育教学改革的深入，影像资料的作用渐显，其运用愈来愈多，为新形势下法学实践教学方式的改革带来了很好契机。但是，由于影像资料在法学实践教学中过快过广的应用，一些问题渐显。

（一）影像资料的选择问题

影像资料回放是一种教学方法，而非教学本身，它必须服务于教学内容和教学目的。这要求教师在授课时围绕教学目标，突出重点，突破难点。如何选择最正确的影像视频，让学生从中得到最大收益，这才是最终目的。而如今，教师在选择影像资料的过程中有时会不经意地选择实际上与教学内容关联不大的视频影像，未做到切实与实际教学内容相吻合，没有突出重点和难点。教师选择影视资料是一项挑战性很大的工作，切忌贪多求全、喧宾夺主。一般来说，适合作为诊所法律教育题材的必须是集中讨论某一类型法律问题的资料，选取的影像必须是有针对性的典型案例，剪辑录像应当简明扼要，主题突出，一般以 3～5 分钟为佳。

（二）努力避免课堂变成视频观赏课

科技可以是一个工具、一位助手，却不能取代教师的地位而成为教学的全部。影像资料的应用确实能给高校法学的实践教学带来极大的促进作用，但是不能就此否定其他教学方法的作用。虽然影像资料为开展诊所法律教育提供了极大的方便，但也绝不能就此放弃原有的方式，正如案例教学法不能完全取代讲授教学一样。实践证明，诊所法律教育的内容并不都适合使用影像资料，如果一个简单的案例解释，本来三两句就能解释清楚，却硬要在课堂上播放相关的影像，就显得有点本末倒置了。因而，过多地引入影像资料容易使课堂变成普通的视频观赏课，从而失去原有教学意义。因此，在实际应用中往往难以把握好一个“度”，当影像资料恰当地融入诊所法律教学方式时，才能有机结合，才能相得益彰，才能使诊所法律的教学方式得以不断完善，达到预期的教学效果。在实践教学中，由于影像资料的过度运用，没有情感的大屏幕成了学生的“新老师”，导致教师与学生的直接交流减少，易使课堂变成普通的视频欣赏课，从而影响到课堂上教师的主导作用和学生的主体地位，这种影响会直接导致教学效果下降。

此外，通过影像资料的学习，确实可以将抽象问题变得具体、形象，可以将抽象的名词概念变成直观和具体的内容，有助于学生对抽象内容的掌握与理解。但是，许多学生往往在这样的教学方式下失去抽象思维的能力，如果只能做到“意会”而不能“言传”，则不利于其日后的法律工作。换句话说，影像资料可以吸引学生迅速进入图像世界，但真正的抽象思维还是要让学生自己深入思考。因此，通过诊所法律教学中影像资料的运用而获得的知识并不能就此代替抽象思维。教师除了精心选择影像资料以外，还要事先布置学生观看录像片断后需要思考和讨论的问题。选取讨论内容的原则应着眼于学生的知识、阅历和能力，以有效引导学生的积极探索、激发学生学习的欲望为目的，教师在采用录像回放前，应当结合案件事实，预测学生在观看录像片断后可能发表的观点和可能存在的问题，找出相应的解决方法和应对措施。在学生对录像内容进行点评时，教师应当尽可能完整地记录学生的主要观点，为准确、有效的点评准备素材。讨论的主题应当直接来自录像片断，既可以是录像所反映的值得学生学习和借鉴的法律技能，也可以是录像所反映的需要改进或者提高的内容。

教师在具体播放音像资料时，可以围绕某一主题，完整地播放录像片断，也可以将相关主题的几个录像片断对比播放。

录像回放教学法的关键在于学生观看录像片断后的反思与评价，一般通常要求学生先对相关录像片断所反映的法律问题发表自己的观点和想法，然后再由教师对学生的观点思路进行完整的点评。教师的指导和建议应当具体而详实，能够为训练和提高学生的实践能力提供最直接、真实、有效的机会。学生在演练中表现的重要内容或争议点，由教师原封不动地加以重复表现，进而更好地理解和体会教师的建议和意见。

（三）同等条件下，尽可能选择真实的学生演练录像

值得提出的一点是，录像回放教学法虽然常选用影视资料，但笔者倾向于选择学生演练的真实录像，尤其是以某一个具体视频影像作为教学研究对象来对其中所涉及的法庭举证、质证能力、法庭论辩能力进行分析时，更应该选择学生实际演练的真实录像。这是因为目前诊所法律教学中直接以影片作为法律教学的对象甚少，不可能涵盖教学所需的实务技能和实务方法，所以难免会有找不到与教学内容切实相关的影像资

料的情况。特别是对于某些热播的美剧和韩剧，由于中西文化差异较大，法律体系和法律理念存在差异，学生不易了解背景，反而会对实际教学产生不利的影响。另外，选择学生的演练录像具有针对性，能够让学生有身临其境的感觉，有效避免影视的商业娱乐性、戏剧性，提升学生的学习积极性。

（四）追求影像资料回放的教学效果的同时，充分发挥教师的主导作用

诊所法律教学过程是一个含有多种因素的复杂过程，要实现和完成的教学目的和教学任务是多方面的，任何单一教学方法都难以全面有效地完成诊所法律教学的目标和任务。教师要抓住实践教学的中心环节，结合学生的各项素质，运用师生互动的教学过程，对各种教学方法加以优化组合，灵活运用，以取得最佳的教学效果。人们常说“教学有法，但无定法”，在教学实践中没有一成不变的固定模式，任何教学方法都是相对的，并且在不断发展变化。无论采用哪一种教学方法，重要的是教师应具有把握教学机制、随机应变的调控能力。在透彻理解教学目标、掌握学生思想动态的基础上，充分发挥自身的特长和能动作用，相机、灵活、创造性地运用教学方法，发挥其综合作用，以获得最佳的教学效果。因此，在充分肯定录像回放教学法的优点和作用的同时，仍需发挥教师在法学实践教学中的主导作用。

诊所式法律教育结合法律援助工作的探索

罗君丽*

摘 要： 从国内外高校诊所式法律教育发展的经验来看，法律援助工作已经成为诊所式法律教育中不可缺少的重要环节。本文从开展诊所式法律教育的实践经验出发，探索诊所式法律教育与法律援助工作结合中出现的主要问题，针对高校法律诊所如何缓解案源稳定性问题、经费保障问题、诊所学生开展法律援助的法律保障问题、人员流动性给案件处理衔接带来的问题，提出了多方面开拓案源、拓宽法律援助经费来源、完善诊所管理以确保援助工作有效衔接等建议。

关键词： 诊所式法律教育　法律援助　教育目标

诊所式法律教育起源于美国大学的法学院，经过多年的发展，这种新的法律教育方式得到了广泛的认可。继美国之后，拉丁美洲、非洲、西欧、东欧、澳大利亚、新西兰、南亚等许多国家和地区的法律院校成功地应用了诊所式法律教育。我国自 2000 年 9 月开始引入诊所法律教育[1]至今，诊所式法律教育已经成为许多高校法学专业重要的专业选修课程。从国内外高校诊所式法律教育发展的经验来看，法律援助工作已经成为诊所式法律教育中不可缺少的重要环节。本文从开展诊所式法律教育的实践经验出发，探索诊所式法律教育与法律援助工作结合中出现的主要问题及解决问题的方向。

---

* 罗君丽，五邑大学政法学院讲师。

[1] 甄贞：《诊所法律教育在中国》，法律出版社 2002 年版，第 3 页。

一、诊所式法律教育与法律援助结合的原因

（一）诊所教育目标的公益性

美国自1830年起，律师在法学院的集中训练开始逐步取代学徒模式，其后案例分析教学法正式确立，并成为美国法律学校占主导地位的教学方法。但自20世纪60年代起，法律现实主义运动学者对案例教学法提出了质疑，他们认为：看似分析实案的教学法，事实上与实际脱离，离开了具体的社会背景，离开了活生生的当事人，离开了办案的真实感受，分析与推理、规则与原则均失去了依托，成了空洞的语言。[1]

另一方面，20世纪60年代美国的民权运动促使律师和法学院学生意识到将法律规则运用于实践以及将书本上的知识转化为实践的重要性。于是，学生自发地为无力负担律师费用的人提供法律帮助，为民事案件尤其是刑事案件中缺乏法律知识的人提供法律咨询。然而学生自发的行为缺乏教师的指导和其他机构的帮助，学生由于在经验上的不足，在提供法律服务过程中显得力不从心，以致不能将当事人的利益最大化。在这些矛盾凸显之后，美国的法学家开始意识到，要解决这些问题，可以借助法学院师生的力量。同时，诊所式法律教育模式的前身——判例教学法已随着法学教育的发展呈现出越来越多的局限。人们开始怀念学徒制，诊所式法律教育在这种背景之下逐步形成。[2]

从上述美国诊所式法律教育的起源可见，从诞生开始，诊所式法律教育就与法律援助工作密不可分。诊所教育目标本身即带有公益性。在西方，诊所法律教育最初的教学目标包括培养学生为穷困当事人服务的责任，传授如何投身于这种服务、法制对社会贫弱者的影响等知识。法律诊所教学日渐成熟后，美国律师协会《麦考利特报告》在确定诊所学生学习律师技能的同时，确立了统一的法律职业四项基本价值目标。其主要包括尽职尽责、努力促进正义、公平与道德，确保那些无力支付费

---

[1] 李傲：《互动教学法——诊所式法律教育》，法律出版社2004年版，第4页。

[2] 温璇："论美国诊所式法律教育模式——兼论诊所法律教育的本土化"，西南政法大学法律史学专业2010博士论文，第3页。

用的人获得充分的法律服务，尽到提高法律及法律机构实现正义的能力的责任，扫除基于民族、宗教、种族出身、性别、性倾向或残疾的偏见，并扭转这些偏见所造成的影响等。

法律人应当具备公益意识，同情并在法律许可的范围内帮助社会中的弱势者。法律人以法律工作为谋生手段，但追求的目标不应单纯是金钱上的收益，公平、正义是法律的应有之义，培养具有深谙法律公平、正义含义的法律人是法律教育的使命。诊所法律教育是一种新的法律教育方式，它的使命就是要通过公益法律实践的方法培养真正理解法律、能有效适用法律乃至具有法律信仰的法律人，通过培养这样的法律人，促进法治的发展，促进人权的保障，促进人类社会的和谐进步。

（二）弥补课堂教学不足的需要

如前所述，尽管与早期的法学教育传统方法“讲义教学法”（Lecture Method）相比，案例分析教学法具有明显的优势，能够使学生获得良好的分析与推理能力，但是它也有明显的缺陷：忽略了法律实践中许多基本技能的训练，例如会见当事人、事实调查、调解、谈判等，也忽略了在判断力、职业责任心以及理解法律和不同的法律职业人的社会角色等方面对学生的培养。

另外，即使是专门面向实践技能训练的诊所式法律教育，其有针对性的课堂教学也同样无法提供真实案件的效果。例如，笔者曾多次在法律诊所课堂上安排关于谈判的模拟训练，但学生反映模拟谈判自我感觉不佳。其中一个重要原因就是明知道是虚拟的场景，没有利害影响的压力，因而不能真正以当事人或者代理人的角色投入其中，容易轻易放弃谈判或者从应有的底线上退却。当然，在模拟法庭中同样存在虚拟带来的影响，但毕竟还有法袍、法锤、律师袍等“道具”带来的形式感，而在模拟谈判中因没有这样的形式存在而使得缺陷更加明显。

开展法律援助工作可以有效弥补这一欠缺。从会见当事人开始，经过咨询，到正式接受委托，事实调查，乃至参与谈判，代理诉讼，都由诊所学生担当主要的角色，更重要的是，这一切都是真实发生的，一个具体处理方案的失策乃至一个细节决定的失当，都可能会产生极其不利的后果，在可能产生的法律责任所加诸的压力下，学生的积极性和投入程度是毋庸置疑的。

在法律援助过程中，学生不再面对充分展现的既有案情，而是要通过会见当事人、事实调查工作自己去挖掘、发现具体案情；除了要解决实体法的问题，还要解决许多相对陌生的程序法问题；除了要求扎实的理论功底和实务知识，还要求很强的应变能力、表达能力；除了要解决当事人的法律问题，还要面对当事人复杂的心态和心理问题以及社会问题；还可能接触到课堂教学中不可能出现的司法环境中的灰色地带甚至司法腐败现象等。这就是从法学院到法院的距离——这些都是课堂教学中无法提供的，而又是法律职业工作者必须应对的。

（三）法律援助的庞大需求与现有法律援助资源相对匮乏

法律援助是一项深受广大人民群众欢迎的“民心工程”。然而目前我国法律援助需求与供给之间的缺口很大。据统计，2010 年全国法律援助机构的平均工作人员只有 3.75 人，法律援助机构平均受理审批法律援助申请 222 件，按照最低审批所需工作日计算，仅这一项工作所牵涉的人力之大就无需多述。[1] 以广东为例，广东是一个人口大省，常住人口达 9194 万，同时也是全国进城务工人员（农民工）最多的省份，约 2000 多万，占全国的 1/4。但政府能够投入的经费有限，据不完全统计，1997～2006 年的 10 年中，全省各级政府投入经费共 1.985 亿元。[2] 按照这一数据，平均每万人的法律援助经费只有约 2000 元/年。上述数据充分显示，无论从投入的人力还是财力来看，法律援助工作仅依靠政府投入是远不能满足现实需求的。

因此，作为政府提供法律援助的有益补充，利用高校师生资源，诊所式法律教育过程中所提供的法律援助能够起到一定的填补缺口、缓解矛盾的作用。

---

[1] 桑宁：“法律发展中结构性矛盾和瓶颈问题研究”，载《中国司法》2012 第 1 期。

[2] 蒲晳祜：“法律援助原则的广东实践”，载《中国司法》2007 年第 8 期。

（四）诊所式法律教育开展法律援助工作的有利条件

一是诊所学生普遍珍惜实践机会，工作热情很高。从实践经验来看，诊所学生非常珍惜接触、代理真实个案的机会。学生还没有直接面对生活的经济压力，赤子之心使他们更能同情当事人的际遇，尽管没有经济收益，但他们投入法律援助工作的热情高涨。

二是诊所法律援助的机制相对灵活，能填补政府法律援助之不足。法律援助的可获得性主要体现在经济困难标准和范围的规定上。然而政府提供的法律援助对于经济困难证明的要求较高，尤其对于外来务工人员，要回到户籍所在地开具经济困难证明不仅手续繁琐，经济成本（主要是来回的交通费）和时间成本也都很高。例如，工伤事故发生后，要求身体已经受到伤害的外来务工人员长途跋涉回户籍所在地办理经济困难证明，实际上是给他/她获得法律援助设置了较大的障碍。相比较而言，高校法律诊所配套的法律援助中心可以通过界定能够施以援助的受案范围确立援助范围，对于经济困难的书面证明并不作硬性要求，这一灵活的机制使相当部分的外来务工人员可以较便捷地获得法律援助，以弥补政府法律援助硬性要求所产生的不足。

三是诊所学生在教师指导下开展法律援助工作，是一种保护下的独立，代理工作的风险大大降低。诊所学生毕竟涉世未深，欠缺实务经验，如果完全放手让其独自面对社会矛盾尖锐激化的局面——诉讼纠纷，很可能出师未捷即已折戟沉戈，搞不好还可能要承担代理失职的法律责任，这不仅可能会使遭受挫折的学生心理上产生阴影，也会给诊所法律援助工作带来负面影响。而诊所教师能够以其丰富的实务经验与社会经验，给予学生必要的指导与支持，使诊所学生获得“保护下的独立”，降低风险。正如雏鸟必须在成鸟保护下才能安全地学会飞翔，诊所学生在羽翼未丰之时，未具备独立开展法律援助工作的能力，诊所教师的帮助是不可或缺的。

二、诊所式法律教育结合法律援助工作存在的问题分析

（一）案源稳定性问题

在我国诊所法律教育实践中，案源不稳定是很多法律诊所开设的法律援助中心面临的困境之一。原因有以下几个方面：首先，由于学生没有执业经验以及缺乏明确的办案身份，即使有教师的指导，部分当事人还是觉得存在办案质量的风险，因此，他们不放心将案件交给学生代理。其次，现实中并不是所有案件都适合学生办理，对接收到的咨询个案必须要加以选择。最后，由于我国诊所法律教育还在起步阶段，宣传力度还不够，社会上对诊所教育以及所提供的法律援助还不是很了解。如果长期缺乏真实案源，学生就无法在真实案件的办理过程中获得实务技巧，更别提法律职业道德以及社会责任感的培养，[1] 诊所教育的效果必然会大打折扣甚至失去存在的意义。故此，案源不足是诊所式法律教育必须要解决的问题。

（二）纠纷类型的单一性问题

诊所式法律教育中开展法律援助工作普遍面对的另一个问题是受案类型的单一性。

一方面，由于法律援助资源不能冲击正常的法律服务市场，只能针对特定人群与特定类型案件提供援助，而这些人一般面对的法律纠纷往往集中于劳动争议、人身损害赔偿、离婚、刑事案件等，案情一般也较为简单，[2] 复杂的案件类型如房地产纠纷、与公司有关的纠纷、知识产权纠纷等则不会涉及。这就使得诊所学生办理案件的类型偏向单一，无

---

[1] 温璇："论美国诊所式法律教育模式——兼论诊所法律教育的本土化"，西南政法大学法律史学专业 2010 年博士论文，第 33 页。

[2] 《司法部关于开展法律援助工作的通知》第 3 条第 1 款规定："（一）法律援助的范围包括：1. 刑事案件；2. 请求给付赡养费、抚育费、扶养费的法律事项；3. 除责任事故外，因公受伤害请求赔偿的法律事项；4. 盲、聋、哑和其他残疾人、未成年人、老年人追索侵权赔偿的法律事项；5. 请求国家赔偿的诉讼案件；6. 请求发给抚恤金、救济金的法律事项；7. 其他确需法律援助的法律事项。"

法获得全面的锻炼。

另一方面，法律援助案件中有相当一部分是刑事案件，但由于诊所学生并非执业律师，不能到看守所会见犯罪嫌疑人（被告人），这使得他们的受案范围进一步收窄。

（三）经费保障问题

与政府设立的法律援助机构相比，高校开设的法律诊所（法律援助中心）更经常面对经费不足的问题。据中国诊所法律教育网站的资料显示，高校的法律诊所援助经费来源主要有三：一是从学校的行政开支中列支，二是来自校内师生的捐款，三是来自社会的捐助。例如，复旦大学的法律援助中心建设初始的经费来源包括：中心成员捐献的自己的奖学金、生活费近1000元，复旦律师事务所捐赠的500元及法律系一些开支的报销。[1] 其都存在经费不足、不稳定的问题。

尽管法律诊所学生是无偿提供法律服务，但法律诊所会发生基础的办公费用，办理案件有交通费、复印费用等支出。经费缺乏保障在一定程度上制约了法律诊所的发展。

（四）诊所学生开展法律援助的法律保障问题

法律诊所开展法律援助工作，主体是学生，但在校学生走出校门从事法律援助工作会经常遭遇各种制约。

一是调查取证权利受限。由于学生并不具有律师身份，到有关部门调查取证的权利就受到限制。这使得学生法律援助工作的效果受到一定影响。

二是出庭代理权利受限。由于社会上有部分不具有律师资格的人非法从事有偿法律服务，许多地区的法院、劳动仲裁委员会都订立了对公民代理的限制规则，例如，有的法院规定公民代理必须与当事人有亲属关系，有的劳动仲裁委员会要求公民代理要当庭提供免费代理的协议。

三是学生代理人身份没有得到尊重。个别法院或者仲裁员不了解诊所学生法律援助的情况，对出庭代理的诊所学生不信任，对其代理人身

---

[1] 中国诊所法律教育网站，http：//www.cliniclaw.cn/，2012—05—04.

份也不认可，在调解过程中绕开学生，这容易使当事人对学生代理人产生误解或不信任，不利于法律援助工作的开展。

（五）人员流动性问题

考虑到法律援助工作对学生专业知识结构完备性的要求，学生参加法律诊所课程和参与法律援助一般已经是大三，而大四学生大多要找工作、考研等，参与办案的时间很难得到保障，毕业后的去向更难确定。许多案件从一审到二审，再到执行，起码是半年至一年，如果涉及发回重审则时间更长，走完全部程序可能会持续两年以上。随着参与办案的学生毕业离校，案件跟进可能会出现衔接上的问题。

此外，法学院有关法律诊所的课程都只安排一学期，而学生的主要任务毕竟还是在学业上，因此，当法律诊所的课程结束后，大部分学生就会将精力重新投在新的课程学习上，并从相关的实践中退出。这样，高校法律援助中心里固定的、有经验的人员相对就会比较少，中心的主要精力就不得不用在培养新的学生上，由此法律援助中心的办案质量、成员能力的提高在很大程度上就会受到限制。因此，如何协调高校法律援助服务和高校法律诊所教育的关系也变得十分重要。[1]

三、完善我国诊所式法律教育的法律援助环节的若干建议

法律援助环节是诊所式法律教育的重要内容，实践中上述问题的存在影响了诊所教育的效果。为此，需要有切实的方案解决或至少是缓解这些问题。

（一）多方面开拓案源

由于没有足够的案源，大多数学生没有参与实践的机会，诊所工作只有单纯的值班等待咨询，诊所课堂教学中的实践技能没有应用的机会，容易使学生产生“无用武之地”的倦怠心理，大大影响教学效果。

高校法律诊所一般设有值班制度，值班学生接受法律咨询，可以获得一定的案源。但法律诊所不能只停留在守株待兔的层面，走出校门，

---

[1] 苗绘：“法律援助式诊所初探”，载《理论观察》2006年第3期。

多方面开拓案源是必要的。笔者所在高校的诊所学生自发组织，通过与社区办事处有效沟通，定期到社区提供法律咨询服务；为了有效吸引更多群众的关注，他们还与本地的社工组织联系，一同组织活动。通过与社区建立长期联系与合作，加大宣传力度，打开局面，是开拓案源的有效途径。

另外，法律诊所还可以与当地司法局的法援处联系，定期组织诊所学生参与法援处的值班，在执业律师的指导下参与值班咨询。由于诊所的机制相对灵活，部分不符合法援处受理条件的案件可以转交给诊所处理。

（二）开源节流，拓宽法律援助经费来源

中国法学会法学教育研究会诊所法律教育专业委员会（CCCLE）制定的《法律诊所课程基本规范（指南）》中明确规定："诊所课程的所需经费最终应当要立足于本校的支撑，倡导多途径地获得诊所课程的所需经费，严禁通过在实践活动中收费或者向当事人募捐获得诊所课程的所需经费。"[1] 法律援助既然着眼于社会服务，就不能因为经费问题而变无偿服务为有偿服务，法律援助经费问题可以从多方面着手解决。

一方面，法学院可以合理配置现有教学资源，整合部分实践课程，适当调拨资源给法律诊所用于法律援助工作。例如，大多数法学院都开设了假期实习、模拟法庭等实践课程，而这些课程内容与法律诊所有所重合，因此可以考虑整合部分课程，从而避免教学资源的重复投放，可以节约部分资金投入到法律诊所中。

另一方面，高校法律诊所应当积极争取各方面社会资源的支持。法学院应当凭借其教师与学生良好的专业素养在其所辐射的地域为社会提供良好的服务，形成较好的声誉以获得所在地域公众的认可，由此，法律诊所对社会的贡献越大，得到各项社会资助的可能性就越大。美国各大法学院的法律诊所对社会的影响力很大，这不仅仅是因为冠以他们的名号响亮，更重要的是他们确确实实为社会、为需要法律服务的人们提

[1] 中国诊所法律教育网站，http：//www.cliniclaw.cn/.2012—05—04.

供了极大的便利与帮助。付出与回报成正比，美国各大法学院法律诊所得到的社会资助相当可观。[1] 但目前我国高校的法律诊所普遍未形成足够的社会影响，社会资助渠道并不畅通。因此，提高诊所专业能力是获得社会资助的条件之一。

各地的律师协会也可以成为诊所争取资金来源的目标，律协的工作之一就是培养律师，而法律诊所是其先行部队，担任了培养“准律师”的角色，为律协造就了不少储备人才，律师协会有可能拨付一些资金或是提供其他的资源支持法律诊所的开展。[2]

（三）各方面协调，保障诊所学生法律援助工作的顺利开展

诊所学生代理人身份问题首先需要诊所的法律援助中心与其他部门协调解决。

以劳动争议为例，对于公民代理，根据《中华人民共和国劳动争议调解仲裁法》及相关法律法规，原则上只要求不能收费，但各地往往另有特别规定。例如，广东省劳动争议仲裁委员会对于公民代理资格的要求就比较严格，其发布的《劳动仲裁委托代理人暂行规定》[3]（以下简称《暂行规定》）第 6 条第 1 款规定：“当事人可以委托下列人员作为代理人：（一）律师；（二）当事人的近亲属；（三）有关的社会团体或者所在单位推荐的人；（四）有正当理由经劳动争议仲裁委员会许可的其他公民。”而根据其第 10 条的规定，学生代理人一般也不属于有正当理由经劳动争议仲裁委员会许可的其他公民，[4] 所以只能以“有关的社会团体或者所在单位推荐的人”的身份担任劳动仲裁案件的代理人。根据《暂

---

[1][2] 徐安：“美国诊所教育的发展善研究及其借鉴意义”，中国政法大学法律硕士 2010 年硕士论文，第 17 页。

[3] 《广东省劳动争议仲裁委员会〈劳动仲裁委托代理人暂行规定〉的通知》（粤劳仲［2003］8 号）。

[4] 《暂行规定》第 10 条：“有正当理由经劳动争议仲裁委员会许可的其他公民，主要指以下情形之一：（一）取得了法律职业资格证或律师资格证的公民；（二）获得企业法律顾问资格的公民；（三）从事法学研究、教育工作的公民；（四）从事劳动保障部门、工会组织、企业协会工作的公民；（五）法律规定的其他法律工作者。”

行规定》和本地劳动仲裁委员会的做法，[1] 笔者指导诊所学生担任代理人时一般按照以下规程：由政法学院与当事人签订免费代理的委托代理合同，政法学院向劳动仲裁委员会提供上述合同，并出具关于指派学生担任代理人的函。

关于民事诉讼的代理人资格，新修订的《民事诉讼法》对于诉讼代理人的要求也趋于规范，[2] 由学校、学院以单位名义推荐是唯一可行的办法。

上述做法只是解决了程序上的问题，而在实际的司法/劳动仲裁过程中，部分法官或仲裁员并没有真正认可学生代理人。例如，笔者就曾遇到以下情况：在一起劳动合同争议案件仲裁过程中，仲裁员在组织双方当事人调解时不通知学生代理人，最后在学生代理人不知情的情况下，案件调解终结。尽管当事人对调解结果基本接受，最后还向诊所赠送了锦旗，但这毕竟反映了学生代理人的身份并没有得到真正认可的事实。可资比较的是，同样的情况很少发生在律师代理人的身上。

另外，学生代理人并非律师，调查取证的权利受到很大的限制。解决的办法暂时只能是申请法院/劳动仲裁委员会调查取证，或者让当事人自行取证。如果上述方案都无法实现，案件处理效果可能会受到影响，直接的影响是当事人可能会因此对学生代理人产生不信任，觉得诊所无法有效帮助自己解决问题。但随着《民事诉讼法》的修改与完善，向法

---

[1] 《暂行规定》第 9 条：当事人委托有关的社会团体或所在单位推荐人为代理人的，应提供社会团体或单位开具的证明。第 13 条：公民代理人参加劳动仲裁活动不得向当事人收取报酬。当事人与代理人应签订不收费的协议书，并提供给劳动争议仲裁委员会。不向劳动争议仲裁委员会提供不收费协议的，劳动争议仲裁委员会有权取消其代理资格。

[2] 新《民事诉讼法》于 2013 年 1 月 1 日起施行，第 58 条第 2 款规定：下列人员可以被委托为诉讼代理人：（1）律师、基层法律服务工作者；（2）当事人的近亲属或者工作人员；（3）当事人所在社区、单位以及有关社会团体推荐的公民。而之前的《民事诉讼法》则规定，律师、当事人的近亲属、有关的社会团体或者所在单位推荐的人、经人民法院许可的其他公民，都可以被委托为诉讼代理人。两者比较可见，之前的法律规定含“经人民法院许可的其他公民”，新法则没有该笼统的规定，代之以更为明确的限制。

院申请调查取证这一诉讼权利得到程序上的保障，学生代理人取证难的消极影响会减弱。

（四）完善诊所管理，确保援助工作有效衔接

如前所述，学生参与办案的时间很难得到保障，毕业后去向就更难确定，随着参与办案的学生毕业离校，审理时间长的案件的跟进可能会出现衔接上的问题。

对此问题，应尽量将学生正常学习时间与法律援助活动时间错开，引导学生合理安排两者的时间，将学生正常学习与法律援助实践学习结合起来，笔者同时鼓励学生选一学期的诊所课，但参加两个学期的活动。同时，应完善诊所管理制度，通过以老带新的方式，让即将毕业的学生与较低年级学生将在办案件及时衔接，确保援助工作的有效推进。

诊所式法律教育结合法律援助工作是关于高校法律教育推行实践式教育模式的积极探索，尽管在实践中遇到不少问题，但随着高校对于这一教育模式的重视与投入的加大以及具体实施方案的改进，相信许多问题可以逐步得到解决。

诊所法律教育与学生法律援助

任学青[*]

摘　要： 诊所法律教育与法律援助存在天然的联系，但由于学生法律援助活动主要以法科学生为主体，从而具有不同于一般法律援助活动的特性与规律。设立学生法律援助组织应当注意设立目的的双重性、管理运作的双系统、成员结构的流动性等特点。学生法律援助在我国的合法化和规范化是诊所法律教育的当务之急。

关键词： 双重性　双系统　流动性　规范化

法律援助，又称法律救助、法律扶助制度，是世界各国普遍采用的司法救济制度。它是指国家为了保证法律赋予公民的各项权利在现实生活中切实得以实现，对某些经济困难或特殊案件的当事人给予减免费用、提供法律帮助的一项法律制度。其类型除政府援助行为外，还有民间性质的法律援助。前者专指在国家设立的法律援助机构的指导和协调下，律师、公证员、基层法律工作者等法律服务人员为经济困难或特殊案件的当事人给予减免收费等法律帮助。后者则是由民间法律工作者组成的非政府组织无偿为社会贫弱者提供法律帮助的社会公益活动。[1]

诊所法律教育所依托的法律援助诊所是在法学院指导下的法律援助组织，它具有双重作用：一是以诊所教育方式提供法学教育；二是作为一种公共服务为贫民提供法律援助。从性质上讲，诊所法律教育所提供的学生法律援助活动可以说是一种民间性质的法律援助活动。

---

* 任学青，山东政法学院经济贸易法学院副教授。

[1] 李傲、许炎："法律援助与法律诊所之甄别与整合"，载《法学杂志》2003年第11期，第62页。

一、美国的历史及其启示

美国的诊所法律教育一诞生就与学生法律援助活动联系在一起。田纳西州大学法学院开办诊所法律教育以后，便在当地的社区中心办了一个免费法律援助办事处，法律诊所的学生每个星期都花一定的时间为当地的贫民和有需要援助的市民提供相应的法律服务；耶鲁大学法学院教授 Jerome Frank 领导的组织“法律诊所或诊疗所”（Legal Clinics or Dispensaries）在给法学院学生提供实践机会的同时，为穷人提供免费法律援助；另外，杜克大学的 John Brardewell 在杜克大学和南卡罗莱纳大学创设了“法律援助诊所”（ Legal Aid Clinic），为需要法律援助的当事人提供法律服务。随后，美国许多大学纷纷仿效，开展了免费为穷人打官司的法律援助活动。正是由于法学院所提供的这种免费的法律援助服务，他们的权利得到了一定的救济和保障。诊所式法律教育的第二个重要阶段是 20 世纪 60～70 年代的形成阶段，当时美国的民权运动蓬勃发展，许多贫困的人拿起法律武器捍卫自己的合法权利，对法律援助的需求更加迫切，这为诊所式法律教育向前迈进提供了更加广阔的空间；同时，诊所法律教育也在法律援助中发挥越来越大的作用。

诊所法律教育与法律援助存在天然的联系：一方面，诊所法律教育中的大量案件来自法律援助机构，法律援助组织是诊所案源的保证和依托。诊所式法律教育主要是让学生办理真实案件与法律事务，让学生在实践中学习。如果没有案源，就意味着法律诊所将没有真实的案件，学生在真实案件中学习法律知识和执业技巧的目的就不能实现，学生参加的热情和积极性会大大降低；更重要的是，作为诊所式法律教育重要目标之一的法律职业道德和社会责任心无法在模拟案件中培养，职业责任心只有在解决具体案件中的两难问题时才能得到最充分的讨论。比如，如何处理矛盾冲突和严守保密准则，如何处理律师与当事人的关系等，只有在办理真实的案件中才能实现这一培养目标。如何保证法律诊所有足够的、适合学生办理的案件，是开展诊所式法律教育的院校必须解决的问题。另一方面，诊所法律教育所提供的学生法律援助是无偿的、合格的，满足了社会的部分需求，学生办理法律援助案件能成为法律援助的补充力量。法律诊所的学生通过向社会弱势群体提供无偿法律服务，能为政府法律援助事业增添力量，既可以解决法律援助中心人力不够的问题，又能够满足社会对政府法律援助的需求，是一个双赢的活动。

目前，美国的法律援助机构可分为三类，一是公共辩护人办公室，属官方机构，办理刑事法律援助案件，主要为刑事被指控者提供无偿法律服务，另外也办理一些家庭法案件、儿童保护案件、精神病人监护案件等。二是民间的法律援助机构，主要为民事案件的当事人提供无偿法律援助。三是法学院成立的各类诊所，学生运用法律知识代理真实的案件。早在 1951 年，法学院诊所教育就被列为全美民事法律援助六大机构之一。[1] 美国的诊所法律教育本身已经成为法律援助中的一个重要组成部分。

美国的历史告诉我们，法律诊所所承载的并不仅仅是教育的任务，同时作为一种服务于社会的模式，法律诊所还可以向社会的弱势群体提供司法平等的法律援助。但由于其法律援助活动主要以法科学生为主体，从而具有不同于一般法律援助活动的特性与规律。

二、学生法律援助组织的设立

（一）学生受理法律援助案件的特点

1. 援助关系的复杂性

在学生法律援助案件中，援助关系的复杂性是针对援助主体而言的。学生法律援助组织一般涉及三方主体，即法学院的学生、指导教师和案件委托人。其中，学生是教学活动的中心、援助案件的办理者。诊所教师是办理援助案件的指导者，其中包括法学院的专职教师，也包括法学院聘请的作为特邀指导教师的其他法律专业人士，如法官、检察官、律师以及妇联、残联和青少年联合会等社会团体中的法律工作者。指导教

---

[1] 李军："法律诊所教育与法律援助"，载《山西师大学报（社会科学版）》2005 年第 4 期，第 39 页。

师的责任是指导、监督学生学习法律工作技巧和办理具体案件。援助案件的委托者是援助案件中不可或缺的主体，他们与法律诊所是委托关系，而学生是具体承担委托案件的承办者。在这种关系中，虽然教师并不直接承担案件的办理及其他活动，但学生针对案件的思维活动及其具体工作一定是在诊所教师的指导和监督下完成的，教师其实在援助关系中具有相应的义务。这应该是我们在今后的诊所工作和研究中进一步研究和关注的问题，当然这有赖于政府和法律制度的支撑。

2. 受理案件的类型化

我国《法律援助条例》规定了政府法律援助的范围，即依法请求国家赔偿的，请求给予社会保险待遇或者最低生活保障待遇的，请求发给抚恤金、救济金的，请求给付赡养费、抚养费、扶养费的，请求支付劳动报酬的，主张因见义勇为行为产生的民事权益的，以及刑事案件中有法定情形的，法定特殊人群需要帮助的等情况，同时也规定省、自治区、直辖市人民政府可以作出补充规定。因此，政府法律援助案件的范围是广泛的。实践中，我国各级法律援助中心的救济范围一般也是没有特别限制的，包括各种类型的案件。与法律援助案件不同的是，诊所受理的案件具有针对性，诊所往往需要确定某一类特殊群体作为援助对象，办理同一类别的案件。这主要是考虑了诊所学生的实际办案能力以及诊所教师的工作领域，目的是在学生的能力范围内使当事人利益得到切实保障。为此，法律诊所受理的案件一般是单一的。比如，美国一般把法律诊所承接的案件都做些分工，一些法学院往往采取设立多个功能不同的法律诊所的办法，有些大的法学院甚至设有十几个不同诊所。在我国，随着诊所法律教育规模的不断扩大，也形成了各具特色的法律诊所，专门从事某一类型的法律实践。

3. 法律责任的独特性

在学生法律援助组织中，除法律诊所外，涉及三方主体，即指导教师、学生和委托人，形成的关系较法律援助复杂。指导教师与学生之间形成教学关系，学生与委托人之间形成委托代理关系，指导教师（或诊所）与委托人之间也形成特定的权利义务关系等。在此种情况下，如何承担因为提供援助案件而产生的有关法律责任就成为必须面对的问题。为了解决这个问题，有必要对美国的有关做法予以思考：为了推动学生在诊所的教育工作，美国许多州制定了学生实践规则。这些规则规范了学生的劳动，并保证具备条件的学生出庭、与未监禁的当事人会面等。任何情况下，学生在有真实委托人的法律诊所的工作必须在执业律师的监督下进行，这些律师对其与客户之间的关系承担最终责任。这样既为学生办理法律援助案件提供了条件，又保证了案件处理的正确性，明确了法律责任。

针对学生受理法律援助案件的以上特点，在实践中笔者认为应当确定相关制度，以有效保证学生参与法律实践并获得应有的培训，切实保障法律援助案件委托人的利益。

（二）设立学生法律援助组织应当注意的问题

1. 设立目的的双重性

学生法律援助的领域和援助目的与政府的法律援助是有区别的，学生法律援助应当强调诊所教育这个范畴的自主性、独特性。这一点首先体现在设立或者说提供法律援助的目的上。

政府法律援助的目的在于为社会贫弱者提供无偿的法律救济，维护他们的合法权益，维护社会正义，因此整个法律援助活动的中心是当事人，以当事人的利益为重心成为设立政府法律援助的基本出发点与目的。学生法律援助组织的设立则不同，它的设立目的即直接目的在于为学生提供一种学习法律、锻炼实务能力的场所，虽然诊所受理的案件的当事人也是社会贫弱者，学生办案的过程实际也在为他们提供法律帮助，但就实质而言，诊所教育所提供的学生法律援助不过是以社会为课堂，以真实的当事人和案件为教材，以谈话、取证、出庭等行动作为学习过程的一门课程，可以说，诊所法律援助是只供给学生观察社会的机会和产地，通过它来感受社会现实层面的法律问题，向社会弱者提供无偿的法律救济仅仅是在这个前提之下的社会目的。[1] 因此，学生法律援助组织的设立不能偏离教学目的而像其他法律援助组织那样单纯追求社会价值和目的。

设立目的的双重性体现为：以教学为目的，以社会服务性为目的。

2. 管理运作的双系统（复杂性）

正如我们上面提到的，学生法律援助组织肩负着双重使命，既是学生学习场地的延伸，也是社会弱者接受法律援助的机构。与其他法律援助组织相比，他们提供法律援助的外在形式没有差别，都是为经济困难或特殊案件的当事人免费提供法律帮助，但就实质而言，学生法律援助不过是以社会为课堂，法律援助是诊所教学的手段之一。因此，其管理运行不同于单纯的法律援助机构。

学生法律援助管理运作的双系统是指，学生法律援助活动存在于教学管理体系和法律救济双重体系中，必须遵循教学管理规则和法律救济规则。其中，教学规则包括授课规则、指导规则、评价规则等日常教学管理中的制度规范；法律救济规则主要是指国家法律救济制度和规范。

3. 成员结构的流动性

成员结构的流动性主要是指在学生法律援助组织中提供法律援助的主体即诊所学生的流动性。学生法律诊所首先是一个教学阵地，以传授实践经验和技能为其教学目的，其中，承担法律援助工作的主体首先以学习为目的，办理法律援助案件是其学习内容之一。学生法律援助组织承担教学任务，其教学任务是以学期或学年为期限的，学期届满，学生即结束在这里的学习。这一点不同于专门的法律援助机构，其通常是独立的组织，有自己固定的组成人员——律师、法律援助工作者、行政工作人员等。

针对成员结构的流动性，在设立学生法律援助组织时应考虑在诊所中配备相对固定的行政人员，从而保证法律援助中行政管理工作的连贯性；同时，诊所师资的相对固定也是必须考虑的问题；另外，应该科学地挑选适合学生在固定的期限内完成的案件。

---

[1] 李军："法律诊所教育与法律援助"，载《山西师大学报（社会科学版）》2005年第4期，第41页。

（三）设立学生法律援助组织的模式选择

1. 法律援助组织与法律诊所一体型

法律援助组织与法律诊所一体型是设立学生法律援助组织的一种选择。在这种模式下，法律诊所与法律援助组织不仅在工作场所、机构设置上相同，而且在运作过程和管理制度上完全一致。许多高校的学生法律援助组织即采用这一形式，不管称呼上是法律诊所还是法律援助中心，或对外称为法律援助中心而对内是法律诊所，都同时具备两方面的职能。

2. 法律援助组织与法律诊所分离型

在这种模式下，学生法律援助组织和法律诊所各自独立，互相合作。法律援助组织和法律诊所是并存的，各有其独立的办公场所、机构设置和管理制度。为了诊所教学所需和解决援助机构人员的不足，二者之间建立长期合作伙伴关系，互为补充，互相促进。诊所的学生经过严格系统的律师技巧训练，可以弥补法律援助人力资源的不足，缓解法律援助供求关系。法律援助机构从接待、咨询、审查到参与代理，丰富的服务形式为诊所学生提供了全方位实践的机会；充裕的、类型各异的案源正好可以满足诊所选择合适案件的需要；法律援助中心的固定工作人员可以协助处理学期间断、学生换届时诊所案件出现的临时问题。这种合作对于促进两者的共同发展十分有益。[1]

对于以上两种模式的选择，可以根据法学院自己的具体情况，如师资的力量、学生的数量和层次以及当地社会的需求予以选择。

三、学生法律援助在我国的合法化和规范化问题

我国是一个有13亿人口的发展中国家，经济发展相对落后，贫困人口的基数较大，导致很多人在发生纠纷、面临诉讼的时候无力支付相关的律师费用。政府从1994年起开始建立法律援助制度，并于2003年颁布了专门规范法律援助制度的法规——《法律援助条例》，目前在全国绝

[1] 李傲、许炎：“法律援助与法律诊所之甄别与整合”，载《法学杂志》2003年第11期，第64页。

大多数地区相继建立了法律援助制度和法律援助中心。法律援助中心主要负责分配和管理由律师完成的、对其具有强制性的工作。虽然法律援助中心制度的建立缓解了部分矛盾，但是资金匮乏、律师严重不足等因素限制和影响了法律援助工作的开展，法律援助机构办理的援助案件数量远远不能满足社会对法律援助的需求，现实中有众多需要并应当得到援助的人没有得到援助。有关统计表明，在人民法院的刑事审判过程中，有“辩护人”参加的案件不足1/10，而其中属于人民法院依法“主动”为被告人指定辩护人的案件更是微乎其微。我国每年需要法律援助的案件超过50万件，而实际得到援助的不足1/3。面对这样的现状，我们必须寻求其他解决困难的途径，而诊所法律教育提供法律援助的模式是一种较好的途径，由学生代理法律援助案件，为社会提供优质的法律服务。

我国已经开展法律诊所教育的几十家法学院与各级政府举办的法律援助中心建立了密切的联系，成立了几十家面向不同援助人群的法律诊所，为选修诊所课程的学生提供了大量参与法律援助活动的机会。例如，北京大学法学院的北京大学学生法律服务中心既是诊所教育的一个载体，又是一个独立的法律服务机构；中国人民大学法律诊所主要依托人大“大学生志愿者法律援助中心”；中南财经政法大学于2000年5月26日成立了“法律援助与保护中心（法律诊所）”，主要通过向社会提供法律援助来培养和锻炼学生；武汉大学法律诊所是一个综合性的法律诊所，是以“武汉大学社会弱者权利保护中心”为基础组建的，目前已经成为极具影响的法律援助中心；华东政法学院的法律诊所依托1997年成立的华东政法学院法律援助中心而成立，其与上海长宁区司法局法律援助中心和长宁区大山街道联手，让诊所学生参与社会法律援助活动；中山大学依托广东省和广州市法律援助中心等机构，开设了以劳动法为主的法律诊所课程和法律诊所。

目前选修法律诊所课程的学生都是本科高年级学生和研究生，他们已经掌握了基本的理论知识，在老师的指导下，在诊所中办理法律援助案件，既培养了学生的职业技能，又为当事人解决了法律问题。如果每所法学院都能建立自己的诊所，为学校所在社区的弱者服务，中国的法律援助服务将不再局限于律师等法律工作者，为社会弱者提供法律服务的队伍将迅速壮大，社会的资源将实现有效的发挥利用。

虽然如此，由于诊所法律教育在我国起步较晚，因此，学生法律援助在我国的发展还缺少制度的保障和配合。首先，学生法律援助组织的地位不明确。我国《法律援助条例》规定，法律援助是政府的责任，县级以上人民政府应当采取积极措施推动法律援助工作，为法律援助提供财政支持。国务院司法行政部门监督管理全国的法律援助工作。县级以上地方各级人民政府司法行政部门监督管理本行政区域的法律援助工作。上述规定表达了我国是政府统领法律援助的模式。虽然《法律援助条例》第 8 条规定国家支持和鼓励社会团体、事业单位等社会组织利用自身资源为经济困难的公民提供法律援助，但实际上，司法行政管理部门为了防止一些打着“法律援助”之名而变相进行有偿法律服务的现象发生，对于法律援助机构的审批和认定有严格的规定。诊所法律教育首先作为一门课程在大学法学院中设立，对比法律援助机构的条件，显然其更像一个组织松散的团体。所以，按照现行的有关规定，从司法行政管理部门的角度看，要确认其作为一个独立或半独立的机构确实有一定的困难。目前，开展法律援助的法学院一般是基于与当地法律援助机构的合作关系而挂靠设立的，作为一个民间法律援助机构，国家法律对法律诊所的法律地位、职能、作用均无明确的规定，从而在一定程度上无法取得官方部门的配合和社会各界的认可，而这种状况对于法律诊所教育独立而有效地选取案例有一定的制约和限制，这个问题不解决，必然给诊所学生在办案过程中带来相当大的阻力和不便。其次，学生办理法律援助案件的身份不明确。我国现行三部诉讼法和律师法都赋予了律师特有的诉讼权利和地位，虽然三部诉讼法并未限制律师以外的公民成为诉讼代理人、辩护人，但普通公民担任诉讼代理人和辩护人所享有的诉讼权利与地位远不及律师。特别是在刑事案件中，公民代理人在查阅卷宗、与被告人会见和通信时，都要事先经过人民法院和人民检察院的许可；在向有关单位和个人调查取证和收集证据时，不如律师那样便利。同样，在民事诉讼和行政诉讼中，公民代理人也存在相似的情况。而法律诊所的学生代理案件，依目前法律规定只能是以普通公民的身份，这非常不利于诊所学生代理工作的开展，许多职业技能得不到训练，也影响到法律诊所的训练目标，可以说，立法机关、司法机关及律师协会的行政规定都没有给诊所式法律教育留有适当的空间。因此，法律诊所学生在从事法律援助时存在身份不清和责任不明问题在所难免。

在美国和东欧，诊所法律教育已部分地将学生为社会提供法律援助的行为合法化、规范化。在美国，通过30年左右时间的努力和发展，法律诊所已经可以“名正言顺”地承办有关的法律案件，甚至是难度较大的移民案件以及为监狱人犯提供法律服务等案件，法院也普遍对诊所学生的代理资格予以承认，这就使法律诊所的学生在真实的案件里能顺利进入司法程序，像真正的律师那样为当事人提供法律服务。

学生法律援助在我国的合法化和规范化已经成为诊所法律教育的当务之急。针对以上两个问题，笔者认为学生法律援助机构的独立化应当予以确认。学生法律援助活动毕竟不同于政府或其他民间法律援助，有其独特的运作原则和规则，在选取案件和具体的结案和办理程序上有自己的要求和目的，独立性是有效开展诊所法律教育和优质办理援助案件的要求。另外，诊所学生的身份问题势必会影响法律诊所与社会的广泛接触，对法律诊所开展的法律职业化教育形成巨大的障碍。因此，国家有关部门应该从职业化教育的角度出发，赋予高校诊所特殊地位，承认学生的“准律师”身份，使其在真正从事法律职业之前充分地参与法律实践，培养其法律职业道德和掌握法律职业基本技能。

参考文献：

1. 甄贞主编.诊所法律教育在中国［M］. 北京：法律出版社，2002.

2. 陈建民.从法学教育方法的目标审视诊所法律教育的地位和作用［J］. 环球法律评论，2005（3）.

3. 王立民，牟逍媛.诊所法律教育研究［M］. 上海：上海交通大学出版社，2004.

4. 李傲，许炎.法律援助与法律诊所之甄别与整合［J］. 法学杂志，2003（11）.

5. 王晨光. 实践性法律教学与法学教育改革［J］. 法学，2001（7）.

6. 王立民. 法律援助与"诊所法律教育"［J］. 政治与法律，2005（1）.

7. 李军. 法律诊所教育与法律援助［J］. 山西师大学报 . 社会科学版，2005（4）.

论大学生法律援助的完善

——以诊所法律教育为视角

戈 琳 徐新意*

摘 要：在我国目前的法律援助实践中，大学生一直扮演着极其重要的角色，在高校开展法律援助活动不仅有助于解决我国法律援助中的供需矛盾问题，同时也有利于法学专业毕业生法务实践能力的锻炼。但大学生法律援助活动存在缺乏权责明确的管理体制、缺乏必要经费的支持、活动形式单一、层次较低等问题。要解决这些问题，可引入诊所法律教育，明确大学生法律援助的专业定位和大学生在法律援助活动中的法律地位，建立大学生法律援助的监督管理体系和长效的激励机制，加强大学生在法律援助方面的经验交流，促进法律援助专业人才的培养。

关键词：大学生 法律援助 诊所法律教育

近年来，随着我国法律援助事业的不断发展，大学生群体日渐成为各种法律援助组织的中坚力量，他们以法律援助志愿者的身份深入社会基层，不仅将法律援助事业在国内大范围地铺展开来，更将法律援助带到了我国最需要的地方。

一、大学生法律援助的价值

同法学理论教育不同，法律援助作为一种法务实践，是需要学生去具体操作的。针对目前我国法学专业毕业生专业技能薄弱、实务能力不

* 戈琳，常州大学文法学院，讲师。徐新意，常州大学文法学院，副教授。

强的现状，让法学院的学生从事法律援助相关活动，对完善法学专业毕业生的专业素质、培养符合社会法制建设需要的法学人才具有极其重要的意义。

（一）增加大学生法务实践机会

法学学生参与法律援助的作用之一，就是能够在实践中加强专业素质的培养。虽然现存的法学教育中也要求法学专业学生开展像模拟法庭等这样的实验活动，但由于其本身与真正的法务实践存在相当的距离而缺乏真实性，无法获得理想的效果。法律援助则能够有效中和其不足，相比于普通的模拟法庭，它能提供真实的案件和办案环境，大学生已完全介入处理一个法律案件所需要经过的复杂的事实调查和人际交往中，需要解决真实案件在事实和职业道德方面的问题，这就为大学生深入法务实践提供了良好的平台，从而给法学专业学生了解司法实践现状、在实践中将理论与现实结合起来、锻炼法务技能提供了机会。[1]

（二）缓解我国法律援助的供需矛盾

让大学生参与法律援助，能够有效缓解法律援助人才紧缺的现状。“据估计，我国每年大约有38万余件法律援助案件需要办理，其中绝大多数需要律师提供帮助，可是按每位律师每年办理1～2件案件来计算，现有的10多万名律师只能办理10多万件此类案件，缺口很大。”[2] 然而目前我国开设法学专业的高校有600多所，在校法学专业学生超过70万，其中具备较为完备法律知识的高年级学生近10万。高校学生积极参加法律援助工作，一方面能够大大缓解我国在法律援助工作中的供需矛盾，另一方面也能够为高校学生提供社会实践机会，提高综合素质，可谓一举两得。

（三）促进法学教育的改革

大学生参与法律援助实践是社会发展的客观要求，有助于法学教育

---

[1] 杨凌珊：“论诊所式法律教育与法律援助”，载《法制与社会》，2009年第6期，第302～302页。

[2] 王立民、牟逍媛主编：《诊所法律教育研究》，上海交通大学出版社2005年版。

改革的推行。随着社会主义法治化进程的不断推进，传统的法学教育所培养的毕业生已经难以满足社会的实际需求，这一现状从近几年法学专业毕业生的就业现状中就可得到很好的体现。因此，我国的法学教育正面临一次由传统的理论灌输式教学向实践应用型教学模式的变革。在这个过程中，各个法学院积极寻求新的教学方法和教学体系，其中之一就是各种实务课程的开设，而法律援助活动的开展正好满足了这一教学上的需求。法律援助为法学院校的课外实务提供了案件来源，并且，以法律援助的形式让学生从事法务实践，从委托人角度考虑更容易被接受和信任。因此，促进法学专业学生深入法律援助实践，对于促进高校法学教育体制的改革，从而促进高素质法学专业人才的培养，具有重要的现实意义。

（四）维护社会稳定

党的十七大工作报告中明确指出，要“最大限度激发社会创造力，最大限度增加和谐因素”。我国正处在转型时期，政治、经济、文化等正在发生结构性的变迁，由此引发一系列的社会问题：利益分配不公，贫富差距加大，社会矛盾错综复杂，冲突加剧，弱势群体规模不断扩大。在这一背景下，如果弱势群体的利益得不到及时有效的保障，将严重影响社会的和谐与稳定。大学生法律援助作为民间法律援助力量，通过向弱势群体提供法律服务，维护弱势群体的利益，发挥减压阀的作用，能够在一定程度上维护社会稳定。

二、大学生法律援助存在的问题

（一）大学生法律援助缺乏权责明确的管理体制

目前国内高校从事法律援助活动主要是在高校自身组织机构下设立相关的部门和人员来展开，相关领域还没有明确的制度体系加以规范，加上各地高校具体情况不一，掺杂很多其他因素，造成目前高校法律援助机构管理无章可循的现象。在这样的情况下，法律援助活动无法长期稳定地开展，相关人员的管理和绩效考核无从着手，缺乏有效的评估和激励机制，从事法律援助的高校组织和人员没有明确的法律地位，得不到社会的认可和信任，严重阻碍了高校法律援助工作积极、持久、健康地发展。

（二）法律援助缺乏必要经费的支持

正是由于高校法律援助机构对高校本身的依赖性，目前国内致力于法律援助相关领域的高校大多属于非营利性事业单位，在没有专项资金提供支持的情况下，高校的法律援助工作往往因经费短缺而无法高效率、高质量地展开。另外，由于法律援助本身就是一项公益性很强的事业，接受法律援助的对象绝大多数都是社会弱势群体，就更不可能从法律援助对象方面去解决经费问题。再从官方角度考虑，高校法律援助的社会效应之一就是缓解国家司法资源紧缺的现状，作为政府机构之一的司法机关当然不可能有预算外的资金去支持高校的法律援助活动。因此，面对种种尴尬局面，高校和师生要想开展有影响力的法律援助活动就陷入了“巧妇难为无米之炊”的困境。

（三）法律援助活动形式单一，层次较低

纵观大学生法律援助活动，普法传单的散发、法律问题的咨询等类似的形式是最为常见的。但随着我国法制建设的不断发展和公民生活水平的不断提高，各种形形色色的法律问题逐渐出现，以往仅仅停留在表层的法律知识普及活动已经无法适应社会的需求，特别是在贫富差距有扩大趋势的情况下，对社会弱势群体的保护需要全方位的更为细致的法律援助工作。但是，上述组织管理、资金来源和体制欠缺等种种问题，加之高校从事法律援助的相关师生专业水平和能力素养存在较大差异，直接导致了高校的法律援助工作无法深入人民社会生活，仅仅停留在表面，停留在做做形象工程的程度。

三、引入诊所法律教育，完善大学生法律援助

法律诊所教育（Clinical Legal Education）是指一种把学生放到具体的办案环境中，在律师或法学教师等具有专业资质的人员的指导和监督下，让学生通过具体的办案实践来学习法学理论知识和办案技能的教学模式。其目的就在于提高法学专业学生的专业素养和实践能力，为其今

后的从业奠定基础。大学生法律援助本身是需要社会实践的，以此为基础将两者结合起来，充分利用各自领域的优势，优势互补，必然会有利于各自的发展。

（一）明确大学生法律援助的专业定位

总结国外法律诊所的发展的成功经验来看，成熟的法律诊所都是以一定的专业方向为发展定位的，例如美国耶鲁大学和密歇根大学就分别设立了环境法和自然资源保护方面的法律诊所。将法律援助方向限定在一定范围内，不论从专业的学术研究角度还是援助本身的教育功能考虑都是必要的，因为任何组织机构所具备的软硬件资源都是有限的：在物力方面，确定一个适当的范围，能够把有限的经费使用到核心项目中，取得突破；从人力方面考虑，在有限的人员中，各人所致力的方向和擅长的领域都是有限的，因人制宜地确定发展方向，能够发挥各自的专长，更好地开展援助工作。事实上，国内现有的法律诊所也都确立了各自的专业方向，如，北京大学法律诊所在其“妇女保护中心”的基础上主要办理妇女权益保护方面的案件，中国人民大学则建立了专门的刑事法律诊所，清华大学的“调解诊所”则主要开展保护消费者权益方面的相关法律活动。因此，要通过法律诊所这样一个组织形式来做好法律援助工作，首先必须明确援助的专业发展方向，确定法律援助的主要对象，否则就无法为援助的长远发展订立明确的发展目标。当然，在具体从事办案活动的过程中，对法律援助的对象和类型可以放宽一些，以谋求大学生有足够的专业视野和经历。

（二）明确大学生在法律援助活动中的法律地位

由于在我国从事法律相关业务必须获得相应的执业资格，而我国目前还没有针对在校学生的相关资格认定，因此在实践中，大学生在从事法律援助工作中常处于身份地位不明的尴尬境地，从而导致其只能从事法律援助辅助性工作且社会评价度不高。“我国学生在办理真实案件时所享有的权利远不及律师所享有的权利，这非常不利于学生代理案件的开展，许多职业技能得不到训练，影响到法律诊所的训练目标的实现，也在一定程度上削弱和打击了诊所学生参加法律援助案件的热情和积极性。"[1] 所以，应当呼吁相关的司法、教育部门及时研究出台相应的政策，通过一定的考核体系赋予法学院学生某种"准律师"资格，允许参与一定的法律实践活动。另外，结合法律诊所本身，也可积极借鉴国外的经验，例如美国的自然资源保护委员会和耶鲁大学法学院教师共同组成的耶鲁大学环境法律诊所、国家野生动植物协会安阿伯大湖区自然资源研究中心与密歇根大学法学院合作设立的密歇根大学环境法律诊所等。这样，通过与一些被社会认可的组织机构合作，提升诊所的社会公信力，进而提高大学生在法律援助中的地位。

（三）依托诊所建立大学生法律援助的监督管理体系

诊所教学与传统的法律课程教学不同，其大部分课程是在课堂外特别是在法律援助案件的办理过程中完成的，因此可以借鉴诊所教学本身的良好监督管理体系来保障大学生法律援助活动的顺利开展。

1. 针对法律援助制定特色课程教学方案

教学方案的建立，也就是对教学内容的确立。不论是诊所的教师还是学生，在从事法律援助的过程中都必须始终明确，法律援助不仅是一种社会实践，还是一门课程，它有预定的教学内容和教学目标需要师生去完成，而完成这些的过程也是按照预先制订好的方案来执行的。当然，建立有特色的方案本身也是一个需要不断在实践中调整的过程，"制订方案是一项复杂的、模糊的、难以被理解的工作，在每个阶段，似乎都有一种倾向使我们去重复早已做过的事"[2]。在这里，西北政法学院在相关方面作出了很好的规划，他们将诊所课程具体划分为多个专题，对教学内容和教学方法都有预期的方案。值得肯定的是，这种方案在教学内容上打破了传统的学科分类体系，通过精心设计的教学实践内容，从法律援助办案实际需求出发培养学生具体的操作能力，构建一体化的教学实

---

[1] 王育红、李慧英："本土化诊所法律教育的问题及对策"，载《河北工程大学学报（社会科学版）》2009年第3期，第88～89页。

[2] Tamara Goriely. The English Approach to Access to Justice [Z]. Paper presented to a World Bank Workshop, Washington, December 11 2002.

践体系，有助于提高学生的办案水平和质量（参见表1）。[1]

表1　西北政法学院法律诊所教学与管理体系

课堂教学	教学的内容	诊所课程与诊所法律教育；接待当事人的技巧；案件陈述；证据方法；策略选定；非诉讼法律事务之一：合同；非诉讼法律事务之二：谈判；诉讼法律事务之一：观摩审判；诉讼法律事务之二：庭审程序；诉讼法律事务之三：模拟审判；判例方法；立法调研与论证；法律实施后的反馈与修改；法律职业操守；法律诊所教学反馈
	教学方法	1. 角色扮演；2. 小组合作；3. 头脑风暴
法律援助	立法援助	立法援助项目的援助对象和范围主要是社会组织和人民团体关于组织社会弱势群体权益的立法建议案和为省、市地方人大以及省、市地方人民政府起草的涉及社会权利保障方案的地方性法规草案和政府规章草案。诊所为其提供立项论证、立法调查、立法草案拟定法律文件起草、筹办和主持立法论证会等
	司法援助	包括老年人法律援助、残疾人法律援助、妇女儿童法律援助、进城务工民工和贫困下岗职工法律援助等不同领域。在具体的司法援助中，由4个学生一组，分组进行个案援助。参加诊所的学生，每2个学生必须在诊所课程进行期间完成一起案件的实际代理或辩护
诊所管理	诊所管理的主要制度	《日常值班制度》、《接案与代理制度》、《财务管理制度》、《档案、图书资料管理制度》、《学生奖惩制度》、《案件的监督指导制度》等
	案件讨论制度	案件小组会议讨论的范围
		案件小组会议的目的与程序

2. 建立以学校为主的监督管理体系

大学生法律援助有人口流动大、人员不稳定的特点，这给长效管理带来了挑战。对此，可借鉴法律诊所的管理模式。在这方面，国外的法律诊所要求诊所成员以课程日志的形式来记录活动的进展情况，并定期由专门人员组织检查和讨论，从中发现问题并及时予以纠正。“如果不加以及时的思考、反馈和计划，所有机构都会面临在日常业务中走下坡路

[1] 西北政法大学法律诊所：“西北政法学院诊所法律教育方案”，载西北政法大学法律诊所网站，2004—11—09［2010—05—28］，http：//www.nwcliniclaw.cn/news/news/37/2004119155549.htm.

的风险。”[1] 国内目前比较流行的做法是将学生分组，由特定的老师专门带领，并对学生的实践活动进行监督和管理。在这一基础上，学校对诊所教师的日常工作制定相关的监管体系，结合所带学生的实践情况，对教师的工作作出评估。

（四）建立法律援助的长效激励机制

法律援助是一项长期事业，要想法律援助达到一个良好的社会效果，必须保障法律援助的相关活动有计划、有规律地长期开展下去。所以，在长期的法律援助办案过程中，大学生需要一个良好的激励机制来保障法律援助活动质量的长效保持。高校应为从事法律援助的诊所配置专兼职律师以及相关的管理人员以缓解上述矛盾，同时为学生代理诉讼提供一定辅导，从而保障所办理的案件的质量。对积极从事法律援助工作的学生给予一定的物质或精神上的奖励，并建立评定机制以调动师生的积极性。[2] 对此，可将法律诊所作为一门课程纳入学生的培养计划，学生除了学到具体的技能和知识以外，还可获得相应的学分。教师方面，负责诊所课程的教师在付出相关劳动之后，必须对其工作量有一个量化的考核，将考核结果纳入教师的工作绩效，考核的标准应当结合具体的教学活动和实践成果由校方予以确立。

（五）加强法律援助经验的交流

大学生法律援助在一定程度上缓解了法律援助专业人才结构性短缺的问题，但由于大学生在专业知识、社会经验等方面存在不足，加强法律援助经验的交流与培训，促进经验和方法的借鉴、学习，是尽快培养人才的有效方法。一方面，大学生可以法律诊所为依托，积极与相关的法律援助机构和人员进行交流、沟通，从他们那里了解法律援助的现状，学习法律援助过程中的一些经验和技能；另一方面，法律诊所本身也要

---

[1] Legal Aid Review, Chairperson: Dame Margaret Bazley DNZM. Transforming the Legal Aid System: Final Report and Recommendations. Wellington: Legal Aid Review, 2009.

[2] 杨钰明、陈字平、张邦铺：“论我国高校法律援助制度的改革与完善”，载《法制与社会》2008 年第 8 期，第 386 页。

加强交流与沟通，虽然不同的法律诊所专业方向可能不同，但作为法律诊所，其在运行模式和操作方法上都有可以值得相互学习和借鉴的东西。例如，2007 年由诊所教育委员会主办、中华全国律师协会法律援助与公益法律委员会协办、北京大学法学院承办的“国际诊所法律教育与法律职业论坛”就有效地推动了相关领域人员的交流与合作，该论坛发出的有关法律援助与法律诊所教育的倡议引起了社会各界的高度关注，推动了这一领域的深入发展。

结　语

法律援助是一项非常有意义的社会事业，它不仅关系着一个国家的社会法制建设，更关系着普通公民特别是社会弱势群体的切身利益。虽然我国真正意义上的法律援助制度同西方发达国家相比建立的时间并不长，但是作为一种缓解我国法律援助资源困境的形式，我国的高校法律援助俨然已经成为我国法律援助领域甚至法学领域的一大特色。在高校积极发展法律援助事业，必将极大地推动我国社会主义法制的完善与发展。

法律诊所学员法律文书制作的问题及对策

——以婚姻家庭纠纷常用文书为视角

顾龙涛*

摘　要：法律文书制作是法律诊所学员办理法律事务中的重要工作。学员在代理诊所法律事务过程中，由于办案经验不足，职业技能欠缺，对民事法律的认知不充分，在制作相应的法律文书时常常不能制作准确而规范的法律文书，使当事人的权利得不到及时有效的维护。诊所教学中应当扩大案源，增加实践机会，加强基础课程与法律诊所课程的衔接，运用多种教学手段提高法律诊所学员的法律文书制作水平，以更好地为社会提供法律服务。

关键词：法律诊所教育　法律文书　问题　对策

法律文书有立法文书、司法文书和民用法律文书之分。民用法律文书是由当事人和律师为解决各类纠纷和处理非诉问题而制作或代书的文书。诊所法律教育通常以法律援助为手段，为当事人提供无偿法律援助。[1] 法律诊所学员制作和运用的法律文书主要是民用法律文书。诊所法律教育主要通过指导老师培训和指导学生进行法律实践来培养学生的法律职业技能和法律实践能力，同时，通过学生为弱势群体提供法律帮助来培养学生作为法律人的职业使命感和正义感。[2] 扬州大学法学院婚姻与家庭法律诊所于2006年4月正式启动，是江苏省高校第一家诊所会

* 顾龙涛，扬州大学法学院讲师。

[1] 蔡彦敏："诊所法律教育"，载《环球法律评论》2005年第3期。

[2] 孙占利、吴修合："诊所法律教育：目标设计与实现"，载《法学杂志》2010年第10期。

员单位和全国最早的婚姻家庭诊所。在诊所教育中，法律文书的制作成为法律诊所学员培训的主要组成部分。通过具体婚姻家庭纠纷法律文书的写作演练，诊所学员加深了对相关法律法规的理解，培养了实践能力，但也暴露出一些问题。本文试以婚姻家庭诊所教学中学员制作法律文书过程中的常见问题为基点，探寻改进法律诊所课程教学方法、提升学员法学综合素质和能力的出路，以求教于各位专家学者。

一、法律文书制作与法律诊所教育的契合性

古语说："工欲善其事，必先利其器。"法律诊所学员从事法律事务时，必然要制作或填写与法律事务相关的各种具有法律效力、法律意义的文书，这也是参加法律实践活动的一项必备技能。法律文书写作训练与法律诊所教育教学模式具有天然的契合性。

（一）法律文书制作是法律诊所教学实践的重要方式

肇始于20世纪初美国的法律诊所教育（Clinical Legal Education），其本质内涵就是借用医科教育中学生在诊所中进行必要实习的教育模式，通过让学生承办真实案件，面对真实的客户和真实的对方当事人，以及教师在学生办案过程中的具体指导，使学生掌握办理法律案件的技巧和技能，了解什么是法律的责任心和敬业精神，学会怎样培养法律人的职业道德，从而为将来成为合格的法律职业人才打下基础。[1] 在法律诊所教学中，学生扮演律师角色，通过提供法律咨询和制作法律文书帮助现实中遇到法律问题的人，而教师的职责是帮助学生从这种经历中获得实践经验，体会律师和法律条文的真正含义，提高职业技能水平。事实上，在现代普通法国家的法学教育中，法学院培养目标主要是律师，法律文书的制作训练主要集中在律师文书的制作技能上。在法律文书的制作标准上，强调满足三个条件：（1）满足客户的要求，并准确实施客户的指

[1] 徐立："美国法学教育及其对我国的启示"，载《法学杂志》2010年第12期。

示；（2）详尽地阐释所有相关的法律及事实问题；（3）明确相关的选择。[1] 诊所法律教育普遍的深度参与性、个体针对性、系统规划性和科学性，可以在很大程度上保证学生付出的时间能得到知识和技能的回报。[2] 这对于培养学生的自主性和创造力具有十分重要的作用，从而能够弥补法学院理论教育与实践间的差距，使学生对所学的各种实体法和程序法进行融会贯通，综合培养学生的职业技能和法律思维能力以及职业道德素质。

（二）从法律诊所受案类型看，适合法律文书制作的训练

从法律诊所发展的历史看，美国最初法律诊所的教育目的是培养公益律师，法律诊所主要是无偿为社会弱势群体提供法律服务。基于服务对象和涉及领域的不同，我国法律诊所的形式多样，包括法律援助诊所、刑事辩护诊所、妇女权利诊所、父母及儿童权利诊所、残疾人权利保护诊所、社区服务诊所、环境保护诊所、移民权利诊所、劳工保护诊所以及其他服务于弱势群体当事人的法律诊所。[3] 诊所受理案件类型具有以下特点：（1）频繁多发，争议标的额小。法律诊所训练要求诊所学员代理真实的案件，由于这类纠纷标的额一般不大，专职律师一般不愿代理，众多弱势群体权益的维护为诊所学员提供了案源，当事人愿意让法律诊所的学员代理。（2）纠纷发生的当地性。法律诊所学员是免费为当事人代理法律事务的，学员还有其他课程需要选修，不到外地调查取证是法律诊所接案的首要条件，诊所受理的纠纷大多能满足这一条件。（3）法律关系比较简单明确。弱势群体的权益维护中所涉及的法律关系一般比较简单，国家为弱势群体利益的维护提供最基本的保障，这使得诊所学员在受理这类纠纷时，对案件的结果有合理的预期，能在保障弱势方基本权益的前提下争取更大的利益。（4）纠纷解决机制可选择性大。诊所

---

[1] ［英］马戈特·科斯坦佐：《法律文书写作之道》，王明昕、刘波译，于丽英审校，法律出版社2006年版，第2页。

[2] 左卫民、兰荣杰："诊所法律教育若干基本问题研究"，载《环球法律评论》2005年第3期。

[3] 蔡彦敏："诊所法律教育"，载《环球法律评论》2005年第3期。

代理的案件主要是民事案件，处理方式有协商、调解、仲裁和诉讼，各种处理方式都有具体的程序规范限制，这样，诊所学员有机会参与接案、调查、起诉（申诉）、出庭、结案的全过程，在这一过程中，学员通过各类法律文书的制作训练，为处于弱势地位的当事人提供法律服务，维护社会正义，有助于培养其法律实务能力。

二、法律诊所学员制作法律文书存在的主要问题

法律文书写作应该是法律人的基本功，也是法律得以在实践中运用的最基本前提。[1] 法律诊所学员法律文书制作的质量高低，直接影响各项法律活动能否正常运作与顺利开展。然而在法律诊所学员的实践中，我们经常发现许多法律文书制作不规范，表达不准确、不精练，极大地削弱了文书本身的法律效力，一定程度上影响了当事人合法权益的维护。从笔者近几年指导的近百名诊所学员所制作的法律文书来看，存在的问题主要体现在以下方面。

（一）主旨不鲜明

主旨就是文书的写作目的和文书的中心意思。法律文书是为了解决一定的具有法律意义的实际问题，所以必须做到主旨鲜明，明确制作文书的目的，否则不利于有效地解决实际问题。例如为当事人代书的离婚诉状，离婚诉状的主旨具体体现在各种诉讼请求的表述上。有些诊所学员初次写作时往往比较含糊和笼统。如，有的学员只根据当事人要求写请求司法机关“主持公道”、“伸张正义”或流行的“给个说法”；有的只写“赔偿原告一切损失”、“请求判令被告支付未成年子女抚养费”等，没有表明具体请求数额。我国民事诉讼法、行政诉讼法都分别把“有具体的诉讼请求和事实、理由”作为起诉的条件之一。因此，对于这种表述，法院或其他司法机关就无从审理，当事人希望通过实现请求事项来维护自己合法权益的目的也就难以达到。

---

[1] 高云：《律师专业思维与写作技能（上）》，法律出版社2007年版，第4页。

（二）结构不合理

法律文书写作非常讲求清晰和准确，结构就是体现这一特征的重要方法。[1] 法律文书不同于普通文章，法律文书结构的特殊性表现为“程式化”，即法律文书在结构形式上有相对固定的格式，内容安排上有比较固定的顺序。法律文书的结构一般由首部、正文和尾部三部分构成，每一部分的内容都由特定的要素构成，制作要求谨慎性和正式性。但我们发现，在实践中不少学员对当事人的基本情况表述不清楚，如缺少联系方式、户籍所在地或经常居住地的表述，影响法院文书的送达和管辖的确定，甚至会引起当事人身份上的误会。有的申请类的文书对受文主体缺少表述，直接影响请求的实现。有的学员在起诉状中缺少对证据和证据来源、证人姓名和住所的表述，使得文书缺少说服力。法律文书具有内容法定性、形式程式性的结构性特点，学员在写作中任意增删内容事项、改变程式性结构都会影响文书的法律效力。

（三）内容不完整

内容的完整性要求写明的内容具有一定的规范性，这种规范性应当符合写作的要素化要求。各类法律文书中都必须包含一定的要素才算符合要求，这些要素既体现法律的要求，也体现写作的要求。如离婚纠纷中，起诉状中的事实叙述往往包括双方婚姻基本情况、夫妻感情破裂的原因、财产债权及债务、子女抚养及探视等情况，但不少学员在文书中往往只重视写双方纠纷的过程和结果，忽视对财产状况和子女抚养权方面的叙述。而在事实叙述之后缺乏对证据情况的列举和说明以及理由的阐述，使得文书的内容不能体现文书主旨的要求，表述相当单一、模糊。有的财产、债权及债务清单只简单列举名称、数量，缺少对相应证据的来源和去向的具体说明以及分割处置意见。而从形式上看，有的文书缺少当事人的签名，使文书不具有法律效力，甚至影响当事人诉权的有效实现。

---

[1] 高云：《思维的笔迹（上）》，法律出版社 2009 年版，第 115 页。

（四）表达不规范

法律文书是具有法律意义的文书，具有高度的严肃性，旨在以理服人，而非以情感人。法律文书的表达主要采用叙述、议论和说明方式，忌用抒情和描写方法。叙述事实要做到要素齐全、关键情节和因果关系要交待清楚，说理讲求充分性、合法性，说明要强调条理性并表述清楚。有些诊所学员在叙述事实时不够清楚。如，在一起包含争夺未成年子女的离婚起诉状中，有的学员对婚生未成年子女只写了姓名，没有说明未成年子女的出生日期和吃、住、学习等情况；在制作诉前保全申请书时，只写明申请保全的财物名称，没有强调“情况紧急”，不列明财产担保的情况。这些都会影响法院对相应法律行为的裁判。有的将“解除婚姻关系”与“判决离婚关系”表述混淆，反映了对两者适用条件的不理解；有的学员在对婚内暴力伤害赔偿请求的事实叙述中没有进行证据说明；有的将《民事诉讼法》表述成《民诉法》、将《婚姻法》第32条第1款表述成《婚姻法》第32条等，在法律名称和条款表述上不规范。

（五）语言不简洁

法律文书写作对语言文字方面的要求很高，必须做到严肃庄重、精确无误。语言严肃庄重要求学员在制作法律文书时一定要正确运用法律的专业术语和惯用语，避免华丽辞藻和方言土语，忌用污言秽语。语言精确无误要求学员字斟句酌，语句结构完整，言简意赅，避免重复语句和口语化现象。诊所学员在制作法律文书语言上的问题突出表现在：（1）内容不明确。如，一份起诉状中写诉讼理由时表述道：“认为女儿由被告抚养为佳，要求原告支付抚养费。但是，如果争取不到，那就归原告”，究竟要不要抚养权并不清楚。有的学员在关于未成年子女的探望权的离婚协议上确定的条款表述为：“在不影响孩子学习、生活的情况下，男方可以每周前往女方住处探望孩子一次。”这种表述在实践中很难执行。（2）叙述不简朴。如，原告的诉讼请求表述成：“因婚后夫妻感情不和，被告常为家庭经济琐事找碴吵嘴打架，使夫妻感情完全破裂，现已分居多年，今后再无法生活下去，请求与被告离婚。”实际上，强调请求法院判决离婚就可以了。（3）风格不庄重。有一份答辩状学员代写道：“婚后不久，因家庭琐碎小事就到娘家告状，而且经常和她父母一起到我家来兴师问罪，发神经。”实际上，改成“原告经常无事生非且性格多疑”的表述可能庄重些。

三、法律诊所学员制作法律文书质量不高的原因分析

法律诊所学员制作法律文书时出现这样或那样的问题，其原因是多方面的：有的是因制作者粗心大意、工作疏忽而带来的笔误；有的是因没有严格执行制作规范而导致的失误；有的则是因法律、写作等理论知识学习不到位，语言文字表达能力欠缺而造成的错误等。结合我院法律诊所教育的现状，归结起来主要有以下几个深层次原因。

（一）诊所案源不足，学员实践机会少

虽然目前有关弱势群体纠纷呈井喷之势，但是法律诊所学员受理案件纠纷的案源仍严重不足。“法律的生命不在于逻辑，而在于经验。”缺乏实践经验是诊所学员法律文书质量较低的重要原因。例如，2011 年下半年，扬州大学法学院法律诊所只受理了 12 件婚姻家庭纠纷案件，与此同时，仅扬州市邗江区人民法院受理的婚姻家庭纠纷就多达 216 起，多数学员缺乏充分实践的机会。这其中的原因主要有：（1）法律诊所学员主动性不足，存在一定的依赖思想。在法学专业课程教学中，教师依据课程内容寻找案例，学员处于被动状态。选修法律诊所课程后，尚未探寻出主动寻找和开拓案源的方法和途径，有不少学员主要是以法律诊所接听电话的方式，等待当事人上门。（2）法律诊所的宣传力度不够，影响不大。法律诊所是近年来才引进的法学实践教学模式，不仅社会公众对此知之甚少，甚至各级妇联、有关行政部门、法律援助机构对此也知之甚少。（3）法律诊所学员身份不够明确，社会的认同感不高。目前，我国各高校对法律诊所学员的定位为“准律师”，但是这种“准律师”的身份并没有得到律师协会及司法管理部门的认同，法律诊所与政府法律援助机构的关系也不明确，也没有得到政府的通力支持。这就造成了一方面政府的法律援助供不应求，另一方面法律诊所的学员“无事可做”。

（二）学员同情心强，缺乏必要的法律思维

法律文书的本质是法律思维的产物。绝大部分选修法律诊所的学员都具有极强的责任心，对社会弱势群体有较强的同情心，在初次接触婚姻家庭纠纷事务时，较易对当事人（尤其是对弱势一方）偏听偏信，缺少必要的法律逻辑判断。一方面，法律诊所的学员崇尚法律的意识不强。虽然在各类法律关系中，妇、幼、老、弱、病、残、伤从总体上讲是处于弱者地位的，但对弱者的保护应当主要体现在基本法律中，而在适用法律时当事人应当是平等的。由于我们比较强调对弱势群体的保护，法律诊所的学员接触此类案件时，理所当然地只注重弱者的倾诉，不能进入“准律师”的角色，不能像律师那样运用法律思维去找法用法。另一方面，中国法学教育的局限性影响法律诊所学员法律思维的培养。由于法律传统不同，中美两国法学院学生获取法律知识的途径与方法是存在差异的。美国法学院的学生从实践特别是通过办案接触各种各样的判例来认识法律、吸收法律理念和感知法律精神；而中国法学院学生获取法律知识和了解立法精神则主要通过课堂中的理论学习，对法律思维的培养是理性有余而感性不足。

（三）学员对法律法规理解不透彻，对各种救济手段不熟悉

由于我国社会经济正处于转型时期，社会关系异常复杂，社会关系中涉及的法律法规数量多，还有大量地方法规以及数量更为庞大的政策。面对内容庞杂、体系尚不健全的法律法规和政策，法律诊所学员很难全面掌握。虽然法律文书课程是综合性非常强的一门学科，但在各高校的重视程度并不高，学科定位为选修课，内容多，涉及面广，但课时少，且大班上课，课堂讨论、模拟训练等教学手段很难得到运用，学生根本没有时间消化吸收所学知识。虽然学习了各类诉讼法程序救济规范，但在具体操作中由于并不熟悉具体环节，各种救济手段不能灵活运用，在法律文书的制作中往往是“盲人摸象”，走一步算一步，缺少准确的办案思路和制作文书的内在动力，如果诊所老师不及时指导，很难在所代理的法律事务中发挥积极作用。

四、提高法律诊所学员法律文书制作水平的基本路径

法律文书的制作须具备丰富扎实的法学理论、法律知识和语言学、逻辑学、写作学等理论，具有一定的文字驾驭能力。正如美国学者加纳所说："不管我们如何将法律称之为'法律科学'，人们都不能脱离写作的艺术，都不能将遣词造句只归结为一个公式。"[1] 法律诊所教育的发展要求我们必须针对学员法律文书制作中存在的问题和症结，探寻解决的对策。

（一）采取多种方式扩大诊所教学案源

法律诊所要与相关部门加强联系，力争获得政府、学校和社会的认可和支持。因此，应当加强与政府法律援助机构、妇联、残联、工会、劳动等部门的联系与合作，可以将法律诊所作为这些维权部门的工作站，将法律诊所学员的工作纳入政府法律援助机构的工作中，从而使法律诊所学员的身份得以明确化。同时，加强与地方律师协会的合作，律协可以推荐优秀的律师作为法律诊所的教师，法律诊所应借鉴律协培养实习律师的手段和方法，在一定程度上实现资源共享。法律诊所学员要克服依赖思想，积极参与法律诊所的学习，主动采取多种形式宣传自己，以期获得社会公众的认可。

（二）注重法律诊所学员法律文书技能的培养

法律文书制作技能的培养贯穿于法律诊所教育的始终，对此应当采取以下措施：（1）完善教学计划，适用新型教学方法。在教学计划中要规定运用模拟训练的方法对一系列司法活动（如会见、调解、谈判、庭审等）进行介绍，并对相关案例的文书进行评价，模拟练习，激发学生的学习兴趣及实务知识运用的能力。有计划地组织学生旁听案件审理，查阅各类卷宗，熟悉办案流程，完成旁听和阅卷心得。在条件允许的前提下，安排诊所学员代理真实案件，使学生在真切的服务性环境中获得

---

[1] ［美］布莱恩·A. 加纳：《加纳谈法律文书写作》，刘鹏飞、张玉荣译，知识产权出版社2005年版，第273页。

角色体验及执业技巧。（2）拓宽诊所师生的选择面，强调互助式学习。在诊所教师的选择上，应当考虑多从实务部门聘请一些经验丰富、办案能力强的人员担任诊所的指导教师，让他们与法律诊所学员面对面地交流，从而使诊所学员能明白在处理相关法律事务时存在的不足，并加以改进。在诊所学员的选择方法上，不拘泥于本科高年级学生，应将部分法律硕士研究生纳入法律诊所的选择范围。在法律诊所学员的编组安排上，应将不同年级的学生编在一起，这样既可以在时间上互补，不耽误诊所学员其他课程的学习，同时更有利于学员对法律文书制作开展讨论式的学习，有利于互相取长补短。

（三）引导诊所学员充分利用各种维权方法

法律诊所的教学过程中，指导教师应当引导学员对各种维权途径进行比较、分析和讨论，并在具体的法律事务中引导学生与委托人充分协商沟通，以谋求委托人利益的最大化。以婚姻家庭纠纷为例，学员在接待相关当事人、了解相关基本情况后，首先就应当向当地政府联系，了解基本情况，组织双方调解当事人纠纷，必要时向相应维权机构投诉，取得这些维权机构的支持。在调解不成的情况下，向当事人阐明诉讼的可行性和必要性，通过调查收集和保全相关证据，确定基本诉讼策略和方法。在这一过程中，学员对于具体环节中所需要制作的法律文书要心中有数，对涉及疑难法律问题的表述及时与指导老师联系，并及时向当事人作出解释和说明。在具体法律文书的制作和运用中，掌握文书写作的技巧和规律。

（四）加强基础课程与诊所课程的衔接

我国引进法律诊所 10 多年来的实践表明，法律诊所无疑是法学实践教学最为有效的教育模式。然而我国其他法学课程的教学仍是传统模式，能够进入法律诊所学习的学员只占法学专业学生的极少部分。只有将法律诊所融入我国法学教育体系，才能更好地发挥其优势和作用，提高学生的职业技能。其他法学课程是法律诊所课程的基础，法律诊所学员通过对其他课程的学习获得系统的法律知识。但在基础课程的教学中，也应加强实践环节的训练，通过完善的教学计划，确立理论知识与实践能力相结合的科学公正的成绩评价体系，提高学生的法律综合素养。应通过法律诊所和各相关法学课程的教学，使诊所学员熟悉法律法规和政策，掌握一定的调查技巧和技术，具备相应的专业知识和技术素质，成为具备准确的判断能力、较严密的逻辑思维能力、清晰的语言表达能力和较强的文字写作能力的准律师，这样才能真正为社会公众提供更好的法律服务。